Jane Cooper

was educated at Cheltenham Ladies' College and Newnham College, Cambridge. After qualifying professionally in education, she has lived most of her life abroad, teaching English in Tanzania and Nigeria, where she acquired her first nineteenth century edition of a book by Mrs Molesworth. She has had a life-long interest in children's books, having collected them since childhood. A further qualification in library studies enabled her, while living in Munich, to work at the International Youth Library on the Schulz Collection of historical children's books. She also mounted an exhibition of her personal collection of books by Mrs Molesworth for the library, accompanied by a lecture to the *Historische Kinderbuchgesellschaft* (Historical Children's Book Society). Serious research on this biography began while she was living in Dakar, Senegal and continued in Brussels. She has published several articles on Mrs Molesworth in *Signal, Folly,* the Children's Books History Society *News-letter* and *The Kipling Journal.* She lives with her husband in Sussex and has two children and four grandchildren.

Jane Cooper

Mrs Molesworth

A BIOGRAPHY

Pratts Folly Press

Pratts Folly Press
Wealden Cottage, Pratts Folly Lane,
Crowborough, East Sussex TN6 1HR

Published by Pratts Folly Press 2002

ISBN 0-9542854-0-9

Typeset by Rowland Phototypesetting Ltd
Bury St Edmunds, Suffolk
Printed in Great Britain by
St Edmundsbury Press Ltd
Bury St Edmunds, Suffolk
Designed and produced by
JAC Design and Print
Clock House Court, Beacon Road,
Crowborough, East Sussex TN6 1AF

To the memory of
Ruth Robertson
Who loved Mrs Molesworth

CONTENTS

PREFACE AND ACKNOWLEDGEMENTS   viii

ABBREVIATIONS   xi

LIST OF UNPUBLISHED MANUSCRIPT SOURCES   xiii

LIST OF ILLUSTRATIONS   xv

1   Beginnings   1

2   Childhood   18

3   Growing Up   53

4   Marriage   73

5   Love Or Friendship?   97

6   1869, A Year Of Troubles   124

7   'We Shall Never Go Back To Cheshire'   151

8   'Tell Me A Story'   178

9   France   204

10   England Again   235

11   A New Friend   265

12   'Nobody Like You'   296

13   Death, Books, And Grandchildren   327

14   Last Years   361

LIST OF BOOKS AND ARTICLES BY
MRS MOLESWORTH   390

LIST OF BOOKS AND ARTICLES CONSULTED   394

INDEX   400

PREFACE AND ACKNOWLEDGEMENTS

Mrs Molesworth was one of the most popular and well thought of writers for children in the last quarter of the nineteenth century. Her books present children with great sympathy and insight, showing both a deep understanding of childish problems and sorrows, and a lively appreciation of fun and mischief, while the power of conveying genuine happiness is one of her great qualities. Her real-life child novels in particular broke new ground in the 1870s. Yet no biography of her has ever been published. Lives have appeared of Mrs Ewing and Frances Hodgson Burnett, who were also popular children's writers of much the same period, but Mrs Molesworth remains ignored. She went on writing into the twentieth century — her last book was published in 1911 — and did not die until 1921. Roger Lancelyn Green has suggested, in his various essays and articles about her, that because she lived for such a long time, she suffered, before instead of after her death, the eclipse so often caused by changing fashion, and that consequently there was, when she actually died, no thought of a biography. Then, in 1937 a librarian called Ruth Robertson, a great fan of Mrs Molesworth's, began to collect information towards writing one. She made contact with a daughter, Cicely Prinsep, and various other acquaintances, friends and relations. After the war she was able to get in touch with one of Mrs Prinsep's twin daughters, Venetia Inglefield, who was particularly helpful. But, although she did a great deal of research, Miss Robertson died in 1988 without having written her book. During this fifty-year period Green and others interested in Mrs Molesworth were aware of Miss Robertson's work and thus left the field to her. This explains the dedication of Green's 1961 Bodley Head monograph on Mrs Molesworth to Ruth Robertson and his acknowledgement of her help, in allowing him access to the material she had collected.

After Ruth Robertson's death, her friend and literary executor, Ellery Yale Wood, asked me to take on the project of producing a life of Mrs Molesworth. I was able to use some of Ruth's research, in particular letters to her from Mrs Molesworth's friends and relations, but I have done further research of my own and have written my own text. I was also fortunate in being able to draw on two large collections of Mrs Molesworth's letters, which had not yet been deposited in the British

Library and the John Rylands Library when Ruth was at work, so that she did not know about them.

My intention in writing this book has been to produce a straightforward, traditional biography, using all the unpublished sources I could identify, personal as well as manuscript, to bring together in one volume all available material on Mrs Molesworth's life. Collectors and fans will welcome such detail, I believe, as one myself. Academic researchers and writers whose interest is in the development of children's literature or innovative approaches to it, should, I hope, find this a useful resource. Out-of-print books can be found in libraries, but it is more of an effort to consult the kind of material I have presented here.

I owe very special thanks to Ellery Yale Wood and the late Benedicta Whistler. To Ellery for first asking me to write this book, and for helping and encouraging me with book loans and information. To Benedicta for reading every chapter as it was written and responding with a helpful blend of enthusiastic encouragement and judicious criticism.

I am grateful to the following relatives, friends and acquaintances of Mrs Molesworth for the help and information they offered to Ruth Robertson, which I have subsequently been able to use.

Valentine Browning, Cynthia Bruce, Gwen Dyson-Laurie, née Molesworth, C. G. Hohler, Venetia Inglefield, M. A. W. Miller, Col. F. C. Molesworth, Cicely Prinsep, Athelstan Riley, Gordon Neil Stewart, General E. C. Walthall.

A. B. Bruce, A. R. Craik, Julia Du Cane, C. M. Hall, L. M. Huil, A. Kedslie, M. H. Noel-Paton, Ranald Noel-Paton, R. M. Paterson, E. G. Robins, A. P. Rogers, O. M. Rogers, C. Roscoe, A. Somerville, H. W. Taylor.

I am grateful to these other relatives of Mrs Molesworth for the help they have given me.

Baronessa Daphne Ando, Fiona Bickersteth, David Bruce, Jean Dunlop, W. Dyson-Laurie, Richard Fremantle, L. G. Mills, Beatrix Molesworth, G. E. Molesworth, Mrs H. D. Molesworth, Allen H. N. Molesworth, Gordon Neil Stewart.

Mr A. H. N. Molesworth, Mrs Molesworth's great-grandson, has very kindly given me permission to quote from all her unpublished letters and I am most grateful to him.

My thanks go to the following individuals for help and advice, or permission to quote from material in their possession or of which they own the copyright.
Brian Alderson; E. O. J. Beck for showing me over Tabley Grange; Nancy Chambers; Chris Coates; The Hon. R. H. Cornwall-Legh; Mary Davidson; Edward Garnett; Jeffrey Garrett; Pat Garrett; Mr A. D. Harper; Hannah Hulton for information about Westfield; Sarah Jardine-Willoughby; Marie-Jaqueline Lancaster; the Hon. Ranald Noel-Paton; Professor Thomas Pinney; Rosi Re Beech (formerly Tessa Rose Chester); Julia Small for information about Bindon House; Alan Smith (of Topham Picturepoint).

I am grateful to the following institutions, libraries and archives for their help in my research, and/or for permission to use or quote from material in their possession or of which they own the copyright.
Archiefdienst, Gemeente Rotterdam; Archives Départmentales de Paris; Bodleian Library Oxford; Bristol University Library; The British Library, Department of Manuscripts; The Brotherton Collection, Leeds University Library; Chatto and Windus Archive (Reading University); Devon County Council, Exeter Central Library; Dunfermline Central Library, with special thanks to the local History Librarian, Margaret Stewart; Edinburgh Central Library; Gwynedd County Council, Deputy County Archivist (Gareth Haulfryn Williams); The Hospitals for Sick Children, Great Ormond Street, London, Museum and Archive Service, Peter Pan Gallery; John Rylands University Library of Manchester, with special thanks to Brenda Scragg; The Kipling Journal; Lancashire County Council, Wyre District Libraries Local Studies Librarian (Martin Ramsbottom); Longman Archive (Reading University); The National Library of Scotland Department of Special Collections, with special thanks to Mrs O. M. Geddes; The Master and Fellows of Trinity College, Cambridge; Reading University Library; The Tabley House Collection Trust, with special thanks to Brenda Folds; Somerset County Council Local History Librarian (David Bromwich); A. P. Watt Ltd on behalf of The National Trust for Places of Historical Interest or Natural Beauty; The Wellcome Institute for the History of Medicine, Assistant Librarian (Claire Cross); Westminster Reference Library, Art and Design Librarian.

Finally my deepest thanks go to my husband, Malcolm, who has had to live with Mrs Molesworth for many years, and has accompanied me willingly on many 'Molesworthing' expeditions. He has read every word I have written, many times over. His support and encouragement have kept me going.

ABBREVIATIONS USED IN NOTES

ACS   Algernon Charles Swinburne, poet, admirer and correspondent.

AJS   Agnes Janet Stewart, *née* Wilson, mother of MLM. AJW in chapter 1.

AH   Adrian Hope, friend and secretary of Great Ormond Street Hospital.

CAS   Charles Augustus Stewart, father of MLM.

CB   Cynthia Bruce, *née* Ainslie, grand-daughter of MLM.

CMY   Charlotte Mary Yonge, business correspondent.

CP   Cicely Prinsep, *née* Molesworth, 2nd daughter of MLM.

DUC   Charlotte Maria Du Cane, *née* Guest, friend.

GDL   Gwen Dyson-Laurie, *née* Molesworth, cousin of RM.

GLC   George Lillie Craik, a partner in Macmillan's.

GM   Gordon Milligan, an editor at Chambers.

GNS   Gordon Neil Stewart, great-grandson of WS.

JBLW   John Byrne Leicester Warren, 3rd Baron de Tabley, friend.

LT   Laura Troubridge, friend and book illustrator. Later LH, as wife of AH.

MAWM   Mary A. Wilson Miller, great-niece of AJS.

MLM   Mary Louisa Molesworth, *née* Stewart.

OM   Olive Molesworth, youngest daughter of MLM.

RLG   Roger Lancelyn Green.

RM   Richard Molesworth, MLM's husband.

RR   Ruth Robertson. (See Preface.)

VMI   Venetia Mary Inglefield, *née* Prinsep, grand-daughter of MLM.

WS   William Stewart, paternal grandfather of MLM.

LIST OF UNPUBLISHED MANUSCRIPT SOURCES

The Claimant, an unpublished manuscript by G. N. Stewart and Stewart Jamieson, great-grandsons of WS, and associated papers, now deposited in the University of Sydney, Australia, Rare Books and Special Collections Library. Quotations from this material are given with permission from GNS.

A Sketch of the Military Services of Lieut: Colonel William Stewart of the 3rd Foot (or Buffs), an unpublished ms written by himself in about 1818. Copy supplied by his great-grandson, GNS.

Letters from MLM to GLC and other members of the publishing house of Macmillan — Macmillan archive in the British Library. BL Add. Mss. 54390. Reproduced by courtesy of the British Library.

Letters from MLM (and a few from other members of her family) to JBLW in the Tabley Papers, held by the Special Collections Division of the John Rylands University Library, Manchester. Reproduced by courtesy of the Director and Librarian, the John Rylands University Library of Manchester.

Single letters from MLM to various recipients. The library or archive holding each letter is mentioned in the relevant note, and acknowledgements are made above.

The Chambers Collection in the National Library of Scotland, Dep. 341/ 101, 103, 143, 168, 170–4, 176, 191–3. Letters from Chambers to MLM are referred to only, as the present owner of the copyright has refused me permission to quote.

De Principe 1547–1830, Vol 2, an ms family history compiled by MLM's son-in-law, James Charles Prinsep, mostly about his own family, but containing 'Notes from information given me by Mrs Molesworth.' Originally copied with permission from Cicely Prinsep.

A small number of privately-owned letters lent to RR specifically for use in a biography of MLM. Letters to RR from MLM's friends and family giving information for use as above. In the notes, detailed references are not usually given to these two sources. Some of these letters were lent by RR to RLG for use in his 71-page essay, *Mrs Molesworth*, The Bodley Head, 1961. Since in all cases I have used the original letters, I do not refer to this essay where RLG has quoted the same passage.

NOTES
Some dates, in the notes and in the booklists, have been put in square brackets — [ ]. This means that the date was not found in the letter or book concerned, but was derived from other sources.

Mrs Molesworth's books are now out of print and only available from libraries and antiquarian booksellers. However, Jane Nissen Books is re-publishing *The Cuckoo Clock* in September 2002, reprinting from the Dent edition with illustrations by E. H. Shepard. Also the complete texts of *The Cuckoo Clock* and *The Tapestry Room* are available online at http://digital.library.upenn.edu/women/molesworth/room/room.html

LIST OF ILLUSTRATIONS
with acknowledgements

Between pages 208 and 209
Mrs Molesworth.
Major-General William Stewart.
Charles Augustus Stewart.
Agnes Janet Stewart, *née* Wilson.
Westnieuwland, Rotterdam, 1836.
Mary Miller, *née* Wilson.
James Horne Stewart.
Hillside House, Saline, near Dunfermline, Fife.
Rusholme Road, No. 92.
Mrs Molesworth as a young woman.
Tabley Grange, Knutsford, Cheshire.
Charles Augustus Stewart in middle age.
J. B. L.Warren, 3rd Lord de Tabley.
Westfield, High Leigh.
St John's, formerly the private chapel of West Hall, High Leigh.
Charles Stewart, 1841–1874, Mrs Molesworth's 2nd brother.
Sir Noel Paton.
Minnie Wilson Maclean, *née* Morgan.
Royal Terrace, Edinburgh, Nos. 25 and 26.
The Rev. Samuel Molesworth, 8th Viscount, 1829–1906.
Agnes Janet Stewart in widow's weeds,
Photograph of Mrs Molesworth published in *Little Folks*, 1894, *Pearson's* 1901 and *The Quiver*, 1906.
Juliet Grant-Duff Ainslie, *née* Molesworth.
Bindon House, Langford Budville, Wellington, Somerset.
Bell and Jean Lorimer, grand-daughters of Minnie Wilson Maclean.
Winkenhurst, Hellingly, East Sussex.

I am grateful to Mr A. H. N. Molesworth for permission to use no. 1; to Mr G. N. Stewart for 2, 3, 4, 7, 12 and 16; to the Archiefdienst, Gemeente Rotterdam for 5; to Fiona Bickersteth for 6; to Mr A. D. Harper for 8; to E. Y. Wood for 9; to Cynthia Bruce and David H. G. D. Bruce for 10; to Mr E. O. J. Beck for 11; to the University of Manchester Tabley House Collection for 13 — Photograph: Photographic Survey, Courtauld Institute of Art; to M. D. Cooper for 14, 15, and 19; to the Hon. Ranald Noel-Paton for 17; to Mrs Jean Dunlop for 18 and 25; to Beatrix Molesworth for 20 — Photograph: M. D. Cooper; to Richard Fremantle for 23; to Julia Small for 24 and to Mr and Mrs Davies for 26.

1

Beginnings

At the height of her popularity as a writer for children, Mrs Molesworth was described by one critic as 'the best story-teller for children England has yet known'.[1] In a private letter towards the end of his life this same critic wrote that he was glad her life was to be written because she had been such a great influence for good and had given so much pleasure to both adult and child readers.[2] Mrs Molesworth's own story began when she was born as Mary Louisa Stewart in Rotterdam. But why should one of England's story-tellers have been born in Holland? This question takes us back at once to the story of her parents.

Mary Louisa, who was known as Louisa or 'Louie' at home, came of Scottish descent on both sides of the family, so she was not after all an English story-teller, but a Scottish one. Her mother, Agnes Janet Wilson, was born in 1810 in Dunfermline, the chief town of Western Fife and centre of the damask linen trade. Her mother's parents, John Wilson and Nancy Black, were both from Fifeshire, though it was said in the family that John Wilson was the ninth generation from a Van Aalsen who had emigrated from Denmark and settled in Fife.[3] Nancy Black (whose given name was, in fact, Mary) was one of six children. Her favourite sister Agnes lived with her after her marriage and, when Nancy died, Agnes continued to live with a niece in Edinburgh, where, later on, her great-niece Louisa would encounter her.[4]

---

[1] Edward Salmon, 'Literature for the Little Ones', *The Nineteenth Century*, 22.10.1887, p. 574.

[2] Salmon to RR, 11.1.1938.

[3] From *De Principe 1547–1830, vol. 2*, an ms family history compiled by MLM's son-in-law, James Charles Prinsep, mostly about his own family, but containing 'Notes from information given me by Mrs Molesworth.'

[4] A family story also suggests that Nancy and Agnes Black were very close. Agnes had been engaged to a sailor who was lost at sea. When her sister Nancy was going to marry John Wilson, Agnes grieved so much at the prospect of further loss in the separation from her sister that their father, John Black of Black Hall in Fife, made Nancy take Agnes to stay with her.

Nancy and John Wilson had four daughters and four sons. Two of the daughters were called after the two grandmothers — Catherine after John Wilson's mother, Kathrene Morrison, (1731–1792)[5] and Marion after Nancy's mother. The third daughter was Mary, after her mother, while the fourth and youngest daughter, the mother of Mary Louisa Stewart, was named for the aunt who lived with them, Nancy's sister Agnes, who couldn't bear to be separated from her. The three aunts appear later on in Louisa's life, but not the uncles.

John Wilson owned an estate, called Transy (short for Transylvania) within the burgh boundary of Dunfermline. A descendant of the family in the 1930s interpreted the name as meaning 'beyond the woods' and suggested that the estate had once been thickly wooded.[6] In 1859 Transy House was listed among the 'Principal Mansions and Houses in the Neighbourhood of Dunfermline'[7] while a description written three years previously, when the property was up for sale, enthused 'This beautiful property, situated about a mile from the Town of Dunfermline, possesses every advantage to render it an agreeable Country Residence. The Mansion House, an Elegant Stone Building, surrounded by Shrubberies and ornamental Grounds, is on a fine exposure to the South-west, and commands a rich and extensive prospect along the Valley of the Forth.'[8] Discounting the house agent's battery of adjectives, it is still possible to picture a pleasant country home where a child might grow up happily with a crowd of sisters and brothers to play with in those shrubberies. The whole estate was 121 acres and had 'a complete suit of farm buildings' with land of 'excellent quality', so John Wilson could either have farmed it himself or let it out. In either case the children had plenty of space to roam. Three years before Agnes was born, her father was Provost of Dunfermline for a year and his father too, also called John Wilson, had been Provost before him from 1789 to 1792, the year of his death.[9] As well as the Transy estate he had owned property in

---

[5] Inscription in Dunfermline Abbey churchyard. Source: John Fowler Mitchell and Sheila Mitchell, *Monumental Inscriptions (pre-1855) in West Fife*, Scottish Genealogy Society, 1972, p. 136, no. 390. See Family Trees at the back of this book.

[6] Maurice James Hartley Wilson, 'Transy Grove' in *Pressed Leaves from the Forest of Dunfermline*, Dunfermline: A. Romanes and Son, 1937.

[7] Peter Chalmers, *Historical and Statistical Account of Dunfermline*, 2 vols, 1844 and 1859, Vol. 2 pp. 323–4.

[8] Notice of sale in *Dunfermline Journal*, 26.9.1856.

[9] Inscription in Dunfermline Abbey churchyard (see note 5); and Alexander Stewart, *Reminiscences of Dunfermline*, Edinburgh: Scott and Ferguson, 1886, p. 288.

Dunfermline itself, an old house in Collier Row known as Provost John Wilson's house.[10] A provost in Scotland corresponds to the English mayor, so the Wilsons were clearly a family of some wealth and standing.

Louisa's mother was christened Agnes Janet in full, and when Louisa came to use the stories her mother related about her childhood as a narrative basis for certain episodes in her own children's books, she gave the name Janet to the fictional character representing her mother. Agnes Janet did, it appears, have a happy childhood, in 'a happy and united family', where the brothers and sisters

> 'all joined . . . in loving and petting little Janet. How well she remembers even now, all across the long half century, how the big brothers would dispute as to which of them should carry her in her flowered chintz dressing-gown, perched like a tiny queen on their shoulders, to father's and mother's room to say good morning . . . how the big sisters would work for hours at her dolls' clothes.'[11]

One of these dolls shared an adventure with her small owner, and later on Agnes told the story to her own children. An infectious fever, probably scarlet fever, which was then so much feared and caused so many deaths, had broken out in some of the nearby villages. Out on a country scramble with one of her brothers, Agnes, separated from him, came upon a sick child by a travelling van and allowed her to nurse the doll, Mary Ann Jolly. Her brother, hearing of this and realizing the danger of infection, threw the doll away to her mystified horror. When she did indeed catch the fever and appeared to be pining for Mary Ann to a degree that increased the severity of her illness, the brother went out and retrieved it from the almost inaccessible rocky slope where he had thrown it.[12] Agnes' daughter commemorated this doll, not only in a children's book but even in one of her adult novels — 'And we had

---

[10] Ebenezer Henderson, *The Annals of Dunfermline*, Glasgow: John Tweed, 1879, pp. 562 and 566.

[11] MLM, 'Mary Ann Jolly' in *Tell Me A Story*, Macmillan, 1875 p. 114. In a letter to Edward Salmon MLM said 'I believe that my best stories are all the really true ones — In "Grandmother Dear", and in several others there are little tales of rather old-world life which are all what were told to me of and by my own grandmother and mother.' (12.10.1887. Privately owned). Together with verbal communication from MLM's daughter and grand-daughters, this statement led RR to be sure that 'Mary Ann Jolly', 'Grandmother's Grandmother' and 'Grandmother's Story' in *Grandmother Dear* and 'A Long Ago Story' in *Carrots* 'may safely be regarded as authentic Wilson family chronicles' (unpublished ms by RR).

[12] *Tell Me A Story*, pp. 119–140.

one dear old-fashioned wooden doll, with a merry face and red cheeks.
We called her Mary Ann Jolly and I almost think we loved her best of
all.'[13]

But Agnes was also a tomboy. Her mother was described as saying
to her 'I really fear, my dear, that you will never be like a young lady
— it is playing so much with your brothers I suppose.' When asked
about her favourite activities she said

> 'Haymaking was delicious, so were snow-balling and sliding . . . and all
> the year round there was another delight that never palled . . . *mischief*
> . . . The scrapes I got into of falling into brooks, tearing my clothes,
> climbing up trees and finding I could not get down again, putting my
> head through window-panes.'

Her daughter, describing these doings for a Victorian audience, did not
seem to disapprove at all, and indeed made one of her child characters
comment 'Grandmother must have been an awfully nice little girl.'[14]
She tore her gowns to such an extent that her mother asked the pedlar
to bring some material that would not tear to dress her in. The stuff
that was brought did not tear, certainly, but the colour was so ugly
that the child was ashamed of it. ' "Birstle peas" colour they called it,
[and] . . . 'Little miss in her birstle-peas gown' was a byword in the
countryside.'[15]

A greater trouble than an ugly dress came to Agnes, however. When
she was quite young she had an accident to one of her eyes, which
meant that all her education came by word of mouth from her father,
so that she did not learn to read until she was twelve.[16]

> 'She was not blind, but her sight was imperfect, and unless the greatest
> care had been taken she might, by the time she grew up, have lost it
> altogether. To look at her you would not have known there was anything
> wrong with her blue eyes; the injury was the result of an accident in her
> infancy, by which one of the delicate sight nerves had been hurt, though
> not so as to prevent the hope of cure. But for several years she was hardly

---

[13] Ennis Graham, *Not Without Thorns*, Tinsley, 1873, 3 vols, vol. 2 pp. 275–6. Ennis
Graham was a pseudonym used by MLM for her first seven published works.
[14] MLM, *Grandmother Dear*, Macmillan, 1878, p. 114; pp. 110–111.
[15] MLM, *Us": An Old-fashioned Story*, Macmillan, 1885, p. 12. The OED defines 'birsle'
as a Scottish dialect word meaning to scorch or toast hard. 'Birsle peas' were dried peas.
The cloth was probably of the faded yellowy green colour characteristic of dried peas.
[16] *De Principe.*

allowed to use her eyes at all. She used to wear a shade whenever she was in a bright light, and she was forbidden to read.'

This trouble had some compensation in what she later described as her 'dearest memory of all', when her father 'would read aloud to her, hour after hour, as she lay on the hearth-rug, coiled up at his feet . . . listening with intense eagerness to the legends and ballads his heart delighted in.'[17] His grand-daughter said he was known as 'a very cultivated man.'[18]

We know something of the books which were read aloud to Agnes, or which she read herself after her twelfth birthday, when she was at last permitted to use her eyes for reading, because she kept her favourites carefully for her own children. Her daughter Louisa wrote of the storybooks she herself had read,

> 'I can recall several belonging to an older generation . . . some actually
> the self-same volumes treasured all those years ago by the then little
> hands, long since resting in the grave — their life work over; some,
> copies or new editions procured with difficulty for us by my mother, . . .
> the favourites of her own childhood . . . Among these the most prominent
> were *The Fairchild Family*, by Mrs Sherwood; one or two of Mrs
> Hofland's; *The Twin Sisters*, published, I think, anonymously; *Ornaments
> Discovered*, also by an unnamed author; and last, but not least, a complete
> collection of Miss Edgeworth's books for the young.'[19]

A country estate near Dunfermline seemed very quiet and isolated to Agnes Stewart looking back, fifty or sixty years later, and this was certainly the impression she gave her daughter who described her mother's situation as a child like this.

> 'She had never travelled fifty miles from her home, and that home was
> far away in the country, in Scotland. And a Scottish country home in
> those days was far removed from the bustle and turmoil and excitement
> of the great haunts of men.'[20]

But Transy was not too far away for John Wilson to supply his daughter with recently published books for children. *Ornaments Discovered* came

---

[17] *Tell Me A Story*, p. 115–6.
[18] *De Principe*.
[19] MLM, 'Story-Reading and Story-Writing', *Chamber's Journal*, 75, 5.11.1898, p. 772. Her mother had died fifteen years before this article was written.
[20] *Tell Me A Story* p. 113.

out when she was five and the first part of *The Fairchild Family* when she was eight.

As well as the books her father read to her, Agnes would have heard stories from her mother, Nancy Wilson, who certainly told tales to her grand-daughter, Louisa. These were tales such as 'The Fair One with Golden Locks' and 'The Brown Bull o' Norrowa' and also 'stories of herself or her own children when they were young.' Louisa described her grandmother as 'unrivalled' at story-telling. Mrs Wilson also did beautiful embroidery, for which she made the designs herself, and sketched and painted with 'unusual talent' though she had never had regular lessons.[21] She would wash her own beautiful old china to make sure it was kept safe to be handed on to her great-grandchildren, using 'a white wood bowl kept on purpose, and a napkin of the finest damask and a large apron of fine holland that she put on, and . . . a pair of embroidered holland cuffs that she used to draw on over her sleeves up to the elbow.'[22] She had lovely hands with what was considered at the time to be very beautiful 'shell' marking on the palms,[23] and watching her wash up her cups and saucers was a treat for any child in the house — 'her hands looked so white and moved so nimbly.'[24]

In 1824, on 17th November, Agnes' father died at Transy.[25] She was fourteen. The family seems to have continued living on the estate until 1829 when it was sold.[26] In this same year, when Agnes was nineteen, her eldest sister, Catherine, married Alexander Colville[27] of Hillside, a house in the parish of Saline about seven miles north of Dunfermline, 'which is situated at an elevation of nearly 800 feet and is almost the highest residence in Fife.' It is described in a guide-book of the 1990s as 'a typical 18th-century classical Scottish mansion later overwhelmed by the gabled additions reflecting Victorian ambition.'[28] Catherine was 28 and her husband was 58 when they married,[29] and they had at least

---

[21] MLM, 'How I Write My Children's Stories', *Little Folks*, 1894, p. 16.

[22] MLM, *Carrots: Just A Little Boy*, Macmillan, 1876, p. 106. Cp. *Us*, p. 32.

[23] *De Principe.*

[24] *Us*, pp. 32–33.

[25] Gravestone in Dunfermline Abbey churchyard, (see note 5).

[26] *Dunfermline Register* 1829–1833 and *Fife and Kinross Register* 1827–1829 and 1823–1835. These show a John Kirk as owner/occupier of Transy for the first time in 1829.

[27] *Dunfermline Parish Register*, Aug. 1829.

[28] David Beveridge, *Between the Ochils and Forth*, Edinburgh: Wm. Blackwood and Sons, 1888, p. 235; Glen L. Pride, *The Kingdom of Fife*, Architectural Guides to Scotland, RIAS 1990, p. 18.

[29] 1851 Census

four children. The house dated from about 1740 and the addition referred to above, a major one in the Scots baronial style, was made some hundred years later, presumably when Alexander Colville was feeling the pressure of an increasing family. Hillside remained in the Colville family until the beginning of the twentieth century and was a centre for Catherine's own family to visit and gather. Alexander Colville was a Justice of the Peace, a sheriff, and also taxation officer for the district,[30] so Catherine married a man of much the same social rank as her father. It is possible that Catherine's marriage was seen by her family as a chance to sell Transy and yet still provide a home for her mother and unmarried sisters.

If this was so, her sisters did not remain with her for long. In 1830 Marion married, as his second wife, a man called Henry Rutherford who was a wealthy merchant in Rotterdam. He was, though, a native of Dunfermline, which explains how she made his acquaintance in the first place.[31] Her sister Agnes visited her in Rotterdam and thus met her own husband, of which more will be said later. The fourth sister, Mary, married (also as a second wife) the Reverend Ebenezer Miller, with whom she lived at first in Saltcoats, but by 1839 they too had moved to Rotterdam where the Rev. Miller was 'Predikant' to the English-speaking Presbyterian community. They remained in Holland for some years and then went further afield, first to the Cape and then to India.[32]

Agnes also went to more exciting foreign parts than Holland, but before she married. Her godfather was Edward William Auriol Drummond-Hay who became British Consul General in Morocco in 1829. Before this he had been Lord Lyon clerk at Edinburgh, a post offered to him by his cousin the Earl of Kinnoull, hereditary Lord Lyon King

---

[30] 1851 Census. Papers found behind the skirting boards of Hillside when it was restored in the 1970s. I am grateful for this information to Mr A. D. Harper who owned the house at that time.

[31] Rutherford's will (Rotterdam archives), dated 21.5.1830, mentions his wife Marion as his heiress. The Rotterdam 1829 population register (taken 31.12.'29) lists him as a widower. So he must have married Marion Wilson in early 1830. This will was probably made on the occasion of his second marriage. The 1829 register also gives Henry Rutherford's birthplace as Dunfermline though the registration of his death in 1833 says he was born in Kinross. Since the two are only ten miles apart, the Rutherford and Wilson families were within reach of each other for purposes of acquaintance, whichever is correct.

[32] Information about Mary Wilson and Ebenezer Miller was given to RR by MAWM, and also obtained from the Rotterdam archives.

at Arms of Scotland.[33] His son wrote in his memoirs that while they were living in Edinburgh 'Walter Scott was a great friend of my family and frequently came to Athol Crescent.'[34] Louisa told her son-in-law that her mother had dined with Walter Scott and this could well have been at Edward Drummond-Hay's table. But Agnes did not just visit her godfather in Edinburgh, she went to stay with him in Tangier. The evidence for this was a large oil painting of her with the inscription 'Agnes Janet Wilson aet. 25, Tangier 1835. Interior of a house in Tangier.'[35] No letters or diaries mentioning this visit have survived, but in Sir John Drummond-Hay's memoirs there is a letter describing just such a visit to his father and the family in Tangier when he himself was a boy of sixteen or seventeen. The visitor was a Miss Shirreff whose mother was a cousin of Edward Drummond-Hay and whose father had been appointed Captain of the Port at Gibraltar in 1830. She wrote to Sir John's daughters when they were editing his memoirs for publication, describing her visit in 1833 accompanied by her sister, which must have been a few months before or after Agnes went there.

'Mrs Drummond-Hay's kind motherly greeting to her two young guests soon set us at ease', she said. 'When the busy mornings were over ['busy' here applied to John Drummond-Hay's study of Arabic, since the letter was written to describe his family background], riding and music were the two delights that drew the young party together. Under Mr Hay's guidance, and with the escort of a Moorish soldier, still at that time necessary for protection, many were the delightful rides that we took beyond the precincts of the old town and along the shore, or through the half-wild country, so new in all its aspects to our eyes.

Then on our return, and often far into the evening hours, the long balcony or gallery as it was called, outside the drawing room windows was our favourite resort. Here we eat [sic] fruit, and talked over our ride, and here guitars were brought out and song and merry talk went on.' *From the beautiful garden could be seen a lovely view of Gibraltar and the*

---

[33] *De Principe* and DNB.

[34] The Right Hon. Sir John Drummond-Hay, *A Memoir Based on His Journals and Correspondence*, London: John Murray, 1896 p. 3.

[35] Portrait of AJW in Tangier. *De Principe* states that it was in the possession of OM. It passed into the possession of VMI, where RR saw it. Despite the date on the picture, the visit must have taken place earlier than 1835, since AJW and CAS were married in July, 1834 and their first child was born in April, 1835. See notes 61 and 62.

straits. 'The enjoyment was only changed for the pleasant circle at dinner, or in the drawing-room.'

Miss Shirreff mentioned a daughter called Louisa, just a year older than herself whose 'bright intellect added force to the pure beauty of her character' and whose 'congenial spirit [and] . . . sympathy in his literary tastes' made her the companion of her father, a position Agnes would have found very natural when she visited in her turn. It might even have been from this attractive-sounding Louisa that she took her eldest daughter's name. French and Spanish were necessary in the society there and, observed Miss Shirreff,

> 'within the small circle of different nationalities the social tone of various countries became familiar and then the intercourse tended to dissipate national prejudices and to lead the young to wider sympathies than generally prevail where all are more or less under the sway of the same habits and associations.'[36]

Agnes too would have received this exposure to languages and multi-racial concord that laid a foundation for her life in Rotterdam and helped her to impart linguistic facility and ease in foreign living to her own children, teaching which would have especially benefited the daughter who lived for many years in Europe, Mary Louisa. Visits in those days were a serious matter. One did not stay for a few days or a week or so. Agnes was in Tangier long enough for her portrait to be painted and probably long enough to learn a language from scratch, though it is very likely that she already spoke French at least.

On her way home from Tangier, Agnes may have stopped in Rotterdam to visit her sister Marion again. Henry Rutherford, her brother-in-law, had a partner in his Rotterdam business called Charles Augustus Stewart. Whatever the details of her growing acquaintance with this young man, whom she must have met while visiting Marion at some time, by 1834 Agnes knew him well enough to marry him. By this time he was the active manager and part proprietor of the business, for Rutherford had died in 1833, some three years after his second marriage. In a worldly sense Agnes' marriage was a good one, for her husband had not only a share in a prosperous business, but also considerable ability, shown by his rising quickly to the status of partner after he was

---

[36] John Drummond-Hay, *A Memoir*, pp. 9–10.

first employed.[37] Charles Augustus' prospects had not always been so fair, for he started life with the stigma of illegitimacy, a burden which would weigh more and more heavily as the century moved into the Victorian age.

His father, William Stewart, came of 'a noted Caithness family' and had a 'brilliant career'[38] in the army. In June 1808, William had reached the stage of Major in this career,[39] and was 39 years old, when, travelling by boat from Gills Bay to Leith, intending to go on to London, he encountered a beautiful young Scots girl[40] called Isabel Innes. She was understood to be on her way to Edinburgh to go into domestic service, but instead, she transhipped at Leith with Major Stewart to a vessel bound for London. The Major was on his way to Devonshire to take up the command of the second battalion of his regiment, The Buffs, which was stationed in the vast camps on Berry Head, near Brixham on the southern tip of Torbay. He clearly took Isabel with him and set her up in some sort of accommodation in the village of Brixham (population 400), since on 11th June 1809 in the parish church of St Mary, Brixham, Devon 'Charles Augustus Stewart, son of Isabell Innes' was

---

[37] *Claimant*, p. 85. Rutherford's death certificate in Rotterdam archives. He died 19.8.1833. His will mentions CAS as partner, owner of one third of the business and in receipt of half-profits. See also note 31.

[38] 'The Stewarts of Strath, Watten' in *John O'Groats Journal*, 23.8.1912. Strath lay pretty well equidistant between Watten and Bylbster, about 4 miles from Wick in the far north of Scotland. Although this headline defines this particular Stewart family as 'of Strath', and Mrs Molesworth's obituaries describe her father as being the son of Major-General Stewart 'of Strath', William Stewart was born in 1769, in Dounreay, Caithness, some 11 miles from Thurso, where his family had lived since an ancestor moved there from Appin in 1680. His father did not buy the estate of Strath until 1801 (John Henderson, *Notes on Family History of Caithness*, Edinburgh, 1884) seven years after he began his military career, and it was sold by William Stewart himself in 1846, sixteen years after he went to live permanently in Australia, so he was hardly 'of Strath' in any settled sense.

[39] William Stewart joined the army in 1794 as an ensign in the 101st regiment. When this regiment was disbanded in the following year he was transferred to The Buffs, the 3rd regiment of foot, in which he served for 36 years. Details of his army career from *A Sketch of the Military Services of Lieut: Colonel William Stewart of the 3rd Foot (or Buffs)*.

[40] Isabel Innes was described as beautiful by two separate lines of family tradition. CP, her great-grand-daughter through her illegitimate son, said this in conversation with RR. Roslyn Jamieson, legitimate grand-daughter of WS in Australia, said 'I believe she was very beautiful' in an oral re-telling of 'the story as I remember hearing it' intended for transcription and transmission to RR.

baptised. No father was mentioned.[41] William only remained near Brixham until January 1809 when he was posted to Plymouth some thirty
miles away to take charge of and re-form three thousand troops landed
there after the defeat at Corunna. The following May he returned to
the command of the second battalion until August when he went to
join the first battalion in Spain.[42] So he might quite well have attended
his son's baptism in June, since he was there on the spot.

William Stewart remained in Spain until October 1812, during which
time he was promoted to Lieutenant Colonel and commanded The
Buffs at the battle of Albuera where the regiment was almost deci-
mated. His performance in this battle won him a gold medal from the
Duke of York. He appears to have been a conscientious and capable
officer. When he returned to England to the command of the second
battalion at the end of 1812, he found that Isabel, having married a
seaman in the Royal Navy, called James Beresford, in the previous
February, was living in the parish of Stoke Damerel, a suburb of
Plymouth in Devon. In the marriage register Isabel described herself as
a spinster and signed only with a cross 'the mark of Isabella Innis'.[43]
This did not appear to upset William, or, if it did, he soon consoled
himself, for we know that he had another illegitimate child in 1814 by
a woman who was in service with his sister in Thurso. He met her
while on leave at Strath, staying with his mother. He already had twin
daughters, born in 1803, by a servant woman of his father's, who later
married a soldier. He recognised all these children, including Charles
Augustus, and gave their mothers financial help. William clearly had an
eighteenth century and Scottish attitude to his bastards at this time —
they were members of the clan, to be acknowledged and supported, not
causes of shame to be hidden away. They all took the surname of
Stewart.[44]

---

[41] Bishop's Transcripts for the parish of Brixham, 1809, Entry No. 98, Devon Record
Office.

[42] *The Claimant* says that Stewart remained in Plymouth until he went off to the
Peninsula war in September (p. 81) but *A Sketch* definitely states that he returned to
the command of the 2nd battalion in May.

[43] Copy of extract from marriage register of Stoke Damerel.

[44] Stewart made a regular allowance to the mother of the twins, which was paid to her
by an uncle of his, Mr John Stewart of Thurso. At one time the twins lived in this
uncle's house as members of his family. *Claimant*, pp. 59–60. His other mistress, who
bore his child in 1814, also received money regularly through his relations. *Claimant*,
p. 64.

William's return to England was 'a circumstance which he will ever deeply regret' as it prevented him from taking a share in what he called 'the important and brilliant operations of the succeeding campaign.'[45] He had to step down because of the arrival of an officer senior to him, and the second battalion, unfortunately for his military ambition, was still in England. When he again succeeded to the command of the first battalion in mid-1814 (through the retirement of this senior officer), it had moved to Canada and he joined it there in October 1814. The following year, with the return of Napoleon, troops were urgently needed, and The Buffs embarked for Europe on 27th May. So William was in Canada for barely eight months, but during this time he managed to get married. The family tradition was that 'one day he saw a beautiful girl riding down the street in Quebec, and he said "That's the girl for me!" '[46] However it happened, the whole event must have been very quick, since the wedding took place in October 1814, the same month that William had arrived, before a Justice of the Peace in a village some distance from Quebec.[47]

So now both Charles Augustus' parents were married, but not to each other. He spent his early childhood with his mother and stepfather in Plymouth. When he was six, he was taken, probably by his stepfather, to see the defeated Emperor Napoleon on his way to exile on St Helena. The 74-gun ship, Bellerophon, with Napoleon on board, sailed into Torbay on the morning of 24th July, 1815. A great crowd of sightseers in boats came clustering round, anxious to see 'Boney' who had for so long been the terror of the world and whose name was regularly used to frighten children into being good. After forty-eight hours, the Bellerophon moved round to Plymouth where again the crowds of spectators were huge, the ship being completely surrounded by boats, though no-one was allowed on board. Napoleon obligingly came on deck and showed himself alternately on each side of the ship, bowing and smiling to the spectators. Surprisingly, the crowds were not abusive; 'on the contrary the spectators generally took off their hats when he bowed.' An eye-witness of these appearances thought that Napoleon had expected, 'and most justly, a very different reception.' Since he was instead greeted with respect, he was induced

---

[45] *A Sketch*, p. 12.
[46] Oral description by Roslyn Jamieson, see note 40.
[47] *Claimant*, p. 17.

'to gratify their curiosity to the utmost, remaining fully exposed to view for nearly an hour' on one occasion.[48] It was a scene that impressed Charles sufficiently, young though he was, for him to recall and mention it years later. He appears to have said to one interlocutor that it was his father who took him to see Bonaparte, but this would have been impossible, since the Buffs arrived back in Portsmouth on 17th July and were ordered the next day to proceed to Ostend, where they arrived on the 22nd, two days before Napoleon came to Torbay.[49]

Soon after this event James Beresford left the navy and moved with Isabella to Rochester, where he became skipper of a sloop called Flora, and sailed regularly to and from Rotterdam with cargoes of cheese. When Charles was nine, his mother took him up to Caithness to visit her family for the first time. They had heard from her occasionally, in letters written for her, and now she and her son stayed for three months with them in the village of Mey, about 7 miles from John O' Groats, where her father, James Innes, was a small farmer. At this time Charles was described as 'a nice gentlemanly looking boy, running in his mother's hand.' It was his first visit to Scotland. He was apparently known as Charles Stewart Beresford on this visit and so was thought to be Isabel's son by her husband, though before she left she told her family that the father was really William Stewart.

Charles Augustus may not have had a very happy childhood at this period, since his stepfather was said to be 'vicious and generally wild.' When he was about 13 his mother left Beresford and went to live in Holland, where she was housekeeper in Rotterdam to a Mr Rutherford, with the special charge of caring for his invalid wife.[50] This was that same Rutherford who would later marry Marion Wilson. Isabel may already have had contact with the Scottish colony in Rotterdam through Beresford's voyages in the cheese trade. A Scottish church had certainly been established there as long ago as 1685 and possibly earlier. The Scots community in

[48] John Bowerbank. *An Extract from a Journal Kept on Board HMS Bellerophon (from Saturday July 15, 1815 to Monday August 17 1815,* London, Whittingham and Arliss, 1815, p. 27ff.

[49] *Claimant,* p. 104 and associated letters.

[50] Information about Charles' stepfather, the visit to Scotland and move to Holland from *Claimant,* pp. 82, 70, 68 and 83.

Rotterdam was reckoned to be about one thousand by the year 1700.[51]

Isabel was not able to keep her son with her all the time now, as William Stewart looked after his son's education and sent him to school in Scotland for about three years, at Inverness Academy, where he was known as 'English Charlie' because he spoke with an English accent. The daughters of the woman he boarded with testified in 1874 that it was always understood that the boy was the illegitimate son of William Stewart. In September, 1824, Stewart, now a full Colonel, was staying in Deptford, waiting to embark for Australia where The Buffs were then stationed. He had successfully petitioned the Duke of York (commander-in-chief of the army) for the post of Lieutenant-Governor of the Colony of New South Wales and received the commission on 4th September.[52] He wrote to Charles at school in Inverness telling him to come to Deptford on a visit, with minute instructions for every stage of the journey. Isabel was very anxious to see her son, and the Colonel had heard of this in a letter from Mr Rutherford. The fact that he was in correspondence with Mr Rutherford prompts the idea that it might have been he who found Isabel her position in Rutherford's household.

He told Charles 'In the meantime you can go to Rotterdam on a visit to your mother by a steam vessel from this place which goes there and returns every week.' Twice in the letter he mentions a special scheme he was planning for his son's benefit, without giving any details.[53] What he had in mind was to take Charles out to Australia with him, to push his fortune in the colony. Isabel, however, did not like the idea of parting with her son so finally, and came to Deptford with him to say so. Both the Colonel and his wife behaved very kindly to her and Charles and it was ultimately decided that the boy should return with her to

---

[51] Some evidence for Scottish settlement in Holland is as follows. In the C17th it was increasingly common for Scottish legal students to finish their studies at a Dutch university. Covenanters sought refuge in Holland from persecution, and there was so much Scottish commercial traffic at the port of Veere that a special dwelling house was erected for Scottish merchants and mariners. John Erskine of Carnock, an exiled Covenanter, recorded in his diary attending the Scottish Church in Rotterdam in March 1685. He also visited the Scots coffee-house and hired a room with a merchant from Stirling. He met with at least 14 fellow Scots in the space of 5 days. Information from *Scotland and the Modern World*, George Pratt, 1932. See also A. J. G. Cummings, 'Scotland's Links with Europe', *History Today*, vol. 35, Apr. 1985.

[52] *Claimant*, pp. 66 and 19.

[53] A copy of this letter exists in the papers associated with *The Claimant* and is quoted there in full, p. 84.

Rotterdam, at least for a time.[54] It seems to have been about now, when he was fifteen, that Charles first went into Mr Henry Rutherford's business at 75 Westnieuwland. Later he moved on to 'Mr Rutherford's branch at the Hague so as to get command of the French language.'[55] His father finally left for Australia alone in January 1825, as the vessel had at first been driven back by autumn storms and medical advice was against his wife and her children attempting the journey.

William's position as Lieutenant-Governor of New South Wales brought him a fine grant of land, a thousand acres more than the amount usually given to settlers.[56] His final post was nearly four years in India where he was 'in command of a Brigade in the presidency of Bengal.' He was promoted to the rank of Major General in July 1830, retired from the army at the end of 1831 and returned to New South Wales in 1832 'to reside on his splendid property near Bathurst.'[57] He never returned to Britain, so he and his son, Charles Augustus, did not meet again but remained in correspondence.

In 1829 the Rotterdam population register shows that Charles was back in Rotterdam, living at 75, Westnieuwland with his employer, a widower at that time, ten other men employed in Rutherford's business, his mother as housekeeper and two servants. It was a large household and mainly an expatriate one, since four of Charles' co-workers were from England and three from Scotland. By this time he could presumably speak Dutch fluently, since most outside business transactions would have been conducted in that language.

We do not know when Charles met Agnes Wilson, but it must have been at or soon after Henry Rutherford's marriage with her sister, Marion.[58] Rutherford's death three years later was perhaps unexpected, since he was only sixty.[59] Marion was left a wealthy widow, inheriting not only her husband's two-thirds share in the business and the right

---

[54] *Claimant*, p. 61.

[55] Unpublished letter from Wigram Allen to J. P. Bunting, Mar. 1874, p. 7; in *Claimant* papers.

[56] *Claimant*, p. 23.

[57] *John O'Groats Journal*, 23.8.1912.

[58] The entry for Henry Rutherford's death in the Rotterdam civil registers gives his widow's name as Marianne, but *De Principe* and MLM in a letter to her sister as a child used the spelling Marion. Similarly, MLM's mother is called Agnes Jeanette in the Dutch registrations of her children's births, but her gravestone in Cheshire has Janet. I have followed family usage.

[59] Registration of death in Rotterdam. He may have been younger, since in 1829 he gave his age for the census as 50.

to receive half of the profits, but also his house in Rotterdam, two houses in the Hague and two in Dunfermline. Charles was relieved of the financial responsibility of his mother's support, for Rutherford left Isabel an annuity of 600 guilders until her death.[60] This help, together with the share of the business that Charles already owned, put him in a position where he was able to marry, which he did, just under a year after Rutherford's death. The wedding took place in St Mary's parish, Edinburgh, 21st July 1834.[61] Agnes went back with him to Rotterdam to live in the house on Westnieuwland, where her first child, Charles May, was born on 19th April in the following year. Isabel had continued to live with the young couple until the baby came, but then, since she was disturbed by the noise, they furnished a house for her in Amsterdam, where she lived until her death in 1836.[62]

Charles Augustus began once more to think about his father's plan of ten years before, for him to go out to Australia. We know this because William Stewart wrote advising him, 'if you are determined on coming out here', that he should leave his mother at first with her friends in Scotland, to follow him later. Only part of the letter survives, so we do not know what William Stewart said about his daughter-in-law. But by the time this letter was written, in August 1836, Isabel had already died, the previous February. Charles Augustus was clearly beginning to feel the pressure of possible public opinion about his illegitimate status, if it should ever come to be known, for in the declaration of his mother's death she was described as 'formerly the widow of William Stewart'.[63] Charles knew this was not true, for he was in correspondence with his father. In order to hide his illegitimacy from the Dutch authorities and his own employee who signed the declaration with him, he was prepared to lie in a very public way. His father, for his part, was also feeling the need to conform to propriety. By this time he had a legitimate growing family with the girl he had married in Canada in such a hurry, and they had arrived in Australia finally in May 1835. Charles Augustus had a half-brother of eleven and three half-sisters aged twenty-one, nineteen and seventeen in the year of his own mother's death. They were his family, though he had probably not met them and around this time he sent the

[60] Rutherford's will in Rotterdam archives. A private communication to RR from MAWM showed that Marion's status as a wealthy widow was a family tradition.
[61] Old Parochial Register of Proclamation of Banns and Marriages, General Register Office, Edinburgh.
[62] Rotterdam Birth Register. Claimant p. 12.
[63] Copy from Amsterdam Death Register.

three girls a present of a silk dress each. This they refused to accept and their father wrote to tell Charles that he must not think of them as his sisters. They were at an age when plans for marriage were being made, and no girl who hoped to make a good marriage could afford to be touched by the slightest whisper of scandal. It is surprising that General Stewart, as he was by then, did not firmly discourage Charles' idea of coming out to Australia, since he was not prepared to let the three sisters know him. This ban did not apparently stretch to the legitimate son, James, and when he grew up there was quite a friendship between the half-brothers. Charles later complained to him of his sisters' attitude and 'alluded with pain to their refusal to accept the present of a dress for each.'[64] One of James' grandsons was to write, in this connection, of 'the stark difference between the easy-going eighteenth century and clan moral standards, and the terrible respectability of Victorian England. I am sure,' he said, 'my grandfather was terribly ashamed of his father.'[65] And General Stewart seems to have become ashamed of himself and of his illegitimate children. Whether this distant attitude had any influence or not, Charles and Agnes decided against going to Australia and by the time they received William's letter of advice, she was pregnant again. Their second son, John Wilson, was born on 21st March 1837 and his two-year-old elder brother died three days later — a terrible time for Agnes.[66]

The following year she had the pleasure of spending several weeks of the summer at her sister Catherine's home, Hillside, near Dunfermline. Her mother was probably living with her eldest daughter and Agnes would have been happy to show John off to them, now nearly a year and a half old and beginning to speak. In a letter to an aunt his father said, 'My little boy . . . is thriving well . . . and bears all the appearance of a hardy healthy little Scotch fellow.' Since his first child had died so young, he was probably reassuring himself as much as playing the proud father. He wrote this letter at Hillside where he had come to fetch his wife and child home. Although Charles had apparently decided against going to Australia, he was uncertain about remaining where he was. In the same letter to his aunt he wrote, 'my residence in Holland is some-what unsettled.' Change was in the wind.[67]

---

[64] *Claimant*, pp. 86, 12 and 8.
[65] Private letter from GNS to RR. Quoted with his permission.
[66] Rotterdam birth and death registers.
[67] Unpublished letter from Charles Stewart to Mrs John Innes, 5.9.1838. Papers associ-ated with *The Claimant*.

2

Childhood

Whatever change Charles had in mind when he wrote to his aunt that his residence in Holland was 'somewhat uncertain' had to be postponed, for soon after he and Agnes arrived home, she became pregnant again.

Mary Louisa Stewart was born, like her brothers before her, at 75 Westnieuwland in Rotterdam, on Wednesday 29th May, 1839, in the afternoon. Her father recorded the birth with the appropriate local authority the next day.[1] Louisa did not live in Rotterdam for long, as her parents moved to England when she was about two, but she retained vivid memories of her birthplace. Years later, when she was fifty-five, she wrote of 'the curious fascination in going back to the beginning of one's own life' as she tried to bring back her 'very earliest recollections'. The first memory of which she was 'almost sure' was of sensations only — the power of a storm of wind and the terror and astonishment it aroused.

> 'Probably enough it was but a passing blast, but it left a strange and awe-inspiring impression upon me — the realization of an actual power I had not till then known of; for it lifted me off my feet. I felt that it was something I could not resist, though it was formless and invisible. I was terrified, but far more astounded. I never forgot it; I never shall forget it.'

Such a passing blast could easily have struck her just outside her home, facing as it did on to a canal not far from the sea. Her other early memory was even more clearly one of Rotterdam, though she calls it 'a vision I have never, curiously enough, been able to localize.' It was certainly curious that she could not do so, when the details fit so well with the large sea port that Rotterdam was and is.

> 'I am walking', she wrote, 'along an unevenly paved road; the large round cobble stones are trying to my little feet, and very slippery. I think they

---

[1] Copy of MLM's birth certificate from Rotterdam archives.

are wet with a coating of greenish seaweed; and though I cannot recall any consciousness of the sea, I think it must have been near, for the strong scent of tar is over all, and in front of me at one side stands the chief feature of the scene — rows and rows of masts stretching up, up, till to my fancy they are lost in the clouds. I hear voices beside me — remarks made by the maids in charge of us children, no doubt — which seem to tell me that these wonderful poles belong to invisible ships. I must have arranged the ideas afterwards, when I knew what ships were, but at the moment I seemed to myself to be alone, quite alone, with the masts stretching up to the sky, and the tar scent in the air. I have always loved the scent. Perhaps the whole combined to prepossess me towards pine-woods!'[2]

Pine-woods and the scent of fir certainly appear over and over again in her writing. The memory of those masts meant so much to her that she had already put a description of them into the mouth of one of her child characters in a story she had written five years before the more deliberate memory-searching undertaken for the magazine article quoted above. Although a simpler and shorter description, the elements are identical.

'"The first thing I can remember in my life," said Armar, speaking slowly, "is a row of tall ships — at least they looked tall to me. Their masts seemed to reach up nearly into the sky. We were walking along a rough stony road close beside them. I remember the smell of tar so well; and if ever I smell tar now, the row of ships comes back to me. I don't know where it was."'

Louisa emphasised that these two incidents were her earliest remembrances, and that there was 'a distinct gulf' between them and the consecutive recollections she had of her life from the age of four. She considered that such early memories were 'important factors in the history of one's self,' and, indeed, that 'their very existence shows that the impressions they record were deep and lasting.'[3]

When Louisa was fifty-eight, she told an interviewer that, although she had left Holland at an early age, 'it was vividly impressed upon her mind by the stories told her by her Dutch nurse.'[4] As soon as she was

[2] MLM, 'Story-Writing', *The Monthly Packet*, no. 522, Vol. 88, Aug. 1894, p. 159.
[3] MLM, *The Story of a Spring Morning, and Other Tales*, Longmans, 1890, p. 6; 'Story-Writing', p 158.
[4] S. A. Tooley, 'Some Women Novelists', *The Woman at Home*, Dec.1897.

old enough to tell herself stories, these were always about Holland — 'my first childish romances were connected with the country where I was born . . . which became to my imagination a land of unspeakable and mysterious delight, a child's paradise.' An interesting inconsistency in one of her most popular books, *The Cuckoo Clock*, can be traced to this strong, imaginative delight in Holland. In the story Louisa at first described the clock of the title as coming from Germany, a plausible and historically accurate statement — the Black Forest was famous for its cuckoo-clocks. Yet in a scene, magically shown to the heroine, of her grandmother's childhood and the making of the clock, the references are to Holland in such phrases as 'the old Dutch mechanic' and 'Mynheer van Huyten'. Louisa had not been able to resist her old childish associations — the land of magic and delight must be Holland. These impressions were further strengthened, she thought, by the arrival 'every Christmas' from some unknown friend in Holland of 'a case of the most entrancing toys.' It is possible that the toys came from her aunt and uncle, Mary and Ebenezer Miller who continued to live in Rotterdam until August 1846, when they left for the Cape of Good Hope where Rev. Miller became minister to the Free Scottish Church.[5] At the time of their departure, the Stewarts had already spent some four or five Christmasses in England and Louisa was seven years old, an age when a 'tradition' that has lasted for only a few years can seem as fixed and eternal as an anniversary kept for fifty years does to someone older. In this way, toys from Holland 'every Christmas' became an unforgettable part of her childhood.

The Stewart family moved to England some time in late 1840 or early 1841. Charles Augustus told his half-brother in 1857 that he was at first 'connected in Preston in business in some subordinate capacity with a very crusty old gentleman.' On a business visit to Manchester he met a fellow Scot, Mr Robert Barbour, a merchant and shipping agent, who asked him how he got on with his employer. Stewart gave a conventional reply which was responded to by an invitation to join Barbour's firm. 'It is not improbable you may some day have an outbreak,' said Mr Barbour. 'Should such occur, I think we could find

---

[5] 'Story-Writing', p. 160; MLM, *The Cuckoo Clock*, Macmillan, 1877, pp 53 and 103. The friend was unknown to her when she was writing the article and she also said 'there is no-one now living who can tell me who he was'. MAWM, grand-daughter of Mary and Ebenezer Miller told RR that her grandmother lost touch with the family because of her long residence in India, where the Millers moved after the Cape.

room for you here.'[6] This is clearly the kind of family anecdote that is remembered from being frequently re-told. However it happened, the family was established in Manchester by May 1841, and Charles had joined the firm of whose head it was said 'In Manchester commercial circles few names commanded more widespread respect for many years than did that of Robert Barbour. He amassed a large fortune.'[7] Charles' fortune was to increase along with Barbour's. Soon after the Stewarts' arrival in Manchester, Louisa's third brother, another Charles, was born on Monday, 24th May. They were living at 86, Bloomsbury, Rusholme Road, Chorlton upon Medlock.

So what was this first English home like? In the nineteen-fifties, fourteen of the original Bloomsbury terrace houses were still standing, three-storey brick buildings with bay-windows on the ground-floor, rather solid and stolid. By then they were all occupied by commercial firms and looked dreary and decayed, but even at its best, no. 86 cannot have been a particularly distinguished or spacious dwelling.[8] 'The house was not a *very* pretty one; but, on the whole, it was nice and comfortable,' Louisa wrote later about the home of a child she called Louisa too, in a story that was almost certainly autobiographical.[9] It seems a suitable description of the Rusholme Road house. A later eye could not see how everyone fitted in,[10] because the house seemed so small, and certainly, by the time the Stewarts left it, there were six children, which must have made a tight squeeze with the four servants and family visitors which we know they had. The 'rather small and dull house in a dull street'[11] faced at the back onto one of the 'narrower and still uglier ones, scarcely indeed to be called streets, so dark and poky were they, so dark and poky were the poor houses they contained.' This was Boundary Street East. Part of this narrow street with its row of slum houses still existed in the late nineteen-fifties. At the front,

'it was not a very pretty prospect; they looked out on to a commonplace street, houses on both sides, though just opposite there was a little variety

[6] Unpublished papers connected with *The Claimant.*
[7] T. Swindells, *Manchester streets and Manchester men,* Manchester, Morten, 1906, series two, p. 12.
[8] RR saw the house around 1952 and wrote this description.
[9] 'The Reel Fairies' in *Tell Me A Story,* p. 9.
[10] R. L. Green visited the house in 1959 and expressed this opinion in a private letter to RR.
[11] MLM, *The Carved Lions,* Macmillan 1895, p. 3.

in the shape of an old-fashioned smoke-dried garden. Beyond that again, more houses, more streets, stretching away out into suburbs, and somewhere beyond that again the mysterious, beautiful, enchanting region which the children spoke of and believed in as "the country", not really so far off after all, though to them it seemed so.

And above the tops of all the houses, clear though faint, was now to be seen the outline of a range of hills, so softly grey-blue in the distance that but for the irregular line never changing in its form, one could easily have fancied it was only the edge of a quickly passing ridge of clouds.'[12]

Quoting this passage in *Tellers of Tales*, Roger Lancelyn Green says, 'Except that the garden was built over long ago, that is still an absolutely accurate description of the view from the top-floor windows of 92 Rusholme Road.'[13]

When she looked back, Louisa saw compensation for the dull, grey, grimy streets and houses not only in the distant view of the country and the hope of getting there sometimes, but also in the contrast between the smoke-filled air outside and the cheerfulness of fires and lights inside. She described such a contrast for instance, in *Robin Redbreast*, where Manchester is rechristened Barmettle.

'At night, when the outer world was shut off, and the dark square hall and wide quaint staircase . . . were lighted up, looking bright and cheerful with the crimson carpets and curtains which Barmettle smoke had not as yet had time to dull, Frances' expression of approval, "Really it looks so nice that you might fancy it wasn't Barmettle at all," could scarcely be contradicted.'[14]

She made the point too in a story for quite small children.

'It was grey and grimy outside, but inside the father and mother made it as bright and cheery as they could. In winter I think they managed this better than in summer, for good blazing fires do a great deal, especially of an evening when the curtains are drawn and the cold north wind,

[12] MLM, *Little Miss Peggy*, Macmillan 1887, pp. 26–7.

[13] R. L. Green, *Tellers of Tales*, Kaye and Ward, 1969, p. 107. The 1841 Census and Manchester directories 1845–1851, show Charles Stewart, merchant, living at 86, Bloomsbury, Chorlton-on-Medlock. The 1852 directory entry is 92, Bloomsbury. There is evidence that the street was re-numbered, so therefore the Stewarts continued to live in the same house. RR and RLG both thought that *Little Miss Peggy* gave an accurate idea of the Rusholme Road house.

[14] MLM, *Robin Redbreast*, Chambers, 1892, p. 256.

howling and blustering outside as if in a rage at not being able to get in, only makes the house seem still cosier. And one of the good things about the north is that coals are cheap and plentiful, so that though the vicar was not rich, there was no need to go without comfortable fires.'[15]

The elderly narrator in *The Carved Lions* recalling her childhood, also delights in this contrast between 'the gloomy, dirty streets of Great Mexington . . . now muddy and sloppy as well' and 'the feeling . . . of our cheerful home waiting for us with a bright fire and the tea-table all spread.'[16] Tea was the meal that Louisa really became lyrical about, whether nursery tea or a grown-up tea-table, temptingly arranged for a tired, home-coming adult. Such descriptions abound in her books[17] and one can guess that the child Louisa really enjoyed those winter tea-times when the curtains shut out the Manchester gloom.

Chorlton, described by a contemporary writer as 'a township in the suburbs,'[18] lay to the south of central Manchester but adjoined it on its own north side. From St Peter's Square in the heart of the city, close by the principal shopping streets and public buildings, the Oxford Road ran out through Chorlton towards the south. About three-quarters of a mile along, on the right, was Grosvenor Square with All Saints Church on one side, and the Scotch church, where later Louisa would be married, was soon to be built facing it on the other. All Saints was in Victorian days one of Manchester's fashionable churches outside which a string of carriages used to wait to take their owners home after the service. On the south of the square in Cavendish Street was Chorlton's 'neat' Town Hall. Rusholme Road led off the Oxford Road almost opposite to Grosvenor Square. In Louisa's childhood the Oxford Road was still

---

[15] MLM, 'Pansy's Pansy' in *The Thirteen Little Black Pigs and Other Stories*, SPCK, [1893], p. 56. 1st pub. in *The Child's Pictorial*, Jan.-Mar. 1892. MLM would not of course have considered the fact that the 'good, blazing fires' themselves contributed to the smoky atmosphere. It would be another 60 years or so before consciousness was raised on that point.

[16] *The Carved Lions*, p. 24.

[17] For example: *The Boys and I*, Routledge, 1882, chap. XI; *Two Little Waifs*, Macmillan, 1883, chap. XI; *The Story of a Year*, Macmillan, 1910, pp. 156–8; *A Christmas Posy*, Macmillan, 1888, pp. 4–6; *The Wood-Pigeons and Mary*, Macmillan, 1901, p. 75; *The Carved Lions*, pp. 24–28; *The February Boys*, Chambers, 1909, p. 31, and many others. See also J. Cooper, 'Just Really What They Do', *Signal*, Sep. 1988, pp. 192–5.

[18] George R. Catt, *The Pictorial History of Manchester*, reprinted from 'The Pictorial Times, [1844], p. 23.

a pleasant place to live. 'The entrance into Manchester from the south, by the Oxford Road, is handsome and striking. The road is broad clean and level; and for two miles above [i.e. south of] All Saints Church elegant country houses and villas on both sides of the road attest that this is a fashionable and healthful part of the town. Plymouth Grove boasts a shady avenue of trees and a more rural aspect.'[19] Rusholme Road, however, was a good ten streets further north than Plymouth Grove, not rural but urban, and lined with terraced houses. Old survey maps of 1850 show that 'Bloomsbury' comprised about twenty such houses fronting the north side of Rusholme Road between the Oxford Road and Brook Street. In the Stewarts' time, Rusholme Road was an ordinary residential street lived in by some of the less wealthy business men and one or two members of the professional classes while of course the inhabitants of the street at the back were much poorer and similar to 'the children at the back' described by Louisa much later on in *Little Miss Peggy*.

The next street parallel to and immediately south of the Bloomsbury section of Rusholme Road was Rosamund Street East, out of which Rumford Street ran southwards at right angles. Chorlton's most famous inhabitant, Mrs Gaskell, lived here from 1842–1850, and her comments in a letter to a friend in 1849 give an idea of the area.

'Our house is a mile and a quarter from the *very* middle of Manchester; the last house countrywards of an interminably long street, the other end of which touches the town, while we look into the fields from some of our windows; not very pretty or rural fields it must be owned, but in which the children can see cows being milked and hay being made in summer time.'[20]

Bloomsbury, being at 'the other end' of Rumford Street from the Gaskells, was definitely considered a part of town, though not in 'the *very* middle'. Years later, the narrator of *The Carved Lions* said something so similar of her own home that one feels Louisa must have been remembering Rusholme Road.

'Our house, though in a street quite filled with houses, was some little way from the centre of the town, where the best shops were — some

[19] Catt, p. 23.
[20] Mrs Gaskell to Eliza Fox, 29.5.1849. In W. Gerin, *Elizabeth Gaskell: A Biography*, OUP, 1976, p. 71.

years before, our street had, I suppose, been considered quite in the country.'[21]

At least the Stewart children could get to the not very pretty rural fields once their legs were long enough to manage the interminable street.

At this period Manchester was expanding rapidly thanks to the cotton trade. By 1841 Manchester parish already had some 185 cotton mills, 28 silk mills and many other undertakings linked to the textile business such as iron foundries, machine makers' and millwrights' workshops, dye works, bleaching works and so on. It was a boom town, becoming more and more industrialised as fast as possible. Between 1831 and 1851 the population had more than doubled. When the Stewarts moved to Rusholme Road the first regular, steam-locomotive-hauled, passenger train service in the world had already been running for eleven years from Liverpool Road station. By the time Louisa was seven, Manchester was served by seven direct railway lines. 'The guides of the time describe these wonders in a tone of almost religious awe'[22] but Manchester inhabitants were already well aware of the disadvantages of the technological progress they admired so much.

> 'Everyone who can possibly afford it hastens to leave the smoky town and pass his leisure hours and his evenings in some dwelling in the suburbs. Not only do all the manufacturers live out of town but a great proportion of the warehousemen and clerks in merchants' offices have their residences as far as possible out of the range of the factory chimneys and may be seen at one o'clock, the universal dinner hour in Manchester, hurrying up the Oxford Road towards their respective homes in some of the streets leading thereout.'[23]

Charles Stewart did not have so very far to go, as Aytoun Street, one of Manchester's main commercial streets where Robert Barbour Bros. had its warehouse and offices, was only about half a mile from Rusholme Road. So the family was not as far as perhaps they would have liked from 'the dense volumes of smoke vomited forth from a thousand mill chimneys' that hung 'in gloom and "palpable air" over the town.'[24] Frances Hodgson Burnett, writing about her childhood in the mid-

---

[21] *The Carved Lions,* p. 7.
[22] W.H.Shercliff, *Manchester, A Short History of Its Development,* Public Relations Office, Manchester, 1977, p. 29.
[23] Catt, p. 23.
[24] Catt, pp. 7–8.

fifties, when she lived in Islington Square, Salford (a mile or so west of St Peter's Square), remembered that she

> 'had always been so accustomed to the ever-falling little rain of "smuts" that it had become an accepted feature of existence. They fell upon one's features . . . They made spots upon one's hat-ribbons and disfigured one's best frock and it occurred to no-one to touch anything or rest against it without previous examination. In fact, one was so accustomed to their presence that the thought of resenting it rarely intruded itself, and one scarcely realised that there existed people who were not so rained upon.'[25]

But already, ten years or more before, according to an 1844 pictorial history, Manchester people had become accustomed to this rain of smuts.

> 'The great drawback to the health and comfort of Manchester as a residence is the coal smoke with which the atmosphere is laden . . . In particular states of the weather it is impossible to walk about Manchester without receiving a lodgement of smut upon one's nose or person; and ladies' dresses and gloves stand no chance against these shadowy ghosts of "black diamonds." '[26]

Reminiscences of this life in 'Smokytown' frequently appeared in Louisa's own writing. In her first book for children she said of one little girl 'her home was not in the country: it was in a street, in a large and rather smoky town' just like Louisa's own home and later in the story the large town was given the proper name of Smokytown.[27] An earlier book, for adults, brought in characters who could remember the days before the ubiquitous smuts, which had obviously already reached out into the surrounding countryside in Louisa's childhood. We can see this from her description of 'a farm-house on the hillside, whose inhabitants could still remember the days when sheep could graze . . . without getting to look like animated soot-bags and it was possible to gather a posy without smearing one's hands with the smuts on the leaves.'[28] She dwelt again on the idea that once the countryside had been clean, in *The Carved Lions.*

> 'It was a rather large town in an ugly part of the country, where great tall chimneys giving out black smoke, and streams — once clear sparkling

[25] F. H. Burnett, *The One I knew the Best of All,* Frederick Warne, 1893, p. 225.
[26] Catt, p. 34.
[27] *Tell Me A Story,* pp. 8–9, 14.
[28] *Not Without Thorns,* vol. 1, p. 190.

brooks, no doubt — whose water was nearly as black as the smoke, made it often difficult to believe in bright blue sky or green grass.'[29]

The feeling that Louisa had as a child about the smoke and the smuts and the dirty town, comes across in a story by her adult self, called 'The White Dove'. The child heroine

> 'could not have explained how the sight of the dark, grey streets of houses dulled her, how the smoke-dried grass that had never had a chance of being green in the fields a little way out of the town, and the dreadful black-looking river that some old, old men in the town still remembered a clear sparkling stream, made her perfectly miserable.'[30]

Chorlton had its river and streams too. It was bounded on the north by the Medlock, and on the south by the Rusholme Brook, a tributary of the Corn Brook which flowed through its centre, so these laments over polluted water in her adult writing were based on what she had actually seen as a child. A writer looking back in 1903 to the Manchester he knew in the 1850s, says 'The Irk was a foul and inky ditch and the Irwell and the Medlock were scarcely less loathesome.'[31]

The Stewarts lived in Chorlton-on-Medlock until Louisa was well on in her teens, so that she had a city upbringing, something quite unusual for her time and class. In 1841 only 17% of the population of England and Wales lived in London and cities with more than 100,000 inhabitants. By 1891 this figure had risen to 32%.[32]

In June 1841 Aunt Marion, Agnes Janet's sister, Mrs Henry Rutherford, was staying with the Stewarts. She might well have been there to help her sister after the birth of Charles, then only a few weeks old. The family had four servants,[33] one of them presumably being a nurse, the Dutch woman who told Louisa stories about the land of her birth. This year a dolls' house was specially made for Louisa. It survived to be passed to one of her grand-daughters, though 'nearly all the original furniture has suffered the fate of being played with by too young children,'[34] which is hardly surprising since Louisa was only two and a half when she received this present. *The Rectory Children* has a delightful

---

[29] *The Carved Lions*, p. 2.
[30] *The Boys and I*, p. 214.
[31] W. E. Adams, *Memoirs of a Social Atom*, 1903, Vol. 2, p. 385.
[32] Asa Briggs, *Victorian Cities*, Penguin, 1982, p. 59.
[33] 1841 Census. Names of household members were not included in this census.
[34] Unpublished letter from VMI to RR, 1951.

description of a family dolls' house being carefully renovated for the youngest girl's birthday, which could be what happened to Louisa's house. 'And only think . . . it is our own old doll-house done up. The one mamma had herself when she was a little girl, you know. Doesn't that make it all the nicer?'[35] Perhaps some such remark was once made to Louisa's own youngest daughter by one of her sisters.

The Dutch nurse may only have stayed for a time as we learn about another nurse from a few facts recorded by Louisa's son-in-law.

'Louisa Stewart (Molesworth) had a nurse, Hannah Jenkinson, who had been in the service of Dorothy Wordsworth, the poet's sister. When Louisa was a child Hannah Jenkinson left and returned to the Words-worths. Soon after, Wordsworth the poet wrote to Louisa on behalf of Hannah Jenkinson, inviting Louisa to come to see them, and sending a Stewart Tartan handkerchief.'[36]

In the Wordsworth family letters there are several mentions of an old servant called Hannah who remained with them after she had ceased to be able to work, and who died in their care. Although her surname is not given, this could have been Louisa's Hannah.[37]

---

[35] MLM, *The Rectory Children*, Macmillan, 1889, p. 196.

[36] *De Principe*. Mrs Molesworth's grand-daughter, VMI, had also heard of this nurse and wrote to RR about her: 'Did you know that my grandmother had as a child a nurse who had been in the service of Dorothy Wordsworth. She returned to their [the Wordsworth's] service and told them about "little Louisa" and the poet wrote her a charming letter. (Alas destroyed).' *The Letters of Mary Wordsworth 1800–1855,* selected and edited by Mary E. Burton, Oxford: Clarendon Press, 1958, contains several mentions of a servant called Hannah. For example, 9.12.1854. 'I wish my Hannah who is with me was as well rid of hers [sc. 'her cold']', p. 349; 22.12.1855, 'Hannah is come to enquire after her [sc. Dorothy Wordsworth],' p. 351.

[37] MLM used this episode in a piece of autobiographical reminiscence. She described an old servant coming to say goodbye to the children of the house, and crying because she had to leave them and go away to take care of her old mistress. '[This] was Miss Dorothy Wordsworth. And though [the children] never saw the faithful servant any more, they heard from, or rather of, her before long. For only a few weeks had passed when one morning the postman brought a small parcel directed to themselves and a letter . . . in a queer somewhat shaky hand-writing, that of Mr Wordsworth himself, now an aged man for it was within a few years of his death; the parcel contained a tempting-looking volume bound in red and gold — "selections for the young" — of the laureate's poems with Jack's name inscribed therein, and even more gratifying from the kindly thoughtfulness it displayed, a little silk neckerchief in tartan — the children's own tartan, for they belonged to a Scotch clan — for Maimie. And the letter written to the old servant's dictation, for she could not write herself, told of her consultation with her master as to the most appropriate presents to choose for her little favourites'.

Louisa was about four when this incident occurred. She would have been experiencing the usual Victorian middle-class childhood, living in the nursery, having regular little lessons with her mother or perhaps a nursery governess, lessons which became longer as she grew older, going for regular walks with nurse or a housemaid when nurse was busy with a new baby. As we have heard from Mrs Gaskell, it was still possible to get into fields from Chorlton. The beginning of *Mary Barton* describes an expedition in such fields.

> 'There are some fields near Manchester, well known to the inhabitants as "Green Heys Fields", through which runs a public footpath to a little village about two miles distant. . . . these commonplace but thoroughly rural fields . . . are popular places of resort at every holiday time.'[38]

They were popular with the factory girls and workmen as well as nurse-maids and children like the Stewarts. Greenheys was a district which began about half a mile south of Rusholme Road, on the other side of the Oxford Road.[39] In one of her stories, Louisa wrote of a walk in fields which might have been these, taken by children somewhat older than she was herself at this time.

> 'We went out a walk that afternoon with the housemaid — quite a long walk though it was winter. We went as far out of town as we could get, to where there were fields which in spring and summer still looked green, and through the remains of a little wood, pleasant even in the dullest season. It was our favourite walk and the only pretty one near the town. There was a brook at the edge of the wood which still did its best to sing merrily, and to forget how dingy and grimy its clear waters became

MLM, 'A Ramble about Childhood', *The Girls' Own Annual,* vol. 20, Oct. 1898-Sep. 1899, 4.2.1899 pp. 292–4. MLM tells this story as though it happened to a third person, naming the children Jack, the short version of John, her eldest brother's name, and Maimie, a recognised diminutive for her own first name, Mary, though she was called Louisa.

[38] Mrs Gaskell, *Mary Barton and Other Tales* Smith Elder, pocket ed. p.7.

[39] 'Greenheys district took its name from "Greenhay":- a country-house built by my father; and at the time of its foundation (say in 1791 or 1792) separated from the last outskirts of Manchester by an entire mile; but now, and for many a year, overtaken by the hasty strides of this great city, and long since (I presume) absorbed into its mighty uproar.' Thomas De Quincey, *Confessions of an Opium Eater*, with introduction and notes by Mark Hunter. London: George Bell and Sons, 1896, p. 21, footnote. Although the *Confessions* was first published in 1822, this note was added to the 1856 edition, so that 'now', 'for many a year' and 'long since' apply to the period of MLM's childhood and youth.

a mile or two further on; there were still a few treasures in the shape of
ivy sprays and autumn-tinted leaves to gather and take home with us to
deck our nursery. . . . It was the favourite walk of many besides ourselves,
especially on a Saturday when the hard-worked Mexington folk were for
once free to ramble about — boys and girls not much older than ourselves
among them, for in those days children were allowed to work in factories
much younger than they do now.'[40]

This is one of several passages in Louisa's books which suggest that
growing up in smoky Manchester gave her a special love for the country.
Her child characters were usually depicted as eager to live in or at least
to visit 'those sweet pure country scenes that children love.'[41] When she
commented as narrator, either direct to her child readers or through the
person of the child narrator she put forward, she emphasised this love
of the country in a way that makes us feel she too, as a child, longed
for the country. From Tib, Gussie and Gerald in *The Palace in the
Garden* to the five-year-old heroine in *Little Miss Peggy* the feeling is the
same. '"Just fancy if we were in the country and could gather primroses
for ourselves — as many as ever we wanted! *Wouldn't* it be lovely?"'
and 'Do you know how beautiful a first waking in the real country is
when you have been a long time in London?' The younger Peggy
complained, '"Everybody's fathers and mothers lived there [sc. in the
country] . . . Why don't peoples let their children live there now?"'[42]
'Everybody' to Peggy meant the few grown-up people who comprised
her small world, but the grand-parents, if not the parents, of almost
everybody who was a child during Louisa Stewart's childhood, had
indeed lived in the country, or in a country town.

The urbanization, (and the industrialization that caused it) which led
to the 17% of the population mentioned earlier living in large towns
and cities, was a comparatively recent phenomenon. Not many decades
had passed since the grand entombment of the countryside pictured in
Walter Greenwood's *History of Lancashire* when

'the little villages in the valley and the country town saw paviours at
work as though on an endless tomb. Beneath the flagstones they laid for
pavements was immured the body of the green fields and the lively

---

[40] *The Carved Lions*, p. 43.

[41] ibid., p. 2.

[42] MLM, *The Palace in the Garden*, Hatchards, 1887, pp. 27 and 52; and *Little Miss
Peggy*, p. 122.

chuckling brook they coffined in a brick culvert. Around and about the parent mill, without plan or design, sprawled the endless wretchedness of the 'homes' of the workers.'[43]

Louisa's walks, whether or not the nursery party managed to get as far as the country each time, were shared at first with John two years older, and Charles two years younger. By the time the latter was old enough to walk some distance on his own there was another baby in the nursery, the first sister for Louisa, Agnes, born in 1845 and the next year came another brother, William Wilson.

Indoors the children shared toys, divided into best and everyday. 'We kept these best toys behind a large sofa in my mother's drawing-room', she wrote, looking back. Some of the best toys had been sent from Holland by the unknown friend mentioned earlier. She remembered one in detail — 'a miniature chariot drawn by four greys, which pranced as we made it run along. And the doors opened, and little steps let down.' But even best toys had their drawbacks, for 'inside sat a doll gentleman and lady who always irritated me because they were only shaped to *sit*, and could not stand upright.'[44] In one interview she gave as an adult, Louisa also talked about a 'wonderful Dutch costume doll' as a toy she specially remembered. But another item she spoke about to this interviewer, which was clearly far more significant in her eyes when she was still a child, was 'a miniature cabinet with unsuspected drawers and recesses.'[45] We can deduce its importance from the number of times she mentioned it in other interviews and in the autobiographical pieces she wrote in the 1890s. To another interviewer she defined the lovingly remembered object as 'the Japanese cabinet [that] belonged to her sister — a wonderful specimen, with steps and cupboards within cupboards and mandarins standing about.'[46] In one of her own pieces, written in 1894, Louisa described it more fully.

'Some years later another friend, a Belgian gentleman this time, whom I remember personally, gave me a miniature cabinet, part of which opened to show unsuspected drawers and recesses inside. Many years afterwards, in a relation's house, I saw a very much larger cabinet — a Japanese one — of a somewhat similar construction, though far more elaborate. It

---

[43] Walter Greenwood, *History of Lancashire*, County Books Series, 1951, p. 7.
[44] 'Story-Writing', p. 160.
[45] Isabel Stuart Robson, *Story Weavers: or Writers for the Young*, Robert Culling, 1900.
[46] Bella Sydney Woolf, 'Children's Classics', *The Quiver*, 1906, p. 675.

recalled to me my own old tiny one, and I think these are answerable for my little story of 'The Nodding Mandarins,' and for some parts of 'The Cuckoo Clock.'"[47]

Clearly the 'relation's house' was her sister's home when grown up. The awakened memory of her own miniature cabinet and the strong feelings she had had about it combined with this newly seen, attractive piece of furniture to form the basis of the chapter of *The Cuckoo Clock* called 'The Country of the Nodding Mandarins'. This was published in 1877, some seventeen years before she wrote the paragraph quoted above, and the gap probably accounts for her seeming to think that 'The Nodding Mandarins' was a separate story from *The Cuckoo Clock*.

For everyday, Louisa's great resource was dolls — not big dolls for dressing or nursing, but little ones as characters in stories.

'No big doll' *she said,* 'ever became a dear friend to me. What I loved was little ones, really very small ones, of which I could have enough to group them into families, or to make them act dramas. And if my collection of small dolls ran short I was never at a loss for other puppets — reels of cotton which I borrowed from my mother's workbox on condition of "putting them all neatly back again," did admirably.'[48]

This account comes from a magazine article, but Louisa also used this part of her own life as the basis for a story, describing her doll substitutes in a more dramatic way.

'Louisa' — *she called the child in the story by her own name because it was first published under a pseudonym, so there was no need to think up a different one* — 'Louisa was sometimes rather lonely and at a loss for companions and this led to her making friends in a very odd way indeed. If you guessed for a whole year I do not think you would ever guess whom, or I should say *what*, she chose for her friends. Indeed, I fear that when I tell you you will hardly believe me; you will think I am "story-telling" indeed. Listen — it was not her doll, nor a pet dog, nor even a favourite pussy-cat — it was, they were rather, *the reels in her mother's workbox.*'[49]

In the article Louisa went on to mention other objects enlisted into the dramatic productions of her childhood.

---

[47] 'Story-Writing' p. 160.
[48] 'Story-Writing' p. 161.
[49] *Tell Me A Story*, p. 10.

'Or shells, of which we happened to have a large collection were charming for this purpose. I almost think I preferred these substitutes for dolls, at one time, to the dolls themselves. They allowed, the shells especially, such unlimited scope for the imagination, the only advantage of the reels being that I could dress them, by tying bright coloured silks or ribbons round them. The shells, I think, gained my greatest affection. I have sobbed for hours at the loss or breakage of some special favourite, a prima donna of my baby dramas.'[50]

This last sentence actually summarizes a story she had written years before in 1877, 'My Pink Pet',[51] not long after 'The Reel Fairies', based on her games with the shells. The two stories demonstrate in detail that what the child Louisa loved about both cotton reels and shells was the acting of dramas, the 'scope for the imagination'. All the cotton reels had names and ranks suited to their physical appearance — for instance, she christened 'two pretty little reels of fine China silk' as the Chinese Princesses, Blanche and Rose, and 'the adventures they had, the elegance and luxury in which they lived, the wonderful stories they told each other!' On the day of which 'The Reel Fairies' tells, 'one of the Chinese Princesses was to be married to one of the Lords Flossy [a larger silk reel].'[52] The shells became characters out of *The Arabian Nights* or all the well-known old fairy-tales.

'. . . Cinderella and dear Beauty and Riquet with the tuft. There was one brown shell with a little hump on its back which did splendidly for Riquet. Then for a change to more sober life I dramatised *The Fairchild Family* and *Jemima Placid.*'

The favourite shell of Lois, in 'My Pink Pet' was described in the same phrase Louisa used in her article — 'the beautiful pale-rose-coloured shell . . . was ever my prima donna and special favourite.'[53] Both Lois in the shell story and Louisa in the reels story are desperate to keep their favourite activity a secret, for fear of being laughed at. This intense, concealed acting out both of made-up and made-over stories must have been a good, if unconscious preparation for the later story-writing. Frances Hodgson Burnett did much the same sort of thing. Dolls were only of interest to her as heroines in an on-going drama. While her

[50] 'Story-Writing', pp. 161–2.
[51] 'My Pink Pet', *A Christmas Posy*, pp. 28–52.
[52] *Tell Me A Story*, p. 16.
[53] *A Christmas Posy*, pp. 38–39.

sisters arranged their dolls' house and played at tea-parties in what we might think of as the normal way, she 'entertained herself with wildly-thrilling histories, which she related to herself in an undertone, while she acted them with the assistance of her Doll.'[54]

A brief event in 'My Pink Pet', which had prompted an aunt to give the child Lois shells to play with in the first place, became the basis for a complete story, called 'The Goblin Face'. This appeared in *The Child's Pictorial* seven years after the earlier story was published in *Aunt Judy's Magazine*. It suggests another element in Louisa's own childhood. The incident common to both tales was an episode of nervous terror in a young child, one aged nine and one five. Louisa often reworked the same happening for another tale, and where she did this, there was probably some foundation in her own experience.[55] In these stories Louisa described the children waking in the night and being terrified by what they thought were mysterious faces alive and moving. What the child really saw was the effect of candlelight on a piece of china. In the one case it was an old Delft vase, in the other, two old Dutch vases, standing on a high shelf where the child had not noticed it, or them, in the daytime. In the longer story the child had already been made frightened and nervous by overhearing ghost stories, told by a servant to her siblings. But, a touch which Louisa often repeated, she told nobody of her trouble. In another of Louisa's short tales for *The Child's Pictorial*, a girl who was unreasonably frightened of a beggar playing a broken barrel organ round the streets of her town, suffered weeks of misery because she told no-one of her fear, and commented 'I really cannot quite explain why I did not tell about it to mamma.'[56] Brave little Denis, in the story of that name, was terrified of the faces of the portraits in the picture gallery he had to pass along to reach his room when on a visit to an elderly relative. But he would not tell, nor allow his sister to tell, partly because he wanted to try to be brave and also not to give trouble, but as well, commented Louisa as narrator, 'partly from the strange reserve one often finds in even very little children. Few but those who have watched them very constantly and closely have any idea how much children will endure rather than complain.'[57]

---

[54] *The One I Knew the Best of All*, p. 47.
[55] This point is commented on further in an account of 'A Ramble about Childhood' in chapter 12 and *The Carved Lions* in chapter 13.
[56] MLM, *The Man with the Pan-Pipes and Other Stories*, SPCK, [1892], p. 19.
[57] *The Green Casket and Other Stories*, Chambers, [1890], p. 102.

Having, in this way, emphasised adult ignorance of childish fears in a story, Louisa enlarged on it eight years after this story was published, in one of her semi-autobiographical articles. She warned would-be writers for children to avoid introducing 'any frightening element' into a story and then described in perceptive detail both the hysterical terror and the reluctance to confide in anyone.

'Unless one knows children intimately, or recalls minutely the experiences of one's own childish days, it would be difficult to believe how even a bright, healthy child may be the victim of nervous terrors. The most sensitive are often the most reserved; partly, perhaps, from a not by any means contemptible feeling of pride, partly from that curious reticence of children, of which — for it often fades as they grow older and could themselves explain it — the root is difficult to discover. For you find it even in the happiest families, where dread of their elders is non-existent, where sympathy is very far from an unknown quantity.'[58]

I think it very likely that Louisa herself, between the ages of five and nine, had some experience of great fear associated with a Dutch vase, a natural item in the furnishings of Charles Augustus' home, since he had lived in Holland for so many years, and that she too did not tell. E. Nesbit in her turn described her inability to tell anyone of her terrors — 'I could not tell anyone the full horror of it while it was over me' — and felt that the inarticulate state of a child in great fear was largely inexplicable. 'I have often wondered what it is that keeps children from telling their mothers these things — and even now I don't know.' Dickens remarked on this same point 'few people know what secrecy there is in the young, under terror.'[59]

One source of nervous fears can be loneliness, and, in writing about her namesake in 'The Reel Fairies', Louisa suggested, as we have seen, that the child resorted to games with her mother's cotton reels because she was 'sometimes rather lonely and at a loss for companions.' In the year that the real Louisa Stewart was eight years old, the age of the story Louisa, her elder brother, John, was ten, Charles was six, and the two smallest members of the family, Agnes and William were two and one respectively. This situation fits 'The Reel Fairies' exactly.

---

[58] 'Story-Reading and Story-Writing', p. 774b.
[59] E. Nesbit, *Long Ago When I Was Young*, Ronald Whiting and Wheaton, 1966, p. 65; Julia Briggs, *A Woman of Passion*, Hutchinson 1987, p. 10; Peter Ackroyd, *Dickens*, Sinclair Stevenson, 1990, p. 50.

'There were two brothers who came nearest Louisa in age, one older and one younger, and two or three mites of children smaller still. The brothers went to school and were so much interested in the things "little boys are made of," that they were apt to be rather contemptuous to Louisa because she was a girl, and the wee children in the nursery were too wee to think of anything but their own tiny pleasures and troubles.'[60]

The town in which she lived, the game she played and her family situation all correspond to Louisa Stewart's own life to such an extent that it is impossible not to feel this really is an autobiographical story, and that Louisa looked back and saw her child self as lonely and companionless at times — times which fuelled the urge to make up stories.

In several other books Louisa described a girl who was lonely and rather looked down on among brothers or cousins devoted to boyish activities. Commenting on Leonora in the short story 'Poor Miss Crawfurd', she said 'in some ways one sister among several brothers is rather like an only child' and that if the brothers 'thought about her at all when she was not actually forced upon their notice, it was with a sort of half-contemptuous pity that she was not a boy!'[61] The eponymous heroine of *Little Miss Peggy* was both teased a lot and left alone among her five brothers, three of school age and two in the nursery. She was also treated to a fair amount of 'rubbish' and 'you silly girl' and she knew very well, like Lois and Louisa, that if any of her fancies were discovered she would be laughed at. Even the three-year-old, Hal, was shown growing easily and unconsciously into masculine contempt for anything female. Peggy tried to tell him how she knew which way to go when nurse told her to turn left. Her pocket was on the right, she explained,

' "and so I know the side it isn't at is the left." Hal listened with some interest but a slight tinge of contempt for feminine garments. "Boys has pockets at each sides, so all boys' sides is right," he said.'[62]

Hal was simply making a straightforward literal statement about life as he saw it, but it is tempting to apply his remark more widely, and to see behind the figure of this three-year-old, a giant masculine shadow, standing astride Victorian England, hands in pockets, gazing with benign contempt on the Lilliputian females at his feet. As another example, the

---

[60]   *Tell Me A Story*, p. 10.

[61]   'Poor Miss Crawfurd', *The Story of a Spring Morning*, p. 253.

[62]   *Little Miss Peggy* p. 62.

same tone occurs frequently in *Miss Mouse and Her Boys*, where the girl is at first puzzled and startled by her five male cousins. A tiny instance is her misunderstanding their reference to 'animals', until her aunt mentions 'pets', but this expression is scorned by the boys as 'a girls' word.'[63] Louisa did not lay any undue emphasis on these situations she so often depicted, where the 'boy-ey' boys look down on the girls and keep them in their place. This was how Victorian society was, and the cult of the superiority of the male began in the nursery. She was only describing normal households, the kind of situation in which she herself grew up. A later Victorian writer, whose first cousin was to marry one of Louisa's daughters, was much more forceful about her misery as her brother succumbed to contemporary social attitudes on being sent away to boarding-school.

'Adrian was now at Mr West's school at Bournemouth where the elder boys had been. We had been constant companions and very great friends up to this time whenever the two elder boys were away and he had not to show his manhood by ill-treating girls, and I was horrified and miserable when he came back for the first holidays and I realised that he had *really* learnt to despise girls and no longer wanted to play with me. I went through several days of anguish and then put him out of my mind. We never were the least intimate after that, though I always had a great respect for him.'[64]

Louisa usually underlined the opposite state of affairs in her stories — if she wanted to portray a boy who behaved kindly, with equal friendship towards girls, she pointed it up as something unusual, as here.

'He was then a boy of twelve and Mary was eight, and boys of twelve sometimes look down on little girls who are four or five years younger than they are. Not so with Michael, he *was* so good and kind'. *Later Mary said of Michael* 'He is my favourite cousin, and there isn't anything I don't tell him. He always understands and never laughs at me.'[65]

Variety came to Louisa and her brothers and sister in the shape of regular visits to the seaside and to Scotland. She once said in an interview that her parents had had a little house at a seaside place where they used to send their children for some part of the year. This has been

---

[63] MLM, *Miss Mouse and Her Boys*, Macmillan, 1897, p. 16.
[64] Annabel Huth Jackson, *A Victorian Childhood*, Methuen, 1932, p. 35–6.
[65] *The Woodpigeons* , pp. 22 and 27.

identified as Fleetwood on the southern shore of Morecambe Bay in Lancashire.[66] It was a new town, founded by the wealthy landowner Peter Hesketh of Rossall Hall. By 1840, on a site valued in 1824 at £50, a town had been built and the railway brought from Preston.[67] Charles Stewart rented a house there for most of his life once he had settled in Manchester. A memorial plaque was erected to him in the parish church, which describes him as 'of Fleetwood' and this would hardly have been done unless he had had a fairly long and close connection with the town. When Fleetwood was laid out, 'the streets were made to radiate from an eminence called the Mount on the north side by the Irish sea.'[68] The house Charles rented was on the north-east side of The Mount and only separated from it by one small street, in a row called Mount Terrace, which had already been built by the end of 1839. It consisted of five solid-looking bay windowed houses immediately overlooking the beach and the sea,[69] facing north-west across Morecambe Bay towards the Lake District. The town immediately became a popular resort after the establishment of the railway. In the first few years the visitors were the wealthy Lancashire manufacturers and mill owners, the better class trades people and even titled people and occasionally minor royalty. 'Whole families complete with servants would arrive for a two or three month's stay, renting a house for the season.'[70] In 1845 'a handsome promenade and carriage drive was completed along the border of the shore from the North Euston Hotel to the west extremity of the Mount Terrace.'[71]

This may have been the point at which Charles Stewart started to visit Fleetwood regularly or anyway to send the children there. Sandyshore in *Carrots*, Louisa said when she was sixty-seven, was a reminiscence of the 'seaside place' of her childhood — Fleetwood.[72] In the

---

[66] *The Quiver*, 1906, p. 675. MLM did not herself say in this interview that the seaside place of her childhood was Fleetwood but it is known from other sources.

[67] Alan Lockett, *Ports and People of Morecambe Bay*, North Lonsdale Publications, 1976.

[68] *The Victoria History of the County of Lancashire*, Constable, 1906, vol. 7, p. 237, note 86. Later quoted as VCH.

[69] Information about the house rented by the Stewarts at Fleetwood comes from C. A. Stewart's death certificate, Lancashire Directories 1871 and 1873, MLM's letters to JBLW, addresses on MLM's letters to Macmillan's and a photo provided by the District Central Library, Fleetwood.

[70] Bill Curtis, *Fleetwood — A Town is Born*, Lavenham; Terence Datton, 1986, p. 29.

[71] John Porter, *History of the Fylde of Lancashire*, Fleetwood and Blackpool, 1876, p. 232. Note that his account came out in 1876, the year *Carrots* was published.

[72] *Quiver*, p. 675.

story she described it as 'not at all a dangerous coast' and then, in another negative,

'it was not what is called "picturesque". It was a long flat stretch of sandy shore, going on and on for miles just the same. There were very few trees and no mountains, not even hills . . . every one said it was such a nice safe place for little people.'[73]

A similar description in a short story for small children is clearly also of Fleetwood.

'The place we were at was called Sandybeach. And it *was* a sandy beach. There were no cliffs or rocks or even sandhills or quicksands. It sounds rather stupid but it was not a bad place. To start with it had the *name* of being "a very safe place for children." '[74]

The boy narrator of this story is pleased at the safe reputation of Sandy-beach as a help in escaping too close supervision from grown-ups and the Stewart children were probably also left to their own devices and pleased to be so. Carrots and his four-years-older sister Floss were finally allowed on the beach by themselves when he was six, only of course where nurse could still see them when she peeped out of the window.[75]

In *Carrots* we also find the statement 'In summer, a few, just a very few visitors used to come to Sandyshore for bathing'[76] which does not seem to match with the accounts of its popularity quoted above. In 1841 the year after the railway arrived, 108,000 people took the trip to Fleetwood — not 'just a very few'.[77] But the town suffered from the fickle public and the equally fickle weather. Serious storms and floods in both 1847 and 1852 caused devastation and the 'handsome promenade' was pounded by heavy seas and fell into dilapidation.

'Huge stones which formerly protected the green sward and road from the waves are now [1876] lying scattered and buried about the beach; while the westerly end of the promenade has not only suffered utter

---

[73] *Carrots*, pp. 13–14.
[74] MLM, 'Where was Tony?', *The Children's Hour*, Nelson, [1899], pp. 123–124.
[75] The safe, sandy beach was certainly a fact about Fleetwood and the neighbouring coastline. 'Sand is the characteristic bottom deposit in the sea off the coast of Lancashire . . . The set of sea currents is such along the sea coast from north of Liverpool to Fleetwood that almost continuous sandy beaches are formed.' VCH, vol. 1, p. 26.
[76] *Carrots*, p. 14.
[77] Curtis, p. 29.

annihilation itself, but serious inroads have been made by the water into the ornamental gardens fronting the houses of Mount Terrace.'[78]

The numbers of visitors recorded decreased while those to Blackpool just down the coast increased. Since the Stewarts were still visiting Fleetwood in the 1870s when Charles Stewart died there, they obviously did not join the faithless majority, and would no doubt have described the devastation just opposite their house and the decrease in visitors to their grown-up children. But Louisa certainly saw all this for herself as we know she continued to visit Fleetwood and stay in the house near The Mount long after she became adult.[79] Her adult knowledge of the place could have combined with childhood memory to produce the statement about only a few visitors.

Louisa also said that the Stewart children were sent to Fleetwood 'for some part of the year' which need not necessarily mean only the summer months. They may well have been there at times other than 'a few weeks in the fine summer time, when it [sc. the sea] looks so bright and sunny and inviting', times when the sea 'looks so dull and leaden that one can hardly believe it will ever be smiling and playful again . . . fierce rough days, when it lashes itself with fury.' Since the Mount Terrace house faced the sea, it had the same position as Cove House in *Carrots*.

> 'Carrot's nursery window looked straight out upon the sea, and many and many an hour Floss and he spent at this window, watching their strange fickle neighbour at his gambols. I do not know that they thought the sea at all wonderful. I think they were too much accustomed to it for that, but they certainly found it very *interesting*.'[80]

In the same interview in which she identified Sandyshore as the seaside place she had visited as a child, Louisa also said that Carrots and his sisters were based partly upon her own children, so that it is dangerous to assume that their thoughts and feelings were necessarily her own, although since the house and the place were founded on fact, we can at least imagine Louisa and her younger brother Charles gazing out of the window of Mount Terrace at Morecambe Bay. We cannot know exactly when Louisa first saw the sea, but she remembered the feeling it gave her — 'the feeling one has the first time one sees the sea — a sort of mixture of plea-

---

[78] Porter, p. 232.

[79] Two letters to Macmillan's in 1875 from MLM are addressed from The Mount, Fleetwood. She also mentions staying there with her children in several letters to JBLW.

[80] *Carrots*, pp. 12–13.

sure and wonder, that makes one almost feel as if one were dreaming.'[81]

In an article for children published in *Little Folks*, Louisa related how, when she went to Scotland, she used to stay with her grandmother in 'a very old-fashioned country house' often for most of the summer — 'the happy summers we spent in the country.' This was probably Hillside, Saline, near Dunfermline, the home of her uncle and aunt Colville where Louisa's maternal grandmother, Nancy Wilson was living or staying with her eldest daughter. These visits began when Louisa was very young, for she wrote 'almost my first recollection is of my grandmother,' and certainly before Agnes was born, since the grandmother sat, Louisa said, 'with my brothers and myself, and later on a little sister, round her in a group.' As we have already seen, her brother John paid his first visit to Hillside at the age of seventeen months and it is quite likely that Louisa was fully as young when she first went there.

Louisa obviously loved and admired her grandmother, recalling her as 'very sweet and very clever,' sure that she would have been a writer herself had she lived at a later period. The grandchildren were specially impressed with her ability to 'sketch for us anything we liked to ask for' and as an adult Louisa commented 'She had never had regular lessons in drawing or painting and yet . . . her sketches and paintings show unusual talent.' So the children 'were very fond of her, but just a little afraid of her too.' This fear or respect stemmed partly from Mrs Wilson's seeming so old to Louisa, 'more like a great-grandmother; and so she was, for I was one of the youngest of a large group of grandchildren.' In 1844 when Louisa was five, her grandmother was seventy-nine and Louisa's mother was the youngest of her four daughters. But the children respected their grandmother also because

'she was so delicate and dainty . . . everything about her was always so beautifully neat and precise that we never thought of rushing in to her with untidy hair or crumpled pinafores; a visit to the nursery "to be made neat" always came before a visit to her.'

Later on Louisa often described children in her stories being made tidy in the nursery before going down to dessert or to see Mamma. There was a special reason for Louisa and her brothers wanting to cluster round their grandmother — 'at story-telling she was unrivalled.'[82]

---

[81] MLM, *Nesta; or Fragments of a Little Life,* W. and R. Chambers, 1889, p. 26.
[82] 'How I Write . . .', p. 16–17. All references in the previous two paragraphs are to this article.

Elsewhere, Louisa emphasised her grandmother's talent even more strongly, saying 'this grandmother was a genius at story-telling, often illustrating her narrations by pictures that she drew for us "out of her head".' It was from this story-telling that Louisa received her first taste of the delight of the fairy-tales which, up to the age of fourteen or fifteen, were the source of her 'most perfect felicity'.[83] She only mentioned two fairy stories by name as ones told by her grandmother — 'The Fair One with Golden Locks' and 'The Brown Bull o' Norrowa'[84] (this last being one she herself re-told in *The Tapestry Room*[85]) — but we can assume that this was how she first became acquainted with 'all the well-known old fairy tales' as she called them in 'My Pink Pet'. Mrs Wilson did not tell her grandchildren fairy-tales only. Sometimes she related stories 'of herself or her own children when they were young,'[86] and if we want to know what kind of stories these were, we have only to look at *Grandmother Dear*. Louisa said in a letter, that this book contained 'little tales of rather old-world life which are all what were told to me of and by my own grandmother and mother.'[87] Such tales, she added, were to be found in 'several others' but *Grandmother Dear*[88] is the title specifically mentioned.

These story-telling sessions were clearly the foundation of Louisa's two kinds of writing for children — fantasy and fairy tale, and the realistic story of everyday child-life. That they made a great impression on her is shown not only by her recalling them in articles she wrote herself but also by her mention of them to interviewers.[89] The material she received from her grandmother was well grounded in her memory through repetition. When 'the happy summers we spent in the country were over' and the children were back in Manchester, Louisa was begged to tell the stories again and again because she remembered them more exactly than the others. By degrees she began to invent ones of her own to supplement her stock, thus taking up the position in the nursery of 'Story-Laureate' as she called it — the same post was held by Mrs Ewing

[83] 'Story-Writing', p. 163.
[84] 'How I Write . . .', p. 16.
[85] MLM, *The Tapestry Room*, Macmillan, 1879, pp. 141–194.
[86] 'How I Write . . .', p. 16.
[87] Letter from MLM to Edward Salmon, 12.10.1886, lent to RR by Edward Salmon in 1938.
[88] See chapter 1, note 11.
[89] F. H. L., 'A Popular Writer for Children: Mrs Molesworth', *Westminster Budget*, 20.10.1893, p. 24; *Woman at Home*, p. 193.

among her brothers and sisters. Obviously in the days before any of our electronic means of amusement, someone who could tell stories on request was really valuable to the nursery and schoolroom community. 'I know I could always bribe my companions,' said Louisa, 'to do anything I wanted by the promise of a story.'[90] When Frances Hodgson Burnett's schoolfriends discovered that she could 'make one up out of her own head,' they were forever pestering her to 'tell some more' of the current on-going exciting serial.[91] Mrs Ewing too had a demanding audience which protested

> 'when she paused for what seemed to us a longer five minutes than usual in the middle of some story she was telling, to think what the next incident should be!'

but which allowed her to re-tell the adventures of a favourite hero when she could not think of anything new.[92] Louisa also went in for instalments or sequels.

> 'I made up stories in plenty, some of them coming to have a permanent existence, so as to be told over and over again, some in parts or chapters supplied according to the nursery demand.'[93]

But unlike Frances Hodgson Burnett, who had been struggling to find enough paper to write on and scribbled on the greasy pages at the back of the butcher's book for want of anything better, before she started telling stories to anyone,[94] Louisa told stories first and wrote them down much later — because she had trouble in actually learning to write. Reading came to her so easily and so early that she could not remember a time when she had not been able to read or when reading stories was not her greatest delight. French, too, was an early acquirement, both understanding and speaking, though she added 'after a very queer fashion, I dare say'. But writing was different — 'it was wretchedness and misery to me'. Because of this difficulty, she did not write down her first stories — 'I think I was past ten before I ever 'wrote out' anything, and then only little plays which *had* to be so treated for convenience' sake.'[95] She recalled in one story the writing exercises she

[90] 'How I Write . . .', pp. 16–17.
[91] *The One I Knew the Best of All*, pp. 193–5.
[92] Horatia Gatty, *Juliana Horatia Ewing and Her Books*, SPCK, 1887, pp. 6–7.
[93] 'Story-Writing', p. 160.
[94] *The One I Knew the Best of All*, p. 167–8.
[95] 'Story-Writing', p.160.

had to do. 'When I was a little girl I remember reading a story about the old proverb which in those days was to be found as one of the model lines in a copy-book. This one stood for the letter 'C' and it was, 'Custom commonly makes things easy.'"[96]

As well as copies, she had to write letters. One of the very, very few of her family letters to survive was a note in capitals between ruled pencil lines to 'My dear Papa'. There is no address or date but the use of capitals and the style suggests she may have been about seven or eight.

Thursday

My dear Papa
    We are very happy & we should be more happy if you were with us. We went to The Botanical Gardens, and have been in the Zoological Gardens a whole evening and saw many animals. And heard the military band playing. Our little cousins drank tea with us on Tuesday. One is called James Henry and the other Charles. With love and kisses from your affectionate Mary Louisa.[97]

Aunt Marion Rutherford had married again before 1849. Her second husband was an accountant called George Meldrum, and they lived in 53, York Place, Edinburgh.[98] Louisa was probably staying with them when she wrote this letter. Edinburgh certainly had a fine Botanical Gardens which was founded in 1824[99] and there was also a Zoological Gardens, that existed between 1840 and 1867, thus being almost the same age as Louisa herself. It was 'a small imitation of the old Vauxhall Gardens in London' which explains why Louisa experienced more than animals there.[100] The Meldrums do not appear to have had any children, but Aunt Catherine Colville had several, including one called Henry. Louisa's mother also had four brothers, any of whose children could have been the 'little cousins' in question.

Another correspondent of Louisa's was her grandfather in Australia. She remembered struggling to write to him.

[96] MLM, *The Oriel Window*, Macmillan, 1896, p. 82.
[97] Letter copied by RR from the original in the possession of CP, afterwards destroyed.
[98] Death certificate of Mary (Nancy) Wilson; Edinburgh Directories; information to RR from MAWM.
[99] Ward Lock's *Guide to Edinburgh*, 1906, p. 187.
[100] James Grant, *Cassell's Old and New Edinburgh*, 3 vols, Cassell and Co., 1883. Vol. 3, p. 88.

'I can even now feel sorry for my poor little cramped fingers toiling away at a periodical letter in large round hand to 'My dear Grand-papa' — 'dear', while those letters were in process, he assuredly to me was not.'[101]

Charles Stewart obviously wanted to keep in contact with his father, in spite of the rebuff over the silk dresses for his half-sisters, so Louisa and her brothers and sisters were at least aware that they had a grandfather in Australia.

Louisa's early education, apart from the easily acquired reading and the troubled efforts over writing, included ancient history and myth-ology, Latin, which she did not take kindly to, and arithmetic which she liked, though she said she was 'intensely dull' at it.[102] As well as the French, already mentioned, German was also an early lesson.[103] Speaking to an interviewer in 1893, Louisa said that 'she received her education privately at home, and thinks that she benefited by the free, happy life, unfettered by too many rules and regulations'. She was obviously glad that she had not been sent to school, and had not been a child later on in the era of 'modern High School education' which she thought hampered all-round development with its emphasis on examinations and working for a career.[104]

One of the most important parts of education of course, is the reading we do on our own, some of which, maybe, we have discovered for ourselves. As we saw when considering Agnes Wilson's library in chapter one, Louisa had a certain number of books handed on from the previous generation. She thought, indeed, that some came from further back — 'I can recall several belonging to an older generation, and an older *still* — those not only of my mother, but of my *grandmother*'. She mentioned Mrs Hofland's books, *Ornaments Discovered*, *Evenings at Home*, *The Twin Sisters*, 'a complete collection of Miss Edgeworth's books for the young' and, 'my favourite by far' among these older books, Mrs

---

[101] 'Story-Writing', pp. 160, 163. The reference is certainly to Charles Stewart's father, first because Agnes Stewart's father, John Wilson, had died in 1824, and then because later in the same article MLM says that 'the awe-inspiring receiver of our round-hand letters' was on the other side of the family from her story-telling grand-mother.

[102] Ibid. pp. 162, 161.

[103] *The Art of Authorship*, compiled and edited by George Bainton, James Clarke and Co., 1890, pp. 93–96.

[104] *Woman at Home*, p. 194.

Sherwood's *The Fairchild Family.*[105] However, none of these titles could have been read by Louisa's grandmother as a child, for Nancy Wilson (née Black) was born in 1765 and the earliest of these books would have been the first volume of *Evenings at Home,* published in 1792. It is, of course, possible that the books Louisa read had once belonged to her grandmother in the sense that Nancy Wilson had used them for educating her own children. As well, Louisa described the titles she listed as 'the most prominent' among these survivals from the past. There could well have been others, unnamed, which were even older.

It is particularly interesting that Louisa read the books of Mrs Hofland (1770–1844). Her work belonged to the genre of moral and didactic tale which had come to dominate children's books by the end of the eighteenth century, but there was more to it than that. Early reviewers praised her for

'her wholesome morality, the way in which her tales are framed so as to teach lessons which will help young readers to lead better lives. Words like 'moral' and 'precept', often juxtaposed with 'excellent' and 'exemplary', occur and recur in the discussion of most children's books of this time, and it is quite clear that these are the qualities for which Mrs Hofland is praised.'

But the modern critic who thus described her typically eighteenth century characteristics, has pointed out other qualities, more interesting to us now. Probably because Mrs Hofland had to support herself for most of her life, there is much attention paid to employment in her stories, with detailed references to money and earning a living.

'The fact that nearly all her characters have a job and that there is an almost endless curiosity about what people do for a living give her books a realism missing from the work of most earlier writers.'

Added to this is what can only be described as early feminism.

'It is, however, when she writes of woman and work that Mrs Hofland writes with real conviction and no little originality.' *She* 'could both

---

[105] 'Story-Reading and Story-Writing', p. 772; 'Story-Writing', p. 162. Barbara Hofland, 1770–1844; Mary Hughes, *née* Robson, *The Ornaments Discovered*, 1815; John Aikin (1747–1822) and Letitia Barbauld (1743–1825), *Evenings at Home*, 1792–6, 6 vols, a collection of stories, poems and dialogues; Elizabeth Sandham, *The Twin Sisters or The Advantages of Religion*, 1805; Mary Martha Sherwood (1775–1851), *The Fairchild Family*, 3 parts, 1818, 1842 and 1847.

see sharply and at times feel strongly about the neglect of woman's talents.'

One further characteristic to be noted is her treatment of family life.

'Her most powerful and recurring motif is the demonstration of family love and co-operation in the face of some crisis or disaster, the loss of a parent for instance, and one can only speculate on the possibilities of the influence of her work on, for example, Charlotte Yonge's *The Daisy Chain*, (1856), Louisa Alcott's *Little Women* (1868) and *The Railway Children* (1906) by E. Nesbit.'[106]

Louisa too, in her turn, often used this theme, usually taking financial hardship or illness, sometimes necessitating the departure of one or both parents, as the crisis eliciting increased mutual help and affection between the family members left behind, as for instance in *Carrots* (1876), *The Boys and I* (1883), *The House That Grew* (1900) and *The Story of A Year* (1909), to name but a few. 'Wholesome morality', though perhaps less conspicuously presented, was also a strong feature of her books. And she herself worked as a writer for a great part of her adult life.

The book that Louisa said she liked best out of this group from the older generation, Mrs Sherwood's *The Fairchild Family*, was by a writer prominent among the religious authors for children of her day. Louisa's mother would have known only the first part of the book in her childhood — the second and third parts were published when Louisa herself was three and eight years old. Mrs Sherwood, with her strong evangelical and Calvinistic fervour, seems to have repelled Louisa as well as attracting her. She commented, without saying exactly which books she was referring to, that 'in certain cases' her mother had taken a lot of trouble to get new editions of the books she remembered only to find that they were 'less appreciated by us than her perhaps too partial remembrance of the favourites of her own childhood (or of *her* mother's) had led her to expect.' But then she specified that although *The Fairchild Family* interested her most, yet she was 'conscious even then of some inward revolt against the *forcedness* of the religious, and even moral teaching it strove to impart.'[107] She expressed this opinion in a simpler and more

---

[106] For a bibliography of Mrs Hofland's books, and an account of her life and work, see Dennis Butts, *Mistress of Our Tears: A Literary and Bibliographical Study of Barbara Hofland*, Scolar Press, 1992. All quotations on Mrs Hofland are taken from this book, pp. 43, 32–3, 46.
[107] 'Story-Reading and Story-Writing', p. 772.

lively manner in a passage which has naturally been quoted before more than once in preference to the staid comment just given, to illustrate both a child's reaction to this book and Louisa's own character as a child.[108] It is too amusing not to repeat here.

> ' "The Fairchild Family" was my favourite by far, excepting for the prayers and hymns at the end of each chapter. These I was too conscientious to 'skip', but they were a sore trial, till at last I hit upon the plan of *reading forward* a certain number of them, so that I could then go back and enjoy the story straight on without the uncongenial break!'[109]

The exclamation mark, Louisa's own punctuation, shows, I think, the amusement, but the sympathetic amusement, with which the adult woman looked back on her over-conscience-ridden self in childhood. Louisa must have had quite hard work to read her 'favourite by far' amongst her mother's books in the way she most enjoyed, for the prayers, hymns and Bible passages are by no means confined to the ends of the chapters, but are liberally sprinkled throughout the text. A slightly younger contemporary of Louisa's, Lucy Bethia Walford, described her very similar reaction to *The Fairchild Family* in a book of memoirs published in 1912. She was at a dinner party during her first London season in 1864, when her neighbour asked if she had been brought up on the book, and then

> 'declared he could still repeat some of the beginnings of the chapters. "But not the ends", rejoined I, slily — and the pith of that observation lay in this, that the end of every chapter in that immortal work is a prayer, and did we not one and all skip that prayer?'[110]

Louisa had felt the same way, but found a different solution.

The books that Louisa discovered for herself even before the age of six sound unbelievably difficult to us for a child of that age as well as very unsuitable, although she herself said later on in this connection, 'I don't think that a child under eight or ten years gets much harm from anything it reads.'[111] These books included Samuel Richardson's *Sir Charles Grandison*, Fanny Burney's *The Wanderer* and several of Scott's

---

[108] R. L. Green, *Mrs Molesworth*, The Bodley Head, 1961, p. 24. Gillian Avery, *Nineteenth-Century Children*, Hodder and Stoughton, 1965, p. 85; *Childhood's Pattern*, Hodder and Stoughton, 1975, p. 93.

[109] 'Story-Writing', p. 162.

[110] L. B. Walford, *Memories of Victorian London*, Edward Arnold, 1912, p. 19.

[111] *Westminster Budget*, p. 24a.

novels. *Peveril of the Peak* defeated her — she was found on her knees 'dissolved in tears' in front of a sofa on which the book lay, and

> 'when cross-questioned as to the cause of my tears, I had to own it was because I "*couldn't* understand the story; it got so muddled after the beginning. And *Ivanhoe* and *The Talisman* and even *Anne of Geierstein*, were so much nicer and easier." '

Even so, 'between six and ten I had read most of the Waverleys'. She came to grief over *Peveril of the Peak* in 'one of my usual dens for reading — a tiny book-room in an uncle's country house' which could have been Hillside.[112] The uncomfortable-sounding attitude in which she was discovered speaks of the true book-worm — one is reminded of Jo March alias Louisa Alcott, although several years older, with her apples and her pet rat enjoying a good cry over *The Heir of Redclyffe* on a three-legged sofa in the garret.

Louisa also read fairy-tales, as well as listening to them. She commented that these had been very few in her mother's childhood, which had coincided with the fashion for didacticism and disapproval of fairy tales as 'something very like lies.'[113] But the Stewart children had 'one perfectly delicious fat little brown volume which we looked upon as an inexhaustible treasury of delight, handed down to us from the end of the last century. . . it contained *all* the dear old stories.' By this Louisa meant *Cinderella, Red Riding Hood, The Sleeping Beauty* and so forth. The brown volume might well have contained a selection or even the collected works of Mme D'Aulnoy and Perrault, which came into English as the tales of Mother Bunch and Mother Goose. She presented this particular volume with great affection in one of her stories as well as in the reminiscence just quoted.

> 'And best of all, perhaps, the dearest, little, shabby, dumpy, dark-brown book of real old-fashioned fairy tales. I have it still — no shabbier for all our thumbing of it: it is so strongly bound, though it is so plain and dingy-looking and I mean to keep it for my children.'

Louisa's own generation, as she said 'were very favoured as regards fairy tales. Grimm and, still more, Hans Andersen, were a library in themselves.'[114] Selections of Hans Andersen's tales first appeared in

---

[112] 'Story-Writing', p. 162, and 'Story-Reading and Story-Writing', p. 773.
[113] 'Peter Parley' (Samuel Goodrich). Quoted in *Tellers of Tales*, p. 23.
[114] 'Story-Reading and Story-Writing', p. 773; *The Palace in the Garden*, p. 15.

English in 1846, just the right timing for Louisa who was then seven years old. The first English translation of Grimm had been around for much longer, having in fact been published when Louisa's mother was thirteen, in 1823. Along with Anderson and Grimm, Louisa put Hawthorne's *Wonder Book* and Kingsley's *The Heroes*, calling them 'less well-known books which I cannot but associate with the 'fairy-tale' department.' In another place she explained why she thought so.

> 'Nathaniel Hawthorne's 'Wonder Book' was a great revelation to me. Till I read it, I had never associated anything classic, anything of 'ancient history,' or mythology with interest and charm. I had looked upon it all as lessons.'

One further example, 'an older book, a translation from the German' that Louisa also classified as fairy-tale and found 'unspeakably fascinating' was *The Nutcracker of Nuremberg*.[115] German fantasy and Hawthorne's Gothic treatment of classical myth were feeding her development of the romantic imagination.

Books were relatively expensive in Louisa's childhood and not simply to be had for the asking.

> 'Well do I recollect' she wrote, 'the slow hoarding of weekly pence or sixpences before the necessary amount was attained for the purchase of some coveted volume. Once in particular I recollect a certain green-and-gold story-book in a shop window, which I had set my heart upon, and my terror of some day finding it gone from its place (for somehow it never struck me that another copy could be procured) before I was rich enough to make it mine.'[116]

She was obviously not indiscriminately indulged, though her granddaughter wrote that 'Louie' was her father's pet.[117] She certainly thought the world of him as the following reminiscence shows.

> 'We were returning late at night, or so at least it seemed to me, from some kind of juvenile entertainment at Christmas time. It was a stormy

---

[115] 'Story-Reading and Story-Writing', p. 773 and 'Story-Writing', p. 162. *The Nutcracker of Nuremberg* must have been a translation either of E. T. A. Hoffman's *Nussknacker und der Mausekönig* (1816), Dumas' 1845 version of this, or Heinrich Hoffman's *König Nussknacker und der arme Reinhold* (1851). The earliest translations of both books in the BL catalogue are dated 1853.

[116] 'Story-reading and Story-Writing', p. 772.

[117] VMI to RR, 16.12.51.

evening; I was a very little girl, and since infancy, high wind has always terrified me, and that night it was blowing fiercely.' *This fear originated in the experience in Rotterdam, already cited, which she mentioned as her earliest memory.* 'I was already trembling when the carriage stopped. My father at once sprang out, for there was no second man on the box; there was nothing wrong, only the coachman's hat had blown off! He got down and ran back for it, and my father replaced him and drove on slowly, for the wind had made the horse restless.

"Oh, mamma," I exclaimed, "I am so frightened. The coachman has gone away."

"Yes, darling," said my mother, "but don't you see papa is driving?"

I shall never forget the impression of absolute comfort and fearlessness that came over me at her words.

"Papa is driving," I repeated to myself. "We are quite, quite safe." '[118]

It sounds as though she was the only child in the carriage with her parents, which suggests that Charles was still too young for such entertainments and Agnes not yet born. We might suppose that the eldest child John was kept in by a cold or invited to some different activity. This surmise, coupled with 'I was a very little girl' suggests that Louisa was about four or five at this time.

The Nutcracker book belonged to one of Louisa's brothers and they found it fascinating together. This was a characteristic of all her childhood reading — it was very much a shared and discussed activity. Both in her articles and in her child novels Louisa emphasised this feature of nursery and schoolroom life and was confident that it resulted directly from the comparatively small number of children's books that were available. Just because they were fewer, they were more carefully read and more dearly loved.

'In those days, as everybody knows, children had far fewer story-books than now, though I well remember my mother and grandmother and aunts telling us how large was our repertory compared with what *theirs* had been.'[119]

These few books

---

[118] 'A Ramble about Childhood', p. 294.
[119] 'Story-Writing', p. 162.

'were not only devoured with enthusiasm, but read over and over again as a matter of course, till the characters and scenes became a reality to us, actual factors in our own existence and experience.'[120]

'We thought about them and got to know them, to like or dislike them, to picture to ourselves all about them. And this 'picturing to oneself' is, of course, the root of invention.'[121]

This imaginative activity sometimes took very practical forms with Louisa.

'When I was a little girl I liked to know exactly about the children in my books, . . . I liked to know their names, their ages, all about their homes and their relations *most* exactly, and more than once I was laughed at for writing out a sort of genealogical tree of some of my little fancy friends' family connections.'[122]

And because all children had much the same stock of books there was no point in lending books to each other.

'Children really *read* their books in those days; they put more of themselves into their reading, . . . they got to know the characters in their favourite stories like real friends, and would talk them over with their companions, and compare their opinions about them in a way that made each book as good, or better, than a dozen.'[123]

In much the same way do children today compare notes over their favourite TV programmes or computer games. So in her earliest experiences both of play and reading Louisa was exercising and developing just those faculties which helped her to write stories later on and looking back she herself recognised that this was so.

---

[120] 'Story-Reading and Story-Writing', p. 772.
[121] 'How I Write . . .', p. 17.
[122] *Grandmother Dear*, p. 7.
[123] *Carrots*, p. 113.

3

Growing Up

In December 1849, when Louisa was ten and a half, her grandmother, Mary (Nancy) Wilson, died in Edinburgh in the home of her daughter and son-in-law, Marion and George Meldrum.[1] This was the end of an era for Louisa, but as we have seen, she did not forget her grandmother and the stories she told. The next year, 1850, her youngest sister Caroline Marion was born, Charles and Agnes Stewart's last child. The family names Agnes and Marion were thus carried on in the two younger daughters. Louisa's own full name, Mary Louisa, obviously came from her grandmother and her aunt, Mary Miller, in part, but Louisa does not seem to occur in the closer family, and may, as conjectured earlier, recall Agnes Stewart's friendship with the daughter of her godfather in Tangier.

Caroline's daughter said she believed her uncles all went to school in Scotland, and in 1850, at the age of thirteen, John, the eldest boy, would have been old enough for this first parting from his family, imposed by boarding-school education. And Louisa, at eleven years old, would also have been old enough to take the girl's part of helping with some of the necessary sewing and errands. She described such activity later in *Carrots*, when 'Nurse was very, very busy, one day; really quite extra busy, for she was arranging and helping to pack Jack's things to go to a new school . . . And there was quite a fuss in the house.'[2]

1850 also brought a visitor from Australia. James Horne Stewart, the only surviving legitimate son of William Stewart, came to England with a letter from his father to Charles Augustus and the instruction to visit him in Manchester. James was twenty-five, meeting for the first time a half-brother, sixteen years older than himself, of whose existence his

---

[1] Agnes Black, her sister, was almost certainly with her, because not only do we know that afterwards she continued to live with the Meldrums, but also that family records say she never left her sister. 1851 and 1861 census returns for 53 York Place. See also p. 1.
[2] *Carrots*, p. 14.

father had apparently come to be ashamed — potentially an embarrassing and difficult situation. Charles certainly thought so, for James later described his reaction.

> 'When I went to his office he kept me waiting for some time and at length came out a good deal excited and said I must expect that he would feel a good deal on meeting me from our relative positions, and he referred to the matter once or twice, but I did not remain long at that period being on my way to Scotland.'

We would take it for granted that not remaining long meant perhaps lunch and conversation for an hour or so, but considering that on later visits James and his wife stayed with the Stewarts for weeks, 'not long' might have meant a day or two. Perhaps James was being tactful by going to the office first (unless he did not have his half-brother's home address) but it seems, though the matter is not completely clear, that he did meet Charles' family on this occasion. On James' later visits, Charles told him that his children did not know his true position, meaning the fact that he was illegitimate. They asked questions about their grandparents and their father obviously had a hard time gratifying their natural curiosity about their own family without giving himself away. We know that the children were instructed to call James Horne 'uncle' from the evidence of a letter to him from the second son, Charles, in 1873, which starts 'My dear uncle'.[3] However little the children were told, it must have been exciting to meet in the flesh a member of that family in the antipodes to whom they had struggled to write dutiful letters. The Victorian family traditions of obedience and respect helped Charles to keep his secret, for years later Louisa wrote to a friend in reference to this matter, 'my father and mother never told us all.'

It seems appropriate here to relate what little is known of Louisa's religious upbringing. We have already seen that she early showed herself to be conscientious, refusing to skip the less palatable prayers and hymns in *The Fairchild Family* although it was the story for which she valued the book. When she was in her sixties she told one writer that 'as a child she had suffered much from excessively Calvinistic surroundings, and determined that no child with whom she was brought in contact should, if she could prevent it, be taught the religion of fear.'[4] This certainly describes the Fairchild atmosphere, and supports her comment,

---

[3] *Claimant*, pp. 11–12, p. 3.
[4] Helena Swan, *Girls' Christian Names*, Swan, Sonnenschein and Co., 1900, p. 354.

already quoted above, about her own distaste for the forcedness of Mrs Sherwood's religious and moral teaching. Her grand-daughter confirmed the nature of Louisa's early religious experience with the remark 'She started life as a v. strict Presbyterian or Calvinist — almost a "Wee Free".' There was also one piece of more direct evidence in the shape of an undated letter from Louisa to her mother. It was really more of a note than a letter, on small, frilly-edged, white writing paper, folded neatly in three with "Mamma" written on the back.

> My dear Mamma,
>   I do not like my birthday to pass without writing a letter to you. I am very sorry I have done anything to displease you today but I think I really mean to keep myself from giving way to bad temper and other things. I know I have done a great many wrong things every day since my last birthday but I think I know better now than I did then the reason why I should try to get over my faults. Dear Mamma please forgive me for all the times I have made you sorry and please believe me that I mean to try. Your Mary Louisa.[5]

This could have been written on almost any birthday from her eighth to her twelfth, though in view of the very clear, quite developed hand-writing, one of the later dates should be preferred. She had clearly been taught to examine her conscience and try to check her faults, and the reticent reference to God and indeed the whole system of Christian belief in the phrase 'the reason why' reflects the nineteenth century attitude to religion in middle and upper-class society. One should be devout but not talk about it — religion was one of the topics that was taboo at the dinner table, although of course not in serious private talks. In her books Louisa often depicted a mother or other figure in charge saying a few serious words to some child in trouble or disgrace, some-thing simple such as 'And you know well that we need never be left to struggle alone against wrong feelings. God has promised to help us.' But she never maintained such a direct religious tone for long — it was woven into the story. The child to whom this remark was addressed did not react with the tears of penitence that would have been the appropriate response in an Evangelical Sunday-school book. Louisa took care not to make *her* presentation of religion forced. 'Tora stood silent. Then her natural honesty came to the front. "Yes," she said, "but just

---

[5] Letter copied by RR from the original in the possession of CP, afterwards destroyed.

now I don't *want* to be helped to be nice about Elinor." [6] Often the moral or religious element was even more underplayed. In *Grandmother Dear*, the grandmother, who was largely based on Louisa's own mother, appeared as a sympathetic figure, conscious of her own faults as well as those of the children in her care. '"Poor little soul"' she said of Molly, who had turned out to be misunderstood rather than plain naughty, '"I wish I had not been so hasty with her. It will be a lesson to me."' Molly's sister, Sylvia, appeared surprised at this remark and grandmother explained that even 'an old woman like me' had lessons to learn right to the end of her life and Sylvia responded '"I know what kind of lessons you mean — not *book* ones — but being kind and good and all things like that."' [7] We can perhaps imagine Agnes Stewart teaching Louisa in a similar way.

Charles Stewart was an elder at the Scottish Presbyterian church in Grosvenor Square. [8] The head of the firm for which he worked, Robert Barbour, was also a Scotch Presbyterian, staunchly so, for not only was he one of the founders of the Scotch Church in St Peter's Square, but he also on one occasion gave £12,000 for the foundation of a professorship in the Presbyterian College in London. [9] However, the Stewart family did not remain rigidly Presbyterian, as is shown by their attending Church of England services both in Fleetwood and in Cheshire where they moved after Louisa's marriage. Both Roger Lancelyn Green and Ruth Robertson thought that in *The Carved Lions* 'many ... of Geraldine's recollections of her early days must be direct scraps of Louisa's own autobiography,' [10] so perhaps the description of Geraldine's Sundays may pass for a reminiscence of one of Louisa's.

> 'The next day, Sunday, was very rainy. It made us feel dull, I think, though we did not really mind a wet Sunday as much as another day, for we never went a walk on Sunday. It was not thought right, and as we had no garden the day would have been a very dreary one to us, except for mamma.
>
> She managed to make it pleasant. We went to church in the morning, and in the evening too sometimes. I think all children like going to church in the evening; there is something grown-up about it. And the

---

[6] MLM, *The Little Guest*, Macmillan, 1907, p. 140.

[7] *Grandmother Dear*, p. 72–3.

[8] Papers associated with *The Claimant*, Wigram Allen to J. P. Bunting, Feb.-Mar. 1874.

[9] Swindells, p. 12.

[10] R. L. Green, *Mrs Molesworth*, Bodley Head, 1961, p. 23.

rest of the day mamma managed to find interesting things for us to do. She generally had some book which she kept for reading aloud on Sunday — Dr Adam's *Allegories*, 'The Dark River' and others, were great favourites, and so were Bishop Wilberforce's *Agathos*. Some of them frightened me a little, but it was rather a pleasant sort of fright, there was something grand and solemn about it.'

In the 1890s, a well-known politician remarked, about one of these favourite Sunday books, 'Who was it who said to me, quite truly, that the Bishop of Winchester, so stirring, so famous in his day, would only be remembered by his little book *Agathos, and Other Sunday Stories?*'[11] Geraldine's description of her Sundays continued

'Then we sang hymns sometimes, and we always had a very nice tea, and mamma, and father too now and then, told us stories about when they were children and what they did on Sundays. It was much stricter for them than for us, though even for us many things were forbidden on Sundays which are now thought not only harmless but right.

Still, I never look back to the quiet Sundays in the dingy Mexington street with anything but a feeling of peace and gentle pleasure.'[12]

In this passage it seems possible to see Louisa's mother softening, as far as she could, the repressive aspects of Scottish Sabbatarianism for the benefit of her children, yet obliged to keep to the veto on Sunday walks and other unspecified forbidden things, which probably included the everyday toys. Certainly the lack of a garden and the dingy street fits Louisa's life, but the 'pleasant sort of fright' does not sound desperate enough to be described as 'the religion of fear'. It might be thought that she was here suppressing any really harsh elements from her own childhood in accordance with her desire, expressed to the author of the passage quoted earlier, 'to make Sundays pleasant for the little people for whom she chiefly writes.'[13] On the other hand it could be that Louisa suffered from 'excessively Calvinistic surroundings' less in Man-

[11] Samuel Wilberforce, successively Bishop of Oxford and Winchester, *Agathos, and Other Sunday Stories*, Thames Ditton, 1840. Sir M. E. Grant-Duff, *Notes From A Diary 1892–1895*, vol. 2, p. 254, entry for 9.9.1895. Samuel Wilberforce is also remembered now for his fierce opposition to Darwin's theory of evolution, notably at the famous meeting of the British Association for the Advancement of Science, held in Oxford on 30.6.1860.

[12] *The Carved Lions*, pp. 46–7.

[13] Swan, p. 355.

chester and more in Scotland during the long holidays with her grandmother in Fifeshire where an extreme form of Calvinism still existed.
Accepting this view, we can still imagine Louisa and her brothers and
sisters enjoying a solemnly pleasant Manchester Sunday with the hymns
and the 'very nice tea' and mamma's stories being the highlights. In the
preface to *Agathos*, Bishop Wilberforce said that a Sunday story should
occupy the imagination, give scriptural instruction and avoid 'all lower-
ing down of holy things.' This was certainly the tone of Geraldine's
religious education, and we may assume of Louisa's too.

One of Louisa's favourite books from this period, published in England when she was thirteen, was *The Wide, Wide World*. This was
another title famous for its religious content, but one which was more
sympathetic to the reader and less rigid than Mrs Sherwood's books.
An author who abridged it for a 1950s audience wrote of it,

> 'Grandmother had loved that book. Mother had loved it. And now I
> loved it. In spite of the long, long, pious discussions so frequently indulged
> in by all the "nice" characters, in spite of the tears — bathfuls of them!
> — shed for every conceivable reason, I read that book over and over
> again.'[14]

Louisa would have had the tears and the pious talk neat and uncut but
she also 'loved that book.' It was the books of her own day, she said,
as opposed to those her mother and grandmother had read and passed
on to her, 'whose influence was the greatest, whose interest was the
most enthralling'. And from these she singled out *The Wide, Wide World*
to describe first to an 1898 readership.

> '*The Wide, Wide World* entranced me, especially the first part, where the
> little heroine's devotion to her mother is so pathetically described. It is
> difficult for me even now to read of Ellen's shopping expeditions without
> tears. I cannot endorse the criticism of present-day readers of this once
> favourite tale, that it is full of weak and unreal sentiment, the hero a
> prig of the first water, the heroine an impossible little personage. There
> may be a good deal of truth in this opinion; nevertheless I cannot bring
> myself to see it — woman-like, very probably, I cannot because I will
> not; and partly, too, because I remember with so much gratitude the

---

[14] Elizabeth Wetherell, *The Wide, Wide World*, edited by Joyce Lankester Brisley. University of London press, 1950, p. 7. First published in 2 vols, 1852, 'edited by a clergyman
of the Church of England.'

many hours of intense enjoyment I owe to it. Yes, I think I loved it better than any other story-book!'[15]

It is interesting to compare Louisa's enthusiastic, almost gushing comments on *The Wide, Wide World* (in another place she said 'I adored it'), with her reluctant praise for Maria Edgeworth's books. They were, she conceded, 'far abler' than Mrs Sherwood's, but there was something missing. She thought them 'hard and dry' and 'too sensible'. What she disliked was 'a lack of sentiment, possibly of sentimentality only!' though she then went on to give full credit to the stories in *The Parent's Assistant* and *Moral Tales*, calling them 'thoroughly interesting, even appealing to the dramatic sense inherent in all intelligent children.'[16] The wryly apologetic tone of her admission that she wanted sentiment in her reading matches up with her defence of *The Wide, Wide World* in the face of the criticism current in the 1890s. It seems that she enjoyed the 'bathfuls of tears'. And this was a taste she shared with many other Victorians — Rossetti wept over Guy's untimely end in *The Heir of Redclyffe*. Mrs Ewing's biographer wrote that she, 'in common with many of her contemporaries, liked to think that she could make her readers weep; and when she sent [*Timothy's Shoes*] to her mother she said, "I think you will weep when they go away."' One of her readers, a clergyman, apparently made a bet with his wife that he could read a particular story aloud without breaking down, but the anecdote ended with his saying '"But after a page or two — I put my hand in my pocket. I said there! take your half-crown and let me cry comfortably when I want to!"'[17] However, it should be noted that Louisa did not over-indulge in this taste for tears and sentiment when she came to write her own stories. There are very few child death-beds in those.

The next actual information we have about Louisa's life does not come until, at 'fourteen or thereabouts', as she wrote in two of her autobiographical pieces, she started to write down some of the 'innumerable stories' she made up.[18] It was about this time too, that is, in the first half of her teens, that Louisa began to be taught by the Rev William Gaskell and his wife the novelist, Elizabeth Gaskell. It appears to have been under their influence that her actual writing of stories began, as

[15] 'Story-Reading and Story-Writing', p. 773.

[16] 'Story-Writing', p. 162; 'Story-Reading and Story-Writing', pp. 772–3.

[17] Georgina Battiscombe, *Charlotte M. Yonge*, Constable, 1943, p. 77; Christabel Maxwell, *Mrs Gatty and Mrs Ewing*, Constable, 1949, pp. 186–7.

[18] 'How I Write . . .', p. 17. 'Story-Writing', p. 160.

opposed to simply telling stories to her nursery and schoolroom audience. At first sight, it would seem more likely that only one of the two taught her, but her own daughter wrote after her death 'I know that both Mr and Mrs Gaskell had a great deal to do with her education and also her beginning to write.' Her grand-daughter also wrote of Mrs Gaskell 'My grandmother . . . always said she owed much of her writing to her [sc. Mrs Gaskell's] encouragement.' This grand-daughter referred twice to Mrs Gaskell as having been her grandmother's governess for a short time and then corrected herself, adding 'Teacher rather than governess.' An interview published during Louisa's lifetime mentioned Mr Gaskell by name as 'taking great pains in helping her to achieve a good literary style.'[19] Since she herself reckoned that fourteen was the age when she began to write down her stories, this, taken with her daughter's statement, suggests that her period of education with the Gaskells began in 1853 or 1854, during her fifteenth year.

From 1850 onwards the Gaskells were living at 42, Plymouth Grove in Manchester, so by the time Louisa began going there for lessons, they had been settled in for several years. It was a handsome, square house with a surrounding garden which 'shed a fresh and verdant air around the house.'[20] A historian of Manchester, writing in the 1930s, described the district and the house in the Gaskells' time.

'Two very desirable suburbs in the eighteen-fifties were Greenheys and Plymouth Grove. Charles Hallé lived in Greenheys Lane, and nearly opposite were Geraldine Jewsbury and her brother. When the Carlyles came to Greenheys to stay with Geraldine, Jane Carlyle was able to pop round to breakfast with Mr and Mrs Gaskell who lived close at hand in Plymouth Grove.'

Charlotte Bronte was another visitor in Plymouth Grove, and she described the Gaskell's house there as

'a large, cheerful airy house, quite out of the smoke . . . a garden surrounds it, and as in this hot weather the windows are kept open, a whispering of leaves and perfume of flowers always pervaded the rooms.'[21]

This must have given great pleasure and refreshment to the young Louisa Stewart, coming from a much more town house, in a street with no

[19] Swan, p. 354.
[20] Gerin, pp. 109–10.
[21] Rachel Ryan, *A Biography of Manchester*, Methuen, 1937, p. 69.

garden. Rusholme Road, where her own home was, cut across Upper
Brook Street, the south end of which runs into Plymouth Grove, so she
was within walking distance of her teachers.

Although her grandmother had died five years before, Louisa continued
to visit relations in Scotland, which must have helped to establish firmly
in her memory and creative thought the stories she had received from her
grandmother and was now beginning to write down. A letter survived that
Louisa wrote to her sister Agnes in July 1854 when Agnes was ten and she
herself was almost two months past her fifteenth birthday.[22]

Edinburgh, Friday, July 21st.

My Dear little Agnes,

Thank you very much for your nice long journal — and as you have
taken the trouble of writing it for me I must do the same for you.

On Tuesday I went to call with Aunt Marion on Miss Savil and on
the Candlishes — afterwards I went with Miss Savil and her niece Annie
Anderson to see the great charity school called Donaldson's hospital,
hardly any children are admitted except those of the name of Donaldson
or Marshall. Donaldson was the gentleman's name who founded it and
Marshall his mother's name.

On Wednesday I went out with Charlie and afterwards to Mr Nas-
myth's. Aunt M. Uncle G. and John went to spend the day at Currie a
little way out of town so Charlie and I were alone with Aunt Black.

On Thursday morning I went to Portobello with Aunt M. to call on
Mrs Kerr and on Miss Kilgour — we walked to the shore, the sea was
beautiful but I could not bathe on account of my hair — so we returned
by the railway. In the evening I called on John Colville's aunts with
John. When we came home I read and then went to bed.

I will write to you afterwards about this evening for we are going to have
a little party — Sometimes when I am going to bed I wish I had you to talk
to but I sleep very comfortably though I am alone — I am going to Kincad-
der tomorrow so I can tell you in my next letter what like little Katie and
Laurence are. Love and kisses to Willie, Carrie and yourself from

Your affectionate Mary Louisa.[23]

---

[22] Unpublished letter owned by CP and copied by RR but later destroyed. The year is
not given, but 21st July was a Friday only in 3 possible years — 1848, 1854, and 1865.
In 1848 Agnes was only 3, and in 1865 MLM had been married for 4 years.

[23] Coloured picture of Newhaven Fishwomen (The Fishwives of Edinburgh) on top of
notepaper.

Although the only address given is Edinburgh, it is clear that Louisa and her next brother Charles were staying with their aunt and uncle, Marion and George Meldrum ('Aunt M.' and 'Uncle G.') at 53 York Place. This is right in the centre of the city, about 300 yards north of Princes Street. The other two children to whom she sends 'love and kisses' were her younger brother and sister, William and Caroline, then aged nine and five respectively. John, the eldest of the family at eighteen, cannot have been at home.

Louisa was well on her way to young ladyhood when she wrote this letter, going calling and not bathing because of her hair, but she was certainly having plenty of outings. Portobello, where 'the sea was beautiful' is almost directly east of Edinburgh, on the shore of the Firth of Forth, about three or four miles from York Place. A guide book of 1907 refers to it as 'Edinburgh's famous watering place' and shows a photograph of a wide, flat, sandy beach.[24] Currie, where Aunt M., Uncle G., and John went to spend the day, is right on the south-western edge of present-day Edinburgh and about six miles from York Place.

One interesting domestic detail is that Louisa was clearly used to sleeping with Agnes — presumably they shared a room, which must have been very necessary in a house where it was difficult to fit everyone in [see chapter 2, note 10]. The Aunt Black referred to is Louisa's great-aunt, Agnes Black who was living with her niece Marion after the death of her sister, Nancy Wilson, Louisa's grandmother. John Colville is John Wilson Colville, Louisa's first cousin, a son of her Aunt Catherine. He also appeared in the 1851 census for 53, York Place, so he might have been living with his Aunt Marion in order to attend the university. In 1851 he was said to be fifteen so at the time of this visit of Louisa's he would have been a young man of nineteen or twenty. Information provided to the census takers could be misleading though — Aunt Marion was recorded as 50 in 1851 but 65 in 1861. The aunts on whom Louisa called with John were probably sisters of his father, since any sisters of his mother would have been her (and Agnes') aunts too and she would have referred to them as such. Nothing is known about the other people mentioned in the letter.

Louisa's outing to Donaldson's Hospital may well have been undertaken in the spirit in which we now visit a National Trust property or other stately home, since it was 'in magnitude and design one of the

---

[24] *A Pictorial and Descriptive Guide to Edinburgh*, Ward, Lock and Co., 1907, p. 201–2.

grandest edifices of Edinburgh'. It had been built between 1842 and 1851 and was specially visited and much admired by Queen Victoria in 1850 before it was quite finished. In 1883 it was described as capable of holding 150 children of each sex, and Louisa's explanation of the entry qualifications was quite correct — 'poor children of the name of Donaldson or Marshall if appearing to the governors to be deserving.' The building was in shape a hollow quadrangle in 'a modified variety of a somewhat ornate Tudor style and built of beautiful freestone.'[25] Perhaps Louisa's experience of this orphanage impressed itself upon her mind enough to be partly the source of the orphanage Mandane's Bounty when she wrote *The Three Witches*[26] more than forty years later.

By 1855, the year after this visit of Louisa's to Edinburgh, the Stewarts had moved house. They did not go far, but it was in the 'right' direction — further away from the centre of Manchester, towards the suburbs. 77, Dover Terrace was some seven or eight streets south of Rusholme Road, down Upper Brook Street. It consisted of five houses at the junction of Upper Brook Street and Dover Street, on the north east corner.[27] Since the terrace, though not the whole of the street, was demolished about 1909, for a description we must rely on a writer whose own grandparents made the same kind of successive moves away from the centre of Manchester as Charles Stewart and at about the same time. He and they were joining the general exodus of merchants and industrialists gradually and steadily out into Cheshire.

Louisa's new home was in one of the

'square built houses of dark red brick along Upper Brook Street . . . Regency houses or at least so early Victorian as to have escaped with years to spare the sham Gothic infection which Manchester took very badly about the middle of the century. They had clean lines and no frills, a solid and suitable dignity of workmanship and design.'

Writing in 1950 this author said

'for as long as I have known them, the Upper Brook Street houses, those of them that remain, have been a draggled travesty of former worth.'

---

[25] Grant, vol. 2, p. 214.

[26] MLM, *The Three Witches*, Chambers, 1900.

[27] Manchester Directories. The dates of the Stewarts' changes of address can only be approximate, because the information provided can be as much as six months or a year out of date. Position of Dover terrace from 1850 survey maps. Letter from Manchester City Surveyor to RR, 11.10.1955.

But, 'occasionally you see one smartened up with a fresh coat of paint for some reason and then you realise what a fine and pleasant approach to Manchester Upper Brook Street must have been in the days when all were turned out in like manner and private cabs with spruce coachmen on their boxes took up their owners and drove them with a show of dignity to their offices.'[28]

In the following year came two sad events for the Stewarts. Contact was renewed with the family of Agnes Stewart's sister, Mary Miller, who with her husband and children had been in India. Mary and Ebenezer Miller were the aunt and uncle living in Rotterdam when the Stewarts were there. Sadly, the only family members to return were two small children, aged three and eighteen months, who had been born in Calcutta. These were Mary Miller's grandchildren, who were sailing back to Britain with their mother Mary Agnes Morgan after the death of their father, Andrew Morgan, in Calcutta. The mother also died, on the voyage home and was buried in Cairo with her latest baby. The two orphans were taken in by the Meldrums in Edinburgh, who had no children of their own, but a close relationship also grew up with the Stewarts, for in his will Charles Stewart referred to Mary Wilson Morgan, 'Minnie', the elder of the two little ones, as having 'for some years been as a daughter to me'. Later on Minnie also lived with Louisa and her family for a time and these links probably began to be forged when the bereaved children arrived in the home of their great-aunt Marion. It must have struck Louisa sadly and forcefully that her own cousin was only 24, seven years older than she herself, when she died leaving these two little creatures to the care of a family she had probably never met.[29]

The year continued sadly for the Stewarts with the death, on 22nd September, of Louisa's eldest brother, John Wilson Stewart, at the age of nineteen, from diabetes. According to the death certificate he had been suffering from this for two years already so the family would have known that he was ill. He was staying at Hillside in Fife at the time, the home of his maternal aunt, Catherine Colville. The death was notified by his cousin, Alexander Colville the younger, the elder brother

---

[28] Katharine Chorley, *Manchester Made Them*, Faber and Faber, 1950, p. 137. Her grandparents 'typified this process of 'moving out'. They moved in sequence from York Place behind Upper Brook Street to Grove House on Oxford Road . . . and then to Bowdon in Cheshire.' Ibid. p. 138. A very similar series of moves to those of CAS.
[29] Information about the Miller family from the Rotterdam archives, MAWM, and personal communication from 'Minnie's' grand-daughter.

of the John Louisa had gone visiting with in Edinburgh. Alexander was described as the occupier of Hillside, so his father was clearly dead, which was not surprising since he had turned 80 in 1851.

Daily life and lessons have to continue no matter what sad events occur, and now that the Stewarts were living in Dover Terrace, Louisa was even nearer to the Gaskells' house in Plymouth Grove, since the terrace was at the south end of Upper Brook Street, just before it ran into Plymouth Grove. There was a great emphasis on translation in her lessons, both from French and German. She recalled this with approval in several of those articles with a biographical element that she was to write in her fifties. It was, she thought, excellent training in 'command of language, just appreciation of words, unconfused with any attempt at using my own crude and immature material.'[30] She used this point, when as a well-known writer for children herself, she was asked to produce an article of advice to young beginners.

'To help you to the acquirement of a good style . . . I would like to repeat the advice I have so often given privately. Drill yourself well by *translating*. It is capital training. You know what you have to say, and there is not for the moment the strain of inventing upon you. The facts and ideas are there ready cut and dry; your business is to clothe them fittingly and gracefully and to this you can give your whole attention.'[31]

As well as translating, she wrote 'essays on given subjects with the heads marked out for me'. She thought this kind of work useful 'as tending to keep the mind to the point'[32] but in another place her tone with regard to it seems slightly dismissive. 'When I did begin to write — 'compositions' was the comprehensive term for our productions — it was as task work *pur et simple.*'[33] She reserved her real enthusiasm for the translation work; 'I think my earliest and best training was by translating'; 'the best work I ever did, up to the age of seventeen or so, was translation.'[34] Yet the compositions as much as the translations were a regular part of William Gaskell's teaching methods, as we know from another pupil who attended his classes at the Manchester Working Men's College in the 1850s. He wrote

---

[30] 'Story-Writing', p. 161.
[31] MLM 'On the Art of Writing Fiction for Children', *Atalanta* VI, May 1893.
[32] Bainton, pp. 93–96.
[33] 'Story-Writing', p. 161.
[34] Bainton, p. 94; 'Story-Writing', p. 161.

'Mr Gaskell encouraged his students to write essays on such subjects as pleased them, and submit the papers to him. The essays having been read and corrected in the meantime, were criticised at the next meeting of the class.'

This pupil also remembered Mr Gaskell's skill in reading aloud. 'I thought at the time that he was the most beautiful reader I had ever heard. Prose and poetry seemed to acquire new lustre of elegance when he read it.'[35] Later in life Louisa was to insist more than once on the importance of reading aloud what one had written as a test of style.[36] Her belief in this technique could have originated in, or at least been reinforced by, the pleasure of her teacher's beautiful reading.

Louisa said nothing in her later essays about any other subjects she studied with Mr Gaskell, naturally enough, since the purpose of all these pieces was to describe, at the request of various editors, for readers of different levels, something of how she wrote and how she had been trained as a writer, with a certain amount of advice for aspiring beginners. We know, if only from the epigraphs to the chapters of her adult novels, that she had a fairly wide acquaintance with English literature — how deep it was, of course this source cannot prove. But certainly she knew something of Chaucer, Shakespeare, Browne's *Religio Medici*, Farquhar, Massinger, Suckling, Swift, Shelley, Tennyson, Browning, Morris and Dickens, to take the epigraphs from one novel only.[37] The teacher in whose company another student

'had made close acquaintance with the persons and writings of England's greatest literary men; had passed from the times of Merlin the Enchanter to the time of Caedmon and Chaucer, on to the age of Shakespeare and Milton and down to the distinguished scholars of the present day,'

had surely taught something of this to young Louisa Stewart. This other student, a trainee Unitarian minister who used to go to the Plymouth Grove house for three or four hours at a time of concentrated study, witnessed to Mr Gaskell's 'pleasant method of teaching' which 'helped

---

[35] W. E. Adams, *Memoirs of a Social Atom*, vol. 2, p. 391 and footnote.
[36] 'On the Art . . .', p. 344; Bainton, p. 94.
[37] MLM *She Was Young and He Was Old: A Novel*. By the author of 'Lover and Husband.' 3 vols, Tinsley Brothers, 1872. This was the only one of her first seven published books in which neither her pseudonym nor her real name were used.

him to bear the strain.'[38] His studies would have been wider and deeper than those normally thought suitable at the time for a girl, but when we consider that the Winkworth sisters had private lessons with William Gaskell on a variety of subjects including Greek, and that in 1852, just before Louisa started with him, he was correcting the proofs of Susanna Winkworth's life of Niebuhr, it seems a little hasty to set too narrow limits to what he would have thought suitable. The very fact that Louisa was having lessons with the man who was tutor in history, literature and New Testament Greek to the new training centre for Unitarian ministers[39] suggests that her parents welcomed for her a wider range of study than could have been given by a governess.

Louisa paid her own tribute to her old teacher when she wrote that her own command of language was 'thanks to the exceptional excellence of the teacher, himself a perfect master of style, a writer far less known by name than he deserved to be.'[40] Louisa's seventeenth birthday fell in 1856, and in the same year she produced her first piece of published work. In keeping with her own account of the importance of translation in the development of her writing ability, this was a translation of a short story, called 'The Bird-mother' that appeared in a magazine. She enjoyed the feeling of being a *published* writer — 'it was very delightful to see my own words in print' and from then on she 'began to send trifling things to magazines — for no pay in those days, but just for the pleasure of their appearance.'[41]

In all this, there is no further reference to Mrs Gaskell and any influence she may have had on Louisa. The only other relevant surviving mention comes from one of Louisa's daughters. 'Mrs Gaskell's daughter used to write to my mother not so very many years ago.' It seems possible from this that Mrs Gaskell never formally taught Louisa, but that, as with the Winkworth sisters, the lessons with William Gaskell led to her becoming friends with the whole Gaskell family — 'friends for life.'[42] The Winkworths became very much part of the Gaskell circle

---

[38] Adam Rushton, *My Life as Farmer's Boy, Factoryhand, Teacher and Preacher*, quoted in Barbara Brill, *William Gaskell 1805–1884*, Manchester Literary and Philosophical Publications, 1984.

[39] Brill, pp. 78–79 and 71–72.

[40] 'Story-Writing', p. 161.

[41] Robson. 'How I Write . . . ,' p 17. Unfortunately 'The Bird-mother' has not been traced.

[42] Brill, p. 78.

and so may the Stewarts have done, though unfortunately we have very little evidence for saying so.

One of the Stewart family's friendships that we do know about was with William Crawford Williamson. In 1851 he became Professor of Natural History at Owens College, Manchester where William Gaskell also taught. Professor Williamson had come to the city first in 1835 as curator of the Manchester Natural History Society Museum for three years. He then went to London to study medicine, qualified in 1840 and returned to Manchester to practise at the beginning of 1841. Very soon afterwards he was appointed surgeon to the Chorlton-on-Medlock dispensary[43] and it seems reasonable to suppose that he first met the Stewarts as their family doctor. We only know of the friendship through a letter from Louisa to Professor Williamson many years later. In this she said 'it cannot surely be *quite* so long as "40 years" since I saw you for I remember you quite well, & I am only 45 now? We left Bloomsbury, I think, in 1853. I was about 13 then. I do not remember ever seeing you again . . . .'[44] But, as we have seen, the Manchester directory indicates that the move was some time in 1855 — anyway, in Louisa's mid-teens. She added 'I was sent abroad soon after for my education, and when I returned we lived, till my marriage, in Whalley Range.' This tantalisingly brief statement implies that she spent at least two years abroad, since the directories show Charles Stewart as resident in Upper Brook Street certainly until 1858, and first mention him in Whalley Range in 1861, the year of Louisa's marriage. It is not possible to be more definite. Memories become vague and confused after thirty years and that Louisa was conscious of this is shown by her use of such qualifying and generalising words as 'I think', 'about' and 'soon after'. In the immediate present 'soon' usually means at most a few hours, but when writing of the distant past it can be several years.

We know practically nothing of what must have been her first stay abroad alone without her family. Apart from her own statement quoted above, there is only a single remark in a letter from one of her daughters to show that she ever went at all; 'my mother I know was at Lausanne for a year'. On her way there, a normal part of the journey would have been an overnight stop in Paris, or even a stay of a few days as part of

---

[43] DNB.

[44] Unpublished letter from MLM to Professor W. C. Williamson, 1.2.1885. Originally copied by RR in the Special Collections Dept. of Manchester Public Library. It cannot now be traced.

the educational experience. One of her early three-volume novels for adults vividly described the impact Paris made on an untravelled, impressionable English girl.

> 'There was novelty and fascination for her at every step, even the sound of a foreign tongue heard for the first time with the dainty crispness of Parisian accent was delightful to her ears; the shops were not shops, but bewildering masses of lovely things arranged to perfection; the churches, above all, were so beautiful, the music so sublime, that Eugenia wondered how any one living within their reach could ever feel anything but "good".'[45]

The zest of novelty in a first experience abroad was mentioned again from a younger girl's point of view in a French reader Louisa wrote some 16 years after the novel.

> 'C'était mon premier repas en France, comme il me parut bon! Le pain était délicieux, le café aussi, tout, même les coussins de la voiture, avait pour moi un aspect *nouveau*.'[46]

Perhaps on the way south. like the heroine of her first novel, written seven or eight years after she was married, she spent a night

> 'in a queer old-world sort of hotel, where the windows of the rooms all looked into each other, and the beds were pannelled into the wall, something like those in old Scotch farmhouses. No doubt imperial rule has by this time "changé tout cela" and travelling in France is probably fast becoming as commonplace as anywhere else.'[47]

One detects here something of that feeling of pride, excitement and slight superiority most travellers experience in the face of anything at all unusual that others may not have known.

Once she got to Lausanne, Louisa probably stayed with a family en pension to improve her languages and did not go to school. It has already been noted that she expressed pleasure in an interview on having been educated at home [see the the description of her early education towards the end of chapter 2]. She would surely have mentioned, in such a discussion, any period, however short, that she had spent in an actual school. Another of her early adult novels opened in French

---

[45] *Not Without Thorns*, vol. 2, p. 231.
[46] MLM *French Life in Letters*, Macmillan, 1889, p. 9.
[47] MLM *Lover and Husband: A Novel*, by Ennis Graham. Charles J. Skeet, 1870, 3 vols, vol. 1, p. 39.

Switzerland, in a pensionnat for ladies where the heroine was staying with her sister and widowed mother, and taking language lessons. Louisa said that this pension was a portrait, meaning a description of somewhere she had actually experienced.[48] She wrote lively descriptions of the company in the pensionnat, and made amusing and understanding comments on the life of English people abroad. A male visitor, for instance, longed for something to read, 'If he had a Times, even the day before yesterday's (one comes to be thankful for small mercies, in the dead of winter, at such out of the world places as Rochette).' When writing about the kind of person we would now define as wanting bacon and eggs or fish and chips in every country they visit, she said 'though a sensible, clear-headed and not ill-natured person in her own country, across the water she became a very silly and objectionable old woman.' A comment about the heroine approved of her education — 'Certainly she has been brought up abroad, which is in many ways an advantage to a girl.'[49] Louisa wrote the novel from which these quotations are taken in her early thirties, when she had already spent several other periods in France. But this time in Lausanne during her teens was her first visit abroad. It was quite a recognised part of education for middle and upper-class girls. For instance, George Eliot, in *Middlemarch*, sent Dorothea and Celia Brooke to be educated in a Swiss family at Lausanne, in about 1830. A later, real-life example was that of Karen Blixen's mother who, as a child in 1864, was taken with her sisters by their mother 'on a program of educational travel,' part of which was living 'en pension at Lausanne' to improve their French.[50]

It was probably during this time in Switzerland that Louisa's love for the climate and landscapes of the more southerly parts of Europe began — a love which is unobtrusively signalled by little references in many of her books, such as

'one day — one lovely day, when it was difficult to believe it was only February, and that up there in the north in poor grey old England, the rain and the fogs, or the snow, perhaps, were having it all their own way'[51] or 'one day in the early spring-time, when the sunshine was already warm and the sky already deeply blue in the genial south.'[52]

---

[48] MLM to GLC, 17.7.[1875].

[49] *She Was Young* . . . , vol.1, p. 50, p. 202, p. 269

[50] Judith Thurman, *Isak Dinesen: The Life of Karen Blixen*, Penguin, 1984, p. 39

[51] MLM, *Silverthorns*. Hatchards, 1887, p. 263.

[52] *Robin Redbreast*, p. 287.

In her adult novels she allowed herself more elaborate descriptions and gave vent to a real enthusiasm.

> 'Spring to our northern ears hardly expresses the warmth and brilliance of these exquisite first touches of summer in the south of France ... Doubtless the north has its own peculiar and precious beauties and fitting it is that its children should appreciate and prize them. But why set ourselves to ignore the more vivid or striking beauties we must turn southwards to see.'

This is a direct personal comment from the author as narrator, a style to which she was much given, and whatever we may think of it as a way of writing, it is a habit very useful to the biographer. In the same novel the heroine also is entranced by the south, speaking of 'the marvellous perfection of those blue skies of the south at which I gazed with a very ecstasy of delight.' To her the sea and sky are 'melted emeralds and sapphires.' Again in her own person, Louisa commented in relation to this enthusiasm that people were accustomed to decry travellers' stories, saying that southern skies are not in fact more rich than those of the north but for herself 'I can only tell of things as they seemed to me.'[53]

While Louisa was away, her uncle from Australia, James Stewart, again visited his half-brother, bringing his own wife and mother with him. He wrote later of Charles Augustus,

> 'I heard nothing more of him until 1857 and 1858 when I had frequent intervals with him when my wife and I stayed at his house ... He told me how carefully he kept his true position from his children and how anxious they were to know all about their grandparents. He asked me not to bring my Mother much to his house as she was apt to speak freely with the children, but on two occasions when my mother was with me, both Charles Augustus and his wife were very kind and attentive to her. He asked me, or rather Mrs Charles asked me, if my wife knew the position of things and if she, my wife, was to be trusted not to say anything to the children on the subject of their relationship with us.'[54]

'The children' at this time were 12, 11 and 7. John was already dead and 16 year old Charles was probably away at school in Scotland. The parents might hope to keep their secret from the younger part of the

---

[53]   *Lover and Husband*, vol.1, p. 59.
[54]   *Claimant*, p. 12.

family and for their peace of mind it was just as well that 18 year old Louisa was in Lausanne and not there in the family circle, old enough to be present at grown up conversations and more difficult to hush up and send off to the schoolroom.

Sometime between 1858 and 1861, the Stewart family moved further out of Manchester, and Louisa returned from abroad. Her statement in the letter to Professor Williamson, 'when I returned we lived . . . in Whalley Range' implied that the move had already happened before her return and that she came home to a different house, Church Croft, Carlton Road, Whalley Range. Her father was taking part in 'the egress of wealthy men . . . [then] in full swing.'[55] Now that he himself was becoming wealthier, he made the next move out and also up the ladder. In the new house, a house with a name and not just a number, they had more servants — a cook and two maids, described as waitress and housemaid, a male servant listed as groom and a governess and nurse. The nurse's name, Julie de Sebun, suggests that she was French and though she and the governess were for the benefit of the younger sisters, Louisa was probably glad of the chance to keep up her French.[56] Home again and grown up. She was on the threshold of a different life.

[55] Ryan, p. 67.
[56] Manchester directories and 1861 census.

4

Marriage

What was Louisa like now, when in the parlance of the time she was 'out', finished, educated? An adjective that frequently recurs, in such descriptions of her as exist, is 'charming'. To give only two instances out of several, one (in reference to a photograph of her, sadly now lost) calls her 'a charming young woman in a coat and cap edged with fur', and the other, with emphasis, says 'She was a most *charming* woman . . . and such really sweet manners.' The authors of these two comments make it clear that the first is referring to her appearance and the other to her character and behaviour. Other blanket remarks are not always so specific. She was apparently 'not beautiful' (though having an 'electric smile'!) but 'certainly good looking with a good profile.' A published description of her later in life calls her 'sweet-faced', but this was contradicted by her grand-daughter. 'Sweet-faced? No. She had too strong a face. Calm. Pleasant. V. intelligent. She was young-looking, probably one of those girls who are never v. young and remain unchanged for years'. The author of the 'sweet-faced' remark also noted her 'youthful air'. Another description calls her 'very attractive looking, tall and dignified.' It seems as though she may have been what would now be called striking. Later photographs show her with a pointed face and high cheek-bones. She obviously did not have the conventional, rounded, pink-and-white prettiness admired in Victorian debutantes. There was also some admiration of her voice — 'a lovely speaking voice,' 'a very quiet soft voice which I always found very attractive.' She had a Scottish accent which survived all her life. Her grand-daughter wrote of this in some detail.

> 'She retained all her life a slight "Scotticism". I was a big child before I realised that "amenities" and similiar words are pronounced in English with a short e. Granny said ameenities. Also she pronounced the H in WH words — why, when etc. She reproved me once for speaking of the cat as furry (rhymed with "surly"). It should be furry as in "hurry".'

'As a young woman she was a keen horsewoman,' and she was also said to be 'very graceful and a fine dancer' as a girl. One of the personal comments she so often inserted into her novels suggests that she was as keen about dancing as she was about riding.[1]

> 'It is something for poor creatures such as most of us are, to be able to do anything perfectly, even so altogether small a thing as dancing. There is a real satisfaction while it lasts in feeling that the thing we are doing could not be done better. And this agreeable consciousness was always Roma's when waltzing with Beauchamp. They were a perfectly matched pair, their movements as harmonious as the blending of two voices in a duet.'[2]

This bears the marks of personal experience, of personal enthusiasm. She herself had felt, while dancing, that what she was doing could not be done better.

Many years later Louisa published an article about girls who had reached the stage we have now come to in her own life.[3] It was indeed addressed to them, by way of advice. And although we cannot assume that she had exactly the same opinions at fifty as at eighteen or twenty, or that she had thought things out in such detail, some attention to this article may give us an idea of how she had begun to consider the world and her own situation, when she was 'Standing with reluctant feet/Where the brook and river meet.' She began her article with this quotation (actually from Longfellow's poem 'Maidenhood', though she did not mention this) and immediately condemned it as hackneyed, if 'pretty and "poetical",' and, she added shrewdly, 'so appropriate to the sort of notion people have long had and like to have about their girls.' But the retiring maiden reluctant to grow up was simply not a true picture, she continued, — the ones who hated the idea 'of long skirts and quiet movements, of "done-up" hair and neatly buttoned gloves' (shades of Jo March!) were far more likely to be tomboys, desperate to retain the freedom of scaling garden walls with their brothers and riding bareback ponies round the paddocks.

She herself does not appear to have been of the tomboy class, but she

---

[1] *Westminster Budget*; M. Laski, *Mrs Ewing, Mrs Molesworth and Mrs Hodgson Burnett*, Arthur Barker Ltd., 1950, p. 58. All other comments in this paragraph come from privately owned letters.
[2] *Not Without Thorns*, vol.2, pp. 31–2.
[3] MLM, 'Coming out', *Atalanta*, May 1890. Later collected in *Studies and Stories*, A. D. Innes, 1893.

saw clearly the social pressure to believe in the ideal of the innocent maiden as opposed to the reality and did not shrink either from pointing out that hoydens might develop into fast, vain and frivolous women. She was also firmly opposed to the traditional idea of how girls should be treated at this stage in their lives. They passed suddenly from a carefully regulated life when 'they have been treated more or less as reasonable beings' with duties, studies and responsibilities, and all amusements 'cautiously selected and but moderately indulged in,' to a period of two or three years of nothing but frivolity and pleasure. The motive might only be 'a sort of thoughtless subscribing to conventionality' but it could also be what she described as 'coarser'. She then proceeded to define, very succinctly, but without actually using any of the key words, what we would call the marriage market. 'The debutante is to be dressed to the greatest advantage, and taken out into society with a very defined though seldom avowed object,' which was of course to make a suitable marriage, although she did not say so. We know that this system had been going on long before she was young, if only from the episode in *Mansfield Park* where Miss Crawford inquires whether Fanny Price is out or not out. The whole passage portrays in Jane Austen's delightful ironic manner the issues Louisa discussed.

The final motive Louisa attributed to parents and guardians was, she thought, 'little short of cruel.' By providing an exaggerated amount of gaiety for 'their newly fledged daughter' they hoped to sicken her of it on the same principle that confectioners 'allow their new apprentices to eat as many sweets as they please, that they may the sooner lose all liking for them.' Why, demanded this girls' champion, should they have to tire of all amusement and did the system work anyway? The better course would be one that resulted in girls being able to partake of amusements 'reasonably and sparingly' so that they need never tire of 'refined and genial social recreation.'

Louisa deplored all the underlying motives for the traditional 'coming-out' system, analysing the root cause of the wrong as making amusement and pleasure, which should be the relaxation of life, into its business. Her solution was not revolutionary. It was not indeed a solution for a social evil at all. She made no suggestion that the system should be scrapped. She merely gave some simple advice to the girls she was writing for as to how they personally might avoid the worst results. They must regulate their time for themselves when released from schoolroom discipline, use some of it to help others both in home duties and in outside charities, continue to read seriously and steadily, be regular and trustworthy in whatever was undertaken. Early rising, punctuality, prompt answering of notes, faithfulness in correspondence with family members away from home, especially 'a Jack or Harry far away' were also all earnestly recommended and finally, although she felt that a girls' magazine was hardly the place to do so, she lightly touched on 'your first and highest and *realest* duties of all,' by which she meant regular prayer, bible-reading, church attendance and the effort to lead a Christian life. Her first readers would have had no difficulty in understanding this, whether they agreed with her or shrugged it off. The whole was a Charlotte M. Yonge recipe for the good life.

And quite possibly Louisa struggled to put these ideas into practice in her own newly-released-from-the-schoolroom life. Certainly later on she had a reputation among her grandchildren for punctuality, meticulousness in all business affairs, an almost comic promptness in replying to notes and an expectation that others should do the same. A granddaughter wrote of her

> 'She never let more than one post go by without answering a letter — or more than one day without paying a bill. If you didn't answer her letters at ONCE, you got another, "Darling, I do not think you can have received etc etc".'

Such characteristics have to be practised from a young age in order for them to become habits. She had other Miss Yonge type rules for herself, such as never reading fiction before lunch. This was her personal habit and she also recommended it in print.

> 'A habit of novel reading in the *forenoon* leaves one in a curiously unready and desultory condition for the day's work, and sitting up late at night over an interesting or exciting tale is equally sure to make one's brain unhealthily tired and listless.'[4]

This is exactly the situation described in Charlotte Yonge's *Scenes and Characters*, first published in 1847, when Louisa was eight. Lily, the heroine, having once been given permission to read Walter Scott's novels, has no idea of moderation and gulps them down to the neglect of all else. Her father has to warn her to 'read them only after the duties of the day are done — make them your pleasure, but do not make yourself their slave.' In response to this she forces herself not to touch one till

---

[4] 'Fiction: Its Use and Abuse', *Girls' Own Paper*, May 1891. Later collected in *Studies and Stories*.

after five o'clock, but then reads so voraciously that she does not enjoy them so much as she might, and finds her more serious reading very dull in comparison — both results also forecast by Louisa who wrote that fiction 'not only unfits one for graver reading . . . but it actually loses its own charm if indulged in too much.' She certainly read Charlotte Yonge enthusiastically, 'Then came the delight of Miss Yonge's books, which seemed to me to open a new world of fiction, as indeed they did, especially, I think, the 'historical' ones,'[5] and *Scenes and Characters* might well have contributed to the formation of her opinions about fiction.

All this could make Louisa sound a dull, priggish sort of girl, but it is clear from many of the stories she later wrote for children that she had plenty of fun in her. High principles and strict control over oneself do not necessarily rule out an attractive personality, as Charlotte Yonge showed when she created Ethel May. Later in life Louisa was described as quiet and reserved, though not shy, having 'a quiet calm manner,' 'a woman of very considerable charm of a quiet, gentle and almost deprecatory kind.'[6]

Louisa herself was not presented at court as her daughters later were — her parents did not move in aristocratic circles — but 'coming out', as used in her article quoted above, did not mean only, or even primarily, being a court debutante. The young girl came out into the adult social milieu of her family. It has been suggested that the Stewarts may have been part of the Gaskell circle and the following brief description of a section of Manchester society gives some idea of the kind of activities in which Louisa could have taken part.

> 'Mrs Carlyle's friend, Geraldine Jewsbury, found the women of Unitarian society dull, but had to suffer them, for such people as the Gaskells were at the time the focus of all the really interesting society in the town. At their house, and at her own nearby, scientists, schoolmasters and journalists, and the most intelligent men of the German, Greek and Italian colonies were continually meeting and mingling. Thackeray lectured and they all went to listen. Macready stayed with them when he came to play at the Theatre Royal. There were dinners, concerts, card-parties, 'regular unsophisticated dances' and Christmas parties at the houses of German friends. Certainly the good life as it was lived in nineteenth century Manchester was not unpleasantly severe.'[7]

---

[5] 'Story-Reading . . .', p. 773.
[6] Private letters.
[7] Ryan, p. 24.

A more general comment, based on much recent research, says of Manchester and Leeds 'There is no doubt, then, that the cultural life of the middle class was lively and sophisticated.'[8]

Louisa was still abroad when the great Manchester 'Exhibition of the Art Treasures of the United Kingdom' took place in 1857, though no doubt her parents had extra visitors for the occasion and perhaps had something of the experience of Mrs Gaskell, who wrote in September of that year 'Our house has been fuller than full, day and night . . . and this last fortnight it will be fuller than ever, as everyone will want to see the Exhibition before it closes.'[9] Opened by the Prince Consort in May, the exhibition lasted until October. James Horne Stewart, Charles Augustus' half brother, with his wife and mother, was, as we have seen, staying with them for some part of this year and it seems unlikely that the Stewarts did *not* take them to the first national exhibition ever to be devoted entirely to art. It was an important example of the 'extensive involvement in, and understanding of, the arts on the part of bankers, merchants, manufacturers and industrialists,' many of whom were colleagues and acquaintances of Robert Barbour and his partner Charles Stewart. A group of them provided the motivation for and planning and organisation behind the event, and the subscription list showed ninety-two Manchester men giving £62,000 towards the expenses of the exhibiton.[10]

Although Louisa could not attend the exhibition itself, she would have benefited with other Manchester citizens from the results. It was something of a turning point in the town's history. From 1857 onwards it began to lead the way among provincial cities in providing public libraries, art galleries and museums. It was now that Charles Hallé started his large public concerts.[11]

But Louisa still continued to visit Scotland and on one of these visits she met a young soldier home on leave from the Indian Mutiny who was having a yachting holiday. We have no further details of the meeting than this. The young man was Richard Molesworth, eldest son of Captain the Hon. Anthony Oliver Molesworth, whose brother was the seventh Viscount Molesworth, a title in the peerage of Ireland, first

[8] Janet Wolff and Caroline Arscott, 'Cultivated Capital', *History Today*, vol. 87, Mar. 1987, p. 24.
[9] Gerin (1976), p. 199.
[10] Wolff and Arscott, p. 23; Ryan, p. 6.
[11] Ryan, pp. 6 and 8.

awarded to Richard's great-great-grandfather. Richard was born 3rd May, 1836 and at the age of eighteen became an ensign in the 1st Yorks North Riding Regiment, on 23rd November, 1854. His daughter described his active military career in a sentence. 'He spent his 3 young years — of 18 — 19 — 20 — in that awful Crimea and Indian Mutiny — & had all his medals.'[12] The Times obituary was more specific.

'He served in the Eastern Campaign [*the usual nineteenth century term for what we now call the Crimean War*] with his regiment from May 1855, having been promoted to lieutenant in March, and was engaged in the attack on the Quarries on June 7th and in the attacks on the Redan on June 18th and on September 8th, when he was severely wounded. He received the medal with the clasps and the Turkish medal for his services.'[13]

A detailed description of the attack on the Redan (a heavily fortified high point) in a book on the Crimean War, tells of Richard's courage in attempting to urge forward his 'stunned and paralysed' men.

'The authority and even the example of the younger officers was insufficient to overcome their men's fears, now increased by the loss of their leaders. Lieutenant Molesworth, scarcely more than a boy, might coolly light a cigar till it was knocked out of his mouth by a shell splinter; the men clinging to the outside of the Redan parapet and there for a time fairly immune from harm, refused to advance further.'

To have a cigar shot out of his mouth in that way, Richard must have been deliberately exposing himself and not lighting it in the shelter of the parapet. A newspaper cutting of 1873, describing 'The Parade of the Commissioners', said

'There is no "19" now on the buttons of this scarred veteran, but the number was there when he followed Massey and Molesworth into the hell-abyss of the Redan on the day when so much good English blood was wasted.'

Richard's heroic behaviour had been conspicuous enough to be remembered as a landmark in this battle eighteen years later. (The

---

[12] CP to RR, private conversation and letters.
[13] *The Times*, 6.4.1900. RM's military career: Entered the Army by direct commission. Created Ensign 23.11.1854, Lieutenant 9.3.1855, Captain 4.6.1861 (all 1st Yorks North Riding regiment). 1st Royal Dragoons 16.7.1861. Retired 29.3.1864. Adjutant 6th Lancashire Militia 25.1.1865. Retired therefrom on retired allowance with Honorary rank of Major 31.12.1873. Information provided by the archivist of Windsor Castle.

number "19" refers to the original name of the regiment to which Richard and the 'scarred veteran' both belonged — the 19th Regiment of Foot. It became the 1st Yorks North Riding Regiment later.)[14]

The Indian Mutiny 'virtually ended with the fall of Gwalior on 20th June 1858.'[15] A young officer would not necessarily have got leave immediately and then there was the voyage home. So it was probably not until the spring or summer of 1859 that Richard was yachting off Scotland — the previous autumn and winter hardly being suitable seasons for such an activity. One of Louisa's grandsons told Marghanita Laski that his grandparents became engaged before Richard went to the Crimea.[16] Since she was not yet sixteen at that time, the story of the encounter when he was home from the Mutiny, which came from her daughter, seems more likely to be correct. It is hardly credible that the Stewarts would have permitted their daughter to become engaged at such a young age, when she was still in the schoolroom, to a very junior officer just setting out on active service. There was time in the remaining months of 1859 for a friendship to develop. In February 1860 he was again in India, a fact established by a bill from a Calcutta store for 'a stiff-brimmed wide-awake hat and two yards of blue sarsanet'. Such are the trivia that survive when the revealing letters have been destroyed! Was there an understanding between them to support them during their parting? Louisa certainly wrote with sympathetic insight in a later novel about a long engagement because of the man's absence in India.

> 'I was very young . . . the one condition my father attached to his consent was that I should not go to India and as Arthur's residence there was not likely to extend over many years, all pointed to the advisability of a long engagement — not in those days looked upon with the dread and misgivings which the mere mention of such a thing now inspires.
>
> But a long engagement, accompanied by a long and indefinite separation must always be a trial . . . happy, intensely happy though I was in the avowed fact of his devotion to me, delightful though it was to have our engagement openly recognised, there was at times a strange weight at my heart which I could not throw off . . . the dark cloud of indefinable apprehensions . . . were only occasional visitors . . . for weeks and months

[14] W. Baring Pemberton, *Battles of the Crimean War*, B. T. Batsford Ltd., 1962, p. 217. I am grateful to Brian Best, the secretary of the Anglo-Zulu War Society, for giving me this reference. Newspaper cutting quoted by RR in unpublished ms.

[15] Percival Spear, *A History of India*, Penguin, 1965, vol. 2.

[16] Laski, p. 57.

at a time I felt quite untroubled. Even now I cannot say that these so-called presentiments or impressions had any real root. If no strange wrench had destroyed the happy placidity of my life's stream, I should no doubt, have forgotten all about them long before this; for I have noticed that, to anyone of thoughtful or imaginative nature, the prospect of great happiness is often accompanied by a curious fear.'[17]

By the following Christmas Richard had returned from India and as a Christmas gift he gave Louisa a book with a formal inscription 'Mary Louisa Stewart from Richard Molesworth, Christmas Day, 1860.' They had evidently become close enough for gifts but were probably not yet officially engaged. Four months later the situation was quite different. He gave her a copy of *The Arabian Nights* in which he wrote 'For my darling Louie from her loving Richard. 18th April, 1861, Jermyn Street.' With our present social customs, to us the only significant words in that inscription are the affectionate adjectives. To the Victorian mind the use of Christian names only would have carried equal or even heavier meaning. An example of this, startling and even shocking to us, is Wilfred Scawen Blunt's admission in his secret memoirs that, although he and Jane Morris were lovers, with 'a love . . . essentially physical and real and indulged as often as we met . . . I do not remember ever having called her by her Christian name.'[18] In the published volume of Jane Morris' letters to Blunt one begins 'Caro mio' and all the rest, even during the period described by the editor as 'the romantic peak of the affair' (in 1889), start 'My dear Mr Blunt.'[19] The Christian name could only be openly used when the relationship could also be publicly acknowledged and even in private interviews and private letters one's guard could not be dropped.

The implication of this for Richard and Louisa seems to be that whatever private understanding there might have been when he returned to India the previous year, or however joyfully she welcomed him on his return, the engagement was only officially acknowledged in the spring of 1861. The copy of *The Arabian Nights* might have been an engagement present. A sword engraved with their joint initials which still existed in the 1950s, in the possession of a grandson, was held by

---

[17] MLM, *Meg Langholme or The Day After Tomorrow*, Chambers, 1897, pp. 200, 201, 202.
[18] Wilfred Scawen Blunt, ms diaries, quoted Fiona MacCarthy, *William Morris: A Life for Our Time*, Faber, 1994, p. 450.
[19] Peter Faulkner (ed.), *Jane Morris to Wilfred Scawen Blunt*, University of Exeter, 1986.

family tradition to have been her present to him on the occasion.[20] Such a gift seems embarrassingly flamboyant now, implying an attitude to war which we cannot share. Pre-First World War, military service could still seem glorious and both their families had a tradition of such service. As described earlier, Louisa's grandfather, Major General William Stewart, distinguished himself in the Peninsula war, and her brother Charles was to have a career in the Royal Artillery. Further back, there had been Stewarts at the battle of Culloden and in later life Louisa once wrote to a friend, 'We have always been like most Scotch people — rather proud of our old Stewart ancestry (it is full of romance as my great-great-grandfather was in the Pretender's army).'[21] A glance at any peerage will show how strong was the military tradition in the Molesworth family. For example, the sixth Viscount, first cousin to Richard's father, reached, like Louisa's grandfather, the rank of Major General, in the 9th regiment of foot. Richard's father, who had died in 1848 at the comparatively young age of 54, long before Richard and Louisa met, was a captain in the Royal Artillery, where he was followed by two of his sons, while Richard's third brother was in the Royal Engineers. Although the horrors of the Crimean campaign had impressed the public mind, scarlet had not yet given way to khaki, either literally or in the general imagination.

On Richard's birthday, just over two weeks after his gift to her in Jermyn Street, Louisa gave him a copy of *The Birthday Souvenir* and inscribed it 'Richard from Louie, May 3rd 1861, The Croft.' It seems as though she was in London probably to meet his family and he then came back to Manchester with her to stay with her family. The Croft was her father's house in Whalley Range.[22] What did the respective families think of this marriage? From a worldly point of view, there were advantages on both sides. It was accepted in the army that unless a young officer had substantial independent means, marriage to a girl without money was impossible. A Lieutenant-General writing in 1889

---

[20] Green, (1961), p. 28. The grandson was H. D. Molesworth.

[21] MLM to DUC, 8.7.1889; cp *John O'Groats Journal* 23.8.1912, 'Major General Stewart of Strath . . . grandson of the Captain Donald Stewart who . . . was an officer of Prince Charles Edward's army, and a zealous adherent of the cause of that unfortunate prince.'

[22] All the books exchanged by MLM and RM were in the possession of VMI and seen by RR in 1952. The 1861 census actually gives The Croft, no. 153 in the record, as the residence of Richard Doncastle, merchant in home trade, and the next entry, no. 154, shows Charles A. Stewart, cotton and woollen merchant, as head of the household of *Church* Croft — a discrepancy which cannot now be resolved.

said that a subaltern 'should not think of marrying before he is thirty-five years old'. The rule of thumb was that subalterns may not marry, captains might marry, majors should marry, and lieutenant-colonels must marry.[23] Richard, young for marriage by army standards, was, however, about to become a captain and was also obeying military custom by marrying into comparative wealth — comfort at least. When his father-in-law died in 1873, his will was proved at under £180,000 — riches in those days, as can be seen from this comment about a character in one of Louisa's novels, published in 1897, 'He died a rich man. His will was proved under fifty thousand pounds.'[24] Twelve years before his death, Charles Augustus Stewart would surely have been worth at least half, if not more, of what he finally left and his increasing wealth has already been indicated by his successive moves to larger houses in better areas. He certainly helped the young couple financially.

On Louisa's side, her father must have seen the marriage as a chance for his daughter to move away from trade and commerce into the aristocracy, or rather, the fringes of it. For, despite the published statement that Richard was heir to the seventh viscount,[25] this was not in fact the case. There was only a very slight chance that he might ever inherit the title himself. Although Richard Pigot, the seventh Viscount, was unmarried and elderly at the time of Richard and Louisa's marriage, he must have been in reasonable health and known by his family to be so, since he lived for another 14 years, dying at the age of 88. His heir, the son of his next brother, was the Rev. Samuel Molesworth, only seven years older than Richard. It is true that he too was unmarried, but he did in fact marry a year after Richard had done so, and proceeded to have seven children in ten years. His first son was born in 1867, nine years before the seventh viscount died, so Richard Molesworth was never direct heir to the title and Louisa's parents can never seriously have thought she would become a viscountess.

'She loved her husband dearly, they were young and happy together' wrote one member of the family, who also emphasised that 'it was a most real love match.' Her youngest sister, Caroline, discussing the marriage with a great-niece after her sister's death, seems to have thought Louisa was swept off her feet 'Young, handsome, gallant — what girl

[23]   Byron Farwell, *For Queen and Country: A Social History of the Victorian and Edwardian Army*, Allen Lane 1981, p. 233.
[24]   *Meg Langholme*, p. 322.
[25]   Laski, p. 57.

could have resisted him?' No photograph of Richard has survived but a witness who saw one of his elder son said he looked 'a handsome youth with clear-cut features.'[26] During the engagement their being happy together would have included the riding and dancing on which she was so keen. Her most popular children's book contains an episode where the heroine, Griselda, is magically shown part of the story of her grandmother, Sybilla, in a series of dissolving views. Griselda watches Sybilla in young girlhood, dancing in

> 'the great saloon ... very different from what she had ever seen it. ... The faded yellow damask hangings were rich and brilliant. There were bouquets of lovely flowers arranged about the tables; wax lights were sending out their brightness in every direction, and the room was filled with ladies and gentlemen in gay attire. ... [Griselda's] attention was attracted by a much younger lady — a mere girl she seemed, but oh, so sweet and pretty! She was dancing with a gentleman whose eyes looked as if they saw no one else, and she herself seemed brimming over with youth and happiness. Her very steps had joy in them.'[27]

Could this scene be built, perhaps, on a reminiscence from the author's own life? At nineteen or twenty, Louisa, tall, graceful, dark-haired, dark-eyed, with a latent vitality called to the surface by young love, may well have been both enchanted and enchanting.

But even in the magic period of engagement, life was not in reality a fairy tale. Richard had been wounded in the Crimea. It was a head wound in which a piece of shrapnel had remained 'and this led to ... years of subsequent ill-health and trouble.' The consequences of this wound were known about before the marriage and caused Louisa's mother to feel very apprehensive. A cousin of Richard's, who later became an intimate friend of Louisa's, wrote about this problem.

> 'I never saw Major Molesworth, but Mrs Molesworth told me herself that he had a very violent temper, and that the mother did not want the marriage for that reason; but she trusted to her own love and tact to keep it under control. She said it was due to the wound he had received in the Crimea on the top of his head.'

This is a variant on the old story of the woman who thinks love will transform a drunkard or a gambler into a sober, industrious fellow.

---

[26] Private letters and conversations.
[27] *The Cuckoo Clock* pp. 105–6.

And she had more to contend with here, for Richard's violence was pathological. His grand-daughter said that her grandfather's rages resembled those of shell-shocked victims. The piece of shrapnel in his head was not discovered until after his death and must have caused pressure on the brain. Modern medicine is fully cognizant of such a state, and modern surgery is capable of dealing with it, but during his lifetime his condition was almost certainly not completely understood. Furthermore, in the army, medical treatment at the time Richard was wounded was of a notoriously low standard and officers and men alike simply had to learn to survive it.[28]

It is possible, too, that behaviour which was really pathological in origin was sometimes attributed to defects of character. Louisa, of course, could not have been aware of all this. All she knew was that her lover had a temper sufficiently violent to arouse her mother's apprehension. She may have played it down to her mother, as her daughter did years later, calling her father 'rather an invalid . . . very irritable and trying at times.' Whether or not Mrs Stewart's opposition led to any rift between her and her daughter, it probably overshadowed Louisa's happiness to some degree. If she had any misgivings herself, she suppressed them successfully, for she married Richard Molesworth on 24th July, 1861, at Grosvenor Square Church, Manchester, the reception taking place at her father's house in Whalley Range.

A few weeks before the wedding Richard transferred with the rank of Captain to the Royal Dragoons which was at that time stationed in Ireland. It seems unlikely that the couple were in Ireland together, since the regiment left there in September 1861.[29] Its next station was Birmingham, where it remained for the following twenty months. Louisa accompanied her husband on his postings, thus living the usual nomadic life of an army wife, like Mrs Ewing. Some years later, in a letter to a friend, when circumstances made it necessary for Richard to leave her behind, she wrote on this very point 'I do not at all like his going there alone — I have never left him all these years . . . Had I been the least stronger I wd. have gone'.[30] Their first child, a daughter, Agnes Violet Grace, was born in her grandfather's house at Whalley Range on 16th

---

[28] Information in this paragraph about RM from letters by VMI, and GDL. Farwell, p. 179. 'Officers and other ranks all seemed to accept the needless pain, the rough handling, the springless ambulances, the crude and insensitive hospital orderlies, and the incompetent doctors as unchangeable aspects of military life.'

[29] C. J. Atkinson, *A History of the Royal Dragoons.*

[30] MLM to JBLW, 18.7.[1869].

April, 1862. At this time James Horne Stewart was visiting America and had left his wife on a long visit to the Stewarts, so that she would have been in the house when Violet was born. There was a family tradition in the Australian branch that Mrs J. H. Stewart was godmother to one of Louisa's children and as she was actually on the spot for the arrival of this one, it would seem to have been the most likely occasion.[31] Violet was in fact named after her two grandmothers — Richard's mother was Grace Jane Crofton — and since Violet, the name that was actually used for her, does not appear on either side of the family, it was probably a personal preference connected with the season. There are many fond references to violets in Louisa's books, a whole chapter, for example, in *The February Boys*, called 'Violets', describing members of a family sending each other little bunches of the first violets through the post from different parts of the country in a friendly competition to see who finds the earliest. If Louisa called her daughter Violet because she liked the flowers, violets increased their attraction for her because she loved her daughter.

Three weeks or so after Violet's birth, Richard's cousin, Samuel Molesworth, the viscount's heir, married Georgina Gosset, youngest daughter of a captain in the 4th Dragoon Guards. The bride's mother, after her husband's death, had by a second marriage become an Italian Marchioness. Her elder sister was already married to a distant Molesworth relation, a descendant of the first viscount. All very suitable.

When Violet was just over a year old, the regiment was posted to Aldershot, in May 1863. It seems certain that Louisa went with Richard, from a comment she made in a letter written in 1869 — when discussing the need to be ready for sudden changes and unexpected postings, she said 'Aldershot probably again next year.'[32] The only scrap of information which survives about this period is that Louisa gave French and German lessons to her husband's batman, Archibald Forbes, who served for a time as a trooper in the Dragoons. A young man of the same age as herself, he had been forced to accept ' "the Queen's shilling" from a fine old recruiting sergeant' when 'follies and extravagance abruptly terminated my university career.' He subsequently became a well-known war correspondent and his initial success in reporting the Franco-German war was perhaps aided by her tutoring. He actually began writing for *The Morning Star* while still a trooper, and also succeeded

---

[31] *Claimant* p. 12.
[32] MLM to JBLW, 18.7.[1869].

in getting several papers on military subjects accepted by *The Cornhill Magazine*.[33] Louisa, as we know, was already writing for various magazines and they may have compared notes on the best way to go about getting accepted.

In December 1863 the second daughter, Mary Cicely Caroline, was born, also at Whalley Range. Cicely's own daughter wrote about this in 1951. 'She went back 'home' [i.e. to her parents] for the birth of most of her children, which was less common then than now.' Her father's house was probably more comfortable than officers' married quarters, but, as well, this habit was mentioned by the grand-daughter to illustrate her statement that 'Louie' was her father's pet. With the naming of this child Louisa seems to have established a family tradition (carried on with two other daughters) whereby the middle name, apparently chosen by the parents simply from personal preference, was the one used and the first and third were family names. Her own grandmother, the story-telling Scottish one, had been a Mary, as had her aunt and cousin, the grandmother and mother of the two orphan children growing up in Edinburgh. Besides which, it was her own name while Caroline was that of her youngest sister.

The following year, 1864, Richard Molesworth retired from the Royal Dragoons, perhaps on account of ill-health, on 29th March, with the rank of Major, and £1,800 in lieu of his commission, which would, of course, have been bought when he was commissioned Ensign in 1854. At that time the proceeds of the sale of a commission on retirement performed the function of the modern pension, but only a few years later, in 1870, this sale and purchase of commissions came to an end. On or soon after Richard's retirement, the Molesworths rented Tabley Grange in Cheshire from the second Baron de Tabley, a friend of the family, who had become Cicely's godfather. He was a friend from the Molesworth side as is shown by a letter from a Molesworth relative to Louisa, referring to Lord de Tabley's 'very flattering reminiscences' of this relative and to a meeting with him at a dinner party. His son, the poet John Byrne Leicester Warren (1835–1895), later the third Baron, became a close friend of both Molesworths and would have been a particularly agreeable one for Louisa, near to her own age and with interests in literature, numismatics and botany. A twentieth century critic writes 'His poetry — and editors keep saying so — has

---

[33] DNB; Archibald Forbes, 'How I Became a War-Correspondent', *English Illustrated Magazine*, Apr. 1884, pp. 450–456.

never quite had its due,' while a contemporary opinion spoke of 'the 'brocaded' . . . stateliness of his diction, the vivid originality of his natural descriptions and an occasional pungency of phrase . . . He will live as an impassioned writer who chose poetry for his medium.' His *Flora* of Cheshire remains the text book used by the university today, and he still stands as the top authority on English seals and bookplates.[34]

Tabley Grange, a pleasant, long, low building, stands close to the main Knutsford-Northwich road in the village of Nether Tabley about 2 miles west of Knutsford. It was originally a farmhouse and has many additions and alterations, some made during the Molesworths' time there. As well as living in the Grange, they managed a farm attached to it, for in one letter Louisa wrote 'Capt. Molesworth has invested in a new cow', and when they gave up the tenancy she said 'The farm of course we must reclaim some of the improvements on separately — & sell the stock'.[35] It was a much larger house and household than Louisa had been used to managing, for when they gave it up she commented on this point more than once, calling the Grange 'a place that entailed so many servants, & so much looking after' & wanting a 'small, easily managed house.'[36] They had not been there long before Richard re-joined the army only nine months after he had retired. His uncle the viscount took an interest in his career and wrote to Louisa about this.

43, Grand Parade, Brighton
3rd Feb. 1865

My Dear Niece,
I have just received your kind letter, communicating the fact of Richard's appointment to the Adjutancy[37] of the Sixth Regiment of Lancashire Militia, and to show you the interest we both of us take in the matter, I sit down instantly to offer our united congratulations — I assure you it affords us sincere pleasure to hear that Richard is at length brought again into active service — I regret to say that Mary's cough is still

---

[34] George MacBeth (ed), *The Penguin Book of Victorian Verse*, 1969, p. 259; DNB article on Warren; letter from assistant administrator, Tabley House Collection Trust, 5.1.1996.

[35] MLM to JBLW, 18.6.[?1867], and 12.4.1869.

[36] MLM to JBLW, 7.4, 12.4, and 18.7.1869.

[37] Farwell, p. 68, 'It was the adjutant's job to arrange the daily routine of the battalion, to issue written orders and to ensure that the drill and dress of the battalion were of the desired standard.'

very troublesome, but we hope it will be less so when we get milder
weather.

>With kind regards to your respected family,
>>Believe me to remain,
>>>Your affect. Uncle,
>>>>Molesworth.[38]

Louisa referred affectionately to the Viscount as 'our dear old uncle' in
several letters, and said to one correspondent 'Lord M. is very kind to
us . . . he is a <u>sort</u> of a father to R.'[39] Here Lord Molesworth is polite
about Louisa's family and clearly on pleasantly polite terms with her.
She was also very great friends with her mother-in-law. Mrs Molesworth senior had been a widow for thirteen years when Richard and
Louisa married, and lived with them for a time in Cheshire. Two little
anecdotes about Cicely and her grandmother were preserved by Cicely's
daughter.

> 'My mother [= *Cicely*] used to slip out of the nursery to come and sit
> with her grandmother [= *Mrs Molesworth senior*] — <u>my</u> grandmother [=
> *Louisa*] must have often listened to them talking. In Cheshire in those
> days butter — even good butter — was v. highly salted and my mother
> used to make fresh butter for her grandmother by swinging a bottle of
> thick cream.'[40]

The thick cream presumably came from the cows on Tabley Grange
farm.

Around the same time that the Molesworths moved to Tabley Grange,
the Stewarts moved to another house in Whalley Range. Their address
was now Whalley House, Withington Road, and according to Manchester directories they were there from 1864 to 1869. If Louisa wanted
to go to Manchester or was on her way to London she would spend
the night at Whalley House, and she and the children often made longer
visits there. But her third child, Louisa Juliet Marion, was born at Tabley
on 17th July, 1865. Named after her mother, her aunt and great-aunt,
she was always called Juliet. Possibly Louisa did not go 'home' for this
birth, because her mother-in-law was already with her. With three tiny
children now and two of them old enough to enjoy simple tales, she
would have been resurrecting her story-telling skills from her own

---

[38] Copy made by RR from CP's papers. Original since destroyed.
[39] MLM to JBLW, 3.8.1869.
[40] VMI to RR.

nursery days. She may even have begun writing some of them down or some of the individual episodes, for she said to an interviewer years later that the stories in her first published children's book had been written for her own children without thought of publication.[41]

As friends of the De Tabley family, the Molesworths would have been well acquainted with Tabley House, a fine Palladian mansion, built of red brick with stone facings and a splendid porticoed terrace, with two meres and a stretch of parkland lying before it. It had been built in 1761 for Sir Peter Leicester (the second Baron's grandfather) by Carr of York. About three quarters of a mile from the house, on an island in one of the meres, stood Tabley Old Hall, a favourite destination for outings with Mrs Gaskell, who spent much of her childhood and youth in Knutsford, only a few miles away. She wrote to Mary Howitt in 1838

'Near the little, clean, kindly country town, where . . . I was brought up there was an old house with a moat within a park called Old Tabley, formerly the dwelling-place of Sir Peter Leycester, the historian of Cheshire, and accounted a very fine specimen of the Elizabethan style . . . Here on summer mornings did we often come, a merry young party, on donkey, pony, or even in a cart with sacks swung across — each with our favourite book, some with sketch-books and one or two baskets filled with eatables. Here we rambled, lounged and meditated: some stretched on the grass in indolent repose, half-reading, half-musing with a posy of musk-roses from the old-fashioned trim garden behind the house, lulled by the ripple of the waters against the grassy lawn; some in the old crazy boats, that would do nothing but float on the glassy water . . . Then if it rained, what merry-making in the old hall. It was galleried, with oak settles and old armour hung up, and a painted window from ceiling to floor. The strange sound our voices had in that unfrequented stone hall!'[42]

The west wing was all that then remained of the original building, but though unoccupied it was kept in a state of preservation with its original furnishings, including portraits and tapestries. The 'painted window from ceiling to floor' was a bay window that showed the Leicester pedigree and arms, and Louisa seems to have had this partly in mind

---

[41] *Westminster Budget.*
[42] Quoted Gerin, (1976), pp. 19–20.

when she made the heroine describe the galleried hall of her home in
Meg Langholme.

> 'The hall here goes right up to the roof — very high for a not very big
> house — and is lighted . . . by pretty, quaintly shaped windows, each
> with a coloured coat-of-arms in the centre, all different — for our family
> has intermarried with other good old stock and we have plenty of respect-
> able quarterings — and each with a border of red, green, yellow or blue
> glass — no two the same. And the effect of either sunshine or moonlight
> coming through is often very curious and picturesque — especially, I
> think, that of moonlight'.[43]

The galleried hall of Old Tabley plays a part in descriptions of old
houses in several of her books, combined for instance with Wistaston
Hall, the home of Edward Walthall Delves Broughton who would soon
be courting her sister Caroline.

Tabley House and the lake are visible today from the end of Tabley
Grange garden, where there is a stream that formed the boundary of
the park. In Louisa's day the garden was not so large and this part
of it was then fields, but fields belonging to the farm that Richard
managed. Possibilities for happy expeditions so near to them, such as
Mrs Gaskell described, must have tempted Louisa and the children to
similar merry-makings. Describing a picnic expedition with loving
enthusiasm in *A Christmas Child*, Louisa commented on such outings
in general 'The tea of course was a great success — when was a gipsy
tea, unless people are *very* cross-tempered and fidgety and difficult to
please, anything else?' Perhaps Louisa took her children to Old Tabley
in a cart like Mrs Gaskell, such as she described in *Nurse Heatherdale's
Story.*

> 'Jacob the donkey was old and no mistake. . . . and the cart was noth-
> ing but a cart such as light luggage might be carried in. It had no seats,
> but we took a couple of footstools with us, which served the purpose, and
> many a pleasant ramble we had with the shabby little old cart and poor
> Jacob.'[44]

They certainly went looking for violets and primroses in the lanes, the
eldest daughter, Violet, in particular, searching 'unweariedly' and crying

---

[43] *Meg Langholme*, p. 97.
[44] *A Christmas Child*, Macmillan, 1880, p. 64; *Nurse Heatherdale's Story*, Macmillan,
1891, p. 68.

out 'in rapture' when she found any. Louisa described this special delight of Violet's in one of her three-volume adult novels, addressing the reader directly in the way that so often marked emotions and ideas that were significant to her.[45]

Louisa's growing friendship with members of Richard's family during this period at Tabley Grange, is also shown by a long and intimate letter to her from the Mary with a cough referred to in the Viscount's letter quoted earlier. It has not been possible to identify this lady exactly apart from her clearly being a relative of the old Viscount's who lived with him. The reference to Lord de Tabley's reading *The Great Experiment*, which, the context implies, Mary must have written herself, makes it virtually certain that she was the Mary Molesworth whose four books appear in the British Library catalogue just before those of Louisa herself, Mary's connection by marriage. The family tree does not help with the puzzle, since all the obvious candidates married in the end, and a note in her last book, a volume of religious and theological essays, shows that she died unmarried in 1869. She addressed her letter from the house listed in the 1870 edition of Burke's *Peerage* as Viscount Molesworth's 'Town House'.

43, Grand Parade, Brighton.   Feb 27 [1867]

My dearest Louisa, The following was the costume worn by the footman who served the Viscount's father: in full dress a blue coat with buff collar edged with braid; buff waistcoat, with blue and buff braid round the edges & pockets; black breeches of velvet or other materials; gilt buttons with crest & *sic fidem teneo*. In undress, a discretion. With dark trousers, a buff stripe is not objectionable; but I need scarcely observe that except in the case of a regular footman the quietest dress is esteemed in best taste. A gold band round the hat, with a black cockade. A groom or coachman wd. wear probably a blue & buff striped waistcoat & make no other display of colour.

I hope Morgan will send his address in Paris to some of us; though I cannot at present give him any information about the De Mallets. I may be able to help him to an acquaintance or two bye and bye.

The French seem behaving very shabbily about this famous show; if people had known beforehand that they were to pay enormous sums for the pleasure of exhibiting, many doubtless would have hesitated to incur the expense. £116,000 is a large bill even for rich England to defray &

---

[45] *Not Without Thorns*, vol. 3, p. 140.

will probably not include all the disbursements. I have quite given up the idea of going over and am not sure if I care to see any more displays of the sort. None will ever come up to the first, at least in the estimation of us fogeys, who were young in 1851. Reference to that enchanting period reminds me of Lord de Tabley & his very flattering reminiscences, so kindly reported by you lately. It is just 15 years since we met him at a dinner party here given by Mrs Kemp (née Thackeray) of Kemp Tower. The Viscount made great way with Lady de T. who sat next him & she wrote him a prescription for a cough he had which caused some merriment & charges of flirtation, billets doux etc. But I do not remember having myself any special notice from my Lord. *The Great Experiment* may have been commended to his favourable attention by his great friend and ally the late Duke of Hamilton who I happen to know read it with much zest.

I like the name of Isabel much; but do not understand or approve the Scotch fashion of turning the middle vowel into O — Isobel. The appellation is, as you are no doubt aware, the Spanish form of Elizabeth but the O destroys what little likeness the indolent Spanish tongue has left.

I rather fancy daughters are in the ascendant this year, but the next in the field of all you ladies may have a son. That is my vaticination[= prophecy]. If you should be first at the post, I hope one of the infant's names will be Charles: 1. In compliment to the living grandfather, who, besides the strongest claim of blood-relationship has established so firm a hold on the gratitude & attachment of the family into which you have married. 2. Because I think it one of the prettiest names in familiar use among Englishmen. 3. Because, as there has never been a Charles Molesworth, the little gentleman would stand out well from the crowd of Richards, Roberts & Anthonys; though of course you might add as many of these as seemed good to you. If you have a daughter during next month you might add Marcia to her other names.

Without re-opening the Source-of-the-Weather question, I will just say in answer to your very just remarks that I do not credit Satan with a particle of creative power. I myself think he gets hold of the exquisite machinery of the atmosphere sometimes & distorts it, just as he attacks us morally through our best instincts & perverts them — Cannot you imagine it sport for a party of friends to let slip great blocks of ice from the Poles and turn the long-expected breath of summer into a freezing blast? Of course the mischief lover is restrained by the Supreme Powers within certain limits but we may suffer a great deal within those limits as we see in the case of Job.

With best love ever your affectionate
Mary Molesworth.[46]

Louisa had presumably asked about footmen's dress, perhaps with a view to using the information in a story, or just possibly on behalf of her father, who in 1861 had a groom but by 1871 had a footman and a coachman.

The Morgan mentioned in the second paragraph was Richard's brother, Morgan Crofton Molesworth (called after his maternal grandfather), a captain in the Royal Engineers, who died five months after this letter was written. He was married with three children at this time but the letter seems to suggest he was off to Paris on his own. The De Mallets were French cousins of the Molesworths, a first cousin of the 7th viscount having married a Baron de Mallet in 1807. Mary was obviously one of those Victorian maiden aunts who kept large families together by their voluminous correspondence and by putting different branches in touch with each other wherever possible. Louisa had perhaps given her the news of Morgan's departure for Paris, along with a request for some introductions.

The Paris exhibition of 1867 was on a very large scale, covering 41 acres. The cost was defrayed partly by the state and partly by private subscription, according to the 11th edition of Britannica. Mary Molesworth had apparently just heard differently and greatly disapproved. 'The first' that she remembered with such enthusiasm was of course the Great Exhibition of 1851, for which the Crystal Palace was built.

Louisa was about to have another baby and must have been discussing possible names with Mary. The crack about daughters being in the ascendant referred to the fact that Richard's cousin, the Viscount's immediate heir, had had three daughters and that his wife was expecting again, that Louisa also had three daughters and that Richard's sister Mary

---

[46] Unpublished letter copied by RR from original owned by CP, afterwards destroyed. Mary Molesworth's books were *A Stumble on the Threshold: A Story of the Day*, Charles Ollier, 1848; *Claude or The Double Sacrifice*, Henry Colburn, 1850, 2 vols; *The Great Experiment*, Newby, 1860; *Stray Leaves from the Tree of Life* by the late Mary Molesworth, London: William Mackintosh, Brighton: G. Wakeling, 1869. With a note 'The writer of the following essays entered upon her 'last sleep' before they could be passed through the press. They are now published chiefly as a short memorial of her and at the request of many kind friends.' Brighton, April, 1869.

Sykes had two daughters and was again pregnant. Mary Molesworth's 'vaticination' failed completely, for Louisa was the first to give birth but the only one of the three not to have a boy. It is interesting to note Mary's voicing of the Molesworth family attitude towards Charles A. Stewart — 'gratitude and attachment' hardly suggest the contempt of the aristocrat for a middle-class merchant. It is clear too that Louisa had recently had a friendly conversation with Lord de Tabley who had entertained her with 'flattering reminiscences' of Mary Molesworth and her books, and that she was on good enough terms with Mary to tease her about it.

The whimsical note of the last paragraph tempered by the slightly tart tone of much of the letter is echoed in Mary Molesworth's final book of essays. For instance, in discussing a daughter's marrying a man she dislikes in order to provide a living for herself and a parent, Mary condemns both daughter and parent in sharp and pithy language, unafraid to compare such behaviour with prostitution —

'while striving after superhuman virtue [she] really places herself on a level little above the vilest of her sex. For why should the wretched creature who sells herself for a meal and a night's lodging be so much more hardly judged than she who barters her whole life for a continuous supply of the same necessaries.'

The sentences that bring this diatribe to a climax have an eighteenth century style and balance.

'Only a parent denaturalized by selfishness, a wooer without a spark of manly feeling in his breast, would permit, much less urge, such a sacrifice; and it cannot be incumbent on one person to offer what it would cover others with infamy to accept.'

No wonder Louisa was on terms of close friendship with a woman who could think and write like this. She must have relished such succinct remarks as this on fasting, 'it is so much easier to dispense with a lump of sugar in one's tea than to suppress the sharp retort that trembles on one's lips.'[47]

In April 1867 Louisa's father became a JP for the county of Lancaster. With this further step into county society he began to look around for a suitable residence in the country, even further away from Manchester smoke. He was preparing to retire and wanted to live nearer his daughter

---

[47] *Stray Leaves*, pp. 151 and 123.

and her family. Since Louisa was anyway often at her parents' house, she was no doubt delighted at the idea of having them even closer. She was very conscious of her and Richard's debt to her father: 'I could never tell you half we owe to my father. And his great motive truly is my happiness.'[48] Louisa's fourth daughter was born on 5th April, somewhat later than expected, and christened Katharine Olive Theodora, so Mary Molesworth's suggestion of Marcia was not taken up. Louisa's own aunt and great-grandmother supplied the Katharine, but the child was always called, like the first three, by her middle name, Olive. Both the 1871 and 1891 censuses give her place of birth as Manchester, so presumably Louisa went back to her parents' house for this birth also.

---

[48] MLM to JBLW, 1.6.1868.

5

Love Or Friendship?

The Molesworths' friendship with the De Tabley family was well established by the end of 1867. They had dined at Tabley House on Christmas day that year, and in letters to Warren, Louisa would send her 'kind remembrances' to Lady de Tabley and his sisters. This, of course, is the usual coin of formal social acquaintance. However, in one letter, written in June 1867, where such a message was sent, Louisa also told Warren she had intercepted 'various hieroglyphs . . . on their way to the post office' from Violet because they were inadequately addressed, 'being only "Miss Margaret, London".' She asked that his sister would not betray her treachery 'by owning that they never reached her.' Margaret was Warren's youngest sister, Margaret Leicester Warren, born in 1847 and so 21 or 22 at this time, and clearly on sufficiently relaxed and friendly terms with Louisa and her children for Violet's attempt at writing to her to be a natural thing.[1]

But the real friendship was with Warren himself. He appears to have spent the larger part of his time in London at this period of his life, but when he was in Cheshire he dined with the Molesworths at Tabley Grange frequently, walked back from church with Louisa and stayed to lunch, sometimes spending the afternoon as well. He wrote to her often, though unfortunately none of his letters have survived. He got on well with the children. A year or so later, on 30th June, 1869, Louisa offered him a picture of Cicely as a keepsake, saying 'I have got such a dear face of Cicely vignetted — Wd. you care to have one?' She continued 'It may remind you of the evenings you & the children told fairy stories

---

[1] M. L. Warren, *Diaries*, 2 vols, 1924, printed for private circulation, p. 165, vol.1, 25.12.1868. This chapter draws heavily on unpublished letters to JBLW, mainly from MLM but also a few from other members of her family, preserved in the Tabley Papers in the John Rylands Library, Manchester. Since the letters are uncatalogued and many are not dated, detailed references are neither possible nor useful. Where the date is known, it is for the most part indicated in the text. Any quotation where the recipient is not mentioned, comes from a letter to JBLW from MLM.

at the drawing room fire'. A few months earlier, in the autumn of 1868, she told him 'You have a particular way of stroking Cicely's head though you don't know'. When she sent the picture in August 1869, she commented 'Is not the enclosed rather nice — & characteristic of the innocent little soul?' To write like this, she must have been completely confident of his interest in, and affection for the child.[2] A note she sent in the summer of 1868, arranging a dinner engagement, emphasised informality — 'You see I am not going to treat you as a "visitor".' In the same summer, Agnes, Louisa's next sister, wrote to consult Warren about some skins that her brother, probably William, had sent from the Cape Colony. She wanted to know where she could get them dressed and made into rugs. In the course of her letter, she said she wished she could go to Tabley that night for dinner because 'my sister & Capt. Molesworth are always so good-humoured when you are there.' In the draft of his reply, scribbled on a blank sheet of her letter, he said 'I am very glad you think my influence a pleasant one at the Grange! I assure you my intercourse with its inhabitants is greatly valued by me.' So a pleasant friendship, which both sides set store by, had been established.

By the beginning of 1868 the Molesworths had been at Tabley Grange for about four years. There had been some discussion as to whether they should remain there and it was finally decided they would not only stay but would build on a new wing. That the planned extension was indeed to be this big is shown by Louisa's comment to Warren on the Christmas Eve of that year, after it was all finished, 'we certainly do not intend to build <u>another</u> wing.' On the first of March Louisa wrote to Warren from Whalley House 'We have made our yearly move in here you see. I have been very busy settling all about the building at Tabley Grange, & locking up there for we shall be quite 3 months away & we have brought all the children here.' In the same letter their longer-term plans are indicated thus. 'You do not say you are either glad or sorry we are likely to stay on at Tabley? — I wonder if we shall really settle there for good.' The tone of this is rather indefinite, but building substantially on to a rented property must have meant that at the time they foresaw a long period at Tabley. Louisa's financial affairs were carefully overseen by her brother, her father and her father's solicitor,

---

[2] Although family sources say that Cicely's godfather was the 2nd Lord de Tabley, these details suggest that a slip of the tongue or a failing memory prompted the statement, and that it was Warren himself who really held the position.

none of whom would have allowed the Molesworths to do anything foolishly short-sighted.[3]

This letter of the first of March is the earliest really long one from Louisa to Warren that we have. The bulk of it is taken up with a discussion of her own writing. He had been helping her by reading and criticising her work, which she referred to throughout the letter as 'my rubbish'. The piece he had seen was a short story that she called 'The Amethyst', which was almost certainly never published. His opinion surprised her — 'Do you know I had not the least idea you would have found as much good to say — were you quite honest? I hope so. But I think you would not have been otherwise to me.' She wanted his help and advice on how to improve her writing, a goal she earnestly desired to reach, even if none of her mss were ever to be published. Although she had one story half done 'long enough, I think for one vol.' and another twice as long which existed only in her head, because she had 'three times burnt the first part', she feared she could only do 'flimsy short things'. She dismissed the idea of attempting a novel with the words 'it is ridiculous of me writing as if I could ever fly so high'. These doubts about her capabilities and about the possibility of publication did not prevent her steadily working away during the year at a novel that was ready to show to a publisher by December.

But she could not have imagined such progress to be possible when she wrote despairingly of her thrice-burnt story 'it won't do', and blamed her ignorance and inexperience. She was aware of her limitations in the area of self-criticism too, which at this stage was only general — 'I am perfectly conscious of my faults in a general way, but I do not know how to correct them.' Her most acute comment about writing novels was one that has often been made — many people have one good story in them, and that is their own. But, she maintained, (without clearly explaining why) 'Anything I write must be essentially from imagination, because I cannot draw from my own experience.' Her attempt to eluci-date this was self-contradictory, for she said both that she was 'rather deficient in the tremendous experiences required by the present school of fiction!' and that 'my autobiography . . . died and I buried it . . . the things I have felt most & been most influenced by . . . are what I never

---

[3] 'I am well looked after by my father and very far-seeing brother, who is my trustee for all,' MLM to JBLW, 21.5.1869; 'I am rather curiously placed — between my brother and my father's lawyer, who knows a good deal more about us than mere business — ,' MLM to JBLW, 24.9.1869.

can write about', which implies that she both had and had not met with experiences suitable for writing about. Since later on both she herself and her family mention characters and events in her books as drawn from or based on real life, it is possible that some of this mystification is part of her developing relationship with Warren.

What she wanted most of all was to talk over her stories with him, and the rest of this letter and the next two are taken up with arrangements for meeting him in London en route for France. She and her sister Agnes (accompanied by a 'middle-aged maid') were going to Pau, spending two or three nights in London and in Paris on the way. This was not just for a holiday, but to visit a friend staying there for a long spell with a young brother who was 'dreadfully delicate'. When she reached Pau in the middle of March, and was able to see for herself, she wrote 'it will be long before he can venture to try England again, so his sister will be kept here for months.' Finally, the boy died in May. Sending their patients to warmer climates was one of the few remedies for any kind of lung disease available to nineteenth century physicians. Many of Louisa's books contain episodes where invalids are sent for their health to 'southern resorts' with fictitious, generalised names such as 'Basse'. Her descriptions of these invalids would have been based on what she had seen herself at Pau, which she visited often, and other resorts in the area. When we read, in *Silverthorns*, of a boy in an invalid chair 'enjoying the sunshine on one of the pleasant terrace walks above the sea', we can feel sure that this is what her friend's delicate brother would have done. The climax in *Robin Redbreast* took place round an invalid's chair.

> 'It was a small and simple place; a balcony ran round the ground floor, and there in a long chair — a deck chair — a gentleman was half lying, half sitting, for the day was mild, and the house had a south exposure. . . . He was a tall thin man with gray hair, and with evident traces of delicate health and suffering upon him, and he walked lame.'[4]

Visitors to Pau would have been used to such sights.

Louisa and her sister were accompanied not only by a maid, but also by their cousin, John Wilson Colville, the son of their Aunt Catherine, who was himself now living in Cheshire. He went with them in pursuit of Louisa's friend, the girl with the invalid brother. In Victorian society he could not have gone to Pau to visit her on his own. We can see that

---

[4] *Silverthorns*, p. 263; *Robin Redbreast*, p. 283–4.

'playing propriety' for her cousin was one of the aims of Louisa's journey, perhaps *the* main one, from her remark in a letter to Warren early in April. 'What I came here for has been accomplished — The two are very happy, though it is only to be known among ourselves as yet.' And when she wrote of the death of the 'dreadfully delicate' boy in May, she was able to refer to him as 'that poor boy, my cousin's fiancée's brother.'

In London Louisa and Agnes stayed at the Brunswick Hotel where Warren visited them more than once. He had given up a visit to Herne Bay in order to see Louisa and on hearing about this she teased him in one of three letters she wrote to him in early March, supposedly about arrangements for meeting in London but with a great deal of other matter besides. 'It is to be hoped,' she said, 'the 3 volumes (which will never see the light of day) will repay you all this self-sacrifice.' Novels were almost always published in 3 volumes at this period, so she was simply joking about her own as yet largely unwritten novel. Her brother Charles came up from Plymouth where he was stationed to see them and the whole party went to the theatre one evening. Writing to Warren from Paris on 11th March, just after she had seen him in London, and in later letters from Pau, Louisa went over their meetings and conversations in some detail. They had had 'an uninterrupted talk about rubbish' on the Sunday morning when everyone else was at church, which she had arranged in the last letter (6th March) before she left Cheshire. He advised her specifically not to write 'with the intention of copying,' meaning that she should try to set down on paper at once what she hoped the final version would be. She found this almost impossible 'for I correct and re-write so much,' but it is interesting to see that she made this advice her own to such an extent that in 1890 she could write as follows.

> 'For my own part I have strictly adhered to the rule of <u>never copying</u>. I write at once as I intend the words to stand; the formation of the sentences being thus the work of the brain unassisted by the sight of the written word. I believe that this leads to great precision of thought . . . In writing with the intention of copying one is apt to think, "Oh, I will set that sentence right afterwards," and one's first time of writing is generally, therefore, slovenly.'[5]

Warren insisted that she would do better if she did not write a rough copy first and she tried to obey him. Presumably, by 1890, she had

---

[5] Bainton, p. 94.

long succeeded in this effort, or thought she had. One wonders if she remembered twenty odd years later where she first got this rule to which she so strictly adhered. Another piece of detailed advice he gave her was to include more direct speech in her stories. This too she found difficult — 'I can't get my people to talk two pages in the ten. Won't two in 20 do?' He warned her about faults such as "periphrases", "general slipshodiness" and "avoidance of Protestant cant" (though she argued against this last that her people had not been Protestants for long and that she hated cant.) But she asked him to tell her of more faults, being determined to benefit from his readiness to act as "friendly critic". He was clearly taking a close interest in her work and he made suggestions too about her reading.

But they did not talk only about her 'rubbish' at these meetings in London. Louisa had, or believed she had, second sight and she was rather sorry that Warren had led her into talking about it to him. This was partly from embarrassment (presumably because of the popularity of seances, mediums and mesmerism) — 'It is so commonplace and silly to go in for that sort of thing' — and yet she would not deny it — 'I am in earnest about it'. Warren had said something about the dangers of a morbid and unhealthy interest in such things and she reassured him in the first letter she wrote after their meetings. 'I am far too sound and healthy to meddle overmuch with those strange mysteries which no doubt we shall understand by & by.' She was also aware of fake mediums and the like for she continued 'but which just now are so desecrated by fools and jugglers.' All the same she was not going to give up her interest in strange or inexplicable events which came into her personal experience. She was making a list of coincidences and actually asked Warren to keep a note for her of any he came across. Stories have been handed down in the family about Louisa's psychic powers. Her great-nephew wrote

> 'I remember stories of how she constantly came down to breakfast in the mornings and quite casually told the others who there was a letter from or of something that was going to occur, usually I think in the fairly near future.'

Such a comment from a member of the third generation suggests that Louisa's second sight was quite widely known about in the family, and was not something that died a natural death as she grew older. 'Strange mysteries' were also quite a frequent theme in her novels and short stories for adults and older girls.

Their talk relating to Warren's own life seems to have centred on his love affairs and possible marriage. This is a blunt statement of something that appears in hints and puzzles, though as the year went on she wrote of it more and more clearly. At first, writing from Paris just after she had seen him in London, she said 'I was unhappy about a friend of mine the other night at the theatre — that made me cross. A new light (or rather a new darkness) seemed to be thrown upon his future.' She enclosed something for this friend to read but was worried that it might make him angry. In a postscript she described the enclosure as 'a sort of dissertation upon marriage in general and one in particular' while saying that she had decided not to send it but might show it to the friend some time or other. The initials of the friend, she said, were W. P. L. This all sounds very strange and roundabout, but when one realises that these are the initials of Warren's pseudonym 'William P. Lancaster' under which he had already published several volumes of verse and poetic drama, the situation becomes clearer. She was trying to be humorously tactful, the more so because she was hurt by his refusal to tell her the name of the person involved. Hurt, because she thought his refusal meant he did not trust her and felt she might gossip — 'do you really think I am so little better than the run of my sex that I would make mischief if I could?'

These topics, of his relationships and her writing occur over and over again in the letters. A further subject which comes up frequently is her concern to keep their correspondence and their friendship as quiet as possible. Because her brother had been with them in London, she wondered if Warren ought not to give his family some hint about her 'literary ambitions' (as a reason for their meeting) just in case anything should filter through to them inadvertently via any friend of Charles', 'though he is not a talker . . . only . . . he knows a good many people.' It is difficult to see why she thought their friendship had to be concealed from his family. Warren was friendly with Richard as well as with Louisa and Richard's being related so closely to Viscount Molesworth must have made the Molesworths socially acceptable to most aristocratic circles. Warren's mother had Irish connections, and the Molesworth title was an Irish one, which ought to have constituted an acceptable link. Besides which, a viscountcy is higher in the peerage than a barony — the nephew of a viscount and the son of a baron were surely on reasonably level terms socially. But several times, over the years of their close friendship, Louisa mentioned Warren's 'peculiar position' as a cause of difficulty in their relationship without ever making clear what she meant by the expression and he does not seem to have questioned it. Still, it is not surprising that the situation should seem puzzling 130 years or so later, when Louisa wrote at the time 'no one who does not know your belongings cd. understand it.' ('Belongings' in this context meant family, relatives — it was often used in this sense together with 'people'.[6])

Louisa had already made Warren promise to burn all her letters and frequently reminded him of this. She certainly burnt all his, however short. 'Happening to read over your last note before committing it to the flames' she wrote on 6th March about a note that was only to do with times and places for meeting in London. Her side of the correspondence has survived because he disobeyed her. It is possible that there were earlier letters which he did burn, because the friendship seems already quite close at the period when the surviving letters begin. Every now and again when she thought she had been more than usually outspoken or gossipy she would write 'Do you always remember to burn?', 'Pray remember to burn' or some such admonition. It makes the biographer feel quite guilty about reading such missives! It should be noted that her insistence on burning did not arise only from fear that letters might fall into the wrong hands. She did not like to think of Warren himself re-reading her letters after the sap had gone out of them. 'Do not be annoyed at my repeating the condition about burning — & please satisfy me that you always do so at once,' she wrote on 27th April, 1868. 'Even for Mr Redrose's own edification, I should not like the idea of his coming upon some shrivelled pods, long after the season for green peas is over.' ('Mr Redrose' was a joke name for Warren himself.)

In Pau, while their cousin was courting, Louisa and her sister enjoyed their holiday. 'This place is really very exhilarating. It makes me feel ten years younger' she wrote, and 'I feel six times as strong down here in the south, as in Cheshire.' They went to meets — there was a hunt at Pau — which were 'great fun' and attended by 'such a medley' of different nationalities. She rode regularly on a pony she called Bumpy but did not follow the hunt — 'such a queer country you never saw'. Agnes gradually started to miss home as a place but Louisa missed only

---

[6] An example from Grant-Duff's diaries illustrates this use. 'I was not aware that he was so warm-hearted and affectionate amongst his immediate belongings as it is clear from this book that he was.' *Notes From A Diary 1896-January 23, 1901*, vol. II, p. 120. 'People' survived at least until the 1950s with this meaning. For instance children at boarding school in the books of Enid Blyton or C.S. Lewis would refer to their own or their friends' parents as 'my people', 'your people'.

the people, 'the friends one has to leave'. 'I like one place quite as well as another and the sunniest the best.' She really loved the sun, finding the English climate depressing, 'I must not allow myself to get spoilt for England though I <u>do</u> wish we could have some of this exquisite air and sun there!' They went to Biarritz which she found 'exceedingly pretty & attractive' and on into Spain. She offered to get Warren dried specimens of any Pyrenean wild flower he liked from a native botanist, but no more is heard of this, so presumably he did not take up the offer. Half jokingly, she suggested he should come to Pau too, tempting him with the cheapness of living — £4 a week — and lots of brambles, a subject he was studying and soon to publish a paper on. Some species of bramble bear his name today, while the farmers on the Tabley estate each knew where his special brambles were and nurtured them for him.[7] Louisa was sufficiently aware of his special interests both to try to help in them and to tease him about them.

As well as enjoying the climate and landscape, Louisa struggled with her novel at Pau.

> 'I have almost re-written my first chapter for the fourth time. It reads more twaddley than ever & I am consequently in a state of depressed disgust or disgusted depression, whichever you think the prettier expression.'

This wry little joke suggests she was not totally downhearted — perhaps the sunshine was keeping her spirits up. When she had done two chapters, she condemned them as 'milk & water'. She did not necessarily keep to the order of events if she felt like jumping to a scene that was to come later in the story. 'A sudden inspiration set me off to attempting one of my stone walls — a very sensational love-scene belonging to the middle of the second volume.' Clearly the main lines of the plot were already straight in her head however many times she re-wrote. But she did not like her sensational love-scene — 'Now it is written I am most horribly ashamed of it — though at first I thought it rather fine'. This is an experience many writers have borne witness to. She could not yet follow Warren's advice about not copying, for 'you see my ideas come so much quicker than my words — So I write a <u>very</u> rough affair first & then pick up all the loose ends.'

Although Louisa wrote to Warren more often than he did to her — she sent him six letters from France during the month she was there,

---

[7] Information from Assistant Administrator, Tabley House Collection Trust.

and he seems to have written to her not more than twice — he was definitely confiding in her about his possible marriage. At first she was very tentative about expressing an opinion. In her first letter from Pau she apologised for writing flippantly (although she was merely being chatty and amusing as we should expect in a holiday letter)

> 'but the truth is I want to keep off any but these surface things, for I have been so uneasy of late about the new light on the subject of you know what — that I am afraid of seeming impertinent or officious were I to tell you half of what has been in my mind. And as people, to the end of the world, will not profit by the experience of their elders (that's me) I think I will just hold my tongue, though like somebody's parrot "I thinks all the more".'

But when, in one of his letters, he told her about a "row" with the person they had started to refer to as 'M. L.' she said more. She thought he was making a mistake and was bold enough (to a man some degree in love) to say she would not have grieved if they had *not* "made up next day".

> 'Better a sharp pang now', she added, 'than a life-long mistake. How much and how sadly I fear you are on the brink of one . . . I tell you my deep misgivings plainly enough, & if I could influence you I would.'

She was still hurt by what she saw as his failure to trust her in the matter of M. L.'s name, and she reproached him for not unsaying the hurtful sentences. She was also upset by something Warren had either told her in conversation or written in the letter to which she was replying — it is not clear which, but he had declared that if ever M. L. were to know Louisa she would dislike her heartily. Louisa did not like this.

> 'If the worst came to the worst (she wd. never know I had known of it at all or called it "the worst") I wd. like her, (or whoever the "her" in the case was) to like me.'

Clearly, in this context, for Louisa, Warren's marriage was 'the worst'. But did she mean his marriage to this particular, unsuitable (as she thought) M. L. or was she really saying that his marriage to anyone at all would be the worst for her? However, despite these serious sentiments, implying quite a deep and complex relationship between them, Louisa was still able to be light-hearted and teasing in other parts of the same letter. She had no doubt about his friendship for her. Her last thought, in a hasty sentence crossing the first page, was 'Don't forget to tell me when your drill for next month is fixed.' Warren was an officer in the Cheshire yeomanry, and this drill would bring him to Tabley and bring also, therefore, the possibility of a meeting.

We know that Warren did not resent what Louisa said about M. L. for in her last letter from Pau she thanked him for his confidence 'because it shows me that you are not offended by my boldness in expressing my view of the case.' He confided further in her about his being 'wretched' over the row he had had with M. L., and this time she was more sympathetic though finding it difficult to understand his 'taking it so deeply'. He had done his best to impress her with his half-heartedness in the affair and then suddenly he told her of real suffering. But she reiterated her former sentiment. 'I should rather have you suffer sharply for a time than have to endure the unceasing ache of a life-mistake.' She obviously thought M. L. unworthy of him in some way but could not quite bring herself to criticise more openly — 'You know what you are worthy of & yet you will be content with — I won't say what. Oh, it so very, very trying to stand by & see it.' This marriage, she thought, would mean his not being appreciated for all his qualities and abilities, and would therefore lead to his drifting and not developing fully. But then she hesitated and drew back — 'All the same my anxiety for you not to share the fate I so shudder at may cause me to exaggerate the warnings of it.' Why did she say 'share' and not something like 'endure' or 'undergo'? Perhaps she was already half-consciously implying that she herself had made a life-mistake.

In that last letter from Pau Louisa also made suggestions for Warren's meeting her again on her return through London. We know that he fell in with them from a reference in the first letter she sent him three days after her return to Cheshire on Easter Saturday. She said she thought their last conversation had been a comfortable and satisfactory one and hoped he felt the same. Once home again she was immersed in social and family affairs. She and Agnes were rather disgusted to find their parents' house full of visitors 'though my mother had tried to get rid of them.' The building works at Tabley Grange had to be visited regularly 'to see how all is going on', besides which 'There will have to be some furniture for the new rooms to see to and all sorts of fusses.' Her father had now found a suitable house in the country and almost decided to take it. He took Louisa to see it on Easter Monday, only two days after she arrived home, so he must have been impatient for her opinion. She was delighted. 'It is not so good a house as this, but still very comfortable and with capabilities. The garden may be made very pretty.' This house was the West Hall at High Legh, much nearer to Louisa and her family than Whalley House, even if it was not so good. The village of High Legh lies just off the Knutsford-Warrington road (the A50), about four miles north-west of Knutsford and five from Tabley Grange, while the Whalley Range area of Manchester is more like thirteen miles from Tabley. If Mr Stewart decided in favour of the West Hall, he would be renting it from Major Egerton Leigh, soon to be MP for mid-Cheshire.

After this visit to High Legh, Louisa went off to Fleetwood to see her children, whom her mother had sent there while she was in France because of an alarm of measles near Whalley House. She was delighted at how 'beautifully well' they were. On their part, the girls, though not demonstrative children according to their mother, completely satisfied her with their way of showing pleasure at her return. They met her at the station, and as they all walked back to Mount Terrace together along the esplanade beside the sea, Cicely, who had said nothing, was quietly and privately kissing her mother's hand. But Louisa was only there for two days and the children remained for some weeks longer. Tabley Grange was not yet ready for them and the seaside with its bracing air was thought to be particularly healthy. Perhaps too, with all the visitors the Stewarts had, their daughter did not want to add to their burdens. All the same, it seems strange to us that a mother, after more than a month's absence abroad, should not remain longer with her children. She had said on setting out 'I am so unhappy about going abroad & leaving my poor little babies.' Of course she belonged to a class and a time which took completely for granted that children should live a life apart with nurse or nanny in their own quarters. For a mother of that class to be completely responsible for her own children at any time was an upheaval needing comment. When it happened to Louisa (in the following year, January 1869), with a child visitor unexpectedly on her hands too, she wrote 'for my nurse had gone off to a dying friend, & when not much disposed for it, I have had a week of children, poor little pets!' The over-burdened mother of today might think she was lucky to have only a week, but all her contemporaries would have understood. Then too, the unexpected child was there because of an alarm of scarlet fever. Her own children had been sent to Fleetwood for fear of measles. We tend to forget how large such fears could loom when there was no inoculation or vaccination available, and no anti-biotics or even aspirin. It was better to keep the children away rather than have them with you and risk their health, which so often then meant their lives.

Back at Whalley House she became absorbed in family business which meant the love affairs of her brother and sister. Louisa took a great interest in these and described events in detail to Warren,[8] though at the same time apologising for 'teazing you with all this'. She had been Charles' sole family confidante for months past in his love for Janetta Tucker, the beautiful 19 year old who had finally agreed to marry him, and sympathised exceedingly with his 'real honest misery' until the happy ending came at last. She was amused at her father's reaction, who, 'having no fault to find, has relieved his feelings by scolding us all round,' and was comically terrified of his 'swooping down on me with the question "have you known anything of this, Louisa?"' 'However', she wrote at the end of April, 'I have no doubt it will be all right in a few days.' Charles Stewart *père* simply wanted to throw his weight around a little, to ensure they did not forget who was the head of the family and Louisa understood this. On May 6 she was able to write 'I really am pleased at my brother's engagement.'

Agnes' situation was more complicated. Louisa had for some months been concerned about her sister's relationship with a young man she referred to as 'the cornet' (ie, the fifth commissioned officer in a troop of cavalry, who carried the colours). She confided her anxiety to Warren, who was 'the only person I have ever talked to about it', since her husband disliked the young man so much that she could not mention the subject to him. Agnes had danced with the cornet at several balls the previous winter but now his family was trying to keep him away from her. They apparently all liked Agnes personally, but 'if only she had a title, she would be all they want.' Louisa also saw their being very rich as 'a horrible complication'. She seemed to think that Agnes' family would be seen as fortune hunters if they encouraged the match. Mr and Mrs Stewart had 'no idea of all this' and Louisa dreaded lest they should find out. She was sure they would dislike the marriage intensely but that 'they would not stand out if her happiness was involved,' by which she meant if Agnes was thoroughly in love.

Since Louisa particularly wanted to know if the cornet really cared for her sister and how he spoke of her, she asked Warren to draw him out tactfully in general conversation 'without his ever suspecting it'. She wanted Warren to discover if the young man was 'staunch and loyal, and . . . trying to bring his father round' or 'if he is mean enough

---

[8] Some 30 letters have survived of those Louisa wrote to Warren between April and December 1868.

(through fear) to affect very slight acquaintance with her or to speak slightingly of her in any way.' If he turned out to be 'mean' Louisa was sure enough of her own influence over her sister to say that she would persuade her to give him up. If on the other hand, he was 'staunch' she could 'for her sake, even yet try to help him.' Despite her apologies for bothering Warren with her affairs, Louisa was expecting a lot of him. She assumed he would do as she asked and she continued to describe all that was going on in detail in her letters, apparently without fear of rebuff. Apparently too, he did co-operate for she wrote at one stage 'thank you for keeping your eye on the cornet.' Her hopes for her sister centred on the possible appearance of a rival to drive the cornet out of Agnes' head. By the end of May she thought the affair was dying a natural death anyway, but she confided to Warren that to help on this desirable result she had 'smoothed the way' to Agnes' leaving home 'on a round of visits . . . beginning with town & ending with Cornwall,' an enterprise which would also give greater scope for an encounter with someone else.

Perhaps she had been unnecessarily anxious, for when, towards the end of June, she was able to report that 'a formidable rival' had indeed appeared, she shrugged off her previous worries with the phrase 'the reign of the cornet, always a feeble affair . . . .' The arrival on the scene of a suitable young man did not lessen her deep interest nor her demands on Warren. Now she wanted him to find out about the new suitor, Craven Goring, (whom her sister did in fact marry). Agnes had confided in their brother Charles as well as in Louisa, and he could be expected to undertake the business of enquiring into position and expectations. What Louisa wanted was some idea of Goring's personal character from an outside source. Perhaps they had been at school together, she suggested, 'so if you have heard anything of the name Goring shake up your memory and give me the benefit thereof.' This appeal brought a quick response for three days later she wrote, 'I fancy the Eton G cannot be he — This one's family belongs to a place called Higham in Sussex.' Warren may have been subtly flattered by her repeated reference to his own special position in her life, in remarks such as this. 'Of course you are the only person I can tell it to as I have no other confidantes.'

While all this was going on, Louisa was also expressing an earnest and continuing interest in Warren's efforts to get his first novel published. He had already published several books of poetry and poetic drama, all under pseudonyms, the first in 1859 together with an Oxford friend whose early death soon after affected him strongly. In a memoir by one of his other friends, it is stated that he took to novel writing simply in order to raise some money, 'and succeeded in producing three which at least fulfilled the purpose for which they were intended.'[9] He certainly needed money at the time for part of Louisa's interest took the form of offering loans or advances to help start his novel on its way. She was apologetic but persistent about this and had apparently got him to promise to tell her if lack of money was a difficulty. Of many references to the subject this one is typical.

> 'I can't get it out of my head that you are meeting with difficulties about the publication of your 3 volumes — Difficulties of a kind that might be overcome by a greater expenditure of capital in the venture — You know how I mean — Now having your promise on the subject I should be content, but I am not — I don't feel sure of your keeping it — & so I send you this reminder . . . if I can have the true pleasure of helping you, do remember my readiness.'

In his response to this he said he had no financial difficulty yet, and she seized on the 'yet' as showing that he didn't mean to snub her but might still take advantage of her offer — 'you may "yet" allow the mouse to nibble a little for you.'

His initial failure to get the book accepted by a publisher, though it only lasted a few months, appeared to depress Warren disproportionately, and he seems to have written severely exaggerated passages of self-criticism to her. She responded 'I wish you believed in yourself more' and took him to task for his reactions to publishers' comments. It is clear that he told her gloomily towards the end of May that Smith and Elder had said his novel was only fit for 'a penny maga.' [sc. magazine] She retorted stoutly 'I don't believe Smith & Elder said a penny maga. I am sure it was "more suited for a periodical".' These fits of depression were not really alleviated when the book was accepted and published. He simply transferred his feelings to the reviewers. Nearly two years later, in November 1870, Louisa accidentally came across a review that had upset him just after publication. It surprised her very much

> 'for from its effect on you I expected something far more of a "castigation" as you called it — Much of it seems to me absolutely encouraging in its

---

[9] *The Flora of Cheshire*, by the late Lord de Tabley, (Hon. J. Byrne Leicester Warren), with a biographical notice of the author by Sir Mountstuart Grant-Duff, Longmans, Green and Co., 1899, p. xxiii.

very fault-finding . . . I do not think you realise the <u>extreme</u> morbidity you must have been in, to have thought that review so discouraging.'

He was reluctant to let even her read his work, dithering between promising to show her his first novel while still in progress and wondering whether she was 'wide-minded' enough to be trusted with it at all. She cut through his hesitations — 'I don't think the effect of the novel could be more to be apprehended than your mysterious way of hinting about it & yourself,' and called his bluff on another excuse, 'don't talk nonsense please about "the labour of wading through 600 pages of M.S." — It wd. be no labour to me, you know.' Despite this, she promised not to read it even after publication if he really did not wish it. She did sympathise, though, with his horror of being misunderstood, thinking it 'excuse enough for seldom telling one's thoughts or ideas.' This seems to be, in part, the explanation for his persistent concealment of himself by pseudonyms or anonymity.

Louisa was careful to respect his wishes and conceal his work even from Richard. One day at the end of May (1868) she was in a little study of her father's in Whalley House, just off his dressing room, where she usually read and wrote undisturbed. On this occasion she was reading a copy of Warren's metrical drama, *Orestes*, which had been published the previous year under his pseudonym William P. Lancaster. Suddenly and unexpectedly Richard appeared and picked up the book. In a terrible fright Louisa snatched it away from him and pretended to be angry at her husband's meddling with her books. Naturally enough he departed indignantly and afterwards told her mother that 'Louisa was in such a bad humour that she would not even let me look at a poem by Matthew Arnold called Orestes.' Louisa told Warren this story simply in order to warn him not to be startled if ever Richard spoke of *Orestes* as a poem by Matthew Arnold. It is not clear why he should have made this mistake, nor even why Louisa should have been so upset, when the author's name on the title page was neither Arnold nor Warren. But she promised to be even more careful in future. This incident throws an interesting light both on Louisa's relationship with her husband and on their way of life at this period. She was still so much at home in her parents' house as to have the regular use of a study there.

The *Orestes* incident also tells us a little of Richard Molesworth's relationship with his mother-in-law. He thought it natural to complain to her about her daughter. When Louisa was away in France, rather worried about Richard's being 'fussed' without her because no-one else could be so useful to him, she relied on the thought of her mother's being 'awfully good to him.' Goodness and usefulness on their part meant coping with the practical details of life. When she had not heard from him for some time in Pau, she assumed he had lost the address because her mother was away — 'he always trusts such matters as addresses to the women of the household.' As she said in the summer of the following year, when he had to be away on some military duty, 'He does not a bit understand "fending for himself".' But he took no notice of their ideas and was indeed likely to cling to the opposite view more strongly if contradicted in any way and was suspicious if their opinions were expressed — 'Anything my mother or I say, he thinks is with a purpose.' Of course Louisa and her mother smoothed things over — that was their natural duty as good Victorian wives and mothers.

Richard's relationship with Charles Augustus Stewart was not so easy. 1868 was the year of the General Election when Gladstone first became Prime Minister. Warren, 'urged by his father, and under the particular aegis of Mr Gladstone,'[10] was going to stand as Liberal candidate for mid-Cheshire. Then Richard was approached by a group of Conservative activists for his support, and decided that he would like to play a part. Louisa was appalled because she was sure it would lead to 'terrible family fuss here, which really might end very badly indeed — with my father.' She also feared that it would cause the 'breaking up of our relations with the liberal candidate's people — (though not himself)', thus indicating the difference between their friendship with Warren and their acquaintance with his family. Her father was a Conservative, so it cannot have been on political grounds that he would have objected to Richard's taking part at the invitation of a Conservative group. Any kind of involvement in politics was expensive, consuming both time and money, and Richard had not only a job needing his attention but also a family that his father-in-law was helping to support. Some such considerations as these could underlie Louisa's certainty that her father would strongly disapprove of Richard's taking an active part in the election. To avoid the 'terrible fuss' she wrote out a statement of reasons why Richard should not be involved, sent it to Warren and asked him to write to Richard incorporating the sense of her statement in his letter. She asked him to 'say it as plainly and strongly, or more so, than I do.' Richard would not listen to her — 'I have no influence and have said nothing,

---

[10] Edmund Gosse, 'Lord de Tabley: A Portrait', *The Contemporary Review*, vol. 69, 1895, p. 86.

as it wd. only strengthen by contradiction' — but Warren's writing on the subject would carry weight and Richard's personal regard for him would ensure that the letter she was asking for would be 'just the touch to the balance wanted.' She showed herself as really manipulative in this matter and also completely confident of Warren's co-operation and trust in her judgement.

In the end Louisa confided fully in Warren over the problem of Richard's relationship with her father as a whole, not just the political issue. There were several letters in May referring to trouble and unhappiness in vague terms, along with apologies for grumbling. 'A cloud I had begun to think was clearing has got as thick as ever lately — I am half setting an example of grumbling!' was the kind of thing she would often write. Eventually she wrote in June 'A great part of my unhappiness has been caused by disagreeables between my father and R in which I must say the latter has been the chief aggressor.' The heart of the problem was Richard's 'unnecessary exaggerated persistence' in 'certain crotchets', which Louisa detailed as 'class-prejudice, dislike to society, sneering at any one not exactly of his way of thinking etc'. Usually 'he storms for hours not merely at dining out, but at dining in this house, [she was writing from her parents' house] if my father invites other guests — especially if the faintest odour of Manchester shd. unfortunately cling to their garments.' Sneering and storming in his father-in-law's house cannot have made Richard Molesworth's staying there for long periods pleasant or agreeable for the rest of the family. No wonder Louisa hoped he would outgrow the habit. She did not expect miracles. He did not need to alter his opinions to make her happy, merely to keep them to himself more and not, as she put it, 'thrust their corners forward.' She enlisted Warren's help again, as with the potential political row, very much aware that she was drawing him further into intimacy and family secrets. 'Of course I am writing in the most perfect confidence, but I know you will not allow anyone to suspect, directly or indirectly, my taking you behind the scenes.' This time she asked him to try to soften Richard's 'peculiar ideas' if he ever obtruded them in conversation when Warren was with him. She had great faith in Warren's powers. 'R respects you and is influenced by you. He thinks you perfectly impartial.' A week or so later, when Richard was in a good mood and even offered to dine out with her at a neighbouring house, she attributed this to Warren's 'exerting a happy influence.'

It seems clear, though, that Richard regularly alternated between good moods and dull ones, when he was irritable and stormy. If he was busy and occupied, he was happy but in a dull mood the slightest thing would make him fly off the handle and Louisa had a set policy of not talking to him about unpleasant things if she could possibly help it.

> 'You know I always keep from him all irritating subjects when I can — & he is so inconsequential & short-sighted that just now he wd probably not see it as I do ... then some day when it flashed upon him he wd. work himself into a mood about it.'

She had known before they married about his uncertain temper — now she was finding what 'trusting to her own love and tact to keep it under control' meant in terms of daily life. Had she been thinking of her own problems when she besought Warren not to make a 'life-mistake'?

1868 and 1869 were the years of Louisa's closest friendship with Warren. They were not lovers. Several of her letters were about her relationship with him and she said more than once quite emphatically that what they gave each other did not deprive anyone else.

> 'Of course it is only very commonplace, narrow-<u>hearted</u> as well as narrow-minded people who think that any strong liking or friendship outside one's immediate circle must <u>weaken</u> what those nearest you have the first claim on,' *and* 'You can give me what I give you without robbing our respective M's.'

are but two of these statements. Whether or not 'M. L.' and Richard M. would have agreed with her, had they known every detail of the friendship, is beside the point. Partners often mind a close intellectual and emotional sympathy more than actual adultery. These statements show that Louisa herself thought her friendship with Warren was not 'robbing' her husband. No woman at that period, of Louisa's social class, who regularly went to church, could possibly have believed that a physically adulterous relationship did not damage her marriage and rob her husband.

Her most intimate letters to Warren seem always to have been written just after they had met, while he was at Tabley and the letters could be delivered by hand, because she thought of more to say just after he had gone or wished to clarify something where it seemed to her she had expressed herself badly. During a visit he made to Tabley in June 1868 she wrote 'You said to me yesterday I must judge for myself if ever I thought your influence over me was unwholesome.' She thought it was definitely not so, and explained that any misgivings she expressed were only self-reproach for allowing herself to discuss Richard's 'provok-ingnesses & so on' with him. If she had serious misgivings about their relationship, she said, 'of course you know, I hope, that I shd. at once give it up — But yr. influence is not unsettling, & I give you nothing that robs anyone.' So she had occasional stabs of guilt at talking over with Warren her husband's temper and bad relationship with her father but saw nothing else to reproach herself with. In this same letter she told him, because she was sure he would be glad of it, 'that things are again, for the time at least, much pleasanter between my people and R — my father of course I mean.' She resolved to be more relaxed about the problem.

> 'By not trying too much, I hope to keep things smoother in future —
> You do help me. You make me more contented — satisfied rather —
> & I am more able to keep strong for difficulties of this kind.'

One of the sources of her contentment was their intellectual congeniality, as can be seen from a passing reference in another letter written during this June visit. She just touched on such congeniality in her usual life being something she missed and needed.

After Warren's visit to Tabley in June, their next meeting took place in Wales where Richard and Louisa, accompanied by her sister Carrie, took a house for three weeks at Bettws-y-coed. Louisa had been planning and looking forward to this holiday for some months. It was to be a completely relaxed time with no formality at all — 'We are going to live like savages — never have any dinner, & forget that such a place as London or the world outside . . . is in existence.' From the first the plan was that Warren would visit them once they were settled there. She had discussed this with him even before she went to Pau in March as is shown in the letter telling him of her safe return to Cheshire when she hankered after the past holiday in these terms, 'I wish I were back at Biarritz (or at Bettws-y-coed).' At the end of May she mentioned three times in the same letter wanting 'to talk over Wales with you as it is getting time to settle it.' It was four months, she said, since they had spoken of it, which means that the first plans must have been made early in February, and she was beginning to wonder if perhaps he had changed his mind. But by mid-June she was writing quite cheerfully and confidently 'I have engaged what Mrs Owen calls "the hole house", from the 16th so we shall have no trouble with fellow lodgers.' In the same letter she sent, at his request, a second batch of suggestions for titles for his novel, so perhaps we can assume he entered more positively

into the Molesworth's holiday plans in the happier mood produced by
the novel's acceptance. The title finally chosen was *A Screw Loose* and
she joked with him about it and the problem of continuing to conceal
his authorship from Richard — 'It takes however some diplomacy to
repeat messages to the Captain out of a letter in which "loose screws"
are mentioned so recklessly.' She scolded him for raising the question
of expense as a possible objection to his coming to Wales.

> 'The expense can't be the consideration — It is only a tourist ticket to
> Bettws-y-coed — It is impossible it should be much at this touristing
> [sic] season — You <u>know</u> your staying with us will not increase our
> expenses — You must not be "horrid" about this.'

What she was really afraid of was that he was reluctant to come and
was making excuses. 'Do be honest about it,' she said.

He seems to have been very sensitive to the slightest hint of not being
truly welcome, or his friendship or interest being a burden in some way,
as in his worry about reading 600 pages of manuscript being a labour
to her. Once, in reference to his visiting her and Richard at Whalley
House, Louisa wrote 'if you are <u>not</u> inclined to come to see us there,
please say so, & don't say it is through any want of cordiality on our
side — or all that about people not liking you.' This view of Warren's
character, together with Louisa's efforts to encourage him and make
him believe in himself, dovetails with the comments in DNB — 'the
sensitive melancholy of his temperament' and 'His most intimate friends
. . . only lament the anguish he inflicted on himself by excessive sensitiveness.' But he did manage to join them, though for less than a week,
in their 'idiotically comfortable condition' where they refused even to
remember what date it was. She looked out the train times for him and
they made plans to climb Snowdon, but the greater part of the time
was spent 'sauntering about . . . the pretty walks here.'

However it was not all sauntering. Just as in Pau, Louisa went on
with her novel in Wales. By the time Warren left them she had nearly
finished it. She had certainly got to the point of counting up pages and
chapters to see if she had enough for three volumes, and saying that
she could only make the book longer if this was needed by adding a
chapter to each volume. It is interesting to see how the three-volume
straitjacket, insisted on by the circulating libraries, was influencing her
as an author even before the manuscript had been offered to a publisher.

By mid-August Louisa was back at Tabley Grange, though uncertain
about having the children at home, because, this time, of an alarm of

scarlet fever. The alterations and additions were finished and despite her remarks about 'all sorts of fusses' over new furniture and other arrangements, she seems to have enjoyed it all, for she wrote in September 1869, after the family had left the house, 'I . . . had some bright hopes at the time I took so much interest in making it bright and pretty.' During the autumn she worked hard at her novel, and by December it was finished. Warren had offered to help her place it with his own publisher, Richard Bentley, who had brought out *A Screw Loose* in the summer. But there was a series of misunderstandings and upsets between them at this time, apparently triggered by a well-meaning gesture on the part of Charles Augustus Stewart that, at first, Louisa knew nothing about. He wrote to Warren in London on 30th November as follows:

> Dear Sir, I have just received from America by steamer a few "canvas-back ducks" which feed on wild celery on the banks of the Potomac & are considered a rarity. I have forwarded today by passenger train a brace of them which kindly present to Lady de Tabley. Though not quite on your side of politics, I sincerely regret that you did not secure your seat for mid-Cheshire. Believe me Yours truly Chas. A. Stewart.

The election for mid-Cheshire had taken place only a few days before, the declaration of the poll having been made at Knutsford on 26th November. Perhaps Stewart thought that his polite attention to Lady de Tabley with a passing reference in the accompanying note to Warren, was a delicate way of sympathising in his defeat. But Warren seems to have been annoyed by Stewart's action, though exactly why it is difficult to gather from Louisa's indignant response:

> 'I have been most <u>exceedingly</u> annoyed by hearing of what I did not know before. Something my father did — intending it in a simple off-hand way — which from your exceptionally uncomfortable surroundings will have annoyed you or worse — That it <u>did</u> do so is traceable in your answer to him — The thing in itself <u>should</u> require no apology — rather the reverse, but all the same as things are I <u>do</u> apologise to you — I also can assure you that such a thing, (or indeed overtures of any kind, for however natural, they wd. be interpreted in a way I writhe to think of) shall <u>never</u> happen again. At all costs of disagreeable [sic] to myself I can & will prevent it — Indeed my father is so essentially proud that my only fear is that I may drive him, by the least hint, too far the other way — For it wd. be very new to him to be suspected of anything

so low & in his independent position so <u>absurd</u> as toadying. You need not fear his ever offending in <u>that</u> way.'

She made a further reference to 'the duck affair' a few days later. It seems as though some kind of slight withdrawal or lack of enthusiasm in response on his part had made her read into his letters and his account of Lady de Tabley's reception of the ducks an accusation of 'sucking up' which infuriated her so much that she could not really see straight. Any suggestion or possible implication that she or her parents were attempting to 'rise' touched a very sore spot with her.

'As to the duck affair, I discerned your annoyance. If I say <u>anything</u> to my father, it wd. probably strike him as too absurd to credit — that so simple and ordinary a thing, cd. involve any man in disagreeables — for he is in this way, quite a man of the world; & I hate exposing any of your surroundings to ridicule, as it <u>assuredly</u> wd., though at the same time it wd. make him determine to have nothing to say to any of you — perhaps to forbid <u>my</u> doing so — Certainly I will say nothing to him just now. I don't suppose he has ever thought of it again.' *In both these quotations 'surroundings', like 'belongings' earlier, means family, relations.*

As well as being up in arms over the mere suspicion that Warren or his family could think her father was trying to curry favour with them, Louisa was also upset with a hurtful letter he had written to her, in which he had 'again mistaken [her] utterly.' He seems to have excused himself on the score of 'troubles' and 'too great pressure of work' (which could have been the additional effort of the recent election). No further details have been found to elucidate this element in the disturbance. The final ingredient was his failure to respond soon enough when she wrote to tell him her novel was ready and to make arrangements for coming up to town to hand over the manuscript and meet the publisher with him. She was clearly not entirely free to travel just when she wished and his silence had caused her difficulty. She reproached him in a way unusual for her.

'It is all very awkward. I can hardly tell you what you wd. have saved me, had you a few days ago sent me a mere <u>word</u>, saying "I shall be at leisure about the 14th." Truly I <u>do</u> think, with all your worries you might have done so.'

She had actually decided to entrust her manuscript to an old family friend without further reference to Warren when her mother, in the usual female role of peacemaker, persuaded her to write to him again. It is clear that, at the time of writing, she was embarrassed and annoyed to be asking him a favour when she felt she had so many causes for silence and withdrawal. There are a series of abrupt instructions in her letter about writing, telegraphing, leaving and collecting the parcel of manuscript which betray her reluctance. His silence was interpreted by her as disinclination on his part 'to give me or my book your attention at present.' If he could help her, he was to telegraph, if not, he was not to bother even to write — 'I think there wd. be very little object in your writing to me.' But he did write, things were patched up and she did go to London, taking the manuscript with her, and was not only very glad afterwards that she had done so but also 'most thankful' for a talk she had had with him.

The manuscript, of what was to be *Lover and Husband*, was handed over to Bentley's reader and then everything hung fire for several months. On Christmas Eve she referred to it casually 'Do not trouble yourself about Bentley — I am not thinking much about it' — but in January she admitted to 'being a little curious and anxious about my story' and suggested that 'if Bentley has refused it, as I expect & I must not trouble you further, it might be made over to my sister when she is in town next week.' But in fact troubles in both the Molesworth and De Tabley families led to the manuscript's languishing in London for some while longer without anyone's paying much attention to it.

Although, after the upset between them just described, Louisa and Warren were once more on amicable terms, Louisa perceived their relationship differently. She had, in one of the intimate notes probably delivered by hand during a summer visit of his to Tabley, talked about the danger of their becoming too dependent on each other, concluding that this was far more likely for her, because his 'rock' (by which she meant 'M') was firmer than hers. She then went on to develop another image in relation to the idea that, if the main relationship failed, anyone would do.

'. . . — If your rock failed (but it won't) — anything with powers of sympathy . . . wd be acceptable — I know that sort of thing. In intense reaction and depression a sensitive person wd. cling to anything. Ivy, torn from a tree, wd. throw itself round a clothes drying post, if it came handy. Never mind. It won't happen. If it did I wd. not be above turning myself into a clothes post — .'

Although she was thus deliberately offering herself as a second-best consolation, ready to support him at need, she still, at this stage, thought she had a place of her own in his life. After the December upset, she did not. She told him that, having realised the 'intermittent nature' of his interest in her, her eyes had now been opened to what she called his mistake and his unintentional misleading of her, in maintaining that she was or ever had been anything but a clothes post. Now that she had come to this conclusion he would not be able to alter it.

There is a slightly ironic flavour to her comment on her position in his life. She had offered to be a 'clothes post' for him when needed, but now she had understood that this was what she had been all the time. 'Any way I <u>have been</u> a good and serviceable clothes-post in my day & I endeavour to cultivate a humble spirit by reflecting thereon with thankfulness.' But she was not sure that she wished to remain in this role — 'I am hardly the stuff for an intermittent clothes post after all. Though I might shape myself even into this, if only I cd. understand it was best.' We may wonder if his 'mistake' had really been unintentional. She said in the same letter 'you have taken immense pains to convince me, not ready to be convinced — that I <u>had</u> a right, a place of my own. . . . I only say to myself "through his impressionability & pity & all that, he thought I had a place & I haven't".' In an undated note, which almost certainly belongs to this year (1868), she had said 'I don't understand you & you <u>must</u> say things you don't mean when we are alone.' It definitely seems that he had encouraged her to invest in a closer and more intimate friendship than he was really committed to himself. She thought at first that they should discuss the situation but then offered to bury the subject — 'So if you like, leave it all for ever. And we shall all the same be very amiable, & I will still not be above asking your help for my book.' An intimate and frequent correspondence continued for over a year, but the tone was not the same. She confided in him about her life and family affairs as before but was more apologetic about claiming his attention.

In describing such a relationship with only one side of the correspondence available, it is difficult not to give the impression that all the running was made by the one whose words remain. But there is evidence that this was not so. As well as her deliberate statement, quoted above, of the 'immense pains' he took to convince her of her place with him, more throwaway phrases scattered in her letters reinforce the impression — 'You greatly overestimate what I have of that' [sc. intellectual power] — 'you have a queer way of drawing on confidence' — 'On Saturday you called me the nicest name!' — 'all this does not affect my <u>best</u> self — what I put in the letter you liked.' So he had admired her intellectual powers, encouraged her to confide in him, called her nice names and told her which of her letters he liked best. And these phrases, which are only a selection from many similar ones, carry the more weight as evidence, since Louisa was not, in their contexts, analysing or complaining about his behaviour to her.

Warren, too, was given to using images in discussing their relationships with each other and with their 'respective M's', although he was more traditional and romantic than Louisa with her mundane clothes post. In referring to his possible marriage and apparently defending 'M's' limited character, he had talked of a garden. Louisa picked this up — 'You say so very few gardens will grow all kinds of flowers that it is best to be thankful if you can get one which has two or three — or even one — really good of its kind.' Then she expanded it further in order to justify the continuation of their friendship.

'And if now and then you would like a sight of some others there is no reason why you should not have it. Certainly not. Having a garden of one's own by no means obliges us never to take a walk in the outside world. Probably it would make you like your own garden all the more.'

But a further twist of the image enabled her to repeat her objections to his marriage.

'All the same no doubt those are happiest who have the most & prettiest in their own, or anyway who <u>think</u> they have. And seeing you about to plant one, taking infinite trouble about it too, it made me sorry to think that yours was only to be an every day sort of one, after all.'

She wrote this in April. During the following Christmas & New Year period, in one of the many notes she wrote to him immediately after a meeting, she went back to the garden image, but we can see the change resulting from the early December upset. He had told her the previous evening of his discovery that 'M' had a beautiful voice and she wanted to confess what she called a mean feeling of jealousy over this, and a fear that

'perhaps you wd. make other discoveries equally unexpected of greater <u>soul</u> than you have hitherto believed in — & that my tiny plot in the corner of the garden wd. after all no longer be cultivated, as you wd. find its herbs wd. after all flourish as well among the roses.'

In other letters she mentioned asking for, or even insisting that she had, 'a place of my own', 'a niche', in his life. In this sad little picture of the tiny herb plot we realise that she knew, although she might not always admit to herself, the real size of that place relative to the rest of his life.

Louisa sometimes used the image of a tie or bond between them which, at the height of their relationship, she described as one of 'essential sympathy' which, 'if it is cherished . . . will . . . outlive circumstances. And when they are favourable it will give you a pull.' But even then she was aware that it could not last. She went on doubtfully

> 'Me, it will at least. I am not so sure of your "out of sight" memory as of my own. I wd. consider you more with respect of outward arrangements — chance of meeting — & so on, than you wd. me.'

By the end of 1869 when it was obvious that the end was in sight, she was saying

> 'I don't think you shd. be hasty in telling me to stop writing; for after all you have gone over a good deal of ground with me that can never be retraced, and this is a tie of actual value, though very probably at present a repulsive one.'

A year later, when she wrote to say goodbye before he went away for a long period, she still maintained that the tie existed.

> 'Only in all conceivable cases, you do know if ever I can be the least good to you, or you the least feel inclined to pull your end of the wire, I shall always be ready at the other — I say this so deliberately & certainly that I hope you will remember it — Even if you don't, it will make no difference in the fact.'

But of course it did, in the outward fact, and the beginning of the difference was heralded by those family troubles referred to above.

6

1869, A Year Of Troubles

The troubles alluded to in the chapter heading were at first quite mild, merely 'fuss'. On Christmas Eve 1868 Louisa listed in a letter to Warren 'a new accession of little troubles.' Her brother Willie, who was turning out to be the scapegrace of the family, had managed to miss the train by which he was coming home for Christmas, and his father had been 'fearfully angry', though by now we are beginning to suspect the seriousness of these paternal rages. Charles was getting married in January at Saltash in Cornwall and there was 'a tremendous fuss about going to C's marriage' which was hardly surprising considering the reluctance we would still feel about travelling from Cheshire to Cornwall in the depths of winter. Besides which the practicalities of the household had been 'rather extra complicated' this Christmas. Then, although she did not mention it in this letter, her father had made up his mind to rent West Hall at High Legh and the Stewarts were about to move house. We can come quite close to an exact date for this, as by mid-January Louisa was telling Warren 'if you have any particular letters to forward, send them to my sister to <u>the new address</u>' and on 26th January she took her children to visit her parents at their new home. The stress rating of moving house then for the servant-employing classes was probably less than it is now for the servantless majority, but it would not have been negligible.

There was also what she called 'a gentle trouble', being the death from scarlet fever of a six year old 'dear little dove of a girl', the daughter of a Scotch friend of Louisa's, who was 'the only friend Violet and Cicely ever played with.' Despite her second sight she saw no omens in the event, even when writing 'Violet sobbed for an hour & Cicely sighed gently, said she felt "sad" & wondered if we shd. cry if she died.' Underlying all this were 'the two great crookednesses,' one of which, she wrote to Warren, 'I can never tell you' and as she seems never to have done so, we also are in the dark. The other was certainly a reference to Richard's 'crotchets' or 'moods', now 'in a chronic state again, after being at its <u>worsest</u> [sic].' But these she regarded as the permanent condition of her life and 'it is better not to dwell thereon.'[1]

During the winter of 1868–9 Lady de Tabley was seriously ill and finally died on 20th February. There are many expressions of sympathy and concern in Louisa's letters to Warren between December and February — 'I was <u>exceedingly</u> sorry to hear of Lady de Tabley's being worse' — 'I am inexpressibly grieved about your anxiety.' This last sentence comes from a letter she wrote, on 7th January, when she was at Trematon Castle, Saltash, near Plymouth, for her brother Charles' marriage to Janetta Tucker. It was actually his wedding day and naturally enough she found it 'difficult to seize a moment to write, in a house full of grand gay people.' She and her family were at Trematon for five days over the celebrations, which could in other circumstances have afforded material for one of her long gossipy letters to him, but she was 'so afraid of saying anything that might jar on you at such a time', very conscious of his sorrow and anxiety and unable to 'write about other things with the thought of how you must be absorbed just now by this.' She did make one comment on the new sister-in-law, whom she met for the first time on this occasion — 'His wife is <u>marvellously</u> pretty & sweet-natured to match.'

But soon she was writing about a new cause for anxiety in her own family. Charles and Janetta had gone to Torquay to begin their honeymoon but the day after the wedding he suddenly fell seriously ill, so much so as to be in danger of his life. Louisa and her parents did not hear about this until two or three days after their return to Cheshire, when the crisis was past. The doctor wrote to Mr Stewart about Charles' great endurance of 'frightful suffering', the operation he had had, and the necessity for another one. Of course they were all 'very wretched,' but Louisa comforted herself with the thought that her brother was 'healthy & wiry, like me' and that 'a short sharp illness is less trying than a weary low sort of one.' Smaller troubles continued to aggravate the situation. The scarlet fever alarm was mentioned again, and 'our dear old dog who has been with all of us all our lives is dead.' She thought this last might seem a frivolous trouble to someone else but, as she wrote herself, 'we don't wear each others' shoes' and present-day

---

[1] There are some 24 letters from MLM to JBLW extant in the Tabley Papers, written in 1869. It is impossible to be completely exact as many had to be dated from internal evidence. As in the previous chapter, quotations where the recipient is not specified are taken from letters to JBLW.

dog-lovers would feel for her. However, Charles soon recovered enough to travel and he and Janetta spent a week at West Hall on their way to Edinburgh where he had 'the final and most important operation on his throat.' Craven Goring was staying at West Hall too, and Louisa was surprised and pleased to see how well they all got on together 'in the most wonderful and unconventionally comfortable way . . . Not at all like relations-in-law.' And perhaps she thought ruefully to herself, not at all like her own husband and his father-in-law. She did not go often to High Legh herself for 'my doing so much gives annoyance here.' She added no further explanation of this fairly guarded comment, but presumably there was disagreement between her and her husband about the amount of time she should spend with her parents and sisters now that they were living so much nearer. One visit that we do know of took place, significantly, when Richard was away on military duty and also 'staying with his own people.' Violet wrote to him, care of his commanding officer.

> My dear Papa,
> I write you this letter to say we are all quite well and very happy. We went to the West Hall yesterday and we were very happy. Love & kisses from us all, Your loving Violet.

Address to:- Capt. Molesworth, Colonel Wilbraham, The Orchards, Blackheath, Kent.[2] [Postmark Knutsford Jan 27 '69.]

West Hall was quite close to an even larger mansion, the Hall, or East Hall, as it was often called to avoid confusion. For many centuries High Legh had had two reigning families, the Egerton Leighs from whom Charles Stewart rented the West Hall and the Cornwall-Leghs who owned the East Hall (and who bought out their rival squires in 1900). The East Hall, a grey eighteenth century building, was larger than its neighbour the West Hall, which was also built of grey stone. It stood in a park of 170 acres, laid out by the celebrated landscape gardener, Repton. The grounds of the two halls were bounded on the south by the Knutsford-Warrington road, and on the west by the Lymm-Arley road, the East Hall drive coming in from the Knutsford road, and the West Hall drive from the Lymm road. It was unusual for the houses of English country gentry to stand quite so close to high

---

[2] Letter copied from original in possession of CP by RR and since destroyed. Written on small size writing paper with a small design of a key in a clenched hand — Molesworth Arms. Paper probably specially made for the children.

roads, and at one time the Knutsford-Warrington turnpike actually ran through the East and West Hall grounds. The squires came to dislike this invasion of their privacy and in 1852 had the road moved further away, thus marooning the village cross in the West Hall grounds. It is even more unusual to find two manorial halls standing cheek by jowl as did these two; there was a dividing wall between but it had a connecting archway and they were only a few hundred yards apart. Each hall moreover had its own chapel of ease for family and tenants, the East Hall sixteenth century St Mary's, and the West Hall, St John's, rebuilt in Grecian style in 1815. The mother church of High Legh and the two chapels was at Rostherne, five or six miles away.

The Stewarts used St John's for family events such as weddings and christenings, but many members of the family were later buried at Rostherne and they probably attended services there. As long as the Molesworths were at Tabley Grange Louisa seems to have gone most often to the De Tabley family's private chapel, which stood on an island in one of the lakes of the park, close to Tabley Old Hall. She refers, in her letters to Warren, to hearing him cough in church, to walking back from church with him or to meeting him there. Tabley Grange was only about half a mile from the chapel. When Richard was away, as he often was on military duties, she found Sundays alone something to be avoided. Before her parents had moved to High Legh, while they were still living in Whalley Range, she wrote to Warren, who had just left Tabley,

> 'if you <u>don't</u> come back by Sunday I may perhaps go to see my mother till Monday. But if you <u>do</u> I won't — for you may be dull, & even my "miserable" face may do for a sort of welcome — I don't care about going, only I want to escape a Sunday here always. I dislike the long day from morning service till night <u>when there is no break</u>.'[3]

Once the Stewarts were at West Hall, during Richard's absences Louisa may well have accompanied them to church at Rostherne and spent the day with them.

Charles Augustus Stewart kept quite a large household at West Hall, suited to his new status as a country gentleman, including a footman and coachman, a butler, a housekeeper, two cooks (though one suspects

---

[3] That services were held regularly in this chapel is shown by Grant Duff's references in his memoir of Warren included in *The Flora of Cheshire* and his account of Warren's funeral in *Notes From A Diary 1892–1895* vol. 2, p. 288.

that the eighteen year old listed was an assistant or even a kitchen maid), two housemaids, a laundress and a lady's maid for his wife.[4] The Stewarts' second grand-daughter, Cicely, was so struck with the butler and the pride he used to take in the dinner parties at West Hall that the memory remained with her into old age. She also particularly recalled some green and red wine glasses that used to adorn these occasions.[5]

The Molesworths' four little daughters ranged from nearly seven years old to one and a half when their grandparents moved to High Legh, so their experience of dinner parties can only have come from watching the preparations or (for the two elder ones) from participation in the Victorian ritual of going down to dessert when they stayed at West Hall or at their own home on special occasions.

> ' "Going down to dessert" continued to be a nursery treat all through the century, all the more valued for its being the sole occasion for the enjoyment of delicacies: a piece of candied fruit, a cluster of grapes, a handful of almonds and raisins.'[6]

It was so taken for granted that Rider Haggard in *Allan Quatermain*, when describing the unusual character and surroundings of a child living with her missionary parents in Africa, could contrast her with what his readers would have thought of as normal girls in these terms. 'She was at an age when in England girls are in the schoolroom and come down to dessert.'[7] Louisa often mentioned the custom in her books, occasionally describing it in detail, and once at least devoting a whole story to it — 'An honest little man' in *A Christmas Posy*. Much earlier in the century it was beautifully depicted by Mrs Gatty.

> 'For when the magical dessert hour had come after the late dinner . . . a signal bell used to ring upstairs to the nurseries, to announce that the "dear ones" might come down. . . . the journey came to an end by degrees and . . . one came into the full blaze of the comfortable old irregularly

---

[4] All, except the butler, listed in the 1871 census. The butler's son wrote to RR in 1937, giving details of his father's employment, and describing the inscription on a christening cup of his sister's - 'E. L. Rogers/ With the best wishes of/ Mrs Stewart/ of the West Hall/ High Leigh/ 1871'. He stated that the sister was born in May 1871, so the butler must simply have been absent from the house on the night of 2.4.1871 when the census was taken.

[5] CP's memories in conversation with RR.

[6] Marion Lochhead, *Their First Ten Years: Victorian Childhood*, John Murray, 1956, p. 10.

[7] H. Rider Haggard. *Allan Quatermain*, Hodder and Stoughton, 1919, p. 107.

built dining room with its bright fire reflected brightly on red curtains, its large old-fashioned chairs, its abundance of lights and the smiling faces round its spread-out table ... And then followed the malt tea tasting, and the fruit and biscuits, till the first exhilaration of spirits was over, besides a little playing with the beautiful purple hand-glasses which threw such wonderful colours on arms and frocks.'[8]

It was, of course, by its very nature, an experience only available to middle and upper-class children, when adults had an elaborate meal in the evening with plenty of servants to prepare and serve it, and children lived in the separate world of nursery life where Nanny ruled in strictness and security, making and receiving visits at preordained times to and from the grown-ups. This was the world Louisa mostly wrote about and it was for its inhabitants that she wrote.

In the first book for children Louisa published, *Tell Me A Story*, there is a story, 'Good-Night, Winny', which she described as 'simply a narrative of my own children, as literal as it can be.'[9] It relates to this period in Cheshire when the Molesworths were at Tabley Grange and the Stewarts at High Legh and, in accordance with her assertion, all the factual details that can be checked match accurately with the real state of affairs. The child narrator, Madge, begins her story

'long ago I used to be called Meg, and the person who first called me so was my sister Winny, who was not quite two years older than I. There were four of us then — four little sisters — Winny and I and Dolly and Blanche, baby Blanche we used to call her. We lived in the country in a pretty house, which we were very fond of.'[10]

We will see later that the story can be dated very specifically to April 1869, and at that time Violet Molesworth was a few days away from her seventh birthday, Cicely was five and a few months, Juliet was three and three quarters and Olive was just two. It is supposed in the story that Madge does not write it until some years after the events described — the last paragraph begins 'I am a big girl now — nearly twelve.' The manuscript was offered to Macmillan in March 1875, the British Library copy is dated November 1875 and Cicely's twelfth birthday was 30th December 1875. Details about the wider family are equally exact.

---

[8] 'The Bachelor Uncle' in *Domestic Pictures and Tales*, quoted in *Mrs Gatty and Mrs Ewing* by Christabel Maxwell, Constable, 1949, p. 30.
[9] MLM to Edward Salmon, 12.10.1886.
[10] TMAS p. 40.

'Have I told you about our aunts at all? We had two aunties we were very fond of. They were young and merry and so kind to us, and there was nothing we liked so much as going to stay with them, for their home — our grandfather's — was not far away.'

This faithfully describes the situation for, at the time covered by this story, Agnes and Caroline, Louisa's younger sisters, who were living at home with their parents, were twenty-four and nineteen. Both were, as yet, unmarried, though as we have seen, Agnes was engaged to Craven Goring, while West Hall and Tabley Grange were only about five miles apart.[11]

An anecdote near the beginning of this tale gives an amusing picture of the two elder girls. Cicely's daughter said years later that the Mr Merton who appears in it was the old Lord de Tabley who was Cicely's godfather (ie the 2nd Baron de Tabley), though it seems to me much more likely that the figure is based on Warren, who we know often dined with the Molesworths and had friendly relations with the children. Here again is the 'coming down to dessert' custom. Accepting the identification of the children in the tale with the Molesworths' own daughters, we hear that Violet was upset with Cicely's outspoken bad manners.

'One day I remember she was very vexed with me for something I said to a gentleman who was dining with our papa and mamma. He was a nice kind gentleman, and we liked him, only we did not think him pretty. Winny and I had fixed together that we did not think him pretty, only of course Winny never thought I would be so silly as to *tell* him so. We came down to dessert that evening — Winny sat beside papa, and I sat between Mr Merton and mamma, and after I had sat quite still, looking at him without speaking, I suddenly said, — I can't think what made me — "Mr Merton, I don't think you are at all pretty. Your hair goes straight down, and up again all of a sudden at the end, just like our old drake's tail".' [*Portraits of Warren later in life show that his hair was like this.*]

Mr Merton laughed very much, and papa laughed, and mamma did too, though not so much. But Winny did not laugh at all. . . . And when we had . . . gone upstairs . . . she said "I am so ashamed of you. I am really. How *could* you be so rude." '[12]

---

[11] TMAS, p. 52.
[12] TMAS, pp. 43–4.

Since the story is about the children, Louisa did not make much of her own reaction, but that understated 'mamma did too, though not so much' tells us that mamma's real feelings were much the same as Winny/Violet's. The children were not being brought up to play to an audience, to be applauded for being impertinently forward like Amelia in Mrs Ewing's story 'Amelia and the dwarfs', published in 1870 and describing a child whose presence was an infliction dreaded by all her parents' friends. Louisa was fond and proud of her children but conscious of the need not to obtrude them on others or seem to be boasting.

> 'Violet and Cicely are here' she had written to Warren some time during the previous summer. 'They are very good and pretty. Violet was very sorry you came when she was away — You will think I have no business to praise them, but I have hardly seen them for months, & I am pleased they are growing satisfactorily in every way.'

With her parents safely settled so much nearer to her, and her brother recovering well from his alarming illness, Louisa's thoughts began to turn back to her neglected manuscript. She wrote tentatively to Warren about it, apologising for being, as she thought, a burden to him. 'And yet I don't know that I <u>should</u> ask you decidedly to give it up and forget all about it — I don't see what to do.' But very soon after she had sent this letter came, first, the news of Lady de Tabley's becoming worse, and then two or three days later, of her death. By the time Louisa wrote again after her letter of sympathy on this event, she herself was immersed in the cares of the sickroom. The alarms of scarlet fever 'around' had now become concrete for her in her youngest child, Olive, who had been 'exceedingly ill — More seriously so than any of them have ever been ... But she is a little better the doctor says, though I can't yet see it. For four days she has only lived on water —.' This was in a note she wrote in answer to a kind message Warren sent by her sister, Agnes. He was at Tabley on a short visit, perhaps on affairs connected with his mother's death, though she had died in London, and Agnes had happened to meet him. Louisa had herself 'not been quite well' and the next we know is that Agnes was writing to Warren, only four days later, to say that her sister was 'very ill — We hope that she may not have caught the fever — but I am sorry to say the symptoms are like it.' She was also four months pregnant, though of course this was not mentioned. Quite possibly Agnes herself did not know it. Agnes' letter shows that both the youngest children had scarlet fever — Juliet as well as Olive. Fortunately Violet and Cicely were already staying at

West Hall and their aunts and grandparents were only too glad to keep them there in the hope that they might escape the infection. Agnes poured all the details out to Warren.

> 'It is a relief to let my fears for my dear sister be told — I dare not tell anyone else all the doctor fears — for it is bad enough to be thinking of the poor children already ill & fearing the others may get it, & I dare not add to my mother's anxiety — Perhaps my sister has broken down from over fatigue for it has been terrible to her to watch the poor child's sufferings —let us hope it may be nothing worse.'

Louisa's family was being kept away from her because of the fear of infection, not primarily for themselves, but for the sake of the two elder children whom they were trying to protect. They found this very hard, just at the time when Louisa most needed help and sympathy. To add to all this, Richard was on the point of going away. 'Captain Molesworth' wrote Agnes, 'is obliged to leave home soon for his usual spring duties — & he is very busy just now — It is very hard on him poor fellow.' These duties were expected to keep him away for six weeks. It is clear that, although it was Louisa who was Warren's close friend, Agnes too was quite confident of the kind sympathy and interest which would receive her flow of 'more particulars.'[13]

The story mentioned earlier, 'Goodnight Winny' is a faithful description of this time from Cicely's point of view. Winny (Violet) and Meg (Cicely) were going to their grandparents' house (West Hall), to stay over Easter with them and the 'young and merry' aunts.

> 'We generally all went there to spend Christmas, but one year something, I forget what, had prevented this, so to make up for it we were promised to spend Easter with them. We did so look forward to it — we were to go by ourselves just like young ladies going to pay a visit.'[14]

Even this could be said to match, for the Molesworths could hardly have spent Christmas with the Stewarts when the latter were just about to move house. In the story also the baby was not well and Winny at the last minute seemed reluctant to leave home but soon cheered up on arrival and when a letter came to say that both the younger children

[13] See Gosse, and Theodore Watts, 'Lord de Tabley', in *The Athenaeum*, No. 3553, Nov. 30, 1895, pp. 754–56, for further details on Warren's kindness, gentleness, sensitivity and sympathy.
[14] TMAS p. 53.

were ill, both girls enjoyed the extra length of their visit. Comparing the details of the story with the letters from Louisa and her sister, we can see why years later Louisa said it was 'as literal as it can be.'

By the beginning of April the situation was worse. In spite of all the efforts at isolation, Violet too had caught the scarlet fever and Louisa was not really well yet. She was going backwards and forwards over the five miles between Tabley Grange and West Hall so as to be with Violet during the day, but returning to the little ones at night. She was tired out with anxiety, with her own illness and with sitting up at night. (In the absence of really effective medicines, the Victorian belief in the importance of watching the patient is attested by every novel in which illness occurs). Richard's absence and the being quite alone without communication with her family had also told on her. 'Now alas there is no more use in separation' she wrote mournfully. Into this miserable situation came what was to her a bombshell of a letter from Warren. It must have been shocking to read that he was pleased at hearing the children were going on well and that he thought she was concerned about the fate of the manuscript of her novel. She had sent him a note enquiring after his own health, and this was the response. It is not surprising that her reply was bitter and angry. In her situation she was not interested in manuscripts — he had better burn it. He was making an excuse to end their friendship, she thought.

> '— I now quite understand that my interest in you now [sic] for some reason has become annoying or disagreeable to you, & you wish to put an end to it — You had much better have said so plainly, than by affecting to think me selfishly occupied with that M.S.'

Warren was again at Tabley House and had received his false news about the children from the agent, Mr Thomas. This appears to have infuriated her.

> 'It is not the case that my children are going on well — I am still very uneasy about the youngest — & now my poor Violet is in the height of it. We cannot possibly tell for some days how it will go with her — Anyone who really cared to know how we were, might have found some way of direct enquiry (without running any risk of infection such as need alarm even the most timorous) & not trusted to the garbled accounts of a heedless person like Mr Thomas, whom I am not in the habit of telling many particulars to, who having secured the safety of his own family naturally feels little interest on the subject.'

These bitter accusations, direct and implied, of cowardly self-concern against both Warren and Thomas are a wild lashing out from the midst of her own pain. That night, 4th April 1869, Violet died, so suddenly there was not time for her mother to get to her.

The next day, in a kind of desperate calm, where agony had washed away bitterness, she wrote the following note to Warren:

> The West Hall, High Legh   Sunday
>
> I wrote bitterly to you yesterday. As long as I can I want to tell you I am sorry I did so — I told you once that the worst sorrows did not make me narrow but made me care more for anyone I cared for — Now this is <u>fearful</u> — agony beyond expression. Do you know it was so sudden I was not even with her? It is so <u>very</u> fearful but I wanted to tell you I was sorry for being bitter — You were kind to my darling and she liked you — You don't know how fearful it is — Yours sincerely   MLM

She obviously assumed that he had already heard of the child's death. News travelled quickly round villages and estates where both indoor and outdoor servants were related to local families. And there was always Mr Thomas. Violet was buried at Rostherne and the inscription on the plain vertical cross over her grave simply gave her full name with dates of birth and death. Louisa was now occupied with brooding over memories of Violet and with 'alternate terror and hope for Cicely'. She was sure that this child too would catch the fever and be taken from her — 'I am not, I think, <u>counting</u> on keeping her.' She was going through some of the classic experiences of bereavement — 'To-day there is a dreadful restlessness come over me — I feel as if every day I might not be able to do anything the next', and 'I have not a very clear impression of the last few days'. She wanted to die so as to be with her beloved daughter — 'You know what I would wish, if it was not wicked — You know I am <u>so</u> tired, & I am sure she wants me.' Only, she recognised, 'the others do too'. Her thoughts of dying were not just the effects of bereavement — women died far more often in childbirth then and she hinted at this obscurely, 'You know if I were the very strongest person, it is certain the chances <u>are</u> against me just now.' It seems very unlikely that Warren knew she was pregnant, so one wonders what he made of this. Perhaps he thought she was referring to the effects of grief and exhaustion on top of having had scarlet fever herself, which must have been included in her assessment of her chances.

It is startling to come upon a letter, dated three days after Violet's death, which begins abruptly 'Dear Mr Warren, Whenever you can will you please send my M.S. to this address.' What could she have been thinking of? Literary ambition in the midst of what was clearly deep and sincere grief? She knew how strange this request would seem — 'You will think I am going out of my mind to speak of such a thing as my M.S. just now' — and we learn that it came out of her brooding on those memories of Violet.

> 'My darling knew about it, & was so disappointed it was not "made into a book". She had read little bits of it — about the children — She even chose the titles of some of the chapters — I used not to like to tell even you of her precocity — It frightened me, & yet I was afraid of seeming to boast, or being partial — And I succeeded of late in making her more of a child — Indeed she was always a child, so happy — but I mean I made her not learn much & I talked nonsense with her.'

'Goodnight, Winny' portrays more vividly and coherently a precocious child who was yet attractive and happy.

> 'I can see now' *says Meg/Cicely,* 'now that I am so much older, that Winny must have been a very clever little girl in some ways, not so much in learning lessons as in thinking things to herself and understanding feelings and thoughts that children do not generally care about at all . . . when I try to remember all about her exactly, what seems to come back most to me is her being always so happy.'[15]

That Louisa's re-awakened desire to get her novel published, just at this apparently unsuitable moment, was entirely on Violet's account is further shown by the whole letter being about her daughter and the effects of her death on the family, apart from the initial necessary brief request about sending the manuscript to a particular address.

It has been suggested that Louisa began to write her first novel as a way of taking her mind off her grief for her daughter, just as Mrs Gaskell started to write *Mary Barton* at the suggestion of her husband, 'to turn her thoughts from the subject of her grief' after the death of her ten month old baby Willie, also from scarlet fever.[16] But, as we have seen, the chronology derived from her letters does not fit this scenario. The book was finished by December 1868 and, as just recounted, she made a renewed effort to get it published only days after Violet's death.

---

[15] TMAS, pp. 40–41.
[16] Green (1961), p. 34. Gerin (1976), pp. 73–5.

Louisa now had a passionate wish to leave Tabley Grange. It would
for ever be associated with agonising memories — 'That most awful
night . . . that fearful room.' She is not referring to the room Violet
died in. The awful thing, to her, was that she had not been there. She
was remembering the agony of waiting through the night with Juliet
and Olive who were still very ill, for news of Violet undergoing the
crisis of her illness without her mother. And when the news of her death
finally came, it left Louisa with a feeling, 'so strong as to be like a
possession, of intensest repugnance' against the house where she had
waited, vainly hoping. At West Hall, on the contrary, she felt that 'all
is hallowed by the sweet dear presence.' There she had hung over her
dead child — 'After she was dead . . . her face grew so very young —
like a baby's — She had a sweet quaint look.' She must have been so
torn between the two sets of children, but her duty was to be with those
who otherwise had only nurses and servants to care for them. Perhaps
she thought, even tortured herself with thinking, that if Richard had
only been there she could have stayed with Violet to the end. There
had been, she told Warren, 'some very bitter outside aggravations of
this sorrow' and one seems to have been a scene of some sort with
Richard. All she said was 'Other things I won't tell you. Essentially
different temperaments must jar under strong excitement, but I believe
I have been good, & have tried to draw good out of it.' 'Being good'
would be a reference to her resolve of the previous summer to keep
things smoother. At the end of the letter, after saying that Richard had
gone away again, she commented 'It is much better that he should.'
Perhaps grief made him angry — another normal part of bereavement.

Louisa's desire to leave Tabley drove her to enlist Warren's help yet
again, in letters written during the first week after Violet's death. She
was afraid that her father and Richard would both think such a move
'insane' because they had just spent a large sum building on to the
house. Secretly her father might be sympathetic. She thought he would
not mind

> 'our losing a proportion of the money we have laid out here — In fact
> at the bottom of his heart he wd. like us to be nearer, but he wd. think
> it folly for us to move in it, unless it came up from the other side.'

So she was sounding Warren as to the likelihood of his father, their
landlord, wanting the house back. If the suggestion came from him, her
own father might acquiesce. Although she said she would 'give worlds
to leave Tabley,' this did not completely obliterate her common sense.

She asked Warren's opinion as to which of two arrangements about giving up the Grange would suit his father best. Should they try to find another tenant, or should they surrender the house direct to Lord de Tabley, leaving him to re-let it? They had, she thought 'sunk in that house & garden about £1,000,' and her father would not mind their losing half of that sum, so they only needed to get back £500, either from another tenant or from Lord de Tabley. She felt Warren's opinion on their 'likeliest and most politic way' from his own knowledge of his father's 'way of looking at such things,' would be a great help. He responded to this with a letter she thanked him for on 21st May, saying that it gave 'just the information I wanted' and provided 'more data to go on in our consultations.'

Whichever course they chose, by 7th May Tabley Grange was 'To Be Let' according to Margaret Warren's diary. The entry which mentions this makes a rather unkind comment about Louisa's reasons for leaving the Grange. The De Tabley family had returned to the Hall after Lady de Tabley's death and Margaret wrote

'the whole of this house is so sad and painful that if we were Mrs Molesworth and had what they all think "nice feelings" we couldn't stay here. She says Tabley is "a painful spot" and has thrown up the Grange — which is now To Be Let.'

Margaret seemed to think that Louisa was putting on a show of proper feeling, which we have seen from her letters to Warren was certainly not the case. One wonders whom she meant by 'they'. Was she referring to the Molesworth and Stewart families, or simply to genteel middle-class opinion? The only other reference to the Molesworths in Margaret's diaries also betrays some dislike. She congratulated herself on missing 'a dinner at home to the Hills and Molesworths' one Christmas.[17] Possibly she knew or suspected something of her brother's friendship with Louisa, and disapproved or was jealous. Louisa seems to have been in some way aware of this. In a letter on 12th April she wrote to Warren 'A letter from your father pleased R exceedingly this morning' — this would have been a letter of sympathy on Violet's death. Over five weeks later, there is a pointed reference to *no* sign of sympathy from his sisters. She commented first that it would have been disagreeable for Warren to go on knowing them had they remained at such close quarters as Tabley Grange. This is apparently a reference to the difficulties of

---

[17] M. L. Warren, *Diaries,* 7.5.1869 and 25.12.1868.

relations with his family, though she only uses general terms — 'R is very irate on several points' — 'these trifles . . . a good deal of pricking annoyance in an outside direction', but then comes the one specific accusation, 'I do think some slight expression of sympathy would have been only womanly from certain young ladies.' And when we remember that Margaret had been on playful enough terms with Violet for the child (then not yet six) to 'write' to her, we may agree with Louisa here.

After Violet's death, the Molesworths never lived in Tabley Grange again. Louisa and the children remained at West Hall, though of course she must have visited the house, however briefly and unwillingly, to oversee packing up. Living completely with her parents was not ideal. The family was 'wonderfully good' but naturally they were 'full of other interests and activities,' which would have included Agnes' approaching marriage and Caroline's courtship by Edward Walthall Delves Broughton[18] of Wistaston Hall, about 25 miles away. The contrast with her own state made her desperate at times, feeling that 'they [her family] must be sick of the bad luck attending all my life.' If this statement is not simply the exaggeration of grief, she was thinking of her marriage not only as 'bad luck', but 'bad luck' of a kind her family were well aware of, for Violet's death can hardly be said to have attended all her life.

Obviously she had to find somewhere else to live, but 'there is nothing in the shape of a suitable habitation to be had anywhere near.' The solution would, in the end, be to build another house, but her trustees and lawyers were throwing cold water on the idea and talking about 'fair investment,' the problem being their reluctance to allow capital to be used for building on land that Mr Stewart was only renting. Louisa preferred the children's present good — 'At most this same building is a very trifling affair, & the children had better be a few hundred pounds poorer 60 years hence, than lose their best chance of a happy growth.' Meanwhile she was feeling 'the wretchedness that must attend the present interregnum' between life at the Grange and another home of her own. She said she had foreseen it but even so 'some things <u>are</u> worse in reality than in anticipation' and her broken heart, as she was not afraid to call her grief, did not prevent her from feeling other things acutely.

---

[18] This was his full name at the time he met Caroline Stewart and for years after. He 'assumed by royal licence 1887 the surname of Walthall in lieu of his patronymic.' Debrett, 1893.

But she, Richard and the children were all going to have a change
and get away from whatever problems there were in High Legh. On 1st
June they went to Buxton for two or three months, to be 'nice and
quiet' in lodgings, with fishing for Richard. Buxton was a spa and this
visit was partly on account of her health — 'I am always suffering more
or less.' They had had to give up the idea of a house in Darby Dale as
it was too hilly for 'a more than half lame person,' as she described
herself. The length of their stay was to be 'according to my health,'
which to her must have meant when the baby was born. She could not
have intended to stay in Buxton for the birth, which was due in August.
When she invited Warren to visit them there she was careful to specify
June and early July. Buxton and the passage of time enabled her to take
an interest once more in her own novel and in Warren's second one.
He sent her a copy at the end of June, which she read closely with great
interest and much enthusiasm for his 'capital title'. (This was *Ropes of
Sand*). At least half of her long letter in response was detailed comment
on this novel. She was very grateful to him for sending it, since 'Any
interest must do me good — for I am still miserable & weary of
endurance.'

She had already made an agreement with Skeet for her own novel,
and Warren had sent her a copy of his agreement with Bentley as a
basis for comparison. Her proofs were due to start coming soon and
she asked whether to correct them in the margin or by interlining. But
although these expressions of fresh interest in life show she was making
an effort, she was also saying

> 'I wish one cd. <u>wake</u> as unconsciously as one falls asleep — The bitter
> concentrated agony of every waking, makes me shrink from ever going
> to sleep — Will this never grow softer, do you think? It is the remem-
> brance of the outside circumstances wh. I have never told you & wh.
> probably I never can, that go on in this torturing way.'

She described this waking experience with equal passion but more art
in one of her novels a few years later.

> 'Who does not know the awful agony of the first waking after some
> overwhelming sorrow has befallen us? The shuddering glimmer of recol-
> lection that *something* has happened, the frantic clutch at the blessed
> unconsciousness of the sleep that is leaving us, the wild refusal to recall
> the truth. And, oh! the unutterable loathing at life, at existence even
> when at last we realize the whole and find that another day has dawned,

that the heartless sunshine is over the world again, that we ourselves must eat and drink and clothe ourselves, and *live*! If we could see that our individual misery made its mark, if the birds would only leave off singing, if the flowers would all wither, if a veil could be drawn over the sun, would it seem quite so bad?'[19]

At least she was spared the terrible thought that, if only some other course of action had been followed, the child would not have died, for the doctor had told her 'nothing could have been done.' In layman's terms she understood him to say that 'something touched the dear little heart and all stopped.' This suggests that Violet had suffered from the less common cardiac complication which made scarlet fever such a formidable disease in the past.

Cicely did not entirely escape. While they were at Buxton she was 'very ill' with low fever, 'something wrong with the tonsils' and general weakness and debility. Louisa herself became 'rather ill again' and was not allowed to walk at all. She wrote of pains in the joints — 'Imagine toothache in every joint!' — and by an unlucky accident she 'sprained the rheumatic joint' which was very painful. This implies that both she and Cicely were suffering from problems related to the scarlet fever germ (Streptococcus pyogenes) which can cause either scarlet fever or tonsillitis. One complication can be a generalized inflammation of the joints, which become swollen and painful and bear a close resemblance to the inflamed joints of acute rheumatism. Cicely's bad throat made her feel so ill that she thought she was going to join Violet, and she found comfort for her aching head in laying it on 'a brilliant magenta handkerchief' which Warren had left at their house long ago and which had somehow never been returned. Cicely liked it because it was so soft and she asked her mother to send Warren a message of thanks —

> 'one day she said "there is no saying that I shall ever see him again. Tell him I did so like his handkerchief" — Fancy if she had not got better, & I had been writing this! You used to think I did not much care for my children & I think I thought so myself. How little I knew!'

While Cicely was still weak, though getting better, all their plans were upset by the sudden news that Richard had been ordered to Hythe on duty from the end of July until October. Louisa found this 'most

---

[19] *Cicely: A Story of Three Years*, by Ennis Graham, Tinsley Brothers, 1874, vol. 3, pp. 57–8.

provoking', since if they had been given more warning, they could have arranged for the whole family to go with him and stay there for several months. As it was, Cicely and the other children were to go to the sea (at Fleetwood, as usual) for several weeks, especially so that Cicely could have the bracing air. Louisa's mother insisted on her returning to West Hall, clearly to await the imminent birth.

The very short notice of Richard's posting to Hythe annoyed Louisa for another reason — the cost. After his return, she twice made passing references in letters to Warren about Hythe's having been very expensive — 'I have had such "complications" lately (money too again — Hythe has been tremendous).' The other reference was occasioned by Warren's having made some joking remark to her about not being able to get new boots. Although she tried to respond in kind, she could not hide (and perhaps did not want to) that she was indeed concerned about money. 'I shall be very poor again this winter' she wrote, 'owing to Hythe and illness — But fortunately I bought two pair of boots last spring as a reserve. You should have done the same — .' Richard stayed in a hotel, 'The Swan', during his duty in Hythe which would, of course, have cost more than lodgings. Before he went, she wrote anxiously 'he does not a bit understand "fending for himself",' which we must interpret here as meaning 'managing his expenses economically,' rather than cooking his own meals or cleaning his own kit. If she were there, she could do better, and she still wrote hopefully 'I can perhaps join R at Hythe later,' even though she was ill and expecting the baby.

Louisa had already prepared Warren for her being incommunicado during this event.

> 'I can't go on writing to you or keeping you informed of our being dead or alive through the summer — & I don't want to seem ungrateful — so if you care to hear about me I will make my sister write once or twice, as she did at the fever time — unless you wd. prefer not, or if possibly you would think it uncalled for or indelicate of me to think you cared to hear.'

'Indelicate' presumably because the news her sister was to send would be, it was to be hoped, of her safe delivery. She was coming very close to mentioning her pregnancy to a male person who was not a member of her family. Not good Victorian behaviour at all! Right up to a day or so before the birth she went on writing to him, correcting her proofs and being involved in disagreeable transactions with the new tenants of Tabley Grange (which fell on her because Richard was in Hythe). She was in quite good spirits about her novel, having got 'a specimen 3 volumes of Skeet's, lately published' which looked 'very business-like' and the idea of actually seeing her own work in the same form was appealing. Several times she mentioned strategies for making people ask for it at the libraries and asked Warren's help with 'its having some sale' because she felt that some small success was necessary to make future attempts possible, and that an unsuccessful first venture would be positively damaging with a publisher asked to consider a second attempt. She wrote, as a matter of course, about sending him duplicates of her proofs once she had several chapters done, so he must already have agreed to look at them, or even suggested or requested it himself.

On 13th August at the West Hall Louisa's first son was born. Her mother and elder sister were with her, while her younger sister, Caroline, had gone to Fleetwood with the children. Within a few days she was writing letters, going on with her proofs and wanting a reference to an article in *The Spectator*, but two weeks afterwards it was Agnes who wrote to Warren, saying that Louisa was making so little progress that they were keeping her quiet for a while. She had already asked Warren to be godfather to the child, apparently as a source of gratification for Richard, who was indeed very pleased, particularly because he thought that Warren had offered this mark of friendly recognition of his own accord. Agnes begged him not to disabuse her brother-in-law because 'Louisa is very anxious for him to be encouraged in every new interest — in having a son.' Louisa was particularly concerned about Richard just then. He had reproached her that, by insisting on leaving Tabley Grange, she had somehow deprived him of Warren's friendship. He had also reacted badly to Violet's death. She therefore wanted to 'rouse him by every means, to some pleasurable interest in this child, which at first he did not feel at all' and to get Warren himself 'to show some active proof of continued interest in us.' So she had been delighted when she heard from Richard just before the baby was born that he and Warren had met up again in Brighton, and that Warren had been 'so nice' to him. She had partly paved the way for this meeting, by the broad hint of giving Warren Richard's address in Hythe and wondering, to Warren, why Richard had not called on him when in Brighton. Asking Warren to offer to be godfather was another piece of well-meaning manipulation. It seemed to be working, for Richard's interest was sufficiently aroused to make him choose the names for the baby — ' "Richard Walter Stewart" — not John or Charles as she wished — "Walter" is the name of the first Molesworth on record' wrote Agnes.

Louisa was too pleased at this sign of attention from her husband to press her own wish for her dead brother's name, or that of her father and elder brother, as recommended by Mary Molesworth before Olive was born.

After Richard Walter's birth, Louisa did not recover very well so she tried a return to Buxton. Writing from there to Warren on 24th September, she said

> 'I came here with Olive and the little boy on Monday, in a sort of despair at gaining no strength — I am supposed to be quite well, but I feel so weak and tired that I am really fit for nothing.'

Her mother had gone with her too. She had enough energy though, to finish her proofs, which she had done by the time she wrote this letter. She had also been able to arrange for their next home, apparently before she left for Buxton. This was a house called The Cottage only about three hundred yards from West Hall. The approach to it led off from the main drive to East Legh Hall, in the grounds of which it lay. From the time of her return from Buxton in early October until the end of 1870, Louisa's letters from High Legh were addressed from The Cottage. She definitely expected to move from West Hall soon after her return, as in trying to arrange how and when to meet Warren she said 'Perhaps it wd. be easier while we are still at the West Hall' and 'There will be no-one at my father's, even if we are detained there a little later than we expected.' She added in brackets after this '(Mrs Edmond L. is later a little of going abroad)' which appears to be a reference to the previous occupant of The Cottage. 'L' may be a contraction for 'Legh' so that Mrs Edmond might be a connection of the Cornwall-Legh family who owned the East Hall estate. When Louisa wrote that there was no 'suitable habitation' near West Hall, she was probably not including The Cottage in her considerations, because Mrs Edmond L. was living there. But this was only a temporary arrangement — building was still in her thoughts and the legal objections were being overcome.

> 'I fancy it will end by a cottage being built for us close to my people's — as a long lease <u>can</u> be secured — And my trustees have the sense to see it is the best thing for me and the children — whatever the future is, it is not a bad investment.'

Louisa's efforts to arrange a meeting with Warren led to another big misunderstanding. She was expecting Richard back from Hythe at the end of the month and very much hoped that Warren would dine with them before he went back south. The invitation in her letter of 24th September was wide-ranging — 'Any day we shall be, as you know, only too glad to see you — & at any hour can arrange to meet you at any point you name.' He replied to this letter apparently suggesting that he should call at West Hall, naming a day when, she told him in her reply, although Richard would almost certainly be there, she would not. She asked him to make the call all the same. He would probably see no-one but her sister Agnes, whom he already knew, as Richard might have had to go to Salford for the day, probably on military business. She made a particular point of his paying this call as a favour to her, though without explaining exactly why she wished it. In a later letter she said that she had 'suggested your seeing my sister for a moment, simply to make the attention to us distinct, unmistakable & open — it was only to us' (ie, to her and Richard). It was to be as easy for him as possible — 'You can make the call as short as you like if you miss R — but I think you don't mind Mrs Craven-to-be now, as she is hardly a "young lady" now! [sic].' His dislike of young ladies was known — his sister wrote that he 'is so bitter about the world and young ladies.'[20]

Louisa wanted him, as well as paying this call, to come to dinner two days later, just after she herself would arrive back, but this she described as 'a simple piece of selfishness on my part' which he could refuse quite freely — he must do just as he liked. She meant that his coming to dinner was simply to give her pleasure, while she thought of the call as a benefit to Richard too. She took a lot of trouble to work out the train he should come by (he would be in Macclesfield at the time) to Lymm, north of High Legh, not Knutsford, where he would be met. But he declined to make the call (and also the dinner visit, presumably) saying he was 'not yet supposed to pay visits', doubtless on account of his mother's death, eight months before. The year's official mourning was not yet over. Louisa was very upset and hurt by this, first because, as she demanded, 'Is leaving a message at a door (wh. had R. been away wd. probably have been all required) a breach of etiquette in the circumstances?' but then, more deeply, because she feared this was an excuse for his real reason — 'At least you might say honestly — "I won't or can't come to see you for fear of possibly being drawn into the slightest contact with your relations."' After all, it was he who had originally suggested making a call, so why else had he suddenly drawn back? There

---

[20] M. L. Warren, *Diaries*, 29.1.1869.

were three more letters on this subject and there had clearly been as many from him, both sides hurt, feeling misunderstood and on the defensive.

As Warren's letters to Louisa have not survived, it is as well to refer to other sources to show that this kind of upset with his friends was not uncommon. It was not all Louisa's fault. There had been, for instance, the episode of his review of Swinburne's *Atalanta* in the *Fortnightly Review*. He felt great admiration for Swinburne's poetry and persuaded G. H. Lewes, the editor, to let him write a review, which was published over his name, but with toning down corrections and slighting additions, such as 'minor poet', from Lewes. Both Edmund Gosse and Theodore Watts mentioned this matter in their obituaries of Warren, and interpreted it in the same way. Because he was subject to a pitiable sensitiveness so that 'the merest trifle pained him,' the thought that he, the admirer of Swinburne, must seem to have belittled him, remained with him like an open wound for the rest of his life.

'He could never be reminded of Mr Swinburne without a shudder at the thought of what he must think that Warren thought he thought. Alas! at times his life was made a perfect nightmare to him by reverberated sensibilities of this kind.'

When Warren first met Watts, he was uncomfortable because he thought there was constraint between them on account of this review, as Swinburne was a friend of Watts. 'He had a habit' commented Watts, after explaining the circumstances in detail, 'of submitting almost every incident of his life to such an analysis as that I have been describing.' Gosse maintained

'I doubt if any friend, however tactful in self-abnegation, got through many years of Lord de Tabley's intimacy without an electric storm. His imagination aided his ingenuity in self-torture, and conjured up monsters of malignity, spectres that strode across the path of friendship and rendered it impassable.'

But his friends would await 'the return of his kinder feelings' with patience.[21]

In this particular 'electric storm' with Louisa, he wrote to explain where he thought she had 'exaggerated and misconceived,' and while maintaining there was justification for her reaction, she apologised 'as

---

[21] Gosse, pp. 95 and 89; Watts p. 754a; Gosse pp. 95–6.

heartily as if there were no excuse for me.' He attended the baby's christening in late October or early November and she was very grateful — 'It was truly kind of you to come, and everybody concerned was pleased with the poor little baby's debut — R particularly.' It was the first time they had met since Violet's death and both seemed to find the meeting painful and awkward. By this time Louisa was feeling that, despite her good reasons on Richard's behalf, she should not have schemed as she did about 'the whole affair of the sponsorship' and she apologised for this too. But those 'reverberated sensibilities'of his show in her reassurances to him in the same letter as she apologised for herself.

> 'I do not attach the slightest weight to your saying if I "knew all" I shd.
> feel different — However I am changed, it is certainly not in the direction
> of being sharper to judge others — certainly not you — I am also certain
> that you are only going through a phase — horribly dark as it is, it is
> only a phase. You are still yourself, though you can't see it.'

She appears to have taken much the same view of his character as Gosse and Watts. Their meeting among so many people at a formal gathering was not conducive to much easy talk and she asked him again to visit them at the cottage before he went away 'for so long.' He was about to go to Rome for several months and was there at the time of the beginning of the Vatican Council which declared the infallibility of the Pope. While there, he wrote a poem called 'At the council' dated November 1869.[22] It is not clear whether they did meet again before he left. Certainly they continued to correspond on friendly terms well into the following year.

But Louisa's attention had now again to be focussed on her family. The baby died on 20th November. He was already ailing when she was in Buxton, and had not improved by the time of the christening, hence the reference to 'the poor little baby'. He was buried in the same grave as his sister, in the churchyard at Rostherne, also with just his name and the dates. There had been other troubles in the year. Earlier on, before April, Mary Molesworth, the relative whose letter was quoted in chapter 4, had died too. Lord Molesworth, Richard's uncle, had been seriously ill at the time of Violet's death — 'I fear my dear old uncle, Lord M, is dying too' wrote Louisa. 'This has seemed the last straw for he was so fond of the child and knew her well.' He did not

---

[22] Quoted in Grant-Duff's memoir in *The Flora of Cheshire.*

in fact die until 1875. Although these things cannot have touched her as nearly as the loss of her own children, yet she had developed a friendship with Mary and was fond of Richard's uncle, so that she must have felt the blows life could deal were crowding very closely together for her.

Her grand-daughter thought that she resented grief, writing

'My grandmother must have been as a young woman v. strong-minded, perhaps too critical both of herself and others, and having perhaps stronger emotions than she herself realised. The troubles in her marriage and the early deaths of her adored first daughter and first son undoubtedly soured her for the time being, and it was many years before the sweetness came back . . . She was [one] of those strong natures who resent grief and only discipline themselves to accept it with great difficulty.'[23]

She said of herself, before any of these blows had fallen, 'I dread suffering and am not brave.' This was in the context of a discussion by letter with Warren during the first half of 1868, on what they both referred to as his 'fickleness theory'. It had arisen from her reading Lewes' *Goethe*,[24] on Warren's recommendation. She ventured to regret, in Goethe, 'what in ordinary people is called fickleness. . . . I can't see the same greatness . . . in his love-affairs . . . the idea of frittering away one's feelings as Goethe did, I cannot . . . think admirable.' Goethe did not marry until he was fifty-seven, the woman he then took as his wife having been his mistress for seven years. But until he was forty, he had indulged in a series of intense relationships with engaged or married women. Over and over again, he became 'obsessively attracted to a sexually unavailable woman.' But because desire rather than fulfilment seemed to feed his genius, he did not attempt to consummate these relationships, and preferred 'the infinite charm of becoming' to the threat of fixity in marriage.[25]

Judging from Louisa's letters, Warren seems to have had similar relationships with unavailable women, including herself. Perhaps he lent her Goethe's biography as a kind of warning against himself. He also seems to have defended the 'changefulness' Louisa disapproved of, which led her to say she thought he did not have a very high standard of

---

[23] VMI to RR 12.12.51.

[24] G. H. Lewes, *The Life and Works of Goethe*, 1855.

[25] Nicholas Boyle, *Goethe, The Poet and the Age, Volume 1, The Poetry of Desire*, OUP, 1992, p. 261.

marriage. She wrote 'you don't seem to think women are ever strong enough or great enough . . . to be worth that sort of whole concentration of friendship & affection.' It is not clear from her side of the discussion how he supported his theory. However, after several months during which it was a regular topic, though not mentioned in every letter, she said that, while not admiring the theory, she would like to be able to adopt it because 'it gives you an immunity against the deepest of suffering.' Her remark about dreading suffering followed on here immediately. She obviously interpreted both Goethe and Warren as holding the belief, whether or not they practised it, that moving on from one woman to another prevented too deep a commitment, and thus reduced the likelihood of great suffering from any one relationship. But she doubted what Warren said of himself. 'Do you really get tired of people after a while?' she asked him. She may have thought she would be glad to adopt this theory, but it is very clear that she did not do so. It was the suffering she experienced over Violet's death which made her realise how very much she had loved her daughter, as we saw in her exclamation to Warren quoted earlier — 'How little I knew!' She had made another remark to Warren about her attitude to suffering, at Christmas 1868, which casts some light on her state of mind in this later period, after Violet's death, the time when her grand-daughter later described her as being soured. 'I can always get up more strength for acute suffering than for chronic' she wrote. For her, it was easier to produce strength in a crisis than to continue in grinding endurance over a long period. Resenting grief, or at least longing for it to be over, appears in that phrase 'weary of endurance' and in her earnest desire that the bitter agony of every waking could cease.

1869 ended more happily with Agnes' wedding to Craven Goring, who was an army officer then stationed at Portsmouth, in St John's Chapel, High Legh on 14th December.[26] This new brother-in-law became a dearly loved and supportive friend to Louisa. Years later, after his death, she dedicated one of her books to him — 'To the dear memory of my brother-in-law, Sir Craven Charles Goring, Bart., whose unfailing interest in my work has been an encouragement through many years.'[27] He and Agnes went abroad for their honeymoon and returned in the spring, when they too decided to settle in High Legh for a time. Louisa was pleased.

---

[26] Parish registers at Rostherne.
[27] *Miss Mouse*, 1897.

'I am glad the Gorings are coming here for all sakes — It is best for them to be quite independent of his cousin . . . & they will be a great addition here. I am very fond of him now, though I was slow about it — He is so very "genuine".'

She described him in one of her earliest books for children as

'*very* nice. He was older than Floss had expected; a good deal older than auntie, whom he sometimes spoke to as if she were quite a little girl, in a way which amused the children very much. At first he seemed very quiet and grave, but after a while Floss found out that in his own way he was very fond of fun, and she confided to auntie that she thought he was the funniest person she had ever seen. I don't know if auntie told him this, or if he took it as a compliment, but certainly he could not have been offended, for every day, as they learnt to know him better, the children found him kinder and kinder.'

This is offered as a description of Major Goring on the authority of Louisa's eldest surviving daughter, Cicely, who wrote 'Yes, Carrots' uncle is a copy of my much loved uncle Sir Craven Goring, (then Major Goring).'[28] The Gorings' home in High Legh was Oak Tree Cottage, in the centre of the village,[29] so their marriage increased the number of family homes for casual visits and social gatherings. This was certainly 'a great addition' for Louisa who would have missed the sister closest to her, the holiday companion whose love affairs she had watched over with such concern, who had looked after her in illness and childbirth and who knew much of her friendship with Warren.

Lover and Husband was finally published towards the end of the year. She had told Warren in July, 'I think it is settled with Skeet — to be completed for the early autumn, when people are supposed to have time to waste on rubbish at the seaside'. There is only one other slight reference to it, when in the letter thanking Warren for attending the baby's christening she said she had wanted to ask him something about her book but could not, because their meeting was so hurried and public. It is not clear from the way she wrote whether the book was actually out then or not. The British Library's copy is date-stamped 9th December, so 'some time in the autumn' is the nearest we can get to a date. Skeet had followed the common practice of dating the title-page 1870, so that

---

[28] *Carrots*, p. 196. CP to RR, 1938.
[29] *The Times* gives this address in a birth notice at the end of 1870.

the book would seem new for longer. The appearance of her first complete book must have given Louisa some pleasure and a sense of achievement, although she so often denigrated it as rubbish. She cloaked her
authorship under the pseudonym of Ennis Graham, which her granddaughter explained as follows — 'My great-grandfather is said to have
disapproved of women writers, young or unmarried ones anyhow, so
perhaps she spared his feelings.' Richard too, on at least one occasion,
had objected to Louisa's writing. When asking Warren to come and see
her in June 1868, she had written 'I think you had better tell R you
are encouraging me with my novel, & that you want to see how I am
getting on. I think he will not dislike my doing it now.' The granddaughter also said that the name chosen was that of Louisa's only
girl-friend who died accompanying her father on an expedition in Central Africa. Louisa herself mentioned to Warren that 'The nom-de-plume
is a real one — of a dead friend,' but the rest of the story must remain
a family tradition only, since she told him nothing further. Probably
his own use of pseudonyms made the practice seem so much a matter
of course that she never thought of offering an explanation. Even the
publisher did not know who the author was. 'He knows nothing about
me, name or anything,' she told Warren in February 1870, which implies
that it was Louisa's own wish, not just her father's, that she remain
unknown. Anonymity or pseudonymity was certainly the practice of
many other women writers at this period.

Further writing plans had to be postponed now, for after the baby's
death Louisa became really ill again. She was bad enough in January
1870 to see an 'Edinburgh "swell" doctor' or specialist. Her references
do not make clear what was the matter with her, but at one stage she
thought she was going to die, which we learn from the remark 'If I
knew I was going to die, I would ask you several things, but I don't
now think I am.' She did not look ill but was weak and easily tired,
and did not herself think of the alarm others were feeling 'except when
it is forced on me by actual pain' and then her reaction was to be cross
rather than nervous. Even Richard had been 'considerably startled at
first' but this did not last long. 'I think he is pretty comfortable now
unless anything brings the impression back . . . He is always inclined
to be spasmodic,' a comment on his character which reminds us of the
moods and rages he suffered from, and indeed inflicted on the whole
family. 1869 had been a bad year for Louisa. She would have hoped
that 1870 would bring better times for her.

7

'We Shall Never Go Back To Cheshire'

In January 1870 the house to be built specially for the Molesworth family was at last begun, 'but of course it will be a long affair' Louisa wrote to Warren.[1] The return of her illness, mentioned at the end of the previous chapter, lasted for many months, well into 1870. At the beginning of February she went to Harrogate with her mother for a fortnight. The visit was to help her mother's rheumatic gout, but she had also hoped the change might do some good to herself and recorded regretfully on her return to High Legh that she was losing weight and that 'Harrogate did me no good'. She went on 'Doctors are marvellously kind, & so patient with one's fancies — but they can't do much.' The mention of 'fancies' might suggest that her illness was psychological, or partly so, but this idea dies away in face of her reference, at the end of March to 'almost incessant pain for months'. A happier family event in March, which, though not mentioned in Louisa's letters, was recorded in the Rostherne parish registers, was the baptism, at St John's Chapel, High Legh, of her first nephew, Charles and Janetta Stewart's first child, — Charles Morier Louis. Charles, a lieutenant in the Royal Artillery, was serving on the staff of the Lieutenant Governor of Jersey at this time. Later in the year, some time in June or July, a second son was born, Noel Ramsay. So Morier must have been as much as eight months old at the time of his christening, which was probably delayed in order that it might take place while Charles Stewart was on leave with his family at his parents' house.[2]

Towards the end of April Louisa went again to Fleetwood with the children, while her mother, who was still 'not well', went with Agnes and Caroline to Bath (another spa town and therefore frequented by the sick). At this time Louisa was 'seldom or ever [sic] getting an hour

---

[1] There are 10 letters from MLM to JBLW in the Tabley Papers which can be dated to 1870 with some certainty. See Chapter 6, note 1.

[2] Census, 2.4.1871 lists Noel Ramsay Stewart as 10 months old. In the dedication to *Carrots*, 1876, MLM refers to these two children as Morier and Noel.

of sleep together.' She also felt very isolated — 'I have never been so alone.' A visit to London was mentioned hopefully, but in May she realised she had to give up the idea — 'I am not able for so long a journey' — even though one of the objects of the intended trip had been to consult another doctor. Throughout these months there were references to her not being able to write properly or only 'in bits' because 'I get to ache rather over it.' Other causes mentioned were having her arm in a sling or 'not sitting up today.' A special frame was made for her, so that she could write 'without leaning or much exertion.' At the same time she was insisting that her general health was good and expressing relief that her condition was not hereditary like consumption 'otherwise I should have dreaded my children's inheriting it.' All this seems to imply that she was still suffering from the very painful rheumatic joints that resulted from a complication of scarlet fever at the time of Violet's death. By the end of May she could say 'I do not know if I am better or not' which suggests some improvement.

She did not allow her painful condition to stop her from writing or from taking an interest in the fate of her novel and making efforts to promote it. The few mentions the novel received had her careful attention, but since they were 'marvellously amiable' she was rather suspicious of them, concluding, not that her novel was good, but that it was 'too unpretending to have anything sharp said.' It had already been mentioned in *The Spectator* at the end of the 'Current Literature' column, but she longed for a real review either in that journal or in *The Saturday Review*, something more than just 'a paragraph or two.' In February she wrote that 'L & H is doing mildly well' but it is impossible to tell whether she means by this that it was selling or that she had evidence of its being read. A week later she wrote to Warren specifically to ask his advice on what she could do to 'help on my story.' In his reply Warren appears to have asked her if she knew who had written about her novel in *The Spectator*. She said

> 'I think I know who wrote that little bit in the Spectator, but I am not sure — If I am right, it is very queer — as the man I mean must have known the book was mine to say it as he did —He is one of the rather odd friends I have made in my life, & I believe Agnes told him [*'made him do it by telling him'* — *crossed out*] — He writes, I think, every week in the Spectator; but my relations to him are not such that I can count him an iron, beyond that little bit, wh. was out-of-the-way kind of him.'

She meant that Agnes had told the unnamed man that her sister Louisa was the author of *Lover and Husband* and that this information had induced him to mention her novel. This man was probably Richard Holt Hutton, editor of *The Spectator* from 1861 to 1897, who wrote and reviewed for it regularly. 'Up till the day of his death Richard Holt Hutton was the most highly honoured of English Journalists.'[3] Later he reviewed at least seven other books of hers in *The Spectator*. Since Agnes knew him too, he was probably a family friend, whom the Stewarts could have got to know in Manchester through their links with the Owens College milieu. As we saw earlier, they knew Professor Williamson and William Gaskell who both taught there. Another tutor there, William Stanley Jevons was a connection of Hutton's through the marriages both of them made into the Roscoe family. Hutton and Jevons were both uncles to two children whom Louisa knew well — Thomas Grindal and Mary Josephine Hutton. Later she was to write a story about Thomas Grindal's life. None of this is proof that this 'odd friend' of hers was indeed Hutton but it seems likely.

Louisa's remark about not counting Hutton 'an iron' relates to her discussion in the same letter about whether she had any other irons in the fire. She meant, was there anyone else she could approach, or anything else she could do 'to get it noticed.' Perhaps she should offer to pay for another week or two's advertisement in *The Saturday* herself, quoting the notice from *The Spectator*? There is a slight tone of embarrassment about her determination to be noticed somehow. Nevertheless, she persisted, 'there must be interest at work to get the hideous nonsense reviewed in those weekly papers, that often is — But how on earth do people get hold of the interest?' Of course, though she did not say so, Warren himself was part of her 'interest', as an author, and a reviewer for the *Fortnightly* and the *Saturday*. He responded to her request for advice with something more concrete. He gave her a recommendation to a Mr Davies, to whom she then sent a copy of *Lover and Husband* for review. It amused her that Mr Davies had asked Warren if he were 'Ennis Graham'.

The genre that Louisa had attempted in writing and publishing a novel was popular and well-established. It was also tightly controlled in subject matter both by the critics and the circulating libraries, of which Mudie's was probably the best-known. Novels had to be fit to be read

---

[3] J. Hogben, *Richard Holt Hutton of 'The Spectator'*, Edinburgh, Oliver and Boyd, 1899, p. 160.

aloud in the family circle and sufficiently blameless to be placed in the hands of Victorian maidenhood or Mudie's would not stock them, and a novel black-balled by Mudie's was condemned to commercial ruin. We know that Louisa was well aware of the importance of the circulating libraries in the fate of a novel from her stated intention 'to do all I can to make people ask for it [sc. her novel] at the libraries.' Publishers relied upon Mudie and his colleagues to take a large part, if not all, of the first edition of any work intended for the general public. This guaranteed sale and easy transaction with one customer meant that publishers did not need to make much effort to advertise their wares widely. Indeed the high price of the three-volume novel, at one and a half guineas (31s 6d) — a week's salary for a London clerk — put it completely out of the range of all but the 27,000 families with an income of £400 or more a year. A skilled artisan in the mid-nineteenth century would be earning about 34s a week — just over the price of a novel! Mudie's subscription was 1 guinea a year for one exchangeable volume or 2 guineas for 4 volumes. So three-volume novels were greatly to his advantage, and library subscriptions were much more economical for the novel-reading public than buying their reading matter. Publishers' contracts often specified the number of volumes, pages and lines to a page, in order to make sure that what they were getting would fill the obligatory three volumes. We saw in chapter five that Louisa calculated in these terms while still writing and before approaching a publisher. Really popular works came out in cheap one-volume reprints, usually after a period specified by the libraries. Textual manipulation, such as reducing the margin and removing leading, meant that as much as two or three hundred words more could be got onto a page, indicating clearly the artificial status of the sancrosanct three volumes.[4]

A contemporary reviewer wrote that 'an English novelist of the average standard is always bound to be moral and to bring about a happy conclusion.'[5] George Moore's first novel was banned by the circulating libraries and he complained that the real authors of fiction were Messrs Mudie and Smith 'not the ladies and gentlemen who place their names

---

[4] More detailed accounts of the 3 volume novel and the circulating library can be found in Richard Altick, *The English Common Reader*, 1957, chaps. 12 and 13; 'English publishing and the mass audience in 1852' in *Studies in Bibliography 6*, 1954, pp. 3–24; Guinevere G. Griest, *Mudie's Circulating Library and the Victorian Novel*, 1970; C. E. and E. S. Lauterbach, 'The Nineteenth Century Three-Volume Novel' in *Papers of the Bibliographical Society of America 51*, 1957, pp. 263–302.
[5] *The Saturday Review*, 12.3.1870, in a review of the novel *No Appeal*.

on the title-page.'[6] What the critics and the libraries meant by being moral was that, whatever might be hinted or suggested about male characters, all ladies must enter marriage as innocent virgins, and whatever the provocation, must remain chaste within it. Adultery was not allowed. Cutting the Gordian knot by melodramatic solutions was not allowed either. A novel in which a virtuous and attractive woman was rescued from a vicious and repulsive husband by his falling into a stream and having a stake thrust into his eye, was castigated as evading the point. 'It is rather annoying' complained the reviewer, 'that the moral question is left after all in uncertainty.'[7] If the problem was raised at all, this reviewer wanted it clearly stated that, whatever happened, women ought to live with their husbands. For evidence of the compulsory nature of happy endings, it is only necessary to refer to Dickens changing the ending of *Great Expectations* at the urging of Bulwer Lytton, or to the pleas for a happy ending to *Villette,* made by both Charlotte Bronte's publisher and her father. Dickens complied, Bronte refused, but both 'veiled the fate in oracular words' so that it requires close reading to be sure of what happened.[8]

It is interesting to see how Louisa worked within these confines in *Lover and Husband.* Wedding bells do not make her happy ending. The wedding is part of the plot complication, not its resolution, for Marion, the heroine, marries a man she does not love at the beginning, not the end, of the third volume. The climax of the book is her chance meeting on her honeymoon with the man she really loves and her discovery that he had not, after all, married as she had been led to suppose. In order to build up plausibly to such a melodramatic situation, Louisa was prepared to use any kind of hackneyed device, for her real interest lay in the characters not the plot. She admitted as much to Warren when he passed on to her some 'really very mild criticism' from Mr Davies. 'I don't mind about the "impossible incidents". Some were so, & others

[6] George Moore, *Literature At Nurse or Circulating Morals,* a pamphlet, Vizetelly and Co., 1885, p. 20. Reprinted, with an article by Moore, 'A New Censorship of Literature', from the *Pall Mall Gazette* and the ensuing correspondence in the PMG, in *Literature At Nurse or Circulating Morals: A Polemic on Victorian Censorship,* edited with an introduction by Pierre Coustillas, The Harvester Press, 1976. A good source of information about contemporary attitudes to the 3 vol. novel and the circulating library.

[7] *The Saturday Review,* ibid.

[8] *Charles Dickens: A Critical Anthology,* ed. Stephen Wall, Penguin, 1970, pp. 156–7. Winifred Gerin, *Charlotte Bronte,* OUP paperback, 1969, pp. 509–11. Mrs Gaskell, *The Life of Charlotte Bronte,* Smith, Elder, 1857 p. 400.

were real ones.' She wanted to explore Marion's reactions not her adventures. So we have a father feared and distrusted, a beloved brother desperately in debt and the eventual solution of Marion's hiring herself out as a governess under an assumed name to earn enough to pay the debt, all liberally sprinkled with spiteful gossip, mistaken addresses and mis-sent letters. The third volume relates Marion's fall into despairing misery and her final emergence into a peace which is not the joyful crowning point of 'they lived happily ever after', intended by *The Saturday Review's* 'happy conclusion'.

Marion's unhappiness is increased by her husband's withdrawal from her because, as she thinks, even he no longer loves her, but in reality because he does not want to force himself on her. She also finds it hard to endure the bathos of daily life with a man incompatible in temperament, a country squire contented with out-door pursuits, a cheerful Philistine, in contrast with her own imaginative, sensitive, poetic, somewhat intellectual nature. Even before their marriage he has been shown as responding to her poetic philosophising about spring with an irrelevant remark on hunting. Now they are actually married, it is 'her duty to listen with patience if not with interest to his commonplace conversation, his stupid talk of weather and crops or his anticipation of the coming season's hunting.' Yet Louisa did not choose to depict the extreme situation of a virtuous woman tied to a villain. This is only incompatibility, and she painted the husband as admirable in his own way. Even after he knows that Marion loves someone else he keeps up his spirits.

> 'He was the possessor of that mysterious and to the mere spectator, somewhat irritating gift, known as 'animal spirits'. There were times when, in spite of all his unspeakable disappointment, his bitter self-reproach, the young man could not help feeling happy. An exciting run, a bracing frosty morning in his fields, filled him for the time with his old joyousness, the exhilaration of life itself apart from all modifying circumstances.'[9]

It is the arrival of misfortune in the shape of a bank failure that stimulates Marion to courage and awakens feeling. She and her husband gradually grow together and she unconsciously learns to love him in poverty. Her recognition and avowal of this, prompted by her husband's serious illness just when he is thinking that his death will at last free her to go to her

---

[9] *Lover and Husband* vol. 3, pp. 68 and 96.

lover, is what makes the 'happy' ending — a low key, muted kind of happiness, more akin to the possibilities of ordinary life than the traditional wedding bells. It is significant that already in her first novel Louisa was writing about incompatibility of temperament in marriage. She must have felt that her heroine's situation reflected her own, at least in the union of a poetic, sensitive nature with a sporting outdoor man, though she did not endow the hero with her husband's temper. Perhaps Richard enjoyed hunting as well as fishing.

Lover and Husband appears never to have been reprinted, which is hardly surprising. It was one among many, not the complete rubbish Louisa was inclined to call it in a low mood, but not distinguished either. The language is straightforward and carries the story on quite well, but if Louisa had not written her children's books, it would never have been heard of again. She was already 'going on with another story' at the time of her son's christening and the concern she showed about getting *Lover and Husband* 'noticed' was, she said (though later we shall see that there was another reason), chiefly with a view to the effect on a possible future publisher. 'If it cd. but have a little success it wd. make it easy for me to write another — to get another published, I mean.' Mentions of this second novel in letters to Warren include asking his permission to use some details from the outward circumstances of his life and a query about the position of rooms and outlook of windows in the De Tabley London house for 'a new story I am amusing myself with arranging.' Reminding him that he had asked her 'not to mind Clara', she said that therefore she did not like to use even a 'mere outside resemblance — not nearly as close as Clara in the Ropes' without asking him. This is a reference to a character in his novel *Ropes of Sand*. The only similarity between Clara and Louisa actually mentioned in her letters is the remark 'It is very nice to make Clara scold him for calling her good-natured' which occurs in the letter thanking Warren for sending her a copy of *Ropes* when she was in Buxton in June 1869. It refers to her own dislike, declared in two letters the previous year, of the expression 'good-natured' — 'Don't call me "good-natured" . . . I had rather be called "designing" than "good-natured".' The other reference is very circuitous, showing that her dislike of this phrase had become an understood joke between them. Writing about 'E's' possible reaction to reading Warren's metrical drama, *Orestes*, she said 'she may . . . like it & think that the author is not altogether as other men, save in his exuberant supply of "good-temper" or "good-nature", which was it? In that sort of way one is as bad as the other.' This harking back to a time when they had jokes together could only be nostalgia on her part, for in the same letter she wrote sadly about his having 'so fearfully suddenly shut the door in my face.' She emphasised strongly that her interest in him was in no way prying or unbecoming curiosity about his affairs, but 'real un-get-over-able anxiety' about him and how he was in himself. The increased distance between them seemed to have become permanent, and feeling this, she showed it by asking Warren not to read her new novel if it were published.

> 'For I think' she explained, 'it wd. now be very painful to me to think you had done so — Had I gone on seeing you often I wd. not have minded the least bit in the world — for I know really you wd. not misunderstand my travesty (is that a right word?) but now, I shd. every now & then fancy you would despise my silliness.'

Although she would not have put it in these terms, she was saying here that a level of discourse and a register suitable to those who meet often and share large parts of their lives, are no longer appropriate when they have drawn apart, and the parody she was planning (which is presumably what she meant by 'travesty') was on a different level from that on which they were now communicating.

She persevered with this second novel, which was eventually to be published with the title *She Was Young and He Was Old*. As she continued, she came to feel the need of some impetus, which she thought ought to have come from reviews. 'I am still going on with another but the utter want of criticism of the first makes me feel rudderless somehow.' She wanted to know exactly what Mr Davies had said about *Lover and Husband* in his correspondence with Warren about her, for, she said, 'I am just now stuck fast & want a shove one way or other terribly — that is why I teaze you to tell me these remarks now.' Even adverse criticism would be helpful — 'a bit of the most contemptuous would do me good and inspirit me.' She told Warren why she did not care for the criticism of a man she had recently met. Something

> 'prevents his liking to cut me up as he cd. do. He is sorry for me, I think. This is tiresome for I hoped for some kindly sharpness from so clever a man. I shall not see him again about it, as he won't be honest.'

We can see from this that critical feed-back was part of the creative process for her and not merely of commercial use.

Her work went steadily on. At the end of May she had 'only just done 1 vol'. She seemed to feel this was slow progress 'I can make my plots in my head, but I have no strength for the steady work . . . I can think alone or work alone but not both together now.' By 'work' here, she clearly meant the actual writing down of episodes in her novel which, she implied, she had already planned out in detail in her head. Years later she was to confirm that this method, which she seems to have adopted rather because of her weakened state than for any more literary reason, became her chosen way. In at least two articles about writing for children she talked about getting to know her characters thoroughly before writing anything down, and in one she specifically stated that this applied to 'stories for either old or young,' that is, both novels and children's books.[10] Ten days later she was getting on faster, would 'soon have finished the second volume' and was wanting to investigate possibilities of publication. By this time she had become disenchanted with Skeet, whom she now described as 'so wretchedly poor a publisher' who had 'behaved very badly.' She was, understandably, particularly annoyed when a friend, trying to get hold of a copy of *Lover and Husband*, found that several of the 'principal bookshops' got the reply from Skeet, that he had no more copies bound and had no intention of binding any more. Louisa had heard of its being 'a good deal read — provincially,' a phrase in which the word 'read' strongly suggests that she meant it had been borrowed from the libraries, not bought. This, together with Skeet's lack of interest in any further sales, is a concrete example of the effect of the mass purchases by Mudie's and other libraries mentioned earlier. Although Louisa had not 'got a halfpenny back' on her first novel she was still prepared to pay to give her second a start, but wondered in fact if money would do the trick. Her object was 'to get a good publisher who would do his best by it' though what she would have liked 'best of all' was, to get it 'into one of the magas'. By this she meant the increasing number of periodicals that serialised fiction, such as *Chamber's Journal* or *All The Year Round*. Later in her career she took great care to use every possible type of publishing opportunity for her children's books — journals, collections, annuals, book form — retaining the copyrights herself so as to maximise the chance of further appearances. In these first efforts over her early novels we see her learning the ropes. It is clear that she was feeling her way, for despite her statement 'I can pay for a chance which I shd. hope wd. repay <u>me</u> eventually,' in February she had declared 'I cd. never again <u>pay</u> anything.' The terms for *Lover and Husband* had been unfav-

---

[10] 'On the Art . . . ,' pp. 344–5; 'How I Write . . . ,' p. 18.

ourable for her — she contributed £50 and Skeet's expenses were the first charge against any profit. Because her correspondence with Warren declined quite sharply after June 1870, we have no further details of the publication history of her early novels. *She Was Young and He Was Old* was eventually published by Tinsley Brothers in April 1872.

In *Lover and Husband*, the heroine lived for some time in a small provincial town that Louisa called Mallingford. The nearest town to Tabley Grange was Knutsford, the protoype of Cranford, and Louisa appears to have drawn 'Mallingford' from the same source but she described it with a sweeping venom far from Mrs Gaskell's gentle and affectionate irony. At this time in her life Louisa could find nothing good to say about small town society as she had experienced it —

'. . . an intensely stupid little town. Dull, with a dullness that, to those fortunate people who have had no personal experience of small provincial town life altogether baffles description. And worse than dull — spiteful, ill-naturedly gossiping and conceited . . . Conservative of course to the backbone, in everything — the more objectionable and undesirable the object of its conservatism, the more stolidly, bull-doggishly tenacious grew Mallingford. Instance the long resistance to the introduction of gas lamps . . . the still prevailing cobble stones in the market place, the stiflingly high pews in the peculiarly hideous church, and last not least, the universally signed petition against that most noisy and blustering of innovations — the railway . . . the prevailing spirit of the little town, the placid stupidity, unrelieved save by occasional outbursts of party spirit, the ludicrous pretensions and would-be exclusiveness of its reigning families, the airs of the half-educated daughters of the same — these and many others of a similar nature would need a keener pen than mine to do justice to them — very laughable, very contemptible no doubt, were it not that from another point of view they strike me as very sad and lamentable.'

That this condemnation was meant as a serious comment on a real society, and not only as a contribution to 'a right understanding of my heroine's life,' can be seen from one of those direct addresses to the reader in her own person which, as has been noted [in chapter 3], was so characteristic of Louisa's writing.

'It may seem exaggerated to speak so gravely of the foibles and absurdities of country town society as it existed in Mallingford some few years ago, as possibly it still exists in other yet more "conservative" places of the kind. If it appears so I can only say that it comes naturally to me to speak seriously of things I have myself felt strongly — absurdities if you like, but worse than absurdities, for they have sprung from deep-rooted error, and their influence, again, has in its turn been an evil one.'[11]

The intense dislike of Knutsford society Louisa showed here was echoed by opinions in her letters. In March 1870 Richard was asked by 'those conservative people' to send them a copy of a circular Warren had written about liberty of voting and to supply them with the exact date of issue. The Ballot Act which secured secrecy of voting as a safeguard against intimidation at elections was not passed until 1872 and Warren's pamphlet was probably on this topic. Since the act was brought in by Gladstone and the Liberal Government, Conservatives would have been against it. These Knutsford Conservatives said they had approached Richard because he was the only Conservative Tabley tenant but Louisa was quite sure that they wanted the information to make mischief against the Liberals in some way, though she could not see exactly how. She was also worried lest any annoyance to or misrepresentation about Warren himself should occur. She wrote 'R is as staunch to you on all occasions, as if he was on your side.' (Warren's side in politics, she meant). This was something she really wanted Warren to know. A decrease in social intercourse between the Molesworths and the De Tableys had apparently caused local gossip.

> 'Of course everybody who has ever heard our small names hereabouts' wrote Louisa, 'thinks we were ignored by your family because of politics —but for this these conservative people wd. never have applied to R for information — & nasty things were and are said which of course I can't contradict, only I say nothing — but now & then I allude to your (you personally) & my husband's continued friendliness.'

Fearing that the conservatives were trying to use the Molesworths to do harm to the Liberal interest in this way did not at all imply that she thought she and Richard had an influential or important position. 'A chimney sweep wd. serve their purpose as well, if he had been a conservative & you had left off having him to clean your chimneys,' she said. It seems that political manoeuvering and efforts to blacken an opponent's name were much the same then as now. Louisa was disgusted. 'I knew the production of the circular shd do you good, not harm, but there is

---

[11] *Lover and Husband* vol. 2, pp. 144–5.

no knowing how the low type conservative (those sneaking, fawning hangers on) might make mischief out of it to spite Latham.' (Mr Latham had been Warren's proposer at the 1868 election.) In the end it appears that nothing came of the request to Richard for a copy of Warren's pamphlet. Louisa, however, continued to be suspicious of the original intention, writing to Warren 'but you see they must have seen a <u>chance</u> of using the circular spitefully or they wd. not have asked for it.' Louisa's opinion of the Knutsford conservatives is supported by Margaret Warren who wrote in her diary at the time of the 1868 election 'I have no heart to write about the Ball. I will <u>never</u> go to another Knutsford one. I cannot describe my feelings of defiance and fury! nor how nasty the Tories all were — all except Piers' and after detailing the 'nice & hearty' behaviour of this man she added 'How different from the spite of the others.'[12]

A further incident which brought Louisa into close contact with spiteful ill-nature was a threat of libel action against her, and perhaps the De Tableys. All the circumstances are not fully explained in her letters but the threat came from a woman who, Louisa said, 'I believe . . . <u>wd.</u> do it, if she thought it wd. injure me, whatever the consequences to herself'. Nothing came of this either, though she told Warren about it by way of warning. She was again disgusted, writing 'The letter is very insolent of course & . . . makes me feel as if some nasty snake had touched me.'

Another warning was about the Knutsford postmaster, who, she thought, was very curious about letters going from his office in the country post-bags. This kind of curiosity about the doings of the landed gentry had been the subject of one of her letters to Warren after their holiday in Wales in 1868. She wrote to tell him that a chance encounter and a chain of gossip meant that his presence with them in Bettws-y-coed had become known to various Knutsford people and the family of the agent, Mr Thomas.

> 'What I had to tell Mr Redrose [*a joke name for Warren himself*] is that that old something, Miss Holland, to whom I never spoke more than once in my life till she turned up here, heard through our landlady of his being here. She called at the door the day he arrived & with the idiotic communicativeness of her class, the landlady volunteered the information that he was with us — *Voilà*, how the thing proceeds! Certain

---

[12] M. L. Warren, *Diaries*, pp. 147 and 149.

Deans of Knutsford are expected to visit the lady aforesaid — She to Deans, Deans to Thomases — Thomases to etc. Disgusting is no word for it. Now you are forewarned. I will say anything you advise if the thing comes up.'

The tone here is the same as in her tirade against Mallingford. Her feelings about the spiteful, gossiping nature of Knutsford society are clear in both, but in the novel the generalised condemnation in a string of adjectives does not provide a sharp or memorable picture. For dissecting the stupidity and malice she inveighs against, her diatribe is a blunt instrument indeed compared with one of Mrs Gaskell's delicately witty remarks about her version of Knutsford. 'As we did not read much, and as all the ladies were pretty well suited with servants, there was a dearth of subjects for conversation.' [13] Louisa was right in saying that a keener pen than hers was needed to depict the disorders of society that aroused her indignation. Yet her attitude was to change. Looking back at this period, she seems to have experienced that nostalgia with which time can endue our feelings about the most unlikely things, even cobble-stones and poor lighting. In 1897 she wrote with tolerant and amused affection of the very things which had so annoyed her in 1869. She described

'a small town which gave one the feeling of its having in no way changed for the last century or two, and . . . of its being scarcely likely to do so for a few more hundred years or so. The railway gave it a wide berth, though the coaches had left off running; the ancient glories had departed, and there was no prospect of new ones replacing them. But it all seemed one to the good people of Bronstanton. The cobble-stoned streets remained in their rugged unevenness, with a good fringe of grass in the untrodden corners; some few and far between lamp-posts, innocent of gas, were all the provision for lighting up in the dark evenings; the shop windows were small-paned, and the show within prosaic enough. It was all old-world to the last degree, and strangely attractive in its way. Since those days it is entirely changed, and is now a busy bustling commonplace little town, with two railway stations on rival lines, and the 'last improvements' of every sort flourishing apace.'

She was even able to write kindly of high pews.

'The church is quite altered now, 'restored' . . . to its ancient and original beauty . . . but, for all that, there was something about the old state of

---

[13] Mrs Gaskell, *Cranford and Other Tales,* Smith, Elder, [n.d.] pocket edition, p. 17.

things, the high pews and all the rest of it, that fills me with a curious sense of pathos when I recall it.'[14]

But of course, her nostalgia for the physical characteristics of Knutsford does not mean that she had learnt to condone those things which, at the time she lived in Cheshire, so angered her as to spread disgust by association even over cobble-stones.

At the time Louisa was warning Warren of the threat of a possible libel action, she also had a 'great trouble' to tell him about — more illness in the family. 'It seems as if we are never to shake it off.' On her return from the visit to Bath with her mother and sister, Carrie, the youngest Stewart daughter, went down with measles, which she had caught there, having never had them as a child. She was 'frightfully ill' and on one day 'it was touch and go, very like my Violet last year.' Louisa must have felt that a ghastly replay was going on but happily the outcome was different and Carrie recovered. She was ill enough for her fiancé, Edward Broughton, to be formally summoned and Louisa much approved of his behaviour. 'I think it speaks well for her & him that he was able to soothe her wonderfully, even when half delirious — He has behaved with unusual unselfishness & good sense, though so very young himself.' So both her brothers-in-law gained her approval and affection. An interesting sidelight is thrown on her relationship with Broughton, and her respect for his opinion, by a remark in one of her letters to Warren during the absence of her mother and sisters in Bath. 'I have such a strong personal dislike to Rhoda Broughton from what ['Ted' crossed out] Edward B has told me that I have not read her red rose [sic], but I shall do so now.' Rhoda and Edward Broughton were distant cousins. Presumably Warren had recommended Rhoda Broughton's novel, *Red As A Rose Is She* (1870) to Louisa. Another echo of the previous year was that Louisa had to stay completely away from her sister so as not to carry the infection to her children. She said that she found this the worst of the whole anxious business. On 3rd June she saw her sister, but only her face at the window, 'for the first time for fully two months.' This does not necessarily mean that Carrie was ill and isolated for two months. The period mentioned could have included the time she was away in Bath. Louisa was again pregnant too — over three months at this time. Carrie 'was slowly recovering but very weak,' but by the end of the summer she was well enough to get married and

---

[14] *Meg Langholme* p. 172 and p. 111.

her wedding to Edward Broughton took place on 8th September at St John's chapel. 1870 was definitely a year of happier events for the Molesworths and Stewarts. After the christening of Charles' son, Morier, and Noel's birth, came Carrie's wedding. Then, in November, there was a double birth, for the middle sister, Agnes, became pregnant at much the same time as Louisa, and the sisters would have been able to support each other and compare notes, living as they did in the same village within easy reach. They had their babies within a few days of each other. Agnes had a daughter, Venetia,[15] who was to be her only child and on whom Louisa based the slightly spoilt little cousin Sybil in *Carrots*.[16] She herself had a son, Richard Bevil, which must have comforted her somewhat for the loss of Richard Walter the previous November. Caroline Broughton (later Walthall), like Louisa, but not Agnes, was to have seven children.

Just before Bevil was born, Louisa wrote a kind of farewell letter to Warren. She would have liked to see him to say goodbye 'more than much' but she obviously accepted that their ways were now drawing even further apart. 'You are going away for a long time, I hear. What may not be happening next, before I see you again, if ever I do!' This almost certainly refers to his move to London on his father's approaching second marriage, which took place on 26th January, 1871. Louisa intended to go on writing to him occasionally, but she knew it would be different. 'There won't be much in common to write about as to outside matters, for you know little of my daily life now, & I, nothing at all of yours — but still it is better than nothing — to me at least.' Her final words were truly valedictory, for it is virtually certain that she never did see him again, though they exchanged a few letters over the years.

> 'I wish I could tell you all I wish for you — or that if I could, it would do you any good — For you have done me a great deal of good, as I have often told you — Anyway you will always find me the same, for I could not be changeable if I wished — Thank you for your letter & everything.'

This letter was still addressed from 'The Cottage' so Louisa's prophecy about slow progress on the new house was being fulfilled. Unfortunately the only two other surviving letters she wrote before leaving Cheshire altogether are addressed merely from High Legh and hence shed no

---

[15] *The Times*, birth notice, 21.11.1870.
[16] VMI to RR, unpublished comments, 1.2.52.

light on the date of completion. In April 1871, according to the census, the Molesworths were living in East Legh Hall itself, but this must have been a very temporary measure to tide them over before their house was finished. Perhaps 'Mrs Edmond L' had come back from abroad and wanted The Cottage again. There was probably no room for them in West Hall either at this time because Charles and Janetta, with their two sons, two nurses and a lady's maid were staying there.[17] The other Stewart son, William, was also in the house, so West Hall must have been pretty full with the Stewarts' ten servants as well. Family sources say that around this time Charles went to China for a period, and it is likely that this visit to High Legh was in order to leave his wife and sons to the care of his parents. In October 1873 he stated in a letter that he was still on the half-pay list of the Royal Artillery and would continue so all his life, and also that he was senior partner in his father's firm (Barbour's, of Aytoun Street, Manchester). This suggests that the visit to China may have been a business trip on behalf of the firm, and not a military posting.[18] The son of a family friend looked back on Charles as 'a hero of my boyhood. I remember well his putting on for our amusement a Mandarin's costume with pigtail etc when he returned from the Chinese war.' This piece of evidence, while confirming that Charles went to China, does not prove beyond doubt what was his position there.[19]

At last the Molesworths moved into newly built Westfield, sometime in the second half of 1871. The name describes its position — in a field west of West Hall. This new home, built specially for them by Louisa's father, was about the same distance from West Hall as The Cottage, just along a short drive almost opposite the West Hall entrance. It was a solid, red-brick, typically Victorian house with lots of gables and chimneys. It had a separate nursery annexe of three rooms and was large enough to hold a good-sized family with a number of servants. The governess and four women servants (three of whom came from Scotland) listed in the census as present in East Legh Hall on 2nd April were almost certainly the Molesworths' own servants, not part of the

---

[17] The 1871 census lists two lady's maids, one of whom was born in Jersey. The assumption is that the first was Mrs Stewart senior's maid, and that the Jersey-born one was brought by the younger Stewarts from their Jersey posting.

[18] Unpublished letter from General E. C. D. Walthall to RR, 10.8.1957. In papers associated with *The Claimant* it is stated that J. H. Stewart 'once got a letter from Captn Stewart — merely a friendly one — from China — but did not retain it.' Letter from CS to JHS, 16.10.1873, *Claimant*, p. 3.

[19] Ranald Paton to RR.

Hall staff. Westfield was described in the 1950s as hideous, but attitudes to Victorian architecture have changed since then.[20] In contrast to the tree-surrounded West Hall, it stood rather bare and stark against the skyline with level views of fields in three directions. The main sitting room had two high windows, the larger facing across the garden towards the West Hall grounds and the other looking over fields crossed by the Knutsford-Warrington road. Louisa liked to sit and write in the latter window while her children were being taught in the opposite corner by the village schoolmaster, borrowed from the nearby schoolhouse.[21] Since they had a governess and presumably the village school had first call on the services of its master, this was probably only for certain special lessons. (The head of High Legh school at this time was one John Scofield Hudson.) It appears that living in their own houses as they did, the Molesworths were not acting in accordance with military regulations. Louisa was worried at the time of the libel threat that, if it was brought to court and so became public, 'it wd. probably raise the question and we shd be ordered in to the barracks, or lose the appointment, as there has been a new fuss about living beyond bounds lately.'

At the time of the move to Westfield, Cicely was getting on for eight, old enough to be excited and impressed by an occurrence relating to the Franco-Prussian war, which was taking place across the channel just at that time. A homing pigeon which had been shot, presumably by some English sportsman, fell into the garden of Westfield, and was found to be carrying a message in French, tied round its leg in the usual way. It was an appeal for help, reading *'O! bons Anglais, succourez-nous!'* English feeling was mostly pro-German then, but Louisa had strong French sympathies and Cicely remembered how upset her mother had been over the incident. She also handed the story on to her own children. Her daughter, who kept homing pigeons herself at one time, commented, when relating the event, 'The interesting detail is that the

---

[20] CP to RR, unpublished letter, 1.6.38, 'I do not remember Whalley Range at all, and only the West Hall and Westfield (the latter I know built for us by my grandfather Stewart before his death) before I was 9!' 1950s description in unpublished letter to RR from C. L. S. Cornwall-Legh, 1.11.52. I saw the outside of the house myself in 1996.
[21] Verbal communication to RR, by Miss M. K. Surridge, daughter of a former incumbent of St John's, who went to live in High Legh in 1884 and heard about Mrs Molesworth from people living there at that time who had known her. The sitting-room now has 3 bay windows, as it has been enlarged since Louisa's time by the demolition of a wall separating it from a former study. Information from the present owner and a sales brochure of the 1980s.

pigeon must have come in the 1st place <u>from</u> England (perhaps with a message) as a <u>French</u> homer wd. not fly back to England but to France.'

Louisa's father was becoming a worry to the family. He wrote such extraordinary letters in response to one business enquiry that his son was forced to complete the transaction on his behalf, writing in explanation that his father's mind was beginning to fail, and asking that nothing should be done to excite him as he was much confused. A memory from another source and a much later period was that he 'went as they say in Lancs "light in the head".'[22] This sounds like the beginning of dementia. Louisa might have been referring to it when she wrote 'I cannot possibly tell you how painfully some other complications have increased.' At least with such a staff of servants, there would have been no problem about looking after Mr Stewart. In July 1869 he had been hurt in a railway accident. Louisa said that it was not serious 'in one sense . . . but in another I am uneasy — His head was cut, & he was much shaken & jarred; & not being well lately, we are afraid of after effects.' It is possible that this could have hastened the onset of the confusion. Mrs Stewart's chronic state of ill-health was also distressing to her family, but as with any condition described generally as rheumatic, sometimes they thought she was getting worse, sometimes they were more hopeful. It was a pleasant contrast for Louisa to be able to write of Bevil as 'pretty and promising' at six months old, though he was 'strangely like' Violet, she thought, and hoped that he would not be so clever.

In 1872 Louisa would have been working on her third novel, *Not Without Thorns,* which was published in May 1873. It was now three years since Violet had died and she felt able to give her sorrow some literary expression. She was probably at last far enough from the event to use it in this way rather than simply to suffer it. Her characteristic direct address to the reader is here an impassioned outcry of grief.

'Oh, but the sunshine can mock cruelly sometimes! . . . And the flowers even! How heartless the daffodils are, and the primroses, and worst of all perhaps, the violets. How can you show your heads again, you terrible little blossoms, and in the self-same spots too, where last year my darling's voice cried out in rapture that she had found you, hidden in the very lane where, day by day, in childish faith she unweariedly sought you? Does she gather spring flowers now? Are there primroses and violets in

---

[22] *Claimant,* p. 13, and associated papers. Unpublished letter to RR from A. P. Rogers, son of the butler at West Hall, 24.11.1937.

the better land? There is "no need of the sun neither of the moon" in that country, we are told; "there is no night there," "neither death nor sorrow nor crying." Should not this satisfy us? But it does not. We long, ah! how we long sometimes to know a little, however little, more, to see if but for an instant the faces of the children playing in the golden streets by the banks of the crystal river.'[23]

Anyone reading this who knew about Violet would have made the connection and even a reader who did not know must have felt that it struck a peculiarly personal note.

In the same novel she described her own experience in the pain and bitterness of the resignation with which a minor character took the loss of her own daughter,

'who was as the apple of her mother's eye, whom she loved as strong natures only can love. And one day — one awful day — the little daughter died suddenly and painfully, and Margaret Hereward's heart broke . . . And all the outside world said "How sad for the poor Herewards" . . . and then forgot all about it, for the chief sufferer never reminded anyone of her woe. . . . In time of course, her mother came to learn that even with a broken heart one can go on living.'[24]

Again, when the heroine of the story said to herself that if something she feared came true, she would die, the author passed stern and bitter judgement on her youthful outburst, mocking

'the innocent arrogance of youth which cannot believe that ever a human being's sufferings equalled its own, or that the worst anguish is not that which kills, but that which is lived through. For in those natures which have the deepest capacity for suffering there is usually an appalling reserve of strength and endurance, and to such, dying is not so easy of achievement, as, fresh from their baptism of woe, they are apt to imagine.'[25]

Writing these passages may have been a kind of relief, but also, perhaps, a grinding on the aching tooth. In view of her grand-daughter's opinion, quoted earlier, about her resentment of grief, one cannot help but think that here she was describing her own nature, and her own reactions. In both incidents she emphasised the deeper suffering of simply going on living after such experiences and we remember that she said she could

---

[23] NWT, vol. 3, pp. 140–1.
[24] NWT, vol. 3, p. 79.
[25] NWT, vol. 2, pp. 63–4.

'always get up more strength for acute suffering than for chronic.' To illustrate her comment about her grandmother's attitude to grief, this grand-daughter told a story about a widow. 'A French priest visiting a lady who had been widowed some two years before — found her still secluded in her room in the deepest mourning — *Quoi, Madame, vous n'avez pas encore pardonné le bon Dieu".*' Louisa did not seclude herself to this extent but she too did not forgive God for a long time.

She was pregnant for much of the time while working on this novel and her second son and last child, Lionel Charles, was born in March 1873, two months before publication day. She must have started work on her fourth novel immediately after finishing the third, for she wrote the dedication to it in December of the same year. She was clearly more satisfied with her publisher, Tinsley, than she had been with Skeet, for they published three of her novels consecutively, as well as a short story in Tinsley's Magazine in December 1873. Writing had become a permanent, on-going part of her life and she may already have established the discipline she described several times in later years, of 'sitting down at a certain hour to your work' and just getting on with it, whether feeling 'inspired' or not.[26]

This was the year that Louisa's father died, at Fleetwood in August. The cause of death was given as apoplexy — what we would now refer to as a stroke — and the whole event was very sudden, a time of thirty minutes being specifically mentioned on the death certificate. The family had not expected it. 'He had been as you know ailing for some time past but we had not the least anticipation that the end was so near' wrote Charles to his half-uncle in Australia.[27] Mr Stewart's body was brought back to be buried at Rostherne in a grave next to his two Molesworth grandchildren. A memorial tablet to him was put up in the church at Fleetwood, and both this and the announcement in the local paper described him as 'of' High Legh and Fleetwood, although he had only ever rented property in both places. The paper gave him the title 'Esq.' and mentioned that he had been a Justice of the Peace for the County of Lancaster. He had definitely arrived in county society, at least in the opinion of those who wrote the notice. His son Charles was home from China, perhaps summoned by the news of his father's death, but anyway in time to prove his father's will as an executor. Charles apparently took over his father's tenancy of West Hall, and certainly

---

[26] e. g. 'Story-Writing', p. 164.
[27] *Claimant*, p. 3.

described himself as residing there.[28] His mother lived with him and his wife and children. Charles Augustus Stewart 'left a large fortune' according to his son. This was an accurate description, for his personal estate was proved at £150,000 and he also left considerable real estate. His son considered that his own position was now such that he would 'have about as much as is good for me' and was very doubtful whether he would bother to carry on the business.[29]

This secure financial position makes it certain that Charles' next action was not taken in order to increase his own fortune. He wrote to his father's half-brother, James Horne Stewart, in Australia, claiming that he had proof of General William Stewart's first marriage and of his own father's legitimacy. In doing this, he said, he was acting in accordance with his father's wishes, and with the advice of his mother, her brothers and his father-in-law. He wanted to be acknowledged as legal head of the family but was indifferent to the property held by his half-uncle in Australia, and suggested that a deed should be executed to vest in J. H. Stewart the legal possession of that property. Of course such a situation, if realised, would involve the acknowledgement by the latter of his own illegitimacy and that his mother's marriage had been bigamous. Naturally he took immediate steps to fight Charles' claim, and it is due to the very thorough investigations of the lawyer he employed in England, J. P. Bunting, that we owe the information about General William Stewart's life, liaisons, marriage and children that was used in chapter one. It is not necessary here to trace Mr Bunting's investigations in detail. He came to the conclusion that Charles believed sincerely in his own claim, although he himself had collected enough evidence to disprove it. The claim never came into the open in court, for less than a year after he had made it, Charles withdrew. No-one ever knew exactly why, though Mr Bunting thought a contributory reason might have been that he was seriously ill with diabetes like his elder brother. He was probably also alarmed at the kind of information being unearthed about his grandfather and father, particularly the undisputable evidence that his father was capable of wilful falsehood as shown by the false statement on his mother's death certificate in Holland.[30]

That Charles was earnestly convinced of the rightness of his father's

---

[28] In a codicil to his own will, 13.1.74.

[29] *Claimant*, pp. 3–4 and 87.

[30] Eventually Mr Bunting sent all the papers about his investigations to Mr J. H. Stewart in Australia. They were preserved by the family and used in the preparation of *The Claimant*, in which this whole story is told in detail.

case is suggested by his own will, made in September 1869. This was the year of his marriage, so it was an obvious step for him to take. The strange thing about it was his effort to make sure that nothing of his could be inherited by anyone, with one exception, connected either by blood or marriage with General William Stewart, 'late of Strath in North Britain.' This was, of course, his grandfather, but the relationship is not mentioned directly in the will. The exception was his own father, Charles Augustus Stewart, and his direct descendants. Charles provided for inheritance by his brother and sisters and their children in case he died without issue himself, but he then went further and named as heirs in, as it were, the third rank, Sir Noel Paton, a friend of the Stewart family, and his cousin John Wilson Colville, the son of his mother's sister Catherine and a trustee of Charles' will. He was living in Cheshire at this time, so he was an obvious relative to choose, even if it seems absurdly careful in Charles to provide for all his siblings and their children dying before he did, when Louisa had three children and Agnes was soon to be married. His own wife was pregnant too. But he did more than this. In case these two men should also die without issue, his estate was to be left to the President of the Royal Scottish Academy at Edinburgh provided there was no connection with William Stewart. And if there were, then it was to go to the next senior member and so on.

His will shows a really intense desire on Charles' part that no member of the Australian branch of the Stewart family should benefit by his own death. This seems very strange in view of the apparently friendly relations described earlier between Charles Augustus Stewart and his half-brother, James Horne Stewart, Charles' uncle. He and his family would be the natural beneficiaries after Charles' immediate family, his siblings and their issue, unless steps were taken to prevent it. It is difficult not to interpret Charles' action as a manifestation at the least of dislike, even of revenge. But for what? I would suggest that what prompted this will at that time was his learning, for the first time from his father, the full story of their relationship with William Stewart. He heard about his father's illegitimacy (or supposed illegitimacy, in his own view) and his grandfather's refusal to allow intercourse between his legitimate daughters and his illegitimate eldest son. He may also have felt that he was not going to enrich those whose wealth his own father would have been entitled to but for that illegitimacy, which was, of course, in his eyes only apparent. It must have been at this time that Charles came to believe his father *was* legitimate, that his grandfather's liaison with Isabel Innes had been a marriage, and this belief must have come from

Charles Augustus. Louisa did not know of all this. She only knew there was a mystery and that her father had promised they might learn all about it after his death.[31]

Sir Noel Paton, the Queen's Limner for Scotland (appointed 1866), appears a little later in Louisa's life as a personal friend and adviser in literary affairs. It is clear from the mention of him in Charles' will that he must have been well known to the Stewart family. He was born and brought up in Dunfermline so it is possible that the link went back to the Wilsons, and that he had first been the friend of Agnes Janet Wilson, the mother of Louisa and Charles. When Macmillan's started to publish Louisa's children's books, in consequence of which she got to know George Lillie Craik, a partner in the firm, and his wife, Dinah Mulock Craik, who were also friends of the Patons, references in her business correspondence with Mr Craik show that she already knew the Patons well and was accustomed to visit them. One of her grand-daughters owned a sepia pen and ink drawing of her, executed by Sir Noel. In 1878 Louisa dedicated a book to Sir Noel's wife, 'my faithful friend, Margaret Gourlay Paton.' The short story mentioned above, published in *Tinsley's Magazine* in December 1873, was based on events told her by Margaret Paton. It was a ghost story, 'Lady Farquhar's Old Lady', very well told, matter-of-fact in its careful detail, convincing and richly deserving re-issue in one of the collections of ghost stories that so often appear now.[32] Louisa liked ghost stories and was to write several during her life. This one used the theme, common to many such stories, of the appearance of a person in loved or familiar surroundings at the time, or the anniversary, of their death. Louisa might have originally 'collected' it from Margaret Paton in pursuance of her interest in strange coincidences. Her belief in her own second sight would have encouraged her both to hear and to write ghost stories.[33]

---

[31] MLM to DUC, unpublished letter, 8.7.1889.

[32] It was, in fact, re-issued in 1992, in *The Lifted Veil: The Book of Fantastic Literature by Women: 1800-WWI*. Ed. A. Susan Williams, Xanadu. 1854801902.

[33] M. H. Noel-Paton, *Tales of a Grand-daughter*, 1970, published by subscription. The story told on p. 25 as having happened personally to Margaret Paton is identical in essential detail with Louisa's 'Lady Farquhar', though much shorter. RR was told by M. H. Noel-Paton that her grandmother's experience was indeed the origin of Louisa's story. A footnote in a publication of the Society for Psychical Research mentions Louisa's story (referring to *Tinsley's Magazine*) as though it were a literal account of a personal experience, but she had clearly used her friend's experience as the inspiration for a literary product. *Phantasms of the Living*, E. Gurney, F. Myers and F. Podmore, 1886, Vol. II, p. 621, note.

In 1874 Louisa's attention was distracted from anything Charles was doing by the sale of Westfield and a move to Wales. Wales might have been chosen because they had enjoyed a holiday there, or perhaps more than one, but also because Louisa's sister Caroline and her family were now settled in North Wales.[34] One brief note from Richard to Warren is all that survives to tell us of the event.

Cae Maen   Penmaenmawr   North Wales   14 April 1874

Dear Warren, We have sold our home at High Legh & have taken this place for a year to see if it suits the children. It's only a small house but has a very fair garden with the sea in front & the mountains behind, with any number of ferns and wild flowers. If you would like to come down for two or three weeks in the summer we shall be very glad to see you (the fresh salmon & Welsh mutton alone ought to be inducements) and it wd. at all events be a change of air & scene. We shall very probably settle down here for some years. We shall never go back to Cheshire, as I have retired from the army as a Major & have given up my adjutancy of Militia. Mrs Molesworth sends kind regards, & I am always sincerely yours, Richard Molesworth.

Penmaenmawr, according to a local directory for 1876, was 'a village which is fast improving', and the mountains behind were the Snowdonian range. Richard's retirement may have been the cause of some discussion, if not downright disagreement, since, when it was mooted a few years earlier, both Louisa and her father were against it.

'R wants to give up his appointment, but now my father & I are against his doing so, unless for a better — It is no profit to speak of, but a young man as he is wd. certainly deteriorate without employment — for he is naturally most desultory — And the thing is more of an appointment & employment than it was — If I were dead he would be utterly broken down without some such interest.'

When she wrote this, in July 1869, Richard was 36 years old. Now, in 1874, retired and living on the Welsh coast, he was a month off his 41st birthday. With her father dead, perhaps Louisa's solitary opposition did not carry so much weight. Her low estimate of his pay is further

---

[34] H. D. Walthall (Caroline's daughter) to RR, 18.11.1937. 'She often stayed with us and she and her family took a house near Penmaenmawr for some time about the time when we came to live in Wales.'

evidence of how much they relied on her father and probably her own marriage settlements. What did this man of desultory and spasmodic character, in early middle age, do all day without employment? This may from now on have been another source of friction in the marriage. Richard tempted Warren to a visit with a vague mention of items he thought would interest him as a botanist — 'ferns and wild flowers' — but also with the delights of the table which he thought *ought* to interest him, probably because they would have been inducements to himself. But he did not come.

Richard's expectation of settling down for some years in Wales was not fulfilled. In October he and Louisa were in Normandy looking at a house they were thinking of taking. Louisa had mentioned to Warren five years before the possibility of going abroad for the whole winter and taking the children, so the thought of living abroad for a while had been in her mind for some time. She had very much enjoyed the holiday in Pau with Agnes, and said several times she would like to go back there. But the present plan came to nothing because, while they were still in Normandy, they received the dreadful news of Charles' death, not from diabetes as might have been anticipated, but from a fatal accident. He had gone to London to meet his brother William. A letter from Agnes to Mr Bunting suggests that this was to be some kind of reconciliation, for she wrote of the anxiety and sorrow 'Willie' had given the family by his 'careless idle life' and their hope for his future based on 'his bitter, and we trust, lasting repentance'. But William did not see his brother alive. Charles was going down the main staircase of the Midland Terminus Hotel at St Pancras Station when he tripped or slipped in some way, and because the balustrade at that point was so low, he fell right over it down to the corridor below, where he fractured his skull on the floor and died almost instantly. The coroner at the inquest said that 'mere architecture must give way to public safety.'[35]

One result of Charles' sudden death was that his own generation never heard the whole story of their father's origins and their true relationship with the Australian Stewarts. Louisa only knew enough to be aware that there was 'a family mystery' and regretted not knowing more. Fifteen years later she wrote

> 'Sometimes I wonder if it is wrong of me to want to know the whole
> of the story, as it does not matter now, & as my father & mother never

---

[35] Agnes' letter is among the papers associated with *The Claimant*. Report of the inquest, *The Times*, 9.10.1874.

told us all — But I know my father said we might know after his death, & but for my brother's fearfully sudden death, I should have been told all as he promised me — & it is rather fascinating to get to the bottom of a family mystery.'[36]

Charles' death was also, of course, a terrible shock to the whole family. They were even afraid it might have been too much altogether for 'our delicate fragile mother,' Agnes told Mr Bunting. But Mrs Stewart survived and begged Louisa and Richard not to go and live abroad during her lifetime. So at the end of the year Louisa wrote to Warren 'we are turning our thoughts to Edinburgh as a home — We hope to go there in the spring.'

During the few months remaining before the Molesworths left Penmaenmawr, Louisa had a wedding to organise. Minnie Wilson Morgan, who had returned from India when a tiny child, as an orphan, was now living with the Molesworths and was married from their house in Wales.[37] Louisa's father, besides mentioning Minnie affectionately in his will, had also left her £1,750, showing that his description of her as 'having been as a daughter to me' was not just fine words. She did not live with the Stewarts and Molesworths altogether, for her home as a child was in Edinburgh, but she was with them often enough and long enough to be mentioned as though she was a recognised and regular member of the household, who needed no explaining, in a letter from Agnes to Warren during the summer of 1868 (when she would have been about 15). This was the letter in which Agnes had asked Warren's advice about treating various skins sent by her brother from the Cape Colony. There were other, more upsetting, items in the box and, wrote Agnes, 'Carrie and Minnie screamed at the skulls and one very ugly monkey'. Minnie's wedding took place in the parish church of Conway on 24th March, 1875, and Louisa and her uncle, George Meldrum, signed the register as witnesses. This uncle, it will be remembered, was a connection by marriage, the husband of her mother's sister Marion, the widow of Henry Rutherford for whom Louisa's father first worked in Rotterdam. George and Marion Meldrum were Minnie's great uncle and aunt, and it was they who gave her and her brother a home on their return from India as orphans.

---

[36] MLM to DUC, 8.7.1889. Because the family was never told the true story, various traditions became current among C. A. Stewart's descendants, for instance, that his father was one of the Royal Dukes.

[37] Unpublished letter from Minnie's daughter to RR, 17.11.1938.

It was at the Meldrum's house in Melville Street, Edinburgh that Louisa stayed in the month before Minnie's wedding, in order to look for a house for her own family. Probably her aunt and uncle returned with her to Wales for the wedding, after the successful conclusion of her efforts. She wrote one of her now very rare short notes to Warren from Melville Street, announcing the projected move. The house she had taken was, she said, 'in most respects, I think, desirable, & very pleasantly situated.' But they could not move into this desirable house until 'quite the middle of the summer.' She was glad to have found somewhere at last — 'I am very wearied of house hunting' — but, she said, she had to do it 'as much travelling or any worry knocks Richard up so.' This suggests another likely reason for his retirement from the army — health, though the mention of worry also links up with her concern to keep annoyance and anxiety from him, because of the effect on his temper. Although Warren had not responded to Richard's invitation to visit them in Wales, Louisa still hoped he might come to see them in Scotland. The inducements she offered were negative ones — that he would not mind their plain ways, and that the children were not spoilt.

The three months the Molesworths still had in Cae Maen after Minnie's wedding included quite a lot of moving around. Louisa went to visit her cousin John Wilson Colville, who was now living in Marple, Cheshire, and both she and Richard spent time in London, though separately. They left Wales at the end of June and went to stay at the Stewarts' house in Fleetwood for the summer months. Louisa's mother, meanwhile, had settled, after her son's death, in Ulverston, just across Morecambe Bay from Fleetwood, and, as Louisa put it, 'a lovely neighbourhood — gateway to the lake country.' One of the Molesworth daughters stayed alone with her grandmother there until the family had completed the removal to Edinburgh, when her mother went to fetch her. In the event, 'quite the middle of the summer' turned out to mean the end of September, when at last they were settled again, intending to stay for a few years.

8

'Tell Me A Story'

A most important event for Louisa's writing career occurred before she left Wales, which was the acceptance of her first book for children, *Tell Me A Story*, by Macmillan and Co. in March 1875. It has more than once been noted in print that she said the idea of publishing for children was suggested to her by Sir Noel Paton.[1] It is clear that she was already writing for her own children from her account to an interviewer in 1893.

> 'I don't know that I should have thought of publishing the stories I wrote for my children if it had not been for a suggestion of my friend Sir Noel Paton. He seemed to think I had a power of making children interested and happy, and by his advice I sent something to one of the publishers, not really at that time caring much whether it was accepted or not.'

She enlarged on this in an article of her own a year later. Without naming Sir Noel this time, she said he had

> 'a clearer instinct than I had myself as to what I could do best . . . "Better do a small thing <u>well</u>," he said, "than a greater thing indifferently," when he had been criticising one of the novels that were my first launches into literature.'[2]

This discussion with Sir Noel could have taken place when she was in Edinburgh in February 1875, looking for a house, and the novel he was criticising was probably the most recent, *Cicely*, which had been published the previous July.

Without arguing about the relative merits of novels and children's books implied by Sir Noel's comments, we may note that he thought Louisa wrote novels 'indifferently'. Not badly, but merely as one of *The*

---

[1] Green (1961) p. 39, and (1969) p. 111.
[2] *Westminster Budget*, p. 24; 'Story-Writing', p. 163.

Saturday Review's group of English novelists 'of the average standard.' Other contemporary reviews gave much the same opinion. The first review of her first book, the paragraph about *Lover and Husband* in *The Spectator*, which she was grateful to Hutton for writing, ended with moderate praise. 'It is written with good taste, naturally and simply; the conversations are easy; the characters, if not profoundly studied, are life-like. . . . On the whole, we can recommend the book.'[3] A reviewer of *She Was Young and He Was Old*, while extremely annoyed at being deprived of a happy ending, still commented 'The author — whom we venture pretty confidently to set down as a woman — is an exceedingly graceful writer with a good deal of literary taste.' The same reviewer disapproved of *Not Without Thorns* because he disliked the view of marriage he thought was being conveyed and spent most of his review on criticism of women in society, not of this novel. He complained about

> 'that tone of mind in the sex which is the cause of half the unhappy marriages afloat — those marriages which begin well and end ill, no one exactly knows how or why. So long as women think that marriage means only courtship consolidated and uninterrupted, . . . & so long as they are unable to enter into the prosaic arrangements of companionable friendliness, they must perforce be unhappy.'

But he did say he was glad the book ended happily.[4]

The Spectator was more perceptive about the same book, seeing that 'the true and real purpose of the story . . . is not one of incident but of character' and praising 'Miss Graham' because she had 'boldly chosen the simple and difficult course of building the troubles of her story solely upon the "incompatibility of disposition".' He disapproved of what he called her 'loose English and provincialisms' and was amused at the mechanics of the plot, but on the whole 'we have not for a long time read a story we so entirely like.' His strongest positive expression of approval was still quite moderate 'It is very complete in its way, — of even power throughout, or rather what is very unusual, increasingly careful, thoughtful and interesting as the story proceeds.'[5] None of these comments could have encouraged Louisa to think she was destined to become a great novelist.

---

[3] *The Spectator*, 22.1.1870.
[4] *The Saturday Review*, 15.6.1872; 1.2.1873.
[5] *The Spectator*, 8.2.1873.

The Saturday Review critic's heavy preoccupation with happy endings in commenting on Louisa's novels encourages further investigation of the point. It is clear from the context that to him a happy ending equalled the marriage of the hero and heroine, but in fact, despite his expressed approval of *Not Without Thorns* in this respect, none of Louisa's first three novels have this kind of happy ending. *Lover and Husband* has already been described. The heroine of *She Was Young and He Was Old* marries a much older man in deference to her dying mother's fears for her future, and despite the introduction of a more traditional style hero-figure, she does not marry again on her husband's death. The marriage in *Not Without Thorns*, is a love match, at least on the heroine's side. But the main male character is 'the sort of man too, to whom it came naturally to try to attract any woman with whom he might be thrown in contact,'[6] and thus hardly qualifies for the epithet 'hero'. The whole thrust of the book is towards analysing how and why the marriage almost comes to grief through incompatibility. The 'happy ending' which gladdened the *Saturday's* critic is a very muted affair, consisting in the fact that the wife, having left her husband, is persuaded to return to him. She expects only dreariness, but another character comments at the end 'She is much happier than I ever hoped to see her,' although adding 'It is not the *sort* of happiness I should long ago have imagined would have contented Eugenia.'[7] Contentment and moderation are the keynotes, not 'living happily ever after;' coming to terms with everyday reality, not achieving a dream.

It was only with *Cicely* that Louisa, for the first time, ended a novel by bringing together a more sympathetic couple than she had hitherto attempted to depict, after a series of problems constructed to keep them apart. She headed her last chapter 'Friend and Wife' and allowed her heroine to whisper the time-honoured phrase 'I never really knew what love meant till I learnt to love you.'[8] But even in this apparently traditional romance, the chief interest lies in the presentation and development of two characters, Cicely and her cousin, a French girl. This has to be done in such a way as to make the most dramatic event of the book, the breaking of Cicely's first engagement, seem thoroughly believable. Cicely must be lovable, a true heroine with whom the reader can sympathize or even identify, and yet with good reason for seeming

[6] NWT, Vol. I, p. 20.
[7] NWT. Vol. III, p. 242.
[8] *Cicely: A Story of Three Years*, Tinsley Brothers, 1874, Vol. III, p. 296.

sufficiently cold and withdrawn to justify her cousin's belief that she is not really in love. The French girl, Genevieve, must be attractive and winning, yet also selfish and mercenary, with both sides of her character based on plausible evidence. And Louisa did achieve this aim, though the plot seems rather disjointed, particularly in the move from France to England in the first volume. She was fond of setting episodes in France, and of using French, not just words and phrases but whole sentences. She was also clever at giving a French air to a speech in English by using literal translations of French structures and word order. However, she recognised herself that there was rather too much of this in *She Was Young and He Was Old*, her second novel. The admission was made in a letter to G. L. Craik of Macmillan's, where, in commenting on a critique of her work, she mentioned some of the points on which she agreed with its author. One was 'there is certainly too much French though it came naturally for I have lived a good deal among French people.'[9] It is interesting, from the biographical viewpoint, that in these 'Ennis Graham' novels Louisa concentrated so steadily on development of character and on difficult relationships, particularly, though not exclusively, between men and women. They certainly seem to be personally revealing in a way that her later, more competent and more commercially successful novels were not, for she continued to produce novels in spite of her move to writing for children.

When Sir Noel Paton gave Louisa that piece of advice about changing from the indifferently written adult novels that gained only moderate praise to children's books, he may, of course, have been visiting her in Wales. The comment about the 'power of making children interested and happy' sounds as though he had seen and heard her telling stories or reading her own stories to her children. The grown-up Juliet had taken part in the 1893 interview when her mother had mentioned Sir Noel's advice, remembering how she and her brothers and sisters loved her mother's stories, and that 'the MSS were read from behind a newspaper, and we never knew at first that they were mother's.' This trying out of her stories first on real children, usually her own, became a permanent feature of Louisa's method of work. It is mentioned in another published interview in 1897, where the place of concealment for her manuscript was described as being between the covers of a book, and she recommended it in her articles on writing for children. She herself was 'greatly helped by seeing the effect' which the stories made

---

[9] MLM to Craik, 17.7.[1875].

on the children, and she thought that 'the criticism, which you may be pretty sure will not be too flattering, of a group of intelligent boys and girls is invaluable.' Later on she was to test her stories on her grand-children and a cousin remembered her telling stories to a family group on holiday.[10] So telling stories, originally to her brothers and sisters, and later to her children, for amusement, merged into reading mss to them with a more utilitarian purpose, which never wholly supplanted the entertainment aspect.

The group of children around her, asking for and listening to her stories, is reproduced in the introduction to *Tell Me A Story*, and also shown in the delightful Walter Crane frontispiece. The Meg or Madge who appears as the narrator of 'Goodnight, Winny', the second story in the collection, is there, 'dear Madge with her thick fair hair and soft kind grey eyes.' The description fits Juliet rather than Cicely, for she did indeed have fair hair and grey eyes.[11] But this is an early and simple example of a habit that Louisa's grand-daughter mentioned several times — the amalgamation or transposition of real people and events for use in her stories. Meg, in the story which Louisa said was literally about her own children, is clearly intended to be Cicely, the next sister to Violet, but Louisa chose to give her Juliet's appearance.[12] Some of the stories that make up *Tell Me A Story* had been published before, or so Louisa said, in one of her articles about how she wrote her children's stories. The same point was made in the section about her in a book on writers for the young, published in 1900, clearly based on a personal

---

[10] *Woman at Home*, p. 193–4; Bainton; p. 344. CB to RR, 6.1.1952; GDL to RR, 4.5.1938.

[11] TMAS p. 1. CB to RR, 6.1.1952, 'Mrs Prinsep [= *Cicely*] the eldest and most beautiful was dark, my mother had masses and masses of wonderful golden hair and green grey eyes'. Eye colour of MLM's children: 'The only blue-eyed ones were Violet the eldest and Bevil the youngest [*prob. mistake for Lionel who was in fact the youngest*] . . . All the others were grey-green or hazel.' VMI to RR, 3.1.52.

[12] Letters to RR from several of Louisa's relations show clearly that they all liked to think some of the stories were about them to the extent of claiming to be the original of a character or event, and denying the claim of another cousin. VMI listed several events as quite true, and particular characters as definitely being real people, writing about *Hoodie*, for instance, 'These children were definitely her children', VMI to RR. But VMI also wrote (which helps to explain the confusing counter claims) 'She really did mix up her characters — her own thoughts & doings — her children's ditto & a little fancy,' and 'my grandmother — her mother her mother-in-law & her children are often mixed up together. I can sometimes make a guess at the original but not always. She not only mixed up the people, but also sometimes the generations,' and 'Herr Baby was Lionel & Bevil "mixed up".' VMI to RR 3.1.52.

interview. But, as yet, no-one has discovered in which magazines these supposedly earliest publications for children appeared.[13] Such very definite assertions about previous publication contradict her earlier statement that she would not have thought of publishing what she wrote for her own children if Sir Noel had not suggested it. Yet her letter to Macmillan's[14] on 2nd March, offering the manuscript of *Tell Me A Story*, made no mention at all of previous publication, which the publisher would have had to know about in order to negotiate the copyright with whatever periodicals were involved. She used Sir Noel Paton's name as her introduction, saying that he 'kindly mentioned to you my wish to have published a little book of children's stories,' and then described the stories themselves as 'exceedingly simple; several of them are not fiction at all, & all of them have in the first place been "criticised" by my own children at home.' In the rest of the letter she discussed the size of the book, offered to write one or two more stories to fill it out if necessary, and mentioned her first four novels. She also enclosed a *resumé* of the various reviews of these, 'by Sir Noel's wish.' Presumably he thought Macmillan's would be impressed by the published criticism of her work so far. All this urges the conclusion that nineteen and more years later, Louisa had forgotten the details of her first children's book, and was mistaken in saying that any of the stories had been published before.

She was pleased when Macmillan's accepted the manuscript within a month and in a letter written on 1st April, thanked them for giving her an answer so quickly. The firm contrasted favourably in her mind with both Skeet and Tinsley Brothers, publishers of her first four novels, for the speed of their response, their offer which she thought 'fully as liberal as I could expect' and their reputation. While not mentioning her earlier publishers by name she made clear her opinion of them and of Macmillan's, writing 'My experience in such matters has not been such as to "spoil" me I assure you, for hitherto I have not succeeded in getting my novels published by first-rate firms'. She must have thought rather better of Tinsley than of Skeet, for she placed three novels in succession with them, but, with one exception, never used them again

---

[13] 'How I Write . . .', p. 17; Robson.

[14] It would seem suitable to refer in the plural to a firm which was founded by two brothers and carried on by their sons and grandsons, and therefore to write Macmillans'. However, since Charles Morgan, in his centenary history, *The House of Macmillan*, (Macmillan and Co. Ltd., 1943) regularly names the firm in the singular — Macmillan's, I have thought it better to follow his usage.

after she had started with Macmillan's, seeking out instead other outlets for work they or she did not think suitable for their own list. The exception was the only adult poem by her that has yet been found in print, published in *Tinsley's Magazine* for August 1875. Called *Nature and Love*, with a stanza for each season, it has been interpreted as expressing the birth and death of her love for Richard,[15] but the Winter stanza could just as easily be read as referring to Violet:

> Where are the flowers? Where the leaves?
> Where the sweet zephyrs' gentle breath?
> Where mellowed fruits and golden sheaves?
> Dead, dead; all icy bound in death!
> Is Love too dead? Hence, needless pain!
> Love dead? Ah no, not so with Love;
> *Love* only dies to live above.

And in the Spring and Summer stanzas, the writer is clearly addressing a woman — 'O maiden mine', 'my queen'. It is hardly great poetry, and after this one effort she seems only to have published sentimental verse for children. Years later, in March 1893, she asked Mr Macmillan (this would have been Frederick Macmillan) to get one of his clerks to help her trace this poem, as she had lost her own copy and had her letter to Tinsleys returned from the Dead Letter office. She wanted to do something else with it, which implies re-publication elsewhere, so she thought well enough of it herself to be prepared to see it in print again. Interestingly she said it appeared under her own name, whereas in fact the name in the magazine was still Ennis Graham. And she could only give the date of publication as sometime between 1868 and 1878, so it probably had no strong emotional association for her. Perhaps it was only an exercise in the romantic style.

Four of the stories in the collection Macmillan's had accepted came into her category of 'not fiction at all.' One of them was the 'narrative of my own children, as literal as it can be,' which has already been used as a source for details about the time of Violet's death. Louisa did not often describe a child's death, unlike many other Victorian writers, and since the weight of the evidence already presented comes down on the side of 'Good-night Winny' being one of a group of stories not originally written for publication but for her own children, it seems likely that its purpose was to give them, and especially Cicely, loving and cheerful

---

[15] Green, (1961) pp. 29 and 38; RR also favoured this interpretation.

memories of Violet, and to help them come to terms with her death. So there is no harrowing death-bed scene, only Meg/Cicely's saying 'good-night' to her sister through the bedroom door, because of the fear of infection, without realising it would be for the last time. Maternal grief is hardly touched on — the focus is on the child's bewilderment and final realisation of parting 'what it would really be to be without her,' her grief precipitated, realistic touch, by a piece of sticking plaster.

'And just then my eyes happened to fall on the little piece of black sticking plaster that [Violet] had put on my thumb only two evenings before, when she had hurt it without meaning. "Mamma, mamma," I cried, "I *can't* stay here without [Violet]."'[16]

In a later story for children Violet's illness is described in much more detail, bearable because Hoodie, the child in the story, survives.[17]

Cicely's daughter wrote 'Of all her children I think Violet was perhaps the most dearly-loved, the first-born — even in my youth 30/40 years later my grandmother (if she would speak of it) cd. remember every little detail of her life and death.' When *Tell Me A Story* was published, six years after Violet's death, Louisa dedicated it to her, 'To a memory, A. V. G. M.' but the story, she told an interviewer, 'was written while the facts were fresh in her mind'.[18] So we may picture Louisa and her children grouped together for a story reading session at any time during those six years. 'Mary Ann Jolly', the fourth piece in the collection, was the story from her mother's childhood, described in the first chapter of this biography, and the factual part of 'The Reel Fairies' derived from her own games with her mother's workbox. Cicely's daughter was quite certain that Violet and her own mother had also played games with the cotton reels in Louisa's workbox, so this is another straightforward example of the amalgamation already referred to. The last story in the volume, 'Charlie's Disappointment', was also based on real life, particularly as far as the child who had crying fits is concerned.[19] 'Con and the fairies' uses the traditional theme of a child stolen by the fairies, who have the spite and childish malice typical of some traditions. 'Too Bad' is an exchange story, in which a complaining child learns the

---

[16] TMAS, p. 64.
[17] VMI to RR. 3.1.52. 'Hoodie's illness was Violet's, but alas it ended in death.' *Hoodie*, Routledge, 1882, ch. 12.
[18] VMI to RR, 3.1.52; *Woman at Home*, Dec. 1897, p 194.
[19] CP told RR that this story was about themselves; see 'A Ramble about Childhood', p. 294, for the crying child.

blessings of her own situation by being made to experience someone else's. In this case the exchange is effected by magic, but Louisa re-used the theme several times, more successfully, both with and without the magic machinery.[20]

In this first children's book, Louisa found one of her many narrative voices for children at once. She writes as though talking to them, in a seemingly artless, almost clumsy manner at times, using a range of linguistic devices, such as childish colloquialisms and made-up words, rambling, interrupted sentence structures, inverted commas or explanations for difficult words and frequent italics reproducing the emphatic intensity of child speech. The direct address of writer to reader which we have already seen as characteristic of her was here and afterwards aimed at the fictional child listeners and through them to the real readers (or listeners being read to), encouraging them to participate in the story. The effect conveyed was that of a 'warmly inviting auntly voice' drawing the reader into the fictive circle of listening children.[21] She also differentiated between narrative personae — the aunt of the introduction, who tells most of the stories, 'speaks' differently from the child narrator of 'Good-night Winny'. And this difference continues and is strengthened in later books, where it is always clear, not only from the specific statement of the author about her characters, but from the narrative style itself, whether the narrator or implied narrator is an adult or a child. Only in one other book, *Summer Stories* (1882), did she ever overtly repeat the device of a group of children brought together specifically in order to listen to stories, and that was a more elaborately planned structure, sustained throughout the book, which was intended for older children. But in all her children's books the implied presence of the fictional child listener, mediating the story to the real reader, is maintained.

It has been said that Mrs Ewing pioneered the technique, in narrative address to children, of adopting the persona of a child narrator, with *A Great Emergency* (1874) offered as the earliest example.[22] But as we have seen, Louisa wrote 'Good-night Winny' in 1869 or '70, while the facts

---

[20] *Great-Uncle Hoot-Toot*, SPCK 1889, *Sheila's Mystery*, Macmillan 1895, and *The Ruby Ring*, Macmillan, 1904.

[21] Sanjay Sircar, 'The Victorian "Auntly" Narrative Voice and Mrs Molesworth's *Cuckoo Clock*,' *Children's Literature*, 17, ed. Butler, Higonnet and Rosen, Yale University Press, 1989 by The Childrens' Literature Foundation. This article offers a particularly interesting, detailed analysis of Mrs Molesworth's narrative style, applicable to all her books for children, not just *The Cuckoo Clock*.

[22] Barbara Wall, *The Narrator's Voice*, Macmillan, 1991, pp. 86–7.

were fresh in her mind. The tone is uneven — some of the sentiments still seem, despite the declared age of the narrator as twelve, to be coming from a lovingly condescending adult. But Louisa does manage to convey the directness and sometimes the bewilderment of a child's experience, and much of the text succeeds in communicating on equal terms with the supposed child reader/listener. 'All our frocks and hats and jackets were exactly the same, and except that Winny was taller than I, we should never have known which was which of our things,' for instance.[23] This first experiment with the form was not an isolated one. She wrote several other short tales with a child narrator, and seven full length child-novels in the same way, trying out different styles for different ages, and in most of them having some very specific reason as to why a child should be writing a story at all, such as wanting a more interesting subject for a schoolroom exercise or making a record of unusual events in the family for other members.

The success of *Tell Me A Story* 'was so great as quite to surprise me, and make me determine to give to stories *for children* all the time I could then spare for writing,' wrote Louisa.[24] So she had hardly had time to settle down in her new home in Edinburgh before the success of her first children's book spurred her on to start another. *Tell Me A Story* came out in November and it was probably the Christmas sales which first made her aware of this welcome result. Her main contact at Macmillan's right from the start was G. L. Craik, whose first wife, Dinah Maria Mulock, was the author of *John Halifax, Gentleman*. Louisa's relationship with Craik moved quickly on to a more than business footing, as can be seen from letters she wrote to him, ostensibly about the publication of her books, which quite often became both lengthy and 'chatty'. Their shared Scottish nationality (and accent) was probably a help towards getting more closely acquainted and she must have admired the energetic way he threw himself into his work — 'a man full of energy and character.' He became a partner in 1865 and 'stayed in the firm until his death forty years later and was still a legend among the older members of staff yet another forty years on. "Is your hearrrt in your worrrk?" he would demand of them as he passed their desks.' His second wife wrote, after they were both dead, that her husband had known Louisa 'very intimately'. [25]

---

[23] TMAS p. 41.
[24] 'How I Write . . .', p. 17.
[25] Morgan, p. 69; A. R. Craik to RR, 3.1.1938.

The easy establishment of friendly relations would have been partly because of her introduction by Sir Noel Paton, whom, as mentioned previously, they both knew well. Sir Noel's diary for 1875 mentioned the Craiks and their adopted daughter several times, referring to them as George and Dinah, on holiday with the Paton family in Western Scotland at a house called Ardmay on Loch Long, near Arrochar. Mrs Craik and the child were there for three weeks. Louisa mentioned this visit twice in her letters to Craik about the publication of *Tell Me A Story*. She had been invited too, but the business of moving house prevented her, though she was expecting to see the Patons for a short time in the week before they left for Ardmay, perhaps because she herself had to go to Edinburgh about the new house. She sounded rather wistful about her missed holiday. 'I am so glad that Ardmay seems to have been decidedly a success — I have longed to join the friends there for a day or two but it is out of the question I fear.'[26]

Craik was also sympathetically interested in Louisa's novels and took the trouble to get some fresh criticism for her on one of them. She was grateful for this and asked if he could do the same for *Cicely*, saying, as she had told Warren, that even adverse criticism would help her — 'I am not cowardly about vivisection.' She told him that she had another novel 'in slow process', being 'barely through the first volume.' This was *Hathercourt Rectory*, and because of her decision to concentrate on children's books the process became slower still and it was not published for another three years. Louisa was also very pleased that Mrs Craik 'liked my little stories' for she had long admired her. The chosen illustrator's work was another source of pleasure to her. She disclaimed any ability to be an artistic judge of Walter Crane's work, but particularly appreciated his 'extreme care and thoughtfulness.' She meant that he had actually taken the trouble to read her stories and had 'forgotten no trifles mentioned . . . Even to the slippers beside "Winny's" cot.' Craik had introduced her to Walter Crane in his office during a visit she made to London in April.[27] Louisa and her children all liked Crane, the two families became friendly and he saw quite a lot of the Molesworths.[28]

The house that Louisa had taken in Edinburgh was 25, Royal Terrace. The terrace had been built in the Regency style some time in the 1820s.

---

[26] Noel-Paton, p. 67; MLM to GLC, 21.8.[1875].

[27] Walter Crane, *An Artist's Reminiscences*, Methuen, 1906, p. 157.

[28] CP in conversation with RR; CB to RR, 12.8.57. Unfortunately this rests on bare statements of fact from the two elder daughters with no anecdotes.

Number 25 rose in three storeys above a basement with iron railings and steps down to a basement area. There were two rows of three sash windows over the ground floor, and a pillared pediment hiding the slope of the roof. The arched front door opened on to broad steps leading directly to the pavement. This was a very different home from the country houses with gardens to which the family were accustomed. But Louisa described the surrounding area to Warren in September 1875, when attempting to persuade him to visit them, as 'hardly like a town . . . being the healthiest & most picturesque & unfashionable side of Edinburgh,' so there were compensations. Royal Terrace was and still is, on the north edge of Calton Hill, with gardens falling away quite steeply in front and behind. There were (and are) houses on only one side of the terrace, so the inhabitants had an uninterrupted view. The national monument on the summit of Calton Hill lies behind the Terrace and a 1907 guidebook says that from this point

> 'one can descry the fair lands of Fife lying across the "Silver Streak", the blue outlines of the Ochils in the far north-east, . . . the straggling lines of the Pentlands and the Moorfoots, the rounded knob of the Bass with the sugar-loaf-like mass of North Berwick Law, while far down at the mouth of the Firth can be traced the faint outlines of the Isle of May looming like a ghost through the haze of distance.'[29]

One can see why Louisa said Royal Terrace was hardly like a town.

She also said, to two different correspondents, that the main reason for the move to Edinburgh was her daughters' education.[30] The school that the girls went to was actually next door to their own house, in Number 26, run by various maiden ladies, at first the Misses Du Plessis and Black and then the Misses Murray and Remmers. In the Edinburgh directory there were forty other schools in the category 'boarding and day schools' where this one was listed, as well as long lists of collegiate institutions, public schools and private schools, so they were spoilt for choice. Number 26 was a little more imposing than Number 25, with a row of classical columns topped by Corinthian capitals along the facade, reaching from the first floor to the roof. Perhaps Louisa chose Number 25 because of the convenience of having a school next door. The girls who were at school with Cicely and her sisters knew of Louisa's writing activities and were rather proud to have 'the daughters of an

---

[29] *A Pictorial and Descriptive Guide to Edinburgh*, p. 130.
[30] JBLW and GLC.

authoress' as fellow pupils. They were remembered as attractive girls. Cicely also had violin lessons in Edinburgh, which might not have been so easy to obtain in Penmaenmawr.[31] Louisa knew this area of Edinburgh from her childhood and youth, for her uncle and aunt Meldrum used to live in York Place, just down the hill from Royal Terrace. Melville Street, where they were now living, was rather further away, at the other end of Princes Street, off Queensferry Street, but not impossibly far for family visits. The Patons too were now just down the road in comparison with the distance between Wales and Scotland, for their house at 33 George Square was about one and a half miles to the south of Calton Hill. As they had lived there since early in their married life, Louisa probably knew the way there well. She may even have been on holiday with the Patons on one of their annual visits to the West Coast when she first met Richard.

New acquaintances as well as old friends made up the Molesworth's social circle. As one example, they got to know their family doctor and his wife and children. Dr William Taylor lived and practised in 67 York Place and the children played together often enough for the doctor's sons to catch whooping cough from Bevil, and pass it on to the whole family. A daughter of William Taylor and his wife wrote in after years that the two families became intimate. She said that the relationship was sufficiently close for the Taylors to have photographs of Louisa and her mother, whom they met when she visited her daughter, for Richard to present Dr Taylor with a large prayer book and for Louisa to confide in him to some extent over her marital problems. Mrs Taylor thought that Louisa was charming and that her mother was a dear old lady.[32] Another old lady, who remembered playing as a little girl with the Molesworth daughters in the Terrace gardens, also remembered the two little boys in short fur coats, going for a walk along Royal Terrace with their nurse, whom Louisa used as the basis for her inset story of 'the two funny little trots' in *Carrots: Just A Little Boy*, the book she was working on during her first months in Edinburgh. The old lady described them as the sons of a doctor who lived near. It is natural to assume from this that these children were Dr Taylor's sons, but in the record

---

[31] Letters to RR in answer to her advertisement in *The Scotsman* in 1938, from a woman who was at school with the Molesworth daughters and from Cicely's violin teacher; Edinburgh and Leith P.O. Directories, 1876/77, and 77/78. Description of Nos 25 and 26 from a personal visit.

[32] Unpublished letters to RR from H. W. Taylor, daughter of Dr Taylor.

of 'a talk' with Louisa, published in 1906, the interviewer wrote 'As to the "tiny trots", they were two children whom Mrs Molesworth used to see in Edinburgh. She never knew them but she always watched them with interest.'[33] Thirty years on she could have forgotten that she knew who they were but the identity of the trots can only be an interesting speculation.

Carrots was written and published within the twelve months following the appearance of *Tell Me A Story*, and since Louisa was writing to Macmillan's about the positioning of the illustrations in August 1876, she must have sent them the manuscript two months or so earlier, for Crane to have had the time to make his contribution. *Carrots* is a full-length book, not a collection, but it does have several inset stories in different styles to suit the narrator. An old nurse tells the children about their mother's childhood in an easy chatting manner with plenty of interruptions from the little listeners, while an older sister reads a story to them from a book which seems to date back to the eighteenth century, so stiff and formal is it, so full of moralisings and long words. The children have to make an effort to understand at all and the younger one, Carrots himself, gives up. They are much more at home with 'the two funny little trots' — a story written by their aunt and read to them partly because 'it would help her to judge if other children would care for [it],'[34] just as Louisa herself would have been reading this very book in manuscript to her own children. But we cannot therefore say that 'auntie' in *Carrots* 'is' Louisa, only that Louisa used some of her own behaviour to build up the character, for we have already noted that Cicely said 'uncle' was a copy of Agnes' husband, Major Goring. As well as this very competent switching of styles in *Carrots*, Louisa showed that she was able to present the world from the child's point of view, as though she remembered exactly what it was like to be four or five. She made clear how puzzling things could seem, how reluctant or even unable the small child was to explain its thoughts and feelings to the grown-up world, how misconceptions could lead to real unhappiness. The very simple plot of *Carrots* is based on this last idea — six-year-old Carrots is believed to have stolen money and to be making his misdeed worse by denying it. The problem turns out to be simply a total mis-understanding of language — he denies he has taken a sovereign (which had fallen into his toy drawer by accident), because he thinks 'sovereign' is the name of a game about kings and queens.

---

[33] *Quiver*, p. 675.
[34] *Carrots*, p. 204.

Carrots was an even greater success than *Tell Me A Story*. It came out in December 1876 and Louisa heard of this 'signal success' while she was at Pau for a period during the winter of 1876–77. She remembered, for the benefit of an interviewer, that Archibald Constable, the publisher, had met her and asked if she knew that the book was selling extremely well. ' "Carrots" had won his way to the heart of the public' said this interviewer.[35] The book certainly became the one by which she was best known during her lifetime. One indication of its popularity was the frequency with which it was used as the book mentioned on the title page of her other works in the little advertising phrase 'Author of . . .'. Macmillan's, her main publishers, had, by the time she stopped writing, produced forty titles by her. Twenty-four of these used the 'author of . . .' phrase, listing two or three of her other books, apparently those considered to be the best-known. (The other sixteen had no mention at all of other books by her on their title pages.) Twenty-one of these examples, including books published as late as 1906, had *Carrots* in first place. *Carrots* remained a Macmillan title during Louisa's lifetime, yet eleven of the 18 other firms who published her work after it came out, acknowledged its popularity by often placing its name on the title page of her books, instead of always using, as might have been expected, another title by her which they had published themselves. A further measure of the affection in which *Carrots* was held can be seen from a survey of the prize and library selections of the London School Board in the twenty years after its inauguration in the early 1870s. *Carrots* and *The Cuckoo Clock* (her next book, 1877) 'were so popular that a stock of two thousand copies was used up within a year and had to be re-ordered.'[36] Louisa herself, looking back from 1906 in a letter to Macmillan's, tried to explain the popularity of *Carrots* in the following way. 'You see when "Carrots" came out, there were very many fewer books for children than is now the case — it perhaps struck a new vein to some extent, for without being conceited, I do think it has been greatly copied!'[37]

The child hero of this most popular of her books, was based partly, Louisa said, on her youngest son, Lionel.[38] The person who chiefly misunderstood Carrots was his father and Cicely wrote after her mother's

[35]   *Quiver*, p. 675.
[36]   J. S. Bratton, *The Impact of Victorian Fiction*, Croom Helm, 1981, p. 195.
[37]   MLM to Macmillan's, 26.2.1906.
[38]   *Quiver*, p. 675.

death, that though her father mostly did not appear in her mother's books, Carrots' father, Captain Desart, was the most like him. He is presented in the story as hot-tempered and hasty, kind but very strict with the children and unable to perceive why all children should not be treated exactly alike, whether they are self-willed, self-confident, bold and matter-of-fact, or timid and fanciful. We do not know that Louisa intended Captain Desart to be a portrait of her husband, but Cicely certainly saw this as her father's character. One of the other, younger, daughters was frightened of her father as a child, and when grown-up told a cousin that all the children had been terrified of him.[39] Perhaps the younger the child, the more frightening were the violent rages Richard could get into.

Another feature of Richard's character, which seems to have come into greater prominence during the Molesworths' time in Edinburgh, was his irresponsibility over money. One of Sir Noel Paton's sons, who remained friendly with Louisa to the end of her life, remembered this period as having been a rather anxious one for her 'with Molesworth's extravagance and eccentricity.' He repeated a story that he had heard from Louisa herself at the time, which we may imagine her telling as a joke against herself. She had apparently warned Bevil not to allow his father to be extravagant. Since Bevil was only five or six at this time, it seems more likely that she had told the child, more simply, not to tease his father to buy things for him. However it was, Bevil had got it into his head that his father must not spend money. Consequently he refused to be taken on a tram. The cable tramway was fairly new in Edinburgh, and because the tramcars were gaily painted and looked important and expensive, Bevil annoyed Richard by making rather a scene in the street. So Louisa's warning recoiled on her in the child's bad behaviour and this may have been the point of the story as she told it. A more serious feature of Richard's extravagance was his habit of buying expensive presents for his wife that they could not afford. She then had the embarrassing task of going to the tradesmen and asking them to take the things back as she could not pay for them. 'The fact was' wrote Mr Paton, 'Major Molesworth had no idea of money.'[40] We remember his living in a hotel instead of lodgings when on a tour of duty at Hythe and Louisa's twice repeated comment on how expensive Hythe had been

---

[39] GDL to RR, 25.5.1938; CB to RR, 28.1.1952.
[40] Ranald Paton to RR. The Edinburgh Tramway Company commenced running November 1871.

and her anxiety about his not being good at 'fending for himself'.[41] All through her life she was careful and exact about money, both outgoing and incoming, punctilious about the prompt payment of bills, and concerned to make the best possible bargain over her books. There are many letters in her correspondence with Macmillan's showing an earnest, almost over-sensitive desire to have all financial arrangements very exactly and punctually carried out.

With such characteristics, Louisa must have found it particularly difficult to fulfill the role of wife to a man who 'had no idea of money.' Cicely's daughter, comparing the characters of her grandmother and great-aunts, wrote that Caroline was 'much more placid and easy-going than either of her sisters.' Since she was the youngest of the Stewart siblings, she had been able to tell her great-niece quite a lot of family history. Agnes had a very lively imagination, a passionate interest in people and their affairs and loved a good gossip. 'She would pull up her chair and settle down to talk with (almost) a 'grin' of delight.' Caroline thought that she would not have minded Richard's financial irresponsibility nearly as much as Louisa did. 'I believe Aunt Agnes was much more like my g.father,' wrote her great-niece. 'I remember Aunt Caroline saying that it was a pity she did not marry Richard as they wd. probably have been quite happy and "gone bust" together. (Aunt C did not say "gone bust" but that was the general idea!)'[42] Agnes, however, had only one child to consider. Few women in Louisa's position, with a brood of young children to bring up, could have contemplated the prospect of 'going bust' with equanimity. The success of her books for children would have comforted her in this respect, with the prospect of another source of income.

In 1877 the Molesworths spent the summer with Mrs Stewart in Ulverston, very quietly. Louisa wrote to Warren from there at the beginning of August to suggest that since he did not seem to want to visit them in Edinburgh, he might prefer the Lake District. After leaving Cheshire, Louisa persisted in trying to persuade Warren to visit, on one occasion writing quite a long letter explaining that he need not be reluctant to come for fear of the painful memories the meeting might evoke, for he 'might absolutely depend' she said, upon her recalling only the pleasant parts of his association with them. It was not just Louisa who tried to keep up the relationship. Richard too roused himself,

---

[41] See the account of Richard's posting to Hythe in chapter 6.
[42] VMI to RR, 24.1.1952.

after the failure of his invitation to Wales, to write from Edinburgh in January 1876, urging Warren to stay with them for a while. The inducements he offered were practical — the journey might be accomplished comfortably and without fatigue in one of the London and Leith steamboats at a quarter of the normal cost, quietness would be achieved by sending the children to stay with their grandmother and old Burgundy and 'capital' black-faced mutton would be on the menu. Typically Richard or typically male? Perhaps a little of both, but neither of the invitations was successful, and we have to recall that friends of Warren's such as Grant-Duff and Watts-Dunton said that the older he grew the more of a recluse he became.

Louisa had at this time already finished a third children's book, *The Cuckoo Clock,* which was in process of publication when she wrote to Warren from Ulverston. She described it to him as 'just coming out', but like the other two, it was published in December to catch the Christmas trade. Her concern with the financial return made her tell Warren that children's books 'pay better than novels, that is to say for about a tenth of the labour I get as much money.' She hoped he might take an interest in this new venture of hers, but was rather doubtful as to whether he could work himself up to reading a child's book. She offered to send him one if he could, 'as I think you <u>might</u> like it — or some of it. You remember the old mouse and lion story?' This was a reference to the story of the mouse who freed a lion from a trap by nibbling through the cords that bound him, which she had more than once used to suggest that she, small and unimportant as she was, might help, entertain or otherwise do good to one as important as he was. This reminiscence immediately brought to her mind a way in which she hoped she might still be of real use to him, namely with Macmillan's, her publishers. Her offer was very hesitant, however, and prompted purely by her own relationship with the firm — 'I am on very intimate terms with some of the firm and have received the greatest kindness from them.' As soon as she considered *his* position — 'your being so appreciated as you are — your poems I mean'— she was sure her being of use in this way was most improbable. In fact she re-opened the letter especially to apologise for her presumption.

'I <u>trust</u> what I say about my connection with the Macmillans' firm will not seem presumptuous or officious to you — for of course you know everything and everybody of literary authorities — But it is not often one meets with such <u>kindness</u> of the kind I now can count upon in this one instance — & sometimes that sort of thing is of use even to great "swells", in a literary sense — I can never forget how kind you were about my first novel, poor old thing — it did pretty well in the end.'

This tentative offer to Warren is of particular interest, in that it shows how early in her career as a children's writer Louisa felt herself to be on close and excellent terms with Macmillan's. She was also obviously thinking of being able in some measure to repay Warren's kindness to her.

It was mentioned in the chapter on her childhood that the story of the nodding mandarins in *The Cuckoo Clock* had been suggested to her partly by the memory of a miniature cabinet she had owned as a child and partly by an elaborate Japanese cabinet belonging to one of her sisters as an adult. When she was small Louisa had often thought how delightful it would be to be able to climb right inside this miniature cabinet of hers, as she made Griselda do in the book.[43] It seems more likely that the larger Japanese cabinet belonged to her younger sister Caroline than to Agnes, and that a visit to the Broughtons at Wistaston Hall could have been one of the seeds from which the book grew, because one of Caroline's daughters wrote 'yes, our cuckoo clock did give my aunt the idea for her book, which was written the year after the clock, a genuine Black Forest one, & still in good order, was given to us as children — She often stayed with us.' This evidence is not as straightforward as it looks, for Cicely contradicted it, saying that her cousin was 'quite wrong about the "Cuckoo Clock" . . . It was written two or three years <u>before</u> they had one, from one <u>we</u> had as children.'[44] And, which must carry more weight than the opinions of any of her children's generation, an interviewer learnt directly from Louisa that 'the ever-delightful "Cuckoo Clock" . . . was taken from a clock possessed by the authoress herself.'[45] But the solution to these contradictory memories may be that the Broughton/Walthall family had a tradition of personal association with the book, which they wrongly linked with their clock, when really they should have made a connection with the Japanese cabinet.

The clock, and the cuckoo in it, is the framing device which links together several fantasy episodes, all also connected by their happening to the same child. The book is more firmly structured than *Carrots*, but

---

[43] *Quiver*, p. 675b.
[44] Helen Walthall to RR, 18.11.1937; CP to RR, 9.5.1938.
[45] *Quiver*, p. 675b.

each section is still sufficiently complete in itself for reading aloud to a child at one sitting. The cuckoo itself is an astringent bird, given to making disconcertingly tart and ambiguous remarks, rather in the style of the Cheshire Cat and the caterpillar in *Alice in Wonderland*, which could well have influenced Louisa, having been published ten years before her own first children's book came out, though there is no surviving reference to her opinion of it, or even to her having read it. The unpredictable, mysterious, sharply-spoken yet kind at heart character is one that Louisa continued to use in her fantasy stories,[46] and one that has origins further back than *Alice* in beast fables and folk tales. E. Nesbit's Psammead, Phoenix and Mouldiwarp, bad-tempered, good-hearted, acid and puzzling of tongue, are later figures in this tradition, and since Nesbit's first biographer said that she was a fervent admirer of Louisa's, it is possible that the cuckoo plays a part somewhere in their ancestry.[47]

The Cuckoo Clock is the one book by Mrs Molesworth that has remained in print, not continuously, but continually, until the present.[48] The Puffin Classics edition of 1988 described it as her most famous book, and now Jane Nissen Books is re-publishing it in September 2002. Judging by the 'author of . . .' test, it began to catch up with *Carrots* during her lifetime, but its position as first has been acquired since her death. It is usually this book which any writer on children's literature who mentions Mrs Molesworth chooses to discuss, whichever other titles are also included. Marghanita Laski called it in 1950 'the book by which she is known to English-speaking children throughout the world' and R. L. Green, also calling it her most famous book, said that it 'set her in the forefront of writers for children.'[49] Since it has received so much attention, I do not propose to discuss it further here.

It was in 1877 also that she published a short story for children called 'My Pink Pet'. It appeared in *Aunt Judy's Magazine* in November, which was probably her first contact with this periodical. In one way it was a kind of companion piece to 'The Reel Fairies' in *Tell Me A Story*, for both stories describe children who are passionately involved in enacting tales from what they have read and heard, using for dramatis personae,

[46] For instance, Dudu the raven in *The Tapestry Room*, North Wind in *Four Winds Farm*, the old woman in *An Enchanted Garden* and others.

[47] D. L. Moore, *E. Nesbit: A Biography*, Ernest Benn, 1933, p. 148.

[48] It is now on the internet. See note at the end of *List of Unpublished Manuscript Sources*.

[49] Sircar; Laski, pp. 65–68; Green (1969) p. 110.

the one her mother's cotton reels and the other a collection of shells. These two stories were almost certainly part of her oral repertoire in entertaining her children, for they are based on her own activities as a child, as we saw when describing her childhood. 'My Pink Pet' links up with her second children's book, *Carrots*, too, in that its rather stilted and elaborate language in places recalls 'The Bewitched Tongue' in that book, which was read to the child characters from an old volume belonging to a previous generation. As a tiny example, the child Lois in 'My Pink Pet', when in a temper with her sisters, exclaimed 'Unnatural sisters that you are, to jeer and mock at me' which might just as well have been uttered by Elizabetha in 'The Bewitched Tongue' who regretted her anger with her brother in a manner hardly more formal — 'my words were but the momentary expression of my vexation.'[50]

At the end of 1877 the Molesworths were again in Pau and this time they had left Edinburgh and made a definite move to France. Several reasons lay behind this decision. Cicely said, late in her life, that the family had lived abroad a good deal for the sake of her father's health,[51] and certainly Richard had been 'rather seriously ill last June' as Louisa told Warren when she wrote to him from Ulverston in August. Her own health had been a problem for a long time after Violet's death, and the arthritic complication associated with scarlet fever from which she had suffered was a condition likely to recur. Pau at that time was a recognised resort for invalids, whom the warmer climate was supposed to help. A later guide-book praised its 'delightful and healthy climate' and asserted that 'at all times Pau is an ideal resort for convalescents and nervous patients.'[52] The choice of this place for their winter home, as opposed to any other suitably warm resort, was presumably influenced by Louisa's knowing and liking it from previous visits. We know that they had been planning to take a house in Normandy for a period in 1874 when the news of her brother's death changed their plans. The fact that her mother then begged them not to go abroad during her lifetime suggests that the Normandy house had been intended as a home, not simply a holiday lodging, so living abroad had been in their minds for some time. A further and more complex cause lay in the increasingly difficult relations between Louisa and Richard. By the end of

[50] *A Christmas Posy*, p. 45; *Carrots*, p. 117.
[51] CP in conversation with RR.
[52] F. Muirhead and M. Monmarche, *Southern France*, The Blue Guides, Macmillan, 1926, p. 385.

another two years or so, they were legally separated and the circumstances leading up to this perhaps encouraged them to move abroad. Such an unusual step might be less uneasily taken if they were not under the immediate eyes of friends, neighbours and relations in Britain. This time, too, Louisa's mother went with them, as we know from Louisa's mentioning the fact in letters to two different friends.[53] As well as not wanting to be separated from her daughter and grandchildren, Mrs Stewart may have thought she could be of use to Louisa during what was clearly going to be a difficult time. It is also possible that Louisa wanted to move to France for financial reasons. She believed they needed to be careful about money and it was accepted that living on the Continent was cheaper for the British, something casually mentioned by Trollope, Thackeray, Charlotte Yonge and other novelists as a fact of life for their characters. From 1821 until the first World War, while Britain was on the gold standard and the London foreign exchange market held an undisputed pre-eminence, acting as a clearing-house for international payments for the whole world, the exchange rate was very much in favour of British travellers and dwellers abroad.

That a possible separation was already in the air at the time the Molesworths were leaving Edinburgh is shown by evidence from Dr and Mrs Taylor's daughter. She said that her parents liked both Richard and Louisa, regretted the separation and hoped that it might be prevented. Mrs Taylor used to say, if the affair was spoken of in her presence, that it was incompatibility of temper and no doubt there were faults on both sides. Dr Taylor never spoke about the matter until just before his death, because as a doctor he had learnt to keep absolute silence about other people's business. Louisa must have valued this characteristic, and years later she celebrated it in one of her children's books by the sympathetic portrayal of a doctor who was extremely careful to discourage gossip about his patients, because 'it might do great mischief.'[54] Louisa confided in Dr Taylor to the extent of asking him to keep a bundle of letters for her. Dr Taylor only mentioned this at the end of his life because he felt he ought to find out what she wished him to do with these letters, which he described as having been given to him at the time of her separation from her husband. This shows that he had known before she left Edinburgh of what might be coming. The letters were returned to her (in 1916) at her request and

---

[53] MLM to JBLW, 14.10.[1883]; MLM to Professor Williamson, 1.2.[1885].
[54] MLM, *The Next-Door House*, W. and R. Chambers Ltd., 1893, p. 33.

probably destroyed. When Louisa went to say good-bye to Mrs Taylor she had with her Lionel, who was then four, and he was encouraged, very reluctantly, to present the Taylors' two and a half year old daughter with one of his toys.[55]

In 1881 Louisa published *The Adventures of Herr Baby*, a story for small children which describes a whole family travelling to the south of France or perhaps Italy, to stay for the winter because of the grandfather's health. Without going into detail about what might be 'true', it is possible to see that her own experience in moving her whole family to Pau must have been drawn on here. She portrayed vividly the getting up 'long before it was light', the drive to the station, the long train journey arriving after dark in London, 'standing together on the bustling platform, dimly lighted up by the gas lamps, which looked yellow and strange in the foggy air of a London November evening,' having tea in 'the strange big station room' and then travelling on to one of the channel ports where they spent the night before crossing the channel and going on via Paris to 'Santino'. This could not have been meant directly for Pau since it was by the sea, but the children's experience of living in a foreign town with a warmer climate was brought in. The whole nature of travelling is summed up in children's terms when, before they set out, the mother reproves one of the girls for being so snappish over having her hair done. 'I don't know how you will bear all the little discomforts of a long journey if you can't bear to have your hair combed.'[56] The children in the book took their pets with them on this long journey, two canaries, a bullfinch, and two dormice, which added somewhat to the difficulties of travelling. In real life, although Louisa was not very fond of animals herself, she loved her children to have them and Cicely told her own daughter that her mother 'was an angel about all their animals in their French and German travels. Everything was always taken.'

The family was established in Pau before Christmas and stayed on for some months into 1878. Louisa was pleased to find that her books were known to some extent there too. She made a new friend who was very enthusiastic about *Carrots* and eager to read the other two. This friend urged her 'to try to start them at one of the booksellers,' so Louisa wrote to Craik giving him the address of a 'very intelligent Italian' bookseller, a Monsieur Ariza. She hoped that Craik could make some

[55] Miss H. W. Taylor to RR, 19.2 and 23.2.1938.
[56] MLM, *The Adventures of Herr Baby*, Macmillan, 1881, pp. 66, 84, 87, 63.

kind of tactful offer to supply her books, for, she pointed out, 'once my story books are started here they might sell every year among the English.' She was aware that such a suggestion was not normally in an author's province for she apologised in case she had done anything against business etiquette, but was obviously sure that Craik would not really mind. She was always eager for her books to sell. The 'very nice' new friend was the Honourable Mrs Haines, twenty years older than Louisa, whose husband had died four years before after a career in India, and whose father 'old Lord Gough' as Louisa described him, had been a distinguished Field Marshal and general, also in India. Although this letter to Craik was, in her eyes, 'a decidedly business letter,' Louisa still knew he was about to go north and sent him 'all sorts of messages to those you will see in Edin.' who will care to hear of me.'[57] Perhaps she was homesick, but, if so, it was, as she told Warren when she and Agnes were in Pau in 1869, clearly for 'the friends one has to leave,' not the place.

The Molesworths rented a house in Pau, the Villa Marie-Jeanne, and it was there that Louisa finished *Hathercourt Rectory* at last, as the dedication to Margaret Paton shows, with the address and date 'Villa Marie-Jeanne, January 1878.' This was the first of her books to be published under her own name, in the form 'Mrs Molesworth,' and all subsequent books by her came out with this name on the title page. Even her first three children's books had been described as by 'Ennis Graham.' She probably decided to make the change at this point, because *Hathercourt Rectory* was her first publication after moving to France. She had also begun work on *Grandmother Dear*, about the adventures of three children travelling to the south of France with their grandmother and aunt, punctuated by stories told to the children by different adults in the book, as in *Carrots*. She dedicated this book 'To *our* 'Grandmother Dear' A. J. S.' that is, Agnes Janet Stewart, and a Molesworth cousin said the grandmother in it was indeed drawn from her own mother. Reading it is like being present at a celebration of Mrs Stewart, both in appearance and character.

> 'When she smiled, all the children agreed together afterwards, she looked more like a fairy godmother than ever. She was really a *very* pretty old lady. Never very tall, with age she had grown smaller, though still upright as a dart; the "November roses" in her cheeks were of their kind as sweet

---

57 MLM to GLC, [Jan/Feb. 1878].

as the June ones that nestled there long ago — ah! so long ago now; and
the look in her eyes had a tenderness and depth which can only come
from a life of unselfishness, of joy and much sorrow too — a life whose
lessons have been well and dutifully learnt, and of which none has been
more thoroughly taken home than that of gentle judgement of, and much
patience with, others.'[58]

Agnes Stewart was sixty-eight at this time, and her photograph suggests
that this description is no exaggeration. She had a fine face, indicating
both humour and tolerance, and the possibility that in her youth she
had been beautiful. The presentation of the relationship between the
grandmother and the children in *Grandmother Dear* suggests that her
relationship with Louisa's five children was both wise and loving. She
must have shared in the story-telling too, for Louisa wrote that in
Grandmother Dear 'there are little tales of rather old-world life which
are all what were told to me of and by my own grandmother and
mother.'[59] She probably listened to her mother re-telling these same
stories to her own children at the time she herself was writing them
down for a wider public. The deeply affectionate relationship between
the grandmother and grandchildren in the story was true for the living
family. Juliet's daughter said that, far from her mother remembering
any particular nurse with affection, ' "Grandmother Dear" who was
with them a lot was the person she really loved, and was <u>definitely</u> the
person the book was drawn from.' In one episode, 'The Six Pinless
Brooches', Grandmother was shown acknowledging that she still had
much to learn, to the surprise of one child. She also much regretted
her hastiness with another child, over the comically eccentric plan she
had made to stop herself from being so careless as to possess, all in the
same broken state, the six brooches of the chapter heading. Cicely said
that this episode was quite true, the owner of the brooches being her
sister Juliet, who 'really loved' her grandmother. One of the foundations
of this affection was perhaps the readiness of her grandmother to admit
herself in the wrong and to try to understand thoroughly what was
going on in Juliet's head.

It was probably during this period in Pau that Louisa, looking in the
windows of an old curiosity shop, was so taken by 'a very pretty old
French pastelle' portrait that she bought it. A few years later she was to

---

[58] *Grandmother Dear*, pp. 6–7.
[59] MLM to Edward Salmon, 12.10.1886.

base her story of the French Revolution, *The Little Old Portrait* on this picture. Since she definitely stated that she owned the original portrait,[60] it seems likely that the episode in *Herr Baby* where auntie was so strongly attracted by the portrait of a very little girl in a shop window, was also drawn from Louisa's own experience, particularly since the description of the pictured child in both books is almost identical. She dwelt in such a lingering way on the discovery of the portrait and the strange feeling it aroused in auntie, and to a certain extent in the children, to imagine the rosy childish face growing old and what its history might have been, that one feels she was showing her readers the genesis of the later book, giving life as it were to her own later words. 'There are instances in which the most trivial incident or impression suggests a whole story — a glance at a picture, the words of a song, a picturesque name.'[61]

But Pau was only a winter home, for warmth during the cold months, and sometime in the spring or early summer the Molesworths moved north again, to Normandy, as they had planned some years before. They took a house in Caen where Richard's and Louisa's ways finally parted.

---

[60] MLM to Macmillan, 18.10.1915.
[61] 'On the Art . . .', p. 345.

9

France

The house in Caen was called the Maison du Chanoine, and although Louisa lived there for barely two years, the dedications of three of her books bear that address. It was in the centre of Caen, near the Abbaye aux Dames founded by Matilda, wife of William the Conqueror, and presumably stood in the similarly named Rue des Chanoines which led directly to the Abbaye. In the 1920s it still existed, 'a typical high-roofed greystone "Gothic" looking Normandy house, evidently very old. Quite "town-y".'[1] But Caen was very largely destroyed in the Second World War and Louisa would not recognise it if she could see it today. The old house in *The Tapestry Room*, one of the three books mentioned above, was based on the Maison du Chanoine.[2] There is no detailed description, only an impression of a large, rambling, old house with thick walls, a mysterious room hung with very old and partly faded tapestry and a beautiful terraced garden shaded by old trees at the back.

The Tapestry Room was dedicated thus: '(By Permission) To H.R.H. Vittorio Emmanuele, Prince of Naples, Crown Prince of Italy. One of the kindliest of my young readers.' This little prince, about ten years old at the time of the dedication, had sent a message to Louisa by a friend of hers who was 'then resident in Italy and acquainted with the Court circle.' Louisa wrote that he had told her friend that

> 'one of my earliest books, *Carrots*, . . . had amused and interested him at a moment when he was specially in want of entertainment, for it was just at the date [*9*th *January 1878*] of the death of his grandfather, the great Victor Emmanuel, and his little namesake had not been allowed to go out riding or driving as usual for several days. He did not know how he would have passed the time but for *Carrots*, he said. He wished Mrs Molesworth to know this, and he also wished to make a request to

---

[1] VMI to RR, 24.1.1952. VMI had seen the house 25 years before writing this letter.
[2] GDL to RR, 4.5.1938.

her. Would she write another book as soon as possible — (not, as one might have expected, of further details of my little hero's boyhood, but) — to tell how "Carrots" brought up his own children when he became a big man and was married!'[3]

Louisa did write another story about Carrots and his own children, but not until 1909, when *The February Boys* was published. It seems very likely that the dedication of *The Tapestry Room* was by way of consolation for the prince, because she had not written the book he had wanted at a time when he could have enjoyed it.

When Louisa went to live in Caen, she already had a contact there. This was Marie Thérèse Hettier, to whom she dedicated *Miss Bouverie*, another of her three-volume adult novels, from the Maison du Chanoine.[4] In the dedication Mme Hettier is described as 'my dear friend', but in 1906 when asking Macmillan to send Mme Hettier a copy of her latest book, Louisa referred to her as one of her old French cousins. A son-in-law of the 8th Viscount said that 'Mrs Molesworth's friends at Caen were the Hettiers. Old Madame Hettier claimed relationship with the Molesworths through the uncle of William the Conqueror!'[5] As the account of the Molesworths in Burke does not go back beyond Edward I, it seems likely that this cousinship was more an affectionate fiction than a reality. But Louisa was probably not just going along with Mme Hettier's ideas about her descent. She loved France and liked to feel that she had some part in the country. The dedication of *Miss Bouverie* to Mme Hettier describes the book as 'this little story of her country and mine,' surely a proud and affectionate claim. There is a tone of pride too, in her remark to Craik, excusing the excessive amount of French in *She Was Young and He Was Old* because 'it came naturally for I have lived a good deal among French people.'[6] The Molesworths may well have chosen Caen to settle in, as opposed to any other town in Normandy, because of this connection with the Hettier family. Possibly Mme Hettier helped them with finding a house to rent.

The statement that the house in *The Tapestry Room* was taken from the real one in Caen, was made by a cousin, Richard's cousin, who first

---

[3] 'A Ramble about Childhood', p. 294. This story also appeared in the *Westminster Budget* article.
[4] *Miss Bouverie*, Hurst and Blackett 1880, 3 vols.
[5] Athelstan Riley to RR, 23.2.1938. He was the husband of the 8th Viscount's eldest daughter.
[6] There is a detailed and appreciative account of *Miss Bouverie* in Laski, pp. 60–61.

came to know Louisa intimately in 1883, when she herself was a girl of eighteen, only three years after Louisa left Caen. Her name was Gwen Molesworth and she was a daughter of the Rev Samuel Molesworth, the 8th Viscount and Richard's first cousin. Their fathers had both been brothers of the old 7th Viscount, whom Louisa had mentioned affectionately in her letters as the old uncle who was so kind to them. The Rev. Samuel also took a kindly interest in their affairs. During the summers of their time at Caen the Molesworths took houses by the sea for a few weeks and the 8th Viscount visited them at one of these near Bayeux. On this visit he 'strongly advocated the separation' between Louisa and Richard 'who had become very difficult.' The main problem was the violent temper but Gwen Molesworth also said that at Caen Richard posed as a bachelor and gave beautiful presents to his lady friends, though he did not bring them to the house. 'I never heard that they were disreputable' she commented, which is probably a politely euphemistic way of saying that these friends were indeed ladies, and not prostitutes or *demi-mondaines*.[7] The presents suggest that his worrying extravagance was continuing. Clearly things had come to such a crisis that Richard's own family felt a separation would be best. This did not disturb the family's relationship with Louisa and she remained on close terms with many of them — the Viscount's daughters, Richard's brother and the Viscount himself. When his second wife died in 1905 Louisa wrote 'she was one of my best friends.'[8] In view of this, the Molesworth family cannot have thought that Louisa herself was in any way greatly to blame.

Separation was a sufficiently unusual step at that period for much uneasiness, pain and even ostracism to result, especially for the woman. Louisa would have needed the explicit support of Richard's family to carry her through. A writer in *The Saturday Review*, whose opinion, that English novelists were bound to be moral, was quoted in chapter 7 in a discussion of Louisa's first novel, illustrates, in the same review, the kind of public opinion she was up against.

'In our opinion wives ought to live with their husbands even if it should be proved that their conduct has formerly been highly reprehensible and that their character is still not so good as it was supposed on the wedding-day, and the fact that great hardship may result from hasty marriages to

---

[7] GDL to RR, 4.5.1938.
[8] MLM to GLC, 22.1.1905.

bad young men is not sufficient to prove that our laws are un-Christian and tyrannical.'[9]

The sister-in-law of a later friend of Louisa's, when writing her memoirs, had this to say about the fate of women who defied public opinion.

'In those days an unwritten law demanded that anyone living apart from her husband should practically be as much guarded and chaperoned as an unmarried woman. How strange it seems now, when people separate on the flimsiest basis and still continue as society queens!'

She was looking back from 1925 to her early teenage days in the 1880s and writing with particular reference to a cousin, Lady Henry Somerset, whose own separation led to her being 'wounded by the coldness of so many former friends.'[10]

The consequences for a woman of separation from her husband was something Louisa had considered very carefully when she was writing *Not Without Thorns*. Her heroine, Eugenia, finally ran away in an access of misery, first to her sister and then to a hotel by herself, with little thought of how her action would appear to the outside world. But events brought home

'even to her uncalculating inexperience, something of the personal suffer-ing, the bitter deprivation, the indefinite suspicion which must attach themselves to the purest and noblest of women, when she voluntarily abandons her home. There may be cases, doubtless there are such, where a wife has no choice, where duty itself, deaf to all suggestions of expediency, relentlessly points out the way to abandonment of the post bravely battled for to the last — but such cases are rare, and the women to whose bitter experience they fall must have suffered too terribly to be sensitive to loneliness or monotony or half-averted looks.'[11]

At the time Louisa wrote that passage, she may not have been applying it to herself, but it shows that she knew what kind of thing to expect when the final decision to separate was made in Caen. She did not run away and she did have her mother with her, as well as the definite advice of the Rev. Samuel. All the same, she probably received her ration of indefinite suspicion and half-averted looks, although her mother's presence, by providing the necessary chaperonage, would have protected

---

[9] *The Saturday Review,* 12.3.1870, review of novel *No Appeal.*
[10] Laura Troubridge, *Memories and Reflections,* Heinemann, 1925, pp. 61–2.
[11] NWT, vol. 3, p. 185.

her from the worst of Eugenia's experience. It is even possible that she and her mother foresaw this necessity when planning for Mrs Stewart to accompany the family to France.

Only one direct comment from Louisa herself has survived to show something of what she felt about the breakdown of her marriage. Many years later, when thanking Craik for his 'kind good words' after Richard had died, she wrote of 'all the bitterness of disappointment and weary anxiety' which she was prepared to admit to 'you, who know the whole.' She mentioned also Richard's 'faults and follies that fell so heavily on those connected with him.'[12] These are the feelings and reactions we are all too familiar with now, when broken marriages are so common.

The separation was a legal arrangement. Cicely in her old age remembered being summoned before the lawyers at the time, and wishing in her heart that she might be allowed to live with her father, though there was no possibility of it.[13] This desire of Cicely's, though probably not expressed then, is a point in Richard's favour and again underlines, as with the opinion of Dr and Mrs Taylor, the Edinburgh friends, the impossibility of allotting blame and innocence in the situation as if they were points in a game. Cicely's daughter also used the term, writing of 'trouble which ended in a legal separation'. Louisa herself, in a letter written some ten months before she returned to England finally, appears to be referring to such a thing.

'Next year I hope in several ways to be feeling more independent of the money part of it, as our affairs will be quite out of court and I shall be settled permanently in England — But this year I have a very great deal before me & upon me.'[14]

This passage from a letter to her publishers, in which she was asking for a manuscript to be accepted and paid for a year in advance because she needed the money, clearly implies that she was looking towards some kind of legal financial settlement. Significantly, between the time that the Rev. Samuel advocated the separation and the final settlement, there occurred the passage of the 1882 Married Women's Property Bill. There could now be no doubt at all about Louisa's retaining control and use of her own property and earnings. It is perhaps necessary here

---

[12] MLM to GLC, 4.4.1900. (University of Reading Archive, MS 1448).
[13] CP to RR, verbal communication.
[14] MLM to GLC, 12.1.84.

Mary Louisa Molesworth, *née* Stewart.

Major-General William Stewart, Mrs Molesworth's paternal grandfather.

Charles Augustus Stewart, Mrs Molesworth's father as a young man.

Agnes Janet Stewart, *née* Wilson,
Mrs Molesworth's mother in middle age.

Westnieuwland, Rotterdam, 1836. Mrs Molesworth was born here, at no. 75, in 1839. The centre of Rotterdam was flattened during World War II, so this street no longer exists.

Mary Miller, *née* Wilson, sister of Agnes Janet Stewart, née Wilson, and thus Mrs Molesworth's aunt. She and her husband were living in Rotterdam when Mrs Molesworth was born there.

Hillside House, Saline, near Dunfermline, Fife. Home of Mrs Molesworth's aunt, Catherine Colville, *née* Wilson. Mrs Molesworth spent time here as a child, being told stories by her grandmother.

No. 92, Rusholme Road, Mrs Molesworth's first home in Manchester as a child. Photograph taken in the 1950s.

James Horne Stewart, legitimate son of William Stewart and half-brother to Charles Augustus Stewart.

Mrs Molesworth as a young woman.
Photograph of an oil painting.

Charles Augustus Stewart in middle age.

Tabley Grange, near Knutsford, Cheshire, where Mrs Molesworth and her family lived
1864-1869. The wing built on by the Molesworths is at the left-hand end.

Modern photographs of Westfield, the house built for Mrs Molesworth and her family in the grounds of West Hall, High Legh, by her father.

J.B.L. Warren (1835-1895), a close friend of Major and Mrs Molesworth for several years while they were living at Tabley Grange and High Legh. This photograph shows clearly the way his hair 'goes straight down, and up again all of a sudden, just like our old drake's tail'. (See the description of his dining with the Molesworths in chapter 6.)

St John's, formerly the private chapel of West Hall, High Legh. Mrs Molesworth's father rented this house (which was demolished in 1964) from 1869 till his death in 1874. His two younger daughters were married in St John's.

Sir Noel Paton, family friend and literary mentor.

Charles Stewart, 1841-1874,
Mrs Molesworth's second brother.

Minnie Wilson Maclean, *née* Morgan, grand-daughter of Mary Miller. She lived for part of her childhood and youth with the Stewarts and then with the Molesworths. She was married from the Molesworths' house at Conwy, North Wales, in March 1875.

Agnes Janet Stewart in widow's weeds, after her husband's death in 1873.

Royal Terrace, Edinburgh, nos. 25 and 26. The Molesworths lived in no. 25 from the autumn of 1875 to the end of 1877. Their daughters went to school next door.

The Rev. Samuel Molesworth, 8th Viscount, 1829-1906, first cousin to Major Richard Molesworth, Mrs Molesworth's husband. He visited the Molesworths in France and strongly advised their separation.

Photograph of Mrs Molesworth published in Little Folks, 1894, Pearson's, 1901 and The Quiver, 1906. She was probably in her early forties when it was taken.

Bindon House, Langford Budville, Wellington, Somerset. Mrs Molesworth spent the summer of 1887 here with the family of Charles Lamport. In August 1887, at Bindon, she wrote the dedication to Little Miss Peggy. 'To the memory of E.L. the dear young friend who suggested its name to this little story, and from whose late home, so intimately associated with her, this dedication is made.' One of the Lamport family daughters, Ella, died at Alassio in February 1887, aged 23. This fits exactly with the dedication.

Juliet Grant-Duff Ainslie, *née* Molesworth, Mrs Molesworth's third daughter, as a young woman.

Bell and Jean Lorimer, grand-daughters of Minnie Wilson Maclean. Mrs Molesworth called herself their 'old Great Auntie', though they were actually first cousins three times removed, kept up an affectionate correspondence with their mother and grandmother, and sent them her books at Christmas.

Winkenhurst, Hellingly, East Sussex. Home of Juliet Ainslie, *née* Molesworth, from c. 1906 to 1913. Mrs Molesworth read her latest stories to her grandchildren here, sitting with them in a circle around her on the lawn.

Illustrations by Walter Crane for Mrs Molesworth's first children's book, *Tell Me A Story*.

The children ask Auntie to tell them a story.

'Wee Janet' lends her doll, Mary Ann Jolly, to a gipsy girl with scarlet fever.

Oh! what sums in addition he gave her!

An illustration by C. E. Brock from the Macmillan 1931 edition of *The Cuckoo Clock*.

Carrots' son in *The February Boys*. Illustration by Mabel Lucie Attwell.

to state that there was no divorce, as the contrary has been affirmed in print, much to the annoyance of the family.[15]

When the Molesworths left Caen, Louisa, her mother and the children moved to Paris, while Richard went back to England. We know that Louisa arrived in Paris some time between March and May 1880, since the dedication of *Miss Bouverie* in March is from the Maison du Chanoine, while that of *A Christmas Child* in May is from Paris. This latter book is rather different from any Louisa had yet written, or indeed was to write, since it is the life of a real child, to whose parents the book was dedicated. 'To the two friends who will best understand this simple little story I dedicate it with much affection.' It was also different in being the only full-length book she wrote in which a child dies. She did not wallow in death-bed pathos. The child was Thomas Grindal Hutton and the title of the story derived from his birth and death near Christmas. He was born on 26th December, 1862, and died on 23rd December, 1875. *The Cuckoo Clock*, published almost exactly two years after his death, had already been dedicated to him and his sister who also features in *A Christmas Child* — 'To Mary Josephine, and to the dear memory of her brother, Thomas Grindal, both friendly little critics of my children's stories.' Several members of a later generation of the Hutton family stated that Thomas Grindal was the original of the Christmas child and that the anecdotes about him were authentic.[16]

The boy's father, John Hutton, was brother to Richard Holt Hutton, editor of *The Spectator*, which had already carried several anonymous reviews of Louisa's work, perhaps by him. *The Spectator's* review of *A Christmas Child* noted a quality that Louisa had herself explained in the book. She wrote

'I blame myself a little for not having told you more plainly at the beginning that it was *not* a regular "story" I had to tell you in the "carrots" coloured book this year, but just some parts, simple and real, of a child-life that I love to think of.'[17]

The Spectator's analysis, in more complex language, said much the same thing.

---

[15] Laski, p 57; VMI to RR, 12.12.1951 — 'Miss L. says there was a divorce there was never any question of such a thing.'

[16] Unpublished letters to RR.

[17] *A Christmas Child*, p. 209.

'This is really a study of a child's character, but one made so fascinating by the various traits and incidents which illustrate it, that many a child we are sure, will prefer it to the orthodox story ... we assume from many hints that Mrs Molesworth drops, that there has been a real original to her vivid picture.'

The different quality of this study from an orthodox story is attributed to the writer's being unable to select or invent incidents.

'It is obvious that Mrs Molesworth in her beautiful study had had to content herself with the sort of miscellaneous incidents which usually occur to the children of our middle class, and that they are neither more nor less adapted to her semi-biographic purpose than such incidents usually are.'

Louisa had more trouble with this book than was usual with her and had to keep re-writing it,[18] probably for the reason indicated by the reviewer — that she could not invent but had to take what was given. 'Indeed it is certain, that had the character she here depicts presented itself to her imagination, she would have found a very different set of incidents from these to clothe it in.'

Thomas Grindal was born in Beaumaris, Anglesey, his sister Josephine in Nevin (nowadays Nefyn), Caernarvonshire, and he died in Ludlow. These places in Wales and Shropshire were within reasonable distance of Louisa's homes during the boy's lifetime. As argued above near the beginning of chapter 7, it seems likely that Louisa first got to know the Huttons, and their Roscoe and Jevons connections, in Manchester, but that she then continued the friendship with John and Lucy Hutton, Thomas Grindal's parents, in Wales and Shropshire. She gives vivid and attractive descriptions of the then very remote area around Nevin on the Lleyn peninsula and the town of Ludlow, which read as though she had visited both places. Grindal's mother, Lucy Anne Hutton *née* Jevons, a grand-daughter of the William Roscoe who wrote *The Butterfly's Ball* in 1806, had two brothers, William Stanley Jevons, Professor of Political Economy at Owens College Manchester and Thomas Edwin Jevons who appears in the book as 'Uncle Ted' who 'writes books with lots of counting and stick-sticks in them.'[19] He was a statistician and economist. The first of these two uncles hurried to Ludlow to be with his sister

---

[18] *The Spectator*, 1880. CP to RR, verbal communication. quoted in an unpublished ms.
[19] *A Christmas Child*, p. 128.

just after her son, 'a most promising boy of 13,' had died of diphtheria. He wrote to his brother Tom 'No-one could know Grindal without becoming exceedingly fond of him. A sweeter disposition no one ever had, and his quaintness and humour were very attractive.' Then, with reference to his own son, he continued 'the pleasure I feel in him only makes me the more sad to think of Lucy's loss.'[20] Jevons' thumb-nail sketch of his nephew confirms the picture Louisa presented in the book she found such a struggle. Her writing and re-writing may well have spanned the move to Paris, and with what relief she would have written 'Paris, May 1880' at the end of the dedication. Louisa's friendship with the Huttons and their children belongs properly to an earlier stage in her life. But although there is firm evidence for its existence, so little detail has survived that it seemed better to place the account here, in a position marking it more as part of her writing career rather than of her personal life.

When Louisa moved to Paris, it is possible that Richard stayed on in Caen for a longer period, since his address in Debrett for 1880 and 1881 is given as Maison du Chanoine. Not until 1882 does Debrett change his address to Weymouth, but the delay in the appearance of this kind of information in annual works of reference means that these dates are only very approximate. A last glimpse of Richard Molesworth, either in Weymouth or Brighton, again in the company of ladies, comes from Sir Noel Paton's son.

'I was only about seven or eight years old when I last saw Major Moles-worth but at home we had a photograph of him taken many years later. In this photograph he was, I think, the only male and he was surrounded by a bevy of "young ladies". I think it was a picture of a very superior school garden party or picnic. Molesworth with a fine fair moustache was wearing a "Boater" straw hat. At that time (probably about '86) he lived I believe in Brighton.'[21]

Once Richard was no longer there, Louisa enjoyed her years in France. She described them in letters on her return to England as 'several very happy years' and said she had lived 'very peacefully alone with my mother and the children.' She had two apartments in Paris, first at 55, Avenue d'Iéna and later at 29, Avenue Kléber. Both these avenues

---

[20] *Letters and Journal of William Stanley Jevons*, edited by his wife, Macmillan, 1886, p. 345–6.
[21] R. Paton to RR, quoted in unpublished ms.

lead directly into the Place de L'Etoile from the south and south-west. According to the property registers made by the Paris communes for taxation purposes, in 1881 a ground floor apartment at 55, Avenue d'Iéna was occupied by Madame Stewart, suggesting either that the registered tenant was Louisa's mother or that she herself was using her maiden name. In the 1883 register, the tenant's name for apartment no. 3 at 29 Avenue Kléber was Molesworth, but she was described as 'veuve'. This would have been a convenient fiction, for the sake of social comfort.

During the time she lived in Paris, Louisa also spent periods in Germany. In the summer of 1881 she was in Coburg, a town in Thuringia, with her two youngest children, Olive and Lionel, staying at the Hotel Vitoria. While there, she made friends with the family of Sir Charles Scott, who was then the British *Chargé d'Affaires* in Coburg. They found her charming and saw a great deal of her. She read them parts of the book she was then writing, *Rosy,* and also accompanied them for some weeks to a little place in the Bavarian Alps. The Scotts believed that her husband was dead, which matches up with the 'veuve' in the Paris register.[22] This time in Thuringia was a fruitful source of material for Louisa. A significant group of her stories had a distinctively German setting with details that point specifically to that area. Her first specially Thuringian story, 'The Toymakers of Bergstein' was actually being written while she was in Coburg, for, in a letter to Craik from there, she mentioned *Summer Stories,* the book in which it appeared, as one she was getting on with well.[23] The story was a purely realistic one, turning on a year's delay by a wealthy English family in collecting a doll they had ordered from a German peasant family who earned their poorly paid living doing piece work for a toy factory, and the hardship that resulted.

Germany was the recognized home of the toy industry until 1914, and doll manufacture centred in Sonneberg and Waltershausen in Thuringia. Sonneberg is about eleven miles north east of Coburg and Louisa might quite well have taken her children to visit doll factories there, or to see piece work being done at home in nearby villages, as described in the story. Between Coburg and Sonneberg lies a town called Neustadt and Louisa obviously transformed this Newtown into the 'Altstatt' (Old-town) she used as the nearest town for her 'Bergstein' villagers. The

[22] A. Somerville to RR, 11.11.1937.
[23] *Summer Stories for Boys and Girls,* Macmillan, 1882.

poverty of the workers clearly made a deep impression on her, for she pointed up the contrast between the pretty picturesque villages with well built comfortable-looking houses and the poverty-stricken interiors, and further contrasted one such interior with the 'delicate beauty' of the row of dolls' heads, waiting for the peasant mother to dress their hair.

The following February another Thuringian story by Louisa appeared in *Aunt Judy's Magazine*, entitled 'The Blue Dwarfs: an adventure in Thuringen.' This time it was a fairy fantasy, but the introductory part again used factual detail about life in the area. It showed two children, the elder a twelve year old girl actually called Olive, travelling on holiday in remote German villages with an aunt and uncle, visiting china and glass factories and noting ways strange to them, such as bullock carts or local dress. The blue dwarfs of the title appeared in a dream Olive had, but they derived from a group of porcelain figures she had seen and admired in 'a very large china manufactory.' The Goebel porcelain factory in Coburg has produced many kinds of figurine since its foundation in 1871, and for a time branched out into toy-making.[24] A visit to this factory and the children's fascination with some of the figurines could well have been the original suggestion that prompted this story. The fairy part took place in a pine forest, one of the 'great stretches of forest land' Louisa had described in the previous story, perhaps with this one already in mind, for she had written 'It is a wonderful land. One could fancy it the home of many strange beings. All the stories of gnomes and kobolds and dwarfs that ever I had heard, seemed to come back into my mind as I journeyed through it.'[25]

Louisa had a passion for pine woods, particularly their smell, which began, as we saw in Chapter 2, way back in her childhood in Rotterdam with the towering masts of ships and the scent of tar — 'Perhaps the whole combined to prepossess me towards pine-woods!'[26] This time in Thuringia, where the ancient Thuringian forest survived in stretches of steep slopes, densely forested with pine trees predominating, helped to confirm that love. She had already made a character in one of her early novels enthuse about the 'strange resinous smell' of charcoal burning,

---

[24] *CBHS Newsletter*, no. 39, Sep. 1989, p. 10. 'Porcelain Children: 'Hummel-Figures' from the Goebel Factory.' A note on a display at the Bethnal Green Museum of Childhood.

[25] *Summer Stories*, pp. 203–4.

[26] 'Story-writing', p. 159.

calling it delicious because 'It makes me think of all sorts of nice things — Black Forest fairy tales, pine woods in summer . . . I do wish I could put some of that pine-wood essence in a scent-bottle and carry it away with me.'[27] In a later book she put a more factual and lovingly appreciative description of firwoods into the mouth of the nurse telling the story.

> ' "There's a charm one can't quite explain about them — the sameness and the stillness and the great tops so high up, and yet the bareness and openness down below, though always in the shade. And the scent, and the feel of the crisp crunching soil one treads on, soil made of the millions of the fir needles, with here and there the cones as they have fallen." '[28]

One of the children cared for by this nurse responded to the firwoods with 'It's like fairy stories.' So here is a third example of Louisa associating the pine or fir woods with wonders, with fairy stories.

In the letter Louisa wrote to Craik from the Hotel Vitoria at Coburg she mentioned both the books she was working on.

> 'I have been getting on well here with two books, one I intended as a sort of pendant to "Herr Baby" — more for quite little girls than boys — to come out Christmas year — The other I was going to write to you about soon — I am calling it "Summer Stories" & thought it wd. do to publish between seasons (as you said you wd. think of for next year at the time I declined Routledge's proposal) — It is more for older children, & I thought perhaps you wd. bring it out rather simply with only a few illustrations, & let it be a sort of summer holiday book for next year.'

"Herr Baby" was *The Adventures of Herr Baby*, which she and Craik were busy arranging to publish in time for Christmas that same year. It is clear that with five previous Molesworth titles on the market, a book by her from Macmillan every year at Christmas was becoming a regular, fixed event, both in her mind and her publisher's. Her publishing activities were widening out — she may have declined Routledge's proposal, whatever it was, but she had accepted two previous ones, and they had produced *Hermy* in December 1880, at the same time as Macmillan's published *A Christmas Child*, and *Hoodie* in August 1881. Both these had previously appeared as serials in Routledge's periodical, *Little Wideawake*. She was also obviously using Routledge's interest in

---

[27] *She Was Young*, vol. 1, p. 76.
[28] *Nurse Heatherdale*, p. 29.

her work to persuade Macmillan's to increase the amount of it that they published.

The letter to Craik just quoted, was chiefly occupied with the problems of publishing *Herr Baby*, or, to be more exact, of illustrating it. Macmillan's were planning a new venture in the field of illustration, referred to in a letter to Lewis Carroll. 'A recent French process has been brought before us and we are going to do Mrs Molesworth's next book in this way. We hope soon to see some proofs of these, and estimates . . . .'[29] The firm that Macmillan hoped would apply the 'recent French process' to *Herr Baby* was the Paris publisher, Quantin, which specialised in colour printing. Louisa had met the publisher, the artist and the engraver, more than once, and had clearly taken a lot of trouble, 'explaining most minutely — & giving photographs for the little boy's dress & describing him in French as a boy of course.' The engraver showed her two proofs of the proposed illustrations which she had doubts about, but, she said,

'as they were quite in the rough I thought they might come out well — he begged me not to judge of them in that state . . . In the two proofs I saw I pointed out great mistakes in the child's clothing, which they promised to correct.'

The greatest mistake had been showing the child as a girl instead of a boy and the only excuse offered was that this matter had been overlooked. Louisa had exchanged several letters with Craik about the whole business, as she reminded him, 'I remember writing all this to you some time ago — & telling you what a good thing it was I had found out their mistake,' although the letters referred to here have apparently not survived.

But when the final proofs and estimates duly arrived in London, Craik was dismayed. He sent them on to Louisa in Coburg, with, it seems, the bald comment 'very bad', for in her reply, on 23rd July (the letter already quoted), she started by saying 'I cannot but agree with you that the proof you send is very bad.' She went on 'It is vulgar & ugly in itself & the work is very bad — the colour just "pitched" on like a cheap nursery tale book illustration.' In fact the earlier proofs she had seen in Paris and been so worried about were 'infinitely better than this they now send.' She did not name the engraver but the artist was Henri

[29] *Lewis Carroll and the House of Macmillan*, edited by Morton N. Cohen and Anita Gandolfo. London: C.U.P., 1987, p. 163n.

Pille,[30] whose work she and Craik had already seen and liked, something which annoyed her all the more in the face of this vexation. 'The provoking thing is that we know Pille can do better . . . He is too much of an artist, & the engraver too much of a workman not to know this work is horrible.' The proofs were accompanied by the estimate Macmillan's had told Lewis Carroll they were expecting and this stimulated her to further exclamations of annoyance.

> 'I think their demand perfectly awful — You cannot be in any way obliged to pay it — & I think for their credit's sake they will not push it to extremes — Quantin's letter seems in a sense reasonable. He too must know it is frightfully bad.'

She wondered whether they might have to go to law 'if they will not be reasonable in their demand' and offered to put Craik in touch with 'an English lawyer, well up in French law — in Paris — should you think it necessary to consult him?' But fortunately the occasion did not arise. Those agitatedly underlined 'know's emphasise Louisa's certainty about the self-evidently poor quality of the work to anyone with eyes to see, and Quantin did not argue.

As to what could be salvaged out of the mess, Louisa was only able to think of trying to get a very small number of good illustrations, or 'even one very good coloured illustration as a frontispiece' which, she thought, 'would be better than a number of bad.' She seriously faced up to the possibility of having to delay publication for a year. 'Or if you think it better to put it off another year, I am quite resigned — only it seems a pity to let a Christmas pass just now while my books are popular does it not? I am so vexed on every account.' She was also very anxious that Macmillan's should not make a loss on the book — 'I cannot bear your losing money by me,' which sounds more like hurt author's pride, than sympathy for the firm's finances. But Craik was equal to the crisis and wrote immediately on receipt of Louisa's letter to Walter Crane, the only illustrator of her books so far. He did not wait for Crane's reply, but sent the sheets of the new book along with his explanation. He was justified when Crane, after emphasising how much work he had on hand, finally got going in September and sent

---

[30] Henri Pille, French painter and black and white artist, 4.1.1844 - 4.3.1897. *Fonds Ancien de Littérature pour la Jeunesse: Catalogue de Livres Imprimés Avant 1914*, Paris, Bibliothèque de L'Heure Joyeuse, nd, p. 208. I am grateful to Rosi Re Beech, formerly Tessa Rose Chester, for drawing my attention to this catalogue.

12 beautiful drawings round to Macmillan's by hand on 4th October
with a triumphant exclamation mark ending the announcement that
they had been finished the day before. And *The Adventures of Herr Baby*
came out when originally planned, in time for Christmas 1881 (the
British Museum received its copy on 15th December). But although this
particular episode had a happy ending, Macmillan's never published a
book by Louisa during her lifetime illustrated in colour. The burnt
children were keeping well away from the fire.[31]

The book Louisa described to Craik as 'a sort of pendant to "Herr
Baby"'' was *Rosy*, the one she had been reading to the Scott family in
Coburg. It is strange she should have said it was intended for 'quite
little girls' as the heroine is more than twice the age of Herr Baby, and
the book is much more complex. Rosy is a cross-grained, suspicious,
bad-tempered child, but Louisa's careful delineation of her nature,
thorough analysis of her motives and vivid presentation of her repeated
trying and often failing 'to be good' make her a character with whom
the reader can truly sympathize.[32] Louisa was particularly good at
depicting the breaking and restoration of relationships between child
and child, and child and adult, and digging beneath the surface to show
what caused such ruptures in the first place. *Hoodie* and *Hermy* had
both been such realistic, analytic child-novels, and this kind of writing
was becoming one of her strengths.

After this time in Coburg Louisa returned to Paris. It is clear that
there were other visits to Germany such as one referred to for instance
in an otherwise strictly business letter to Craik in January 1883 — 'we
shall be going to Germany in May' — but Paris remained her base.
During the autumn and winter of 1881–2 she had to finish off *Rosy*
and *Summer Stories* for Macmillan as well as writing 'The Blue Dwarfs'
for *Aunt Judy's Magazine*. A third story for Routledge had been appearing
over the year as a serial in *Little Wideawake* and she would have been
corresponding with them over its forthcoming appearance as a book —
The Boys and I. It looked as if a regular arrangement with Routledge
was growing up, similar to her relationship with Macmillan's, but it
was nipped in the bud, as she seems never to have written for them
again after *The Boys and I*. The rupture appears to have arisen from a
disagreement over a fourth book that Routledge offered to take for *Little*

---

[31] See also J. Cooper, 'Penny Plain or Twopence Coloured?', *Newsletter No. 55*, Children's Books History Society, Jul. 1996.
[32] See Cooper (1988) for a more detailed analysis of this book.

Wideawake. This time Louisa wanted to allow Routledge the serial rights only but was unsuccessful, so, she said, 'I refused to let him have it, as I could get no <u>thorough security</u> that it wd. not be republished as a book.' Her change of mind almost certainly arose from financial considerations. She probably hoped to make more by having Macmillan's publish the book after Routledge had done the serial version. Until nearly the end of her life, Louisa did not sell her mss outright. She was very particular about retaining the copyright herself and making as much as possible out of her work. Since she began to publish with Routledge around the time of her separation from her husband, or at least when she knew it was imminent, it seems likely that the increase, more or less doubling her previous annual output, was chiefly due to her need of more income when on her own with five children to support and educate.

By the time they were settled in Paris, Louisa's children were fast growing up, and Cicely was on the verge of adulthood. During this period she went back to England to be presented at court by her god-mother.[33] In May 1880 the ages of the five children ranged from seventeen and a half to six — quite a handful. Cicely looked back on the family's move abroad as marking a change in the way she and her sisters and brothers were being brought up. They had not had a very happy childhood, she thought, but it was better after they went abroad. She described both her parents as being very strict, although many of the restrictions she mentioned were part of normal Victorian family routine, not specially harsh rules laid down by unusually stern parents. They included not being allowed to go out alone, or without saying where she was going and what time she would come in, not being allowed to read novels until after tea (a rule Louisa imposed on herself as we have seen) and not being allowed a dog of her own till she was twenty. It would have been difficult to keep a dog in a Paris apartment anyway. Budgerigars, bullfinches and guinea pigs would have been easier to cope

---

[33] There is a puzzle about this. VMI said her mother was presented by her godmother Lady Molesworth. She also described GDL as 'a daughter of the Lady Molesworth who presented my mother'. GDL's mother, the first Lady Molesworth, *née* Georgina Charlotte Cecil Gosset, died in January 1879, when Cicely was only just 15, hardly of an age for court presentation. The 8th Viscount married again in 1883, Agnes Dove. There is evidence to suggest that AD was already a friend of MLM and so could have been Cicely's godmother from that connection, but this still contradicts VMI's definite statement that it was the first Lady Molesworth, Gwen's mother, who was Cicely's godmother and presented her.

with, and to travel with, and as was noted in the last chapter Cicely did remember that her mother was generous about such pets. When discussing the little story 'Charlie's Disappointment' from Louisa's first children's book, Cicely said that the picture of the small boy trying to put on his socks, 'sitting on the floor, shaking with sobs and cold' and running 'all shaking and shivering to his nice warm mother' who had come to the nursery on hearing his sobs and then took him to her own room to be dressed by a 'beautiful fire', was quite true. She was emphasising the cold in the nursery in contrast with the fire in the mother's room, underlining that this was true in her own experience. There was even ice on the bath water in the mornings, she said, though one notices that the child in the story was eventually taken to the warmth.[34]

But a severe, indeed spartan, regime, was common for children in Victorian days. A woman writing about her own upbringing in Scotland earlier in the century said 'That winter was very severe, and the water in our bedroom used to be frozen in the morning. It was not then considered the proper thing for young people to use hot water in their ablutions, and there were very few fixed baths in those days.'[35] Charlotte Yonge wrote 'My nursery would frighten a modern mother. It was like a little passage room, at the back of the house, with a birch-tree just before the window, a wooden crib for me, and a turn-up press bed for my nurse; and it also answered the purpose of workroom for the maids.' The nursery at Tabley Grange, however, where Cicely spent her early years, was more spacious and pleasant than this. Food was very plain, bread and milk figuring largely — 'As to eggs, ham, jam and all the rest, no-one dreamt of giving them to children.'[36] However, the childhood of these two writers was contemporary with that of Louisa herself, not of her children, although she referred to Grindal Hutton's having a 'nice cold bath' as a matter of course, and this must have been in the late '60s.[37] But during the Molesworth children's time in the nursery, custom was becoming somewhat gentler and this gradual softening, together with her own growing up, may have partly caused the change Cicely remembered.

It was also likely that Louisa's grief over Violet's death and her troubles with her husband made her, as Cicely's daughter thought, 'a strict, even

---

[34] CP verbal communication to RR, quoted in unpublished ms.
[35] M. E. Haldane, *A Record of a Hundred Years*, Hodder and Stoughton, 1925, p. 65.
[36] Christabel Coleridge, *Charlotte Mary Yonge*, Macmillan, 1903, pp. 57–8.
[37] *A Christmas Child*, p. 137.

a stern mamma' although 'a more dearly loved grandmother never lived,' adding 'it was many years before the sweetness came back.' Her father's illness and death and her brother's terrible accident must also have contributed to a mood at least of preoccupation and tension, which a child would interpret as 'crossness'. But although she was 'so sweet a grandmother,' she was not demonstrative. 'I never remember her kissing or petting my sister or me' wrote this grand-daughter, and Cicely also remembered that her mother was not a petting mamma.[38] The mother in *Carrots* was like this — 'she was not generally a very petting or kissing mamma, but rather quiet and grave.'[39] We know that Louisa did love her children deeply, and before Violet's death had also rejoiced in outward signs of their affection. After it, when Cicely was ill, we saw that she realised how very much she cared. As well, when sending Warren a picture of Cicely just after her illness, she wrote 'I miss my gentle little Cicely, but I am glad she is growing strong. Is not the enclosed rather nice — & characteristic of the innocent little soul?' By 1880 Violet had been dead for eleven years, and Richard was no longer there. Perhaps, when Cicely said that things were better abroad, she was remembering the beginnings of the returning sweetness.

Gwen Molesworth said that Louisa 'adored her girls,' and that Cicely 'was like a sister to her,' though she could not imagine her 'romping on the floor with small children.' She was, remembered Gwen, 'very attractive looking, tall and dignified with quiet calm manner . . . Her manner was distant and one worshipped from afar.'[40] But outward calm and distance does not necessarily mean lack of inward sympathy. Her writing for children displays a deep comprehension of childish thoughts and feelings. Although it may seem a trivial example, since we know something of her real attitude to dogs and pets, it is worth continuing with this theme. 'She was not very fond of animals' we noted, according to Cicely's daughter, and she did not allow Cicely to have a dog of her own till she was twenty, but she wrote several short stories about dogs, showing real affection for and knowledge of them, and great understanding of children as pet lovers. One in particular, 'Lost Rollo' in *A Christmas Posy* depicts vividly the intense, consuming desire of the two child characters to have a dog of their own. The mother in the story 'does not care much about pets, particularly not in town. She always says

---

[38] VMI to RR, 12.12.1951; CP to RR, verbal communication.
[39] *Carrots,* p. 160.
[40] GDL to RR, 25.5.1938.

they are not happy except in the country. At least she used to say so. I
think she has rather changed her opinion now.'[41] 'Now' is after the
children have acquired a very beautiful collie which the mother can't
help admiring too. An interesting pendant to this is a story about Louisa
in old age, contributed by someone who simply met her in the street
several times. 'She took a great fancy for my dog, a very fine spirited
Welsh terrier and wanted me to sell him. I think she offered me £30
for him! But he was not for sale!'[42] Evidence about a person's thoughts,
feelings and tastes can be very complex and contradictory. Did Louisa
change her attitude to dogs very markedly? Or is it that her daughter
and grand-daughter misinterpreted rules based on convenience and
necessity as a matter of personal taste? The real affection and insight
shown in her dog stories suggests the latter.

A little anecdote about the time in Paris illustrates in a small way her
more relaxed attitude to the children. Lionel, aged about six, had a pet
mouse that he carried around in his pocket. A really stern mother would
not have allowed that, to begin with. Then, in addition, as his niece
recounted the story, Louisa even bore with his producing this mouse in
the middle of a 'ladies' "day".'[43] The expression 'bore with' suggests he
was not punished. Perhaps she thought it was funny.

A ladies' day would have been a regular day for visitors, when Louisa
was 'at home', in this instance to ladies only. She had many friends and
acquaintances in Paris. One whom she saw a lot of was Lady Pine,
whom she described to Craik in 1901 as 'my dear French-Scotch cousin
. . . I cannot tell you how good she has always been to me.' She was
asking Craik to send Lady Pine a book called *The Crisis* which had had
an extraordinary success, because, since she was 'very wealthy' and had
'everything she wants except new English books,' this kind of gift was
about the only thing Louisa could do in return. Lady Pine and her
husband, Sir Benjamin Chilley Campbell Pine, lived in Versailles. Sir
Benjamin was retired at the time Louisa was in Paris, but had been a
colonial governor of such places as Sierra Leone, Natal, the Gold Coast
and Antigua.[44] Another set of people in Paris, connected with the Molesworths, whom Louisa most probably saw, was the De Mallet family,

[41] *A Christmas Posy*, p. 150.
[42] E. G. Robins to RR, 17.2.1938.
[43] VMI to RR, 12.12.51.
[44] GDL to RR, 4.5.1938, 'Lady Pine, I think a connection, she saw a lot of.' MLM to
GLC, 31.7.1901.

the French cousins mentioned by Mary Molesworth in a letter to Louisa as possible contacts for Richard's brother on his visit to Paris in 1867, but whom she could not at that time produce any information about. At one time Louisa worked a set of chair seats and backs in a design, Cicely remembered, 'copied by special permission from Versailles chairs through my father's French cousins.' It is most likely that the De Mallets obtained this permission for Louisa while she was actually living in Paris, so there must have been some contact between them. One of Cicely's daughters knew about these chair covers but had a different association with them. Her grandmother, she wrote,

> 'did not care for needlework & told us this dislike often got her into trouble as a child, in later life she did some "petit-point" & "gros-point" chair covers but more I think as an occupation than anything else.'[45]

It is surprising to us to think of a professional writer, the busy mother of a large family casting round for 'occupation' in this way, but one has to remember that Victorian custom decreed that ladies should not sit idle when gentlemen were visiting. Nor could the necessary 'work' be useful shirts or sheets — some kind of decorative needlework was essential.

A near neighbour and close friend was Mrs Milner-Gibson who lived in the Rue de Traktir, just off the Avenue du Bois de Boulogne at the Etoile end. She was in her late sixties when Louisa came to Paris, and had been well-known in London for her political and literary salon, where many distinguished Europeans could have been met, such as Mazzini, Louis Blanc and Victor Hugo, as well as leading English literary celebrities like Thackeray, Monckton Milnes and especially Dickens, to one of whose sons she stood sponsor. She still 'received' regularly in Paris on Thursday afternoons, and for closer friends on Sunday evenings. These details about visiting appear in letters Louisa wrote to her, introducing other friends, letters that she signed most warmly 'with much love, Yours very affectionately.' Contemporaries described her in attractive terms as someone with 'a genuine instinct of hospitality, an innate good feeling, the pleasure that arises from giving pleasure to others, the happiness of seeing those around her happy,' a person in whom, whatever

---

[45] Athelstan Riley also mentioned this connection — 'There was a Baron in Paris who <u>was</u> a relation.' Postcard to RR, 23.2.1938. Anne Molesworth, eldest daughter of the 5th Viscount, and thus first cousin to Richard's father, married Baron de Mallet in 1807 and died leaving issue. CP to RR, 19.12.37; VMI to RR, 12.12.51.

experiences she went through, 'the generous heart, the loving nature, the wide full charity of divine sympathy and pity remained unchanged.' And she did go through very varied stages of thought — ' the widest Liberalism, the most marked Bohemianism, the most mystical spiritualism and the most fervent Catholicism.'[46] Louisa would no doubt have been interested in the spiritualist side because of her own second sight and fascination with ghost stories. Cicely and Juliet were on friendly terms with Mrs Milner-Gibson's son, George Gery Milner-Gibson-Cullum, who was in his last year at Cambridge when Louisa and her family arrived in Paris, and the girls in her household, Poppy, Maud and 'Thusie', probably nieces or cousins. There was a regular exchange of hospitality — parties, dances, theatre-going and informal dinners.[47]

The family also went in for amateur theatre. In early 1882 Louisa was writing to a friend asking urgently for 'comedies for drawing-room acting' as she had promised the friends who were arranging these 'private theatricals' to have some texts for consideration in a few days' time, and could not get hold of her usual contact in London. The event was to include material in French as well as English, implying that actors and audience would be of both nationalities. Cicely was going to act — she was 18 at the time — and had specially asked that if her part included any love-making her uncle, Major Goring, who was visiting just then, should be her lover. He acted very well, Louisa said. Only two gentlemen's parts were wanted — perhaps the other man was to be Gery Cullum — but three or more ladies, a situation always common among amateurs, now as then. Louisa showed no objection to this amusement, her only specification apart from technical ones of length and complexity being 'lively, but not of course at all "slangy".'[48]

Louisa had contacts among painters too. One letter she wrote to Mrs Milner-Gibson was to introduce another friend of hers, Madame Lacretelle, the wife of an artist who had met Mrs Milner-Gibson twenty years before at a dinner in London, but who was afraid she would not remember him. Jean-Edouard Lacretelle was a portrait and history painter who lived and worked both in London and Paris. Louisa said in her letter that he was probably better known in London, which seems likely, judging by the large number of pictures he sent to the Royal

[46] Edmund Yates, *Recollections,* Harper, 1885, vol. 1, pp. 252–3; Elizabeth Lynn Linton, *The Autobiography of Christopher Kirkland,* Richard Bentley, 1885, vol. 2, p. 15.
[47] MLM to Milner-Gibson, letters in Cullum collection, Trinity College Library.
[48] MLM to Mrs Seddon, 8.2.1882. Privately owned letter.

Academy and the Royal Society of British Artists in Suffolk Street, though he also exhibited in the Paris Salon. He seems to have specialised in society portraits, and on Louisa's visit to his studio he showed her several that she thought very interesting and the subjects of which she was sure Mrs Milner-Gibson would know. Louisa was very enthusiastic about young Mme Lacretelle, calling her 'perfectly lovely . . . charming, as nice as she is beautiful.'

As one might expect, Louisa made friends in the literary world as well as among artists. She knew the Paris correspondent of *The Times*, M. de Blowitz, well enough for him to ask her to introduce and recommend him to her publishers. She wrote to Craik in November 1883 describing a book de Blowitz had written about a journey to Constantinople earlier in the same year, on the inaugural train of the Orient Express.[49] His idea was to bring it out more or less simultaneously in French and English. It appears that nothing came of this, since although the third edition of *Une Course à Constantinople*, by H. G. S. A. Opper de Blowitz, published in Paris in 1884, appears in the British Library catalogue, there is no English edition. De Blowitz is referred to in Alice James' diary as an eminent European journalist.

Recommending her friends to her publishers was something Louisa liked to do. After she returned to England Craik suggested to her that she might write a French text-book. Feeling that she really had no time for the work just then, she proposed the name of a friend, Kathleen O'Meara, 'in Paris, where she has lived many years, who cd. do it, & well — She has great literary taste. You have seen her "Madame Mohl?"[50] This was a reference to *Madame Mohl: Her Salon and Friends: A Study of Social Life in Paris*, which was published by Bentley in 1885. Mme Mohl, *née* Mary Anne Clarke, was a noted *salonniére*, inheritor of the Recamier mantle, of Scottish Whig background. Louisa would have heard much about her in Paris, if not before, during her period of teaching from the Gaskells, of whom Mme Mohl was a great friend. She was unlikely to have met her, since Mme Mohl died in 1883 at the age of 90.[51] Kathleen O'Meara had lived in Paris since the 1850s, when her mother settled in France with her and her sister for the sake of their education. The family already had a link with the country, since

[49] H. G. S. A. Opper de Blowitz, *My Memoirs*, Edward Arnold, 1903, p 269.
[50] MLM to GLC, 4.2.1888.
[51] J. Uglow, *Elizabeth Gaskell*, Faber, 1993, pp. 347–350; Gerin, (1976) pp. 150–1, 155–8.

a close relative, Dr Barry O'Meara, had been Napoleon's physician at St Helena. Kathleen did not really need Louisa's recommendation, since she published much and successfully in French and English, both history and biography under her own name (including a life of the Curé D'Ars), and novels under the pseudonym 'Grace Ramsay'.[52]

The Irish O'Meara family was Catholic, and they were also friends of a very well-known Catholic, Mrs Augustus Craven, *née* Pauline de la Ferronnays, whom Louisa also came to know. Mrs Craven was famous in English Catholic and Anglo-Catholic circles for the book, *Le Récit d'une Soeur, (A Sister's Story)*, an account of the life and death of her brother Albert and his Russian wife, Alexandrine d'Alopeus. This was not only a romantic personal story but also a chronicle of the de la Ferronays family and the aristocratic, Catholic and diplomatic society in which they lived. Charlotte Yonge knew and referred to the book as something loved and familiar, which her readers would also recognise with ease.[53] Sir M. E. Grant-Duff, the eminent politician and statesman, and Governor of Madras from 1881–86, with whose family Louisa later became connected through the marriage of her daughter, Juliet, was captivated by *Le Récit*. After reading it, he became a life-long friend and admirer of Mrs Craven. This latter position was one Louisa also held, judging by a reference in her essay 'Fiction: Its Use and Abuse' where she mentions Mrs Craven's novels as pre-eminent among modern ones, with a sad little aside — 'whose death her many friends are still mourning.'[54] Louisa knew Mrs Craven well enough to write on her behalf to Mrs Milner-Gibson, with her apologies for not visiting. 'She says it has lain on her heart to think of never having gone to see you — she put it off at a time she was very much occupied & then she felt ashamed to go.' She also urged a meeting — 'you would feel such thorough sympathy with each other.' The casual survival of notes like this, which performed a function now totally usurped by the telephone, gives no deep insight into the friendships they bear witness to, but does prove their existence. There is also one mention of Louisa extant in a letter of Mrs Craven's, some years after the Molesworths had left France and settled again in England. Louisa and Juliet had written letters of admiration and congratulation about a novel by Mrs Craven, who wrote to another friend

---

[52] M. C. Bishop, *A Memoir of Mrs Augustus Craven*, Richard Bentley, 1894, vol. 1, p. 372–3, and BL catalogue.

[53] C. M. Yonge, *The Pillars of the House*, Macmillan, 1873, vol. 1, p. 55.

[54] MLM, *Studies and Stories*, A.D. Innes, 1893, p. 252.

'Pray thank Mrs Molesworth and Juliet for their very kind letters. I am very glad they liked the "Valbriant". The characters and incidents alluded to are so French — so unfamiliar to foreigners — that I did not expect it to be cared for by any outside *le terroir*.'[55]

Here is another indication of how much Louisa not only loved but understood France and the French.

The letter quoted above was addressed to Marie Catherine Bishop, *née* O'Connor Morris, another Irish Catholic, who wrote a memoir of Mrs Craven after her death. She had also written a novel, and other memoirs, and wrote reviews for such periodicals as the *Pall Mall Gazette*. She had been a friend and correspondent of Mrs Craven's since 1869, and was often in Paris. It is clear that she was also in touch with Louisa since she was expected to be able to pass on a message, and Louisa knew her well enough to stay with her at her home. A letter to Craik in 1891 asking him to send Mrs Bishop a copy of her own latest book, mentioned such a visit — 'I have just been staying with Mrs Bishop at Tunbridge Wells.' It seems likely that Louisa first got to know her in Paris as one of Mrs Craven's circle of friends.

Mrs Craven, it should be noted, despite her English husband, was completely French by birth and upbringing. Acquaintance with her brought Louisa into the heart of French Catholic society. There never seems to have been any question of this influence converting her to Catholicism herself. Gwen Molesworth said that she was a staunch Anglo-Catholic though only confirmed after her marriage, a far cry from the Calvinism of her childhood. Her grand-daughter too supported this view, saying that 'she became — if not Anglo-Catholic — very near it', and suggesting that 'her life in and her love for France may have influenced her views.'[56] Either knowing Mrs Craven and her friends encouraged Louisa towards the more Catholic branch of her own church, or, already leaning in that direction, she found their circle sympathetic.

But she also had French Protestant friends in Guillaume Guizot and his family. He was the son of Francois P. E. Guizot, the celebrated French historian and statesman. Louisa had mentioned him in her letter to Craik about the problems of illustrating *Herr Baby*, in terms which suggest that they both knew him well. Should they consult him 'about this bother,' she wondered, since he must be experienced in 'all sorts of

---

[55] Bishop, vol. 2, p. 263.
[56] VMI to RR, 3.1.1952.

book concerns.' As well as this, she said he would 'do a good deal to oblige me and he is an old friend of yours.' This old friendship probably came through Dinah Mulock, Mrs Craik, for she had translated several books by Guizot's father, and also translated or wrote prefaces for books by his sister, Henriette Guizot de Witt. When Mrs Craik and Mme de Witt met, 'they discovered in one another a sympathy of values and tastes that made them feel immediately like old friends.' Then, too, in her preface to *A Christian Woman*, a book by de Witt which came out in 1882 while Louisa was in Paris, Mrs Craik wrote in terms that show it had standards and an attitude to life similar to *Le Récit d'une Soeur*, allowing for the difference in denomination. All de Witt's books celebrated family, home-love and moral responsibility, something which Mrs Craik praised and Louisa too showed were her standards in all that she wrote. But further than that, Mrs Craik saw in her friend's books evidence that there were women

'in France as in England . . . who while nobly fulfilling all home duties, have the courage and capacity to stretch out beyond home, and carry out in the external world worthy schemes of usefulness and benevolence.'[57]

Mrs Craik visited Paris often for reasons of her work, and we know, from Louisa's letters to Craik, of one particular visit in the first half of 1883, when Louisa was deliberately making her own plans so as not to be away when Mrs Craik was there. One of the reasons for this and other visits was to look at the life of a group of British and American women artists who studied together at the same atelier and lived in rented rooms in the same house. The result was an article, 'A Paris Atelier' which appeared in 1886.[58] In this article she wrote with approval of the group who had had to break with the conventions of bourgeois femininity in order to establish an independent working life. Louisa must have known of this interest — she may even have visited the atelier with Mrs Craik. No letters between them have so far been discovered, but there is frequent mention in Louisa's letters to Craik of messages, letters and enclosures for his wife. Louisa admired Dinah Craik and looked up to her as she said to Craik when she first came to know him over the publication of *Tell Me A Story*.

[57] S. Mitchell, *Dinah Mulock Craik*, Boston, Twayne Publishers, 1983, p. 102.
[58] *Good Words*, 1886, p. 309. Quoted in D. Cherry, *Painting Women: Victorian Women Artists*, Routledge, 1993, p. 49.

'I would like, if I could do so without seeming intrusive, to send some sort of message to Mrs Craik — for I was so pleased that she liked my little stories — But I have only seen her once & I am sure she cannot remember me, & I do not know what message I can send. May I tell her that I seem to have known her & looked up to her for a great many years? She must have a great many friends (I will not say "admirers", it is such a horrible word) she does not know, so perhaps she will not dislike to hear of another.'[59]

Admiring Mrs Craik as she did, Louisa would have read her books. In *A Woman's Thoughts About Women* she would have found ideas to encourage her in her own career. Mrs Craik 'insisted that women's cultural work should be judged on its artistic or literary merits, not on the sex of the maker. She claimed that art was a neutral realm, not a domain governed by sexual difference.'[60] In this context it is interesting to note that Louisa 'could not bear "feminising words". Author*ess* was TABOO. "As well say groom*ess* or paint*ress*".'[61] This dislike stemmed from a correct realisation that 'ess' words were perceived as derogatory, not just denoting sex. 'Paintress' was actually used in a negative sense by Ruskin who, in a letter of 1858 to the painter Sophia Sinnett wrote 'the feminine termination does exist, there never having been such a being yet as a lady who could paint.'[62] Such a climate of thought implied that to be called 'authoress' meant one could not really write. Naturally Louisa withstood the word, probably without ever articulating the underlying reasons. I am not here saying that Louisa was an early feminist — she appeared to live for the most part easily within the conventions of her time. But now separated from her husband, she earned her own living and wished to be seen as a professional writer, circumstances that would have aroused her sympathy with Mrs Craik's views on women's work.

By the beginning of 1883 Louisa had half finished two books for Macmillan's. This situation had come about, she explained to Craik, because, while writing a 'semi-fairy story' for the following Christmas, she had been struck by the thought that perhaps Craik 'would not like it as much as a completely real story again'. So she set to work on what

[59] MLM to GLC, 17.7.[1875].
[60] Cherry, p. 67, summarizing from *A Woman's Thoughts About Women*, Hurst and Blackett, 1858, pp. 50–57.
[61] VMI to RR, 12.12.1951.
[62] Cherry, p. 66 and p. 237 note 8.

became *Two Little Waifs* and was now offering him the choice, promising to finish first whichever he preferred. She also asked his advice on where best to place the other one. She could always get it into *Aunt Judy's Magazine* but was reluctant to do this because 'they pay poorly.' Could he suggest an American paper that would pay better for an original story? Between these two possibilities she slipped in, as an aside, the idea that the second story could be held over for a year and be published at Christmas 1884 by Macmillan's themselves.[63] There are several themes here that recur throughout Louisa's working life. Craik's preference for 'real' stories over fairy ones, and also, though not mentioned in this connection, for a full-length book over a collection of shorter tales, definitely influenced what Louisa wrote. She felt she had to argue him into accepting his less-preferred forms each time she produced one. Here too she uses competition again, this time only suggested, to spur him over any reluctance in taking what she offered. Asking his advice was also something she did frequently. She expected from him, and he apparently supplied willingly, services which, in a later period, would be provided by a literary agent. Looking ahead, not just to next Christmas but to the one after, is also characteristic of her. She liked the feeling of having the next story finished and ready, as she told Craik during the negotiations over her 1888 Christmas book, *A Christmas Posy*. Another theme is her continued search for better paying outlets for her work. *Aunt Judy* ceased publication a few months after Mrs Ewing's death in 1885, and Louisa had first had a story published there in 1878, but during that period the magazine only had four of her stories altogether, very likely because of the poor payment.[64]

As Louisa expected, Craik took the real life story for her 1883 Christmas book. *Two Little Waifs* was one of her best child-novels, with convincing character studies and an integrated plot-structure. The small hero and heroine are moved clearly and compellingly through successive and utterly realistic and convincing deprivations of those taking care of them, to the dark climax of being completely lost and alone in Paris. This is sustained only long enough to make the subsequent peripeteia all the more delightful. Once Craik had made the choice, Louisa worked fast to finish the book, as can be seen from the fact that the story half done in mid-January was completed and printed in time for proof sheets

---

[63] MLM to GLC, 21.1.1883.

[64] MLM stories in *Aunt Judy*:- 'My Pink Pet' (1878); 'The Blue Dwarfs' (1882); 'Basil's Violin' (1883); 'Grandmother Dear's Old Watch' (1884).

to be sent to Walter Crane in early April. Louisa was particularly eager that this book should be a success because in that same April Macmillan's were making plans for a cheaper edition of *Herr Baby* to try to recoup the loss they had so far sustained on it. The original edition, in quarto rather than octavo size, bound in dusty pink cloth quite different from the orange colour normally used for Molesworth titles, had been an unsuccessful attempt to start a different series for younger children. But once brought into line with her other Christmas books, *Herr Baby* seems to have flourished — eleven reprintings between 1886 and 1908 do not suggest a failure.

Nor did Craik allow the fairy story to go to some American paper. It was *Christmas-Tree Land*, and it became the Molesworth/Macmillan title for Christmas 1884. This book was Louisa's most complete celebration of her love for pine woods and fir-trees, their smell, their strangeness, their association with gnomes, kobolds and all kinds of fairy lore. The fir-trees *are* the story in *Christmas-Tree Land*.[65] They dominate the scene from the outset, when the two children wake to their first sight of their new home at the end of a long journey, thrilled with pleasure at 'the hills rising ever higher and higher, clothed from base to summit with fir-trees, innumerable as the stars on a clear frosty night.' The girl exclaims 'It is a land of Christmas trees!' and the climax of the story is a vision of these same trees, rising tier upon tier up the slopes of a valley, lighted, decorated, toy-laden, each crowned by a Christmas angel with gleaming wings.[66] Pine-woods and fir-trees appeared regularly in Louisa's later books, but this is the fullest and deepest expression of her feeling for them. 'The pine forests of that country had been celebrated as far back as there was any record of its existence . . . Beautiful and wonderful . . . in their solemn majesty.'[67] It is possible that the story was actually written in Thuringia among the pine-woods, for when proposing to send Craik the manuscript in January 1884, Louisa told him it had been written 'in an out-of-the-way place'. This was by way of explanation for the bad 'crushable paper' and the poor quality ink that was already fading. She was eager for it to be set up in type and to have proof sheets before the fading process went any further.

---

[65] Anita Moss discusses *Christmas-Tree Land* in some detail in 'Mrs Molesworth: Victorian Visionary', *The Lion and the Unicorn*, vol.12, no. 1, Jun. 1988, pp. 105–110.

[66] MLM, *Christmas-Tree Land*, Macmillan, 1884, pp. 2 and 217.

[67] *Christmas-Tree Land*, p. 23.

Later in that year, 1883, on 20th June, Agnes Stewart, Louisa's mother, died. It was an unexpected blow as Louisa made clear in a letter to a member of the Macmillan family a few months later.

'Thank you very much for your kind letter — I was not sure till I received it, if the death I saw in the papers was that of Mr Craik's mother. I am very grieved for him, & I can peculiarly sympathize with him, as I have quite lately lost my own mother, whom we had every reason to hope would have been spared to us for many years still.'[68]

Mrs Stewart was 73 at the time of her death. But Louisa thought that her husband's death and the early deaths of her three sons had had something to do with it, as she wrote nearly two years afterwards.

'Our family history has been a sad one — all my three brothers died prematurely. My father's death was followed by that of the two younger ones, one by an accident. My most dear mother died only two years ago; I think troubles had exhausted her, for she was barely 70.'[69]

She probably skated over the missing three years half consciously, wishing to emphasise her feeling that her mother had died early, too early. She had loved her dearly. Writing in October 1883, to tell Warren of the death and her own approaching return to England, she said, 'You may remember how very much she was to me.'

It is possible that Mrs Stewart was no longer living with Louisa in 1883, or that she had at least gone to visit her other daughters, for in a letter at the very beginning of the year Louisa wrote 'there was some question of my going over to see my mother as I shall not see her next summer.'[70] A letter from Guillaume Guizot in October implied that she was in London after the death and funeral, as he explained he had heard of her 'grand malheur' only just before he left London himself and apologised because he had thus been prevented from visiting her there. She had written to him, a letter which had touched him deeply, and he assured her how well he understood the grief she described, because he still felt the deaths of his father and sister although he had lost them more than nine years before. She appears to have bewailed the suddenness of her mother's death, for in reply he said that even the long illnesses which seem intended to prepare us for the departure of our

---

[68] MLM to Macmillan, 3.11.1883.
[69] MLM to Professor Williamson, 1.2.1885.
[70] MLM to GLC, 21.1.1883.

loved ones, afterwards only look like time doubly lost when we have not been able to enjoy their company. There were griefs that were like bullets, which one ought not to try to extract, but had to carry in the wound throughout life. That she should have written a letter that evoked such a response five months after Mrs Stewart's death, shows how deeply Louisa was still mourning the loss of her mother. Guizot wrote to her from Nîmes, and promised to visit her in a few days, as soon as he arrived in Paris.[71]

Mrs Stewart was buried at Rostherne in the same grave as her two younger sons. William had died in November, 1879, when Louisa was still living in Caen. The width of another row of burial plots separated this grave from that of her husband, who lay beside the eldest son and the two Molesworth grandchildren. Rostherne had become the family burial ground. Probably Louisa and her sisters chose together the inscription carved on their mother's gravestone, 'Death the minister of love, the servant of eternal life.' Caroline's eldest son remembered attending the funeral with his father. He remembered his grandmother too, very well, as 'a frail, white-haired very Scotch old lady who used to stay with us in N. Wales.'[72]

Grandmother Dear, the book whose title character was based on Mrs Stewart, had a little sequel first published in *Aunt Judy's Magazine* just a year after her death, 'Grandmother Dear's Old Watch: A Fragment'. The actual plot of the story, turning on the loss and recovery of a watch that had belonged to 'Grandmother Dear' who was now dead, may be mostly invention. But it seems likely that the grief of Auntie and the two girls, now grown-up, for their mother and grandmother, truly depicted Louisa's and her daughters' feelings after the death of Agnes Stewart. The girls were twenty and eighteen, with chestnut and fair hair, and in 1883 Cicely and Juliet, dark and fair, were also twenty and eighteen. They were shown living in an apartment on 'one of the wide handsome avenues in the new part of Paris,' a description which matched the Avenue Kléber. From the balcony of this apartment the girls watched their aunt's figure 'in its deep mourning dress — not *quite* so erect or active as it used to be, for Auntie was no longer young, and this year, so nearly ended now, had brought her the greatest sorrow of her life.'[73]

---

[71] Guizot to MLM, 24.10.1883, typewritten copy of a letter in the possession of CP, now destroyed.
[72] E. C. Walthall to RR, 18.8.1957.
[73] *A Christmas Posy*, pp. 2–3.

This does seem to be a glimpse of Louisa, at forty-four, in her grief for her mother. The vividness of the description of losing the watch, and the efforts to find it, the intimate acquaintance with every detail of the Parisian lost property system, the visits to the *Préfecture de Police* and even the *Mont de Pieté*, the great central pawnbroker, do suggest that Louisa had had some such experience, though the finding by a poverty-stricken family, to whom the offered reward brought immeasurable relief, seems more likely to be fictitious. It is 'Auntie's' excessive depression over the loss and her thoughts of her mother that seem to bring Louisa most clearly before us. She could not sleep.

> ' "It is really wrong of me to fret so about the loss of any *thing*," she would say to herself. "I seem more overwhelmed than even during the first few terrible days after mother's death. Though, after all, *were* those first few days terrible? Just at the first when the door seems still as it were half-open, and we feel almost as if we could see a little way *in*, where our dear ones have gone — no, those first days are *not* the worst." '

The reversion here to the plural 'dear ones', although 'Auntie' was supposedly thinking only of her mother's death, suggests that Louisa's mind had gone back to Violet's death as well. 'Auntie' became calmer and

> 'then came before her the remembrance of "grandmother dear's" sweet quiet face as she had seen it the last time, in the beautiful calm of holy death. "It is *wrong* to fret so, my child," the well-known voice seemed to say.'

After this 'Auntie' fell quietly asleep and woke in the morning to hear that the watch had been found.[74]

In one of her articles about writing for children, published ten years after her mother's death, Louisa described how the child's early and absolute trust in its parents is gradually replaced by the realisation that 'neither father nor mother, best of teachers or dearest of friends, is infallible.' She suggested that 'the bonds of the old childish love and trust [are drawn] yet closer by the addition of that of understanding *sympathy*.'[75] It seems as though she was here drawing on the memory of her own relationship with her mother, who meant so *very* much to her, as she told Warren.

---

[74] *A Christmas Posy*, pp. 20–21.
[75] 'On the Art . . .', p. 343.

Over a year passed after her mother's death before Louisa finally left Paris. In the March of 1884 her first book aimed specially at teenage girls appeared under the imprint of the SPCK, a firm with which she was to have a long association. In terms of numbers it was her third most important publisher after Macmillan's and Chambers, (for whom she did not start to write for another five years). *The Spectator's* review of *Lettice*, this first girls' book, singled out what most readers feel about this class of her writing — that she loses 'a great part of her power when she depicts the doings of youth rather than those of early child-hood.'[76] Later in the year SPCK also produced *The Little Old Portrait* for children, Louisa's only attempt at historical fiction. It was unusual for her too, in that it was the only story she wrote that was set entirely in a foreign land without any English protagonists at all. So she was able to contemplate her return to London with the comfortable knowledge of an established working relationship with two publishers ready to take whatever she offered, having already tried and moved on from four others.[77]

She was thinking and planning about her return for quite a long time beforehand. In October 1883 she had told Warren that she intended to bring her sons over to England for their education.[78] She was also worried that all the children had become too French — 'After so many years in France I am afraid my children are not very patriotic, but I am sure they will like England when they know it a little better.'[79] Behind this blandly polite sentence to Mr Macmillan (whom, at that time, she had not met personally) seems to lie disagreement, perhaps even a family row, about returning to England at all. However that may be, by the autumn of 1884 the family was settled in 85, Lexham Gardens, off Earl's Court Road, just north of West Cromwell Road and within walking distance of Kensington Gardens.

---

[76] *The Spectator*, 5.7.1884, p. 889. It would be possible to argue that *Hathercourt Rectory* (1878) and *Miss Bouverie* (1880) are teenage novels, but since they both appeared first in 3 vols, and since *The Spectator's* reviewer writes as though *Lettice* were an entirely new departure, I have accepted that as the contemporary view.

[77] These were Skeet, Tinsley, Hurst and Blackett, and Routledge.

[78] Draft letter JBLW to MLM, 20.10.1883, in Cheshire Record office.

[79] MLM to Macmillan, 3.11.[1883].

10

England Again

85, Lexham Gardens had been found and taken for Louisa while she was still abroad. After she had lived there for two years she wrote about the new house and her first coming to England, 'I had lived too little in London to realise the inconvenience of the situation, as the house itself is nice.' What she meant by inconvenience was that Lexham Gardens was too far from the centre of town. She apologised more than once on this point to prospective visitors in such phrases as 'It is a very long way out, I know!' and 'I wish you did not feel this so far out.' To our way of thinking, Kensington is pretty well in the middle of London, but things looked different to a society dependent on horse-drawn transport. She never really resigned herself to the position — 'I do dislike Kensington' and 'We do find this "quartier" so gloomy and out-of-the-way!' she complained in different letters to one close friend.[1] There were at least four servants in the household, including a cook, a manservant and Louisa's personal maid, Fanny Jordan, who was with her for many years and afterwards went to work for the family of one of Viscount Molesworth's daughters. Louisa did not keep a carriage of her own in London and would thus have had to use cabs, which would have underlined to her the 'far-out' position of her house.[2]

Just at the point of Louisa's return to England there appeared an article in *The Nineteenth Century* which must have pleased and encouraged her considerably. The poet and critic A. C. Swinburne, in the course of an article about Charles Reade, now chiefly remembered as the author of *The Cloister and the Hearth*, produced a lyrical paragraph on writing about children, in which he expressed great admiration for Louisa's work. After praising Reade's presentation of a child in one of his novels, Swinburne continued,

---

[1] MLM to DUC, [3.1887]; MLM to GLC, 22.2.[1888]; MLM to DUC, 21.10.1887; ibid., 9.11.1887.
[2] Census, 1891 and VMI to RR, 3.1.52. The Census lists 4 servants while VMI mentions 6.

'the child . . . commends himself to all readers of experience as a Reality and no Phantasm. It seems to me not at all easier to draw a lifelike child than to draw a lifelike man or woman: Shakespeare and Webster were the only two men of their age who could do it with perfect delicacy and success: at least, if there was another who could, I must crave pardon of his happy memory for my forgetfulness or ignorance of his name. Our own age is more fortunate on this single score at least, having a larger and nobler proportion of female writers; among whom, since the death of George Eliot, there is none left whose touch is so exquisite and masterly, whose love is so thoroughly according to knowledge, whose bright and sweet invention is so fruitful, so truthful or so delightful as Mrs Molesworth's. Any chapter of *The Cuckoo Clock* or the enchanting *Adventures of Herr Baby* is worth a shoal of the very best novels dealing with the characters and fortunes of mere adults.'[3]

Swinburne had not met Louisa but he had been taking an interest in her work at least since 1880 when her name first appeared in his letters in a request to his publishers to send him a copy of *A Christmas Child*. From then on he ordered her books regularly. The first letter that survives of the many he wrote to her, dated 14th November, 1884, makes it clear that they were already acquainted on paper. He referred to a long letter he had previously sent in acknowledgement of one from her, which shows that she had written to him first, probably to thank him for his enthusiastic mention of her in *The Nineteenth Century*.

When Louisa first made Swinburne's acquaintance, he had already been living for five years at The Pines, Putney Hill, a house he and Theodore Watts took on a joint tenancy. Before that time, his health had been undermined by heavy drinking and other excesses and it was through Watts' tactful care and unobtrusive control that he was weaned off all stronger intoxicants than beer and his health and spirits were restored, so that the man Louisa met was, as well as a poet and critic, a formidable scholar leading a disciplined life. Photographs of him taken at The Pines

'show a poise and dignity, a calm nobility and self- possession quite lacking in those taken of him in earlier years, and might almost be photographs of a different person. His days were now regulated by a fixed

---

[3] A. C. Swinburne, 'Charles Reade', *The Nineteenth Century*, Oct. 1884, vol. XVI, p. 563.

and unvarying timetable, which he followed with an almost mechanical regularity, and in this he apparently found peace and contentment.'[4]

Although Louisa probably never knew what Swinburne had been, if she had encountered or heard of him in his earlier years she might well have felt she could not then properly have known such a man. But, considering his present way of living, Society could not frown on the friendship now. And of course the admiration and praise of this well-known poet delighted her. But what was her attraction for him? At this stage of his life he had developed 'a sort of idolatry' for babies. Max Beerbohm, in his essay 'No. 2, The Pines' gives a vivid impression of this.

> 'Well do I remember his ecstasy of emphasis and immensity of pause when he described how he had seen in a perambulator on the Heath to-day "the most BEAUT-iful babbie ever beheld by mortal eyes." . . . After Mazzini had followed Landor to Elysium, and Victor Hugo had followed Mazzini [*earlier heroes of the poet's idolatry*], babies were what among live creatures most evoked Swinburne's genius for self-abasement. His rapture about this especial 'babbie' was such as to shake within me my hitherto firm conviction that, whereas the young of the brute creation are already beautiful at the age of five minutes, the human young never begin to be so before the age of three years. He could as soon have imagined a man not loving the very sea as not doting on the aspect of babies.'[5]

It was not only babies that called forth this enthusiasm — Swinburne adored children too. Gosse described one occasion of ecstatic experience with them.

> 'He was never happier than when passively enduring the tyranny of babes, and some of the most delightful recollections of him which we possess are connected with the infancy of our own little ones. I shall never lose from my memory the picture of the poet seated stiffly on the edge of the sofa (his favourite station) in our house in Delamere Terrace with one of my small girls perched on his little knees, while my son, just advanced to knickerbockers, having climbed up behind him, with open

---

[4] Philip Henderson, *Swinburne: The Portrait of a Poet*, Routledge and Kegan Paul, 1974, p. 232.
[5] Max Beerbohm, 'No. 2, The Pines' in *And Even Now*, Heinemann, 1920, pp. 57–88.

palm was softly stroking his bald cranium, as though it had been the warm and delicious egg of some enormous bird. At that moment the rapturous face of the poet wore no trace of the "Olympian".[6]

It is clear from Swinburne's praise of Louisa's writing that he liked her books because they portrayed so vividly the children and babies he worshipped, and from his first surviving letter to her that he believed she must share his passion, or at least be sympathetic to it. Having related a touching and funny story about a child, he said

'To any other personal stranger but the author of your books I should feel bound to apologise for bestowing all my tediousness upon you like a Dogberry of the nursery or schoolroom,'

and then immediately continued with another such story, because 'I cannot help thinking that *you* may be interested.'[7] The child who was the subject of the first touching story in Swinburne's letter to Louisa was Bertie Mason, the nephew of Theodore Watts. A few months after Watts and Swinburne moved to Putney he also came to live in the house.

'"And now" Swinburne wrote to his mother on 11 November 1879, "we have got my small friend, Watt's little five-year-old nephew, with his mother and an aunt . . . and he is a sweet thing in infants. . . . It makes such a pleasant difference having a child in the household to rule over you. It makes everything bright about him." '[8]

Swinburne's penchant for baby-worship made him write some very sentimental verse, and of his other poetry at this stage of his life Gosse said 'He poured forth stanzas in which great lines were frequent and luminous passages occasional, but the total effect of which was merely foggy and fatiguing.'[9] But this did not disable him from scholarly research and critical writing. While making friends with Bertie he was, for instance, writing articles for the *Encyclopaedia Britannica* on Landor,

---

[6] Edmund Gosse, *The Life of Algernon Charles Swinburne*, Macmillan, 1917, p. 305.

[7] *The Swinburne Letters*, vols I-VI, ed. C.Y.Lang, Yale UP, New Haven, 1982, vol. V, pp. 85–7. There are twenty letters from Swinburne to MLM in these volumes, of which 16 were rescued from oblivion by RR. She transcribed them with the permission of CP, and after CP's death when it was found all personal papers had been destroyed (VMI to RR, 21.12.51), her transcriptions were the only source for them, and they are so marked in the published work.

[8] Henderson, p. 233.

[9] Henderson, p. 236.

Marlowe and Keats. He was, too, conducting a lengthy and learned correspondence with Sidney Colvin (then Slade Professor of Fine Art at Cambridge) over the proofs of Colvin's *Landor*, giving him the benefit of his own bibliographical research. Writers and artists like Gosse, Madox Brown, William Rossetti, William Morris and Burne Jones visited The Pines and corresponded with him on literary matters. Andrew Lang wrote of him, shortly after his death

> 'As a critic Swinburne had a transcendental knowledge of literature and a power of appreciation only rivalled by Charles Lamb; but whether he loved or hated an author, his language was certainly too violent in praise or dispraise.'[10]

On balance, Louisa might well be proud of his praise, even though it was violent in adulation.

Bertie, with his family, was still living at No. 2, The Pines, aged eleven, when Louisa first corresponded with Swinburne. In April 1885, she wrote offering to dedicate to the child her next Macmillan title, *"Us": An Old-fashioned Story*. Swinburne was delighted by this 'great compliment', and most upset at having to refuse it, because, as he explained in his reply, the child's mother and uncle were 'afraid lest the dedication of a book to him "might lead him to think that he is somebody in particular".' He also mentioned the delight both he and Bertie took in all her books, particularly 'your most lovely and touching story 'Goodnight Winny',' which he had just re-read, and the enjoyment they anticipated from *Us*.[11] He and Louisa had still not met, although she had invited him to bring Bertie to visit her family the previous November. Swinburne had countered this both by doubt over Bertie's being allowed to go and by a vague, general invitation to lunch 'one of these holidays' to her and 'any little friend whom you were kind enough to bring,' mentioning only Lionel by name, naturally enough as he was the same age as Bertie.[12] Now (in May) she issued another invitation, to call, which Swinburne accepted, while explaining how unusual a step this was for him.

> 'If you can receive a visitor in the morning, I hope I may be able to come on Wednesday week (the thirteenth) about eleven or so; afternoon calls being quite out of my unfashionable line. As a rule I never go

[10] Andrew Lang, *History of English Literature*, Longmans, 1912, p. 605.
[11] C. Y. Lang, V, p. 103.
[12] C. Y. Lang, V, p. 85.

anywhere: but of course I would not on any account forego the pleasure of meeting you, even if I had to go to the house of a third person for that purpose: and that — for a deaf recluse — is saying something. I long to see your children — so many of your large family (in print) have been dear to me for years that I shall feel almost as if I were coming among friends long since familiar to me.'[13]

Interestingly, Swinburne here appears to have taken it for granted that the children in her books were based on her own family (unless she had told him so herself). He also mentioned his delight in the 'triple prospect' of more stories from her. One of these was clearly *Us*. The most immediate prospect of other stories for children was her contributions to *The Child's Pictorial*, a new monthly periodical from SPCK, which began in May 1885. It continued until the end of 1896 and every issue but three contained a new story or part of one, by Louisa. All these were later published as collections of stories, the majority in nine books issued by SPCK and the rest in one from Nelson and one from Fisher Unwin.[14] The odd items that escaped this net eventually appeared in Nister collections of stories by various authors. Only two of these contributions to *The Child's Pictorial* seem never to have been re-published.[15] Louisa said she was well-paid for this activity, and described it as 'these little stories [which] are reprinted by the S.P.C.K. as, so to say, nursery books, in paper backs & coloured pictures.'[16] The third member of the 'triple prospect' is more difficult to identify. Another story of hers was published in two parts in May and June 1885 in *Macmillan's Magazine*, but it was a ghost story for adults and Swinburne definitely associated Bertie with himself in his letter, saying he had not told him of the pleasure to come 'for fear of exciting too keen an impatience.' The other possibility was *The Palace in the Garden*, which was going to start as a serial in *Little Folks* the following January, and which, therefore, she had presumably at least begun to write, and would have been able to mention to Swinburne as something in store.

---

[13] C. Y. Lang, V, pp. 106–7.

[14] *Five Minutes' Stories*, 1888; *A House To Let*, 1889; *Twelve Tiny Tales*, 1890; *Family Troubles*, 1890; *The Lucky Ducks and Other Stories*, 1891; *The Man with the Pan-Pipes and Other Stories*, 1892; *The Thirteen Little Black Pigs and Other Stories*, 1893; *Opposite Neighbours and Other Stories*, 1895; *Friendly Joey, and Other Stories*, 1896; *The Children's Hour*, Nelson, 1899; *The Blue Baby and Other Stories*, Fisher Unwin, 1901.

[15] These were a poem, 'Secrets' in CP, May 1888 and 'An Odd Fancy' in CP Jul. 1892. Note by RLG in his unpublished bibliography.

[16] MLM to GLC, 30.1.[1893].

The meeting arranged in Swinburne's letter quoted above did take place and must have been a success as another was fixed for 26th May only ten days later. Swinburne did not manage to attend this one, and wrote to apologise for missing it, which happened because he was unwell, and also because 'I have had a very heavy blow since we met'. This was the death of Victor Hugo on 22nd May, for whom he had a very great respect and admiration. This second abortive meeting seems also to have been arranged in part to bring them together with a mutual friend, Annie C. Ogle, a novelist and a friend of Browning's. Louisa replied to Swinburne's apology with news of Miss Ogle's being in bad health and in his reply he said that he himself would 'not be in visiting trim for some time to come. Indeed I hardly go out once in six months.' This sounds like the recluse justifying his retreat into his shell, but in fact two days later he wrote again with a definite invitation to Louisa and Lionel to visit himself and Bertie, with specific instructions for finding the house from Putney Hill station. He also acknowledged with thanks two numbers of *Macmillan's Magazine* containing the ghost story mentioned above, which he found 'beautiful and interesting.'[17]

Another friend who found this story interesting was Gery Cullum, whom the Molesworths had known in Paris. Louisa sent him a copy at Cicely's request, because Cicely had half promised to see that he got one if ever her mother wrote it out. The girls and Cullum 'used to talk on such subjects.'[18] From this we see that it was a story told to and known among family and friends well before it was prepared for publication. Gwen Molesworth remembered spending the summer of 1883 at Hohwald in the Vosges with 'Cousin Louisa' and her children, when Louisa would sit on a log with all the family around her and tell them ghost stories.[19] 'Unexplained', the story just published in *Macmillan's*, may well have been among them. It was another member of the group set in Thuringia, showing Louisa's personal knowledge of the area. This is evident from the vivid and minutely detailed description of the 'stupid and stolid and ungenial' people, unlike any the narrator encountered elsewhere in Germany, and their rough, remote village where the characters are marooned and have their ghostly experience. There are pine forests, a china factory and an unnamed town with an old fortress 'on the borders of the Thuringian Forest,' which could be Coburg. These

---

[17] C. Y. Lang, V, pp. 111–12 and 116–17.
[18] MLM to Gery M-G Cullum, 19.7.[1885] Trinity College, Cambridge.
[19] GDL to RR, 4.5.1938.

touches of local colour appear in even more detail than in the account
of the same features in the Thuringian stories for children described in
the previous chapter. The other striking point about this story is the
thoughtful, careful consideration of the nature of ghosts and tales about
them. This story was not written for the sake of causing sensation and
raising a shudder — indeed none of Louisa's ghost stories could be
accused of this. She was clearly deeply, earnestly interested in the matter.
It may be that points in the discussion the characters had about ghosts
derive from conversations she and her daughters had with Cullum,
Gwen Molesworth and other friends and relations.

Louisa and Lionel did visit The Pines on 8th July. Although no description of her experience has survived, Swinburne's life and surroundings
remained so much the same during his last thirty years that we can
imagine what it was like from Max Beerbohm's account of a visit he
made in the spring of 1899.

'It is but a few steps from the railway-station in Putney High Street to
No 2, The Pines. . . . No. 2 — prosaic inscription! But as that front
door closed behind me I had the instant sense of having slipped away
from the harsh light of the ordinary and contemporary into the dimness
of an odd august past. Here, in this dark hall, the past was the present.
Here loomed vivid and vital on the walls those women of Rossetti whom
I had known but as shades. Familiar to me in small reproductions by
photogravure, here they themselves were, life-sized, 'with curled-up lips
and amorous hair' done in the original warm crayon, all of them intently
looking down on me while I took off my overcoat . . . That they hung
in the hall, evidently no more than an overflow, was an earnest of packed
plenitude within. The room I was ushered into was a back-room, a
dining- room, looking on to a good garden. It was, in form and 'fixtures'
an inalienably mid-Victorian room, and held its stolid own in the riot
of Rossettis. Its proportions, its window-sash, bisecting the view of garden,
its folding doors . . . its mantel-piece, its gas-brackets, all promised that
nothing would ever seduce them from their allegiance to Martin
Tupper. . . . Swinburne's entry was for me a great moment. . . . here he
was shutting the door behind him as might anybody else, and advancing
— a strange small figure in grey, having an air at once noble and roguish,
proud and skittish. My name was roared to him. In shaking his hand, I
bowed low of course — a bow *de coeur*; and he in the old aristocratic
manner, bowed equally low . . . You do not usually associate a man of
genius, when you see one, with any social class; and, Swinburne being

of an aspect so unrelated as it was to any species of human kind, I wondered the more that almost the first impression he made on me, or would make on any one, was that of a very great gentleman indeed. Not of an *old* gentleman either. Sparse and straggling though the grey hair was that fringed the immense pale dome of his head, and venerably haloed though he was for me by his greatness, there was yet about him something — boyish? girlish? childish, rather; something of a beautiful well-bred child. . . . Watts-Dunton leaned forward and "Well, Algernon", he roared, "how was it on the Heath today?" Swinburne . . . threw back his head, uttering a sound that was like the cooing of a dove, and forthwith, rapidly, ever so musically, he spoke to us of his walk; spoke not in the strain of a man who had been taking his daily exercise on Putney Heath, but rather in that of a Peri who had at long last been suffered to pass through Paradise. And rather than that he spoke would I say that he cooingly and flutingly *sang* of his experience. The wonders of this morning's wind and sun and clouds were expressed in a flow of words so right and sentences so perfectly balanced that they would have seemed pedantic had they not been clearly as spontaneous as the wordless notes of a bird in song. The frail, sweet voice rose and fell, lingered, quickened, in all manner of trills and roulades. That he himself could not hear it, seemed to me the greatest loss his deafness inflicted on him. One would have expected this disability to mar the music; but it didn't; save that now and again a note would come out metallic and over- shrill, the tones were under good control. The whole manner and method had certainly a strong element of oddness; but no one incapable of condemning as unmanly the song of a lark would have called it affected.'[20]

We can only conjecture how Louisa managed to conduct a conversation with the deaf poet — her lovely but quiet and soft speaking voice cannot have helped. Probably she had to rely on interpretative roars from Watts. We know some of the topics of those conversations — obviously her own books, and baby anecdotes to begin with. He also wanted to show her 'the last photograph Victor Hugo sent me of himself and his young grandson, a very fine-looking boy,'[21] so she probably heard a trilled monologue about his adored second father. An old black-letter book full of woodcuts of animals 'in whose existence I am sorry to say that

---

[20] Beerbohm, 'At the Pines'. Theodore Watts had added the name of Dunton to his own by deed-poll before Beerbohm first visited The Pines. He was still Watts when MLM first went there.

[21] C. Y. Lang, V, p. 117.

Bertie, the child of a sceptical and scientific generation, stoutly refuses to believe' was another treasure he had promised to show Lionel. But probably after an inspection of the 'mermaid with her tail in her left hand' and 'a lion, an eagle and a snake with human faces, unlovely in feature but amiable in expression,'[22] Lionel and Bertie spent most of the visit playing outside in the 'good garden.' Louisa and later her family treasured letters from Swinburne (and Watts, with news of the poet's health) written over nearly twenty years, so it seems clear that the friendship lasted to the end of Swinburne's life.

Another friend Louisa made during her first months in London was Anne Thackeray Ritchie, the daughter of William Thackeray. Only one piece of direct evidence links the two. In March 1885, A.W. Kinglake, traveller, historian and author of *Eothen*, wrote affectionately to Mrs Ritchie in reply to her request for information on Madame Mohl, hoping to meet her soon and promising to talk about Madame Mohl to her and her friend Mrs Molesworth if she were there.[23] This topic is one that would have formed a natural bond between Louisa and Mrs Ritchie. They both loved France and in her childhood and girlhood Anne Thackeray, as she was then, had spent much of her time in Paris with her grandparents. She still visited the country frequently, as Louisa was to do now she had returned to London. Thackeray had visited Madame Mohl's salon and twice in her published letters his daughter also mentions doing so. One of these visits was at the height of the Paris commune in 1871.[24]

For Christmas 1888 and January 1889 Mrs Ritchie and her family took a house in Lexham Gardens. They urgently needed somewhere to live in order to receive relations home on leave from India, having just packed up the house where they had been living, on the death of Mrs Ritchie senior.[25] It is tempting to suppose Louisa might have helped in finding them this temporary home so near to her own.

Mrs Ritchie was, too, a close friend of Swinburne, whom she had first met as a young man in 1863, and they exchanged affectionate letters. With her, as with Louisa, he shared his love for babies and small children. Congratulating her on becoming a grandmother he wrote 'To

[22] C. Y. Lang, V, pp. 85–6.

[23] From a list of autograph letters, mss. etc, offered for sale in August 1997 by Henry Bristow of Ringwood.

[24] Hester Ritchie, ed., *Letters of Anne Thackeray Ritchie*, Murray, 1924, pp. 146 and 164.

[25] W. Gerin, *Anne Thackeray Ritchie: A Biography*, OUP, 1981, p. 216.

have a baby at hand or within reach is to belong to the "Kingdom of heaven" yourself.' Friendship with Anne Thackeray Ritchie could have opened the way to contacts with very many of the great names of the day — men and women who knew and loved Mrs Ritchie first for her father's sake and then for her own — the Tennysons, Julia Margaret Cameron, Thomas Hardy, Henry James, Mrs Oliphant — 'outside her own family . . . perhaps the person Anny loved and admired most'[26] — to name but a few. Leslie Stephen became her brother-in-law through his marriage with her sister Minny, and his second wife Julia Duckworth, already Anne's friend, brought Prinsep cousins into the family. Cicely Molesworth, Louisa's eldest daughter, was to marry a Prinsep. That one phrase in Kinglake's letter suggests that Louisa may have had some entrée to these circles of family links and friendships. She could at least have felt in touch with the literary lions. There is no point in speculating further here, for no letters between any of these famous people and Louisa have been found.

During this first year in London Cicely and Juliet went into society and 'enjoyed the season very much.' Lady Randolph Churchill, in her reminiscences, described the Season in the 1880s when it had been considered so important that 'no votary of fashion would willingly miss a week or a day.' Between October and February

'the town was a desert. Religiously, however, on the 1st of May, Belgravia . . . would open the doors of its freshly-painted and flower-bedecked mansions. Dinners, balls and parties succeeded one another without intermission till the end of July, the only respite being at the Whitsuntide [parliamentary] recess.'[27]

Juliet's daughter, describing all three girls as they were around this time, said that

'As a mother [*Louisa*] must have been rather proud of her three daughters as they were very good-looking and all different. Mrs Prinsep [*Cicely*], the eldest and <u>most</u> beautiful, was dark, my mother had masses and masses of wonderful golden hair and green grey eyes, and the youngest, Olive, deep auburn hair and the same green grey eyes.'

---

[26] Gerin (1981), pp. 246 and 263.

[27] MLM to Cullum, 19.7.[1885]; Mrs George Cornwallis-West, *The Reminiscences of Lady Randolph Churchill*, 1908, pp. 39–40. Quoted in Pamela Horn, *High Society: the English Social Elite, 1880–1914*, Alan Sutton, 1992, p. 15.

Their mother was indeed proud of their looks and hardly able to credit herself with such grown-up daughters as the following extract from a letter written in July 1885 shows. 'People seem to think they have by no means "fallen off" in English air — I think it must be true — Cicely is, I think, prettier than she was — & now she has attained the dignity of twenty-one!' She wrote this to Gery Cullum, the son of her friend in Paris, Mrs Milner-Gibson. She had died in February and Louisa remembered that 'she was, I like to think, very fond of both Cicely and me — dear loving heart that she was.' Sympathising with his loss made her recall her own mother's death, which, she said, 'seems as fresh and acute a sorrow to me as ever.' Cullum had invited her and the family to visit him in Venice but she did not think it would be possible to accept, enjoyable though such a visit might be, because 'I am so much tied by having my little boys at home.'[28] Bevil and Lionel were at this time fourteen and twelve and were mostly being educated at home with tutors, although Bevil did go to Westminster School for a time. When Lionel was grown up, or nearly so, he told a story about this time of his life to one of his cousins. In common with many small boys he had always hated new clothes. But, he said, 'our tailor always used to put a sixpence in the pocket of our new suits.' Then, as he suddenly re-alised what must have been the case, he added 'Oh, I never thought of it till this instant, but, of course, it was my mother who put them in.'[29]

Louisa managed to chaperone her daughters to parties but found she could not accompany them on visits outside London because of the boys, so that the country-house visiting part of the season was curtailed for them, except for staying with relations. In this connection she found, as she told Cullum, that her mother's death had made life terribly difficult. She seems to have meant by this, in the context, that there was now only one adult member of the household to chaperone the girls, oversee the boys, and look after Olive who had not yet 'come out' although she was eighteen — three groups all engaged in different pursuits. When Mrs Stewart was alive Louisa had, for instance, been able to go off to Germany with only two of the children, leaving the others in Paris in her mother's care.

As well as these concerns, the normal overseeing of a household and the balls, parties, dinners and other events which made up a London social life, there was the everlasting business of calling. Louisa once

[28] MLM to Cullum, 19.7.[1885], Trinity College, Cambridge.
[29] F. C. Molesworth to RR, 19.12.1951.

lamented to a friend 'I am frightfully in arrears with my calls!'[30] Paying
calls at the right time and leaving the correct number of cards was an
important part of being in society. To get any detail wrong 'showed
ignorance of polite manners and therefore brought the caller's whole
social position into question.' The whole process

> 'for those who were assiduous about it, probably accounted for a couple
> of afternoons a week. It was really a two-way affair, for most of the ladies
> set aside an afternoon a week when they dressed up and produced extra
> cakes for tea and sat in their drawing-rooms awaiting the callers.'

The writer of this description, born in 1897, remembered her mother
reluctantly co-operating with this social demand.

> 'Those like mother . . . who did respect their time and had plenty of
> occupations on which they would have been glad to use it, . . . went
> forth about three o'clock in the spirit of drilled and disciplined soldiers
> parading for fatigues whose necessity they do not see but whose perform-
> ance they cannot question. Even the tone in which they would announce
> their intentions at lunch betrayed their real feelings — 'I *must* pay calls this
> afternoon,' mother would say and go upstairs with stern determination to
> change into her calling things. On the whole it would be a more successful
> afternoon if most of her hostesses were out. That meant getting through
> more in the time, because the cards could be left and the score counted
> just the same.'[31]

Louisa was one of those, who, like this writer's mother, respected her
time and had plenty to do. She always had her writing work, which
generally took up part of each day. Gwen Molesworth remembered that
she sat down to write regularly every morning after breakfast. Regularity
in writing was a principle with her. Whether she felt like it or not, she
did it. 'My rule is to sit down and begin to write, even though I am
not feeling at all "inspired".' And this habit helped her work.

> 'Concentration of thought, even mechanical regularity — the sitting
> down at a certain hour to your work, the very feeling of the pen in your
> fingers — help to bring the material.'

Usually after writing a page or two she could continue with ease and
pleasure. On the rare occasions when this did not happen, when she

---

[30] MLM to DUC, 30.1.[1888].
[31] Chorley, pp. 152–3.

was 'too tired or too much occupied with real life to have any fancy to spare for story-telling' she put the writing away, feeling that at such times 'to persist would be wrong, unfair to your readers and yourself.'[32] This account of her writing discipline comes from two articles she wrote herself, both published in 1894, when she had been back in England for nearly ten years, with habits for London life well established. She had expressed herself more emphatically about it the previous year, to an interviewer who wrote, 'Her own rule is to compel herself to write to the end of two pages. If by that time she finds she has not got into the spirit of her work, she lays it aside.'[33] The section about her in a book on 'writers for the young' published in 1900 also mentions this rule.[34] Public repetition of it so often must mean that she really did work in this way.

It is more difficult to accept a statement from an article published in 1906 that 'she has never worked more than an hour and a half a day.'[35] The author of this article wrote, 'it was my good fortune to enjoy a talk with Mrs Molesworth about her books,' so Louisa must herself have said something to prompt the 'hour and a half' remark. The solution seems to lie in the method of work she set up when writing her early novels, as described in chapter seven. We saw that she referred to invention and planning, of both character and plot, as 'thinking'. Only the actual writing down of what was already clear in her head did she call 'work'. So she presumably came to her 'hour and a half' with plenty of well-planned material ready to write at once, a result that had been achieved at other times. This conclusion is supported by her description of the way she would live with her characters for weeks with the only thing about them actually written down being their names.

> 'And so day by day I seem to be more in their lives, more able to tell how, in certain circumstances, my characters would comport themselves. And by degrees these circumstances stretch themselves out and take vague shape, which like the at first far-off and dimly perceived heights above one in climbing a mountain, grow distinct and defined as one approaches them more nearly.'[36]

---

[32] 'How I Write . . .', p. 18; 'Story-Writing', p. 163–4.
[33] *Westminster Budget*, p. 24.
[34] Robson, *Story Weavers*.
[35] *Quiver*, p. 675b.
[36] 'On the Art . . .' p. 345.

With all this worked out before she put pen to paper, the hour and a half a day becomes more credible.

At the end of their first season in London, Louisa and the family set off to spend their summer holiday in St Davids, South Wales, having begun to feel reasonably settled; as she told Gery Cullum.

> 'We are getting accustomed to London, — in <u>many</u> ways we like it better than Paris. Still it is always more or less of an uprooting to leave a country one has lived in for a good many years.'[37]

In one of her later books for girls, the youngest daughter of a family that moved from France to England expressed this more settled feeling in a way that Olive or Juliet might have done. 'London in November, with a fog, in a horrid hotel, and without a creature to speak to, isn't exactly the same thing as London in May, in a bright open street like this.'[38] Just before they went away, Louisa and Cicely made the acquaintance of Jean Ingelow, who lived in Holland Villas Road, the other side of Holland Park from Lexham Gardens. The only surviving evidence of this is a little note from Miss Ingelow thanking Louisa for lending her 'pretty daughter to grace my party' and thus permitting the 'hope you will allow me to make your acquaintance.' It seems strange that an invitation should have been issued and accepted by a hostess and a guest who did not know each other, but there was probably a mutual friend involved. Miss Ingelow invited Louisa to call on her, having said 'It would give me great pleasure to know the writer of stories so beautiful as yours.' We may be sure an invitation baited with such a compliment was accepted, and also that the compliment was not empty, for Jean Ingelow was shy and reserved and would surely not have courted the acquaintance of a writer unknown to her if she did not admire the writing.[39]

No doubt on holiday Louisa continued with her regular writing sessions both in obedience to her rule, and to fulfil her obligations. There were the stories for *The Child's Pictorial* needed monthly, the first instalment of *The Palace in the Garden* due in January, another ghost story coming out in the *English Illustrated Magazine* in January (her first contact with this periodical), and her second 'teenage' book for SPCK,

---

[37] MLM to Cullum, 19.7.[1885].
[38] *Blanche: A Story for Girls*, Chambers, [1893] 1894, p. 340.
[39] Copy of letter from JI to MLM, 30.7.1885, typed with permission of CP, who owned it, since destroyed.

A Charge Fulfilled, due out in May. This last was something of a thriller, with a plot turning on kidnapping, attempted murder and wrongful inheritance. It also differed from many of her later books for older girls in that the narrator was a farmer's daughter, the action taking place mostly in her milieu, so the book was far less concerned with trivial details of Victorian etiquette for young ladies. The climax of the story depends on an uncanny episode, in which a dream leads to a rescue. Clearly at this period Louisa's mind was working a great deal on such lines. The old conviction of her own gift of second sight, the old interest in coincidences that she confided to Warren, still influenced her. Another story that she may well have begun to plan this summer was a fantasy tale. This was a class of writing for children that relates to her general interest in the uncanny and mysterious, to which she was much drawn and which she might have written more of had it not been that her publisher preferred real-life stories. She had referred to this issue during the negotiations over *Christmas-Tree Land* — 'I know you prefer not fairy tales' she wrote to Craik and then after a sentence on its prospects, she added 'I have not written a fairy-tale for several years.'[40] She did not enlarge on this remark, but it has a wistful tone, as though she would like to have done so. The fantasy she was probably thinking out that summer in St Davids was worked on with Olive as the dedication shows, 'To my youngest daughter Olive I inscribe this little story which we thought of together,' and this was dated June 1886. The remote Welsh coast (and it was remote in those days) was an appropriate setting for the preliminary getting to know the characters and circumstances of *Four Winds Farm* shared with her daughter.

That autumn or soon after Louisa became involved in a different kind of activity — charitable appeals on behalf of Great Ormond Street children's hospital. It was customary for Victorian women of the middle-class and above to go in for charitable work, and those who had a live, as opposed to merely conventional, Christian faith to support their activities were the more vigorous in pursuing them. She started simply by becoming an annual subscriber but this soon drew her in to a more personal involvement, since this and the active help she gave to a special and urgent appeal in 1886 resulted in her becoming an Honorary Governor of the hospital. The significant thing about this position was that it carried the privilege of recommending patients to the hospital — two in-patients and twelve out-patients a year. It is clear from correspondence

---

[40] MLM to GLC, 12.1.[1884].

in the hospital's letter books that she exercised this privilege with care, and spent time investigating and following up cases. At that period very often the only chance of treatment for a sick child of the poor was a recommendation from a subscriber to the children's hospital. With no state provision for medical care, voluntary contributions were vital. Children and young people were encouraged to help by the periodicals they read. Readers of *Aunt Judy's Magazine* and *The Quiver* were among the best friends of the hospital, special cots being named after these two magazines and supported by subscriptions of at least £1,000 per cot. Louisa would of course have been aware of this since she contributed stories and articles to both periodicals. She remained a Governor to the end of her life. It seems very likely that her continuing interest in children, fuelling and fed by her books for them in a mutual interchange, together with the memory of Violet's illness and death, prompted her interest in this particular form of charitable work.[41]

Louisa continued gradually to widen her literary contacts. She approached Charlotte Yonge with the offer of a story for *The Monthly Packet*, obviously written on purpose for that periodical with its aim clearly in mind, of helping its readers 'to bring your religious principles to bear upon your daily life.' It is the working out of a comment by the vicar's wife at the beginning of the story, that 'if an angel from heaven came down to preach one Sunday morning . . . he would be found fault with or sneered at, or criticised'. The various fault-finders are all sketches of different contemporary schools of religious or anti-religious thought.[42] It appealed to Miss Yonge for she accepted it and also welcomed the offer of a 'free translation from the French' which Louisa made soon after returning the corrected proofs. This was 'Felix — an outcast' from 'Le Parigot' by Madame de Pressensé, a French version of the ever-popular street-arab story. Louisa was particularly pleased to discover that Miss Yonge had accepted the first story, 'One Sunday morning', without knowing that the author was the Mrs Molesworth who had written *Carrots*. She had had to apply to Mr Craik for information about Louisa's identity.[43] Louisa sent one more tale to *The Monthly Packet* while Charlotte Yonge was still the editor, and later on one article on story-writing. That she did not do more is probably for

[41] Information from the archives of Great Ormond Street hospital.
[42] MLM 'One Sunday Morning', *The Monthly Packet*, 1, no. 1 [Jan. 1851] pp. i-iv.
[43] MLM to C. M. Yonge, 26.2.[1886], National Library of Scotland, MS9752/57–8; 2 letters from CMY to MLM, formerly owned by CP, now destroyed.

the same reason she was reluctant to contribute to *Aunt Judy* — 'they pay poorly.' 'Circulation was a matter of little moment' to Charlotte and *The Monthly Packet* could not hope to pay its contributors competitively when it was run 'on these charming but unbusinesslike lines.'[44] Mrs Gatty had complained about the low rate of pay — 'Why does Miss Yonge's publisher pay authors so badly?' When she made this protest, in the sixties, magazines such as *Good Words* were paying her eight times as much as *The Monthly Packet* — '£1 per page and copyright reserved — instead of 2s 6d.'[45]

In May 1886, *The Contemporary Review* published an article of Louisa's on Mrs Ewing. She cannot have known her subject personally for she wrote

'More may be written of her in the future by those who had the best opportunities of knowing her intimately and thoroughly, and who, as friends only, and not relations, may feel able to let their enthusiasm have full vent, but in one not so privileged it would be presumption to say more.'

But a few words later in the article suggest that there had been some contact between them, perhaps just a letter from Mrs Ewing of appreciation and encouragement on the publication of one of Louisa's books. 'I myself' wrote Louisa, 'can speak to her ever ready interest in the work of others, lying along similar paths to her own.' But although she did not know the writer, she knew, loved and admired her stories. She called them 'full of charm and merit,' saying that they 'never fail to attract and interest and impress,' that they are 'brightened by touches of humour never long absent from Mrs Ewing's pages' and yet also contain 'many serious passages of great beauty.' And in the detailed comments on each story, the lovingly lingering quotations introduced by some admiring remark like 'What can give a more perfect picture of an owlet than this?', it becomes even clearer how very much Louisa appreciated Mrs Ewing's books.[46] Later on, in a private letter to the critic Edward Salmon, she confirmed her opinion simply and directly.

'In your new book or article,' she wrote, 'I hope you will say a great deal about Mrs Ewing — I myself wrote a pretty exhaustive article on her

[44] Battiscombe, p. 157.
[45] Maxwell, p. 133.
[46] 'Mrs Ewing's Less Well-Known Books', *The Contemporary Review*, 49, May 1886, pp. 675–86.

<u>lesser known books</u> in last May's "Contemporary" — I wish you cd. get it. <u>On the whole</u> her stories are for older children than mine — some perhaps are not really for children, but I allow this reluctantly: I admire everything she ever did so thoroughly.'[47]

The article brought her into contact with Mrs Ewing's family as we see from a letter to Theodore Watts. 'I am exceedingly pleased that you like my Mrs Ewing. I have some touching letters from her family about the article which I will show you.'[48]

The references that survive show that Louisa's social life was active. In March she had been expecting to meet Craik at the Holman Hunts, a party she could not after all attend, because several of the children were ill.[49] It was probably the Craiks who introduced her to the Hunts, since Mrs Craik was a particular friend of theirs. She accompanied Edith Waugh to Switzerland in 1875 for the latter's marriage to Holman Hunt, her dead sister's widower. Such a union was illegal in England until the passage of the Deceased Wife's Sister's Marriage Act in 1907, and the total breach between the Hunts and Edith's family caused by it shows that Dinah Craik braved quite a degree of social disapproval to support her friend.[50] Louisa's mention of the Hunts was so slight and casual, yet coupled with her friendship with Swinburne and Watts it is enough to make one wonder how many of the Pre-Raphaelites she came to know. Did she meet William Morris for instance?

A somewhat better documented friendship was that with Edwin Arnold (later Sir Edwin) the poet and journalist, who was by many confidently expected to become poet laureate after Tennyson's death. He owed most of his fame to his epic poem *The Light of Asia*, about the life and philosophy of Gautama Buddha. It was a poem so well-known that pet guinea pigs were named after it, much as if a favourite animal now were to be called after a Booker prize winner, or a film with a string of Oscars.[51] Louisa headed the first chapter of *Four Winds Farm* with a quotation from this poem. She wrote of Arnold 'He is the

[47] MLM to Salmon, 12.10.[1886].

[48] MLM to Watts, 13.5.[1886], Brotherton Library Leeds.

[49] MLM to GLC, 8.3.[1886], University Library Bristol.

[50] Diana Holman-Hunt, *My Grandfather, His Wives and Loves*, Columbus Books, 1969, p. 284 and chap. XXI.

[51] *The Journal of Beatrix Potter*, F. Warne and Co., 1966, p. 304 — 'a still more illustrious animal named the Light of Asia.' General information about Arnold from DNB.

best and kindest of human beings and a great friend of mine and my children.' Two notes from him to Louisa survived,[52] both from 1888, one on the occasion of his becoming a KCIE in the New Year Honour's List of that year, which assured her of his 'profound regard' and 'faithfullest friendship' and the other a note of thanks for flowers and a visit after what sounds like an operation. Lexham Gardens, where the Molesworths were living, leads into West Cromwell Road from which Arnold's note was addressed, so visiting him would have been easy.

In May 1886 Louisa gave a party where Arnold and various French friends were among the guests, and to which she invited Swinburne and Watts. They were unable to come but Watts begged for an introduction to Arnold anyway.

'Between ourselves I do not at all share your liking for French people and French ways: but I should much like to see you again and I have a great wish to meet Mr Edwin Arnold, whose character, from what I hear, is as fine as his work. . . . Could you not let us meet Mr Arnold alone some day?'

Louisa was delighted with this idea, and she arranged the meeting for a few days after her larger party. The details of her reply to Watts about this show that she was in close and easy touch with Arnold. Watts' prejudice against 'French people and French ways,' prompting him to complain 'And why does he [Lionel] (who has the privilege of being an English boy) write his letter in French?', throws a sidelight on one of Louisa's aims for Lionel's education. His complaint elicited an explanation from her. She wrote

'You wd. find Lionel a thorough English boy at heart — his French proclivities are only on the surface and fast disappearing, only I don't want his French language to disappear, so I rather encourage his speaking it at home & writing it to any friend who likes it. It is still easier for him to write than English.'[53]

A casual reference in a letter of Mrs Humphry Ward's shows that in June Louisa, described by Mrs Ward as 'the child's story-teller,' met her at dinner at a Mrs Susan Jeune's and endeared herself by admiring Mrs Ward's second book *Miss Bretherton* (1884) as 'a gem'. 'A whole gaggle of novelists' attended this dinner and Louisa had the opportunity of

---

[52] Long enough to be copied by RR, but both destroyed by CP.

[53] Watts to MLM, 10.5.1886, copy of letter owned by CP, now destroyed; MLM to Watts, 13.5.[1886] Brotherton Library.

meeting Thomas Hardy, Mrs Campbell Praed and Justin McCarthy.[54]
Mrs Jeune was on one of the Great Ormond Street Hospital committees
and they probably met through their common interest in this charitable
work.

In the autumn, while Louisa was preparing for a visit to Scotland,
she was interested but surprised, and, as she later admitted, 'exceedingly
disappointed,' to read an article in *The Nineteenth Century* entitled
'What Girls Read,' which made no mention at all of her own books.
This omission disturbed her so much that she actually wrote to the
author, Edward Salmon, to ask the reason. Salmon was then well known
as an authority on children's books and Louisa wrote that she would
have been glad to profit by his criticism. She also feared that his leaving
her out meant he disapproved of her work — 'If you object to my
books I should like to know on what grounds'. And she was piqued
enough to point to her good sales — 'Of course if one is to judge by
practical results in such matters, it would be false modesty in me to
deny that my books are <u>exceedingly</u> popular.' To an impartial reader,
not annoyed by neglect, it would seem obvious that she was reserved
for later treatment as a writer for younger children, but this we can
never know, for her intervention has naturally prevented us from seeing
what Salmon would have done without it. She herself was unable to
mention the titles of more than four of her books up to that time as
having been 'specially written for girls,' and such books were, after all,
the subject of Salmon's article. His response to her letter must have
been tactful, for she said it was kind, and also thanked him for writing
so cordially. He clearly asked for information about her work, since in
a second letter she provided a detailed list of her books with comments,
analysed into sections by age and offered to tell him 'anything more
you may possibly wish to know.' He used all that she told him in a
second article published in *The Nineteenth Century* a year later, called
'Literature for the Little Ones' which was afterwards included, with
some alteration, in his book *Juvenile Literature As It Is*. In this article
he said, among much other detailed praise,

> 'I have left till last any mention of the lady who, by right of merit, should
> stand first. Mrs Molesworth is, in my opinion, considering the quality
> and quantity of her labours, the best story-teller for children England
> has yet known.'

---

[54] J. Sutherland, *Mrs Humphry Ward*, OUP 1991, p. 112.

Louisa was naturally delighted by this and wrote as much to a great friend — 'It is so kind of you to feel so interested in the Nineteenth Century article. It is very nice, & gave me extreme pleasure — & it is delightful to find my friends sympathising with me in this.'[55]

Immediately after her second letter to Salmon, Louisa, accompanied certainly by Olive and probably by the rest of the family too, went to Edinburgh to spend several weeks with the Patons. *Silverthorns*, one of the books she mentioned to Salmon as written 'expressly for girls' which, she told him, was just coming out, had four illustrations by Sir Noel and it seems very likely that during her visit she would have discussed them with him. This was the only one of her books that he illustrated. The letter she received from Sir Noel after the visit is worth quoting in full, particularly since it appears to be the sole survivor of his letters to her.

Nov. 11th 1886   33, George Square, Edinburgh.

My dear "Marie Louise",

Thanks for the sight of Swinburne's interesting and characteristic letter — herewith returned. In the light of his fervent periods, how tame and frigid my approval of the "Farm" must have seemed to you! And yet I venture to maintain that my poor "worthy of its predecessor and of its Author" was praise not less strong than his! for you cannot but know what I think of them — and of her.

I had much quiet satisfaction in showing the letter to the Skeltons, who were here yesterday afternoon. Indeed I retained it for that purpose — not a breach of confidence I trust. Olive is working away like a Trojan (though why the Trojans should be quoted as the typical workers is more than I know!) at her little St Jerome; and I am greatly mistaken if her work does not indicate a very remarkable faculty of imitative art, which you would be fully justified in cultivating. Whether she has the inventive faculty, up till now I have not the means of guessing.

I am more glad than I can tell you that you were really "happy" with us, — quiet and stupid people as we are. But can we ever be so happy

---

[55] MLM to Edward Salmon, 5 and 12.10.1886 (letters made available to RR by Salmon himself); 'What Girls Read' and 'Literature for the Little Ones' in *The Nineteenth Century*, vol. XX, no. 116, pp. 515–529, Oct. 1886 and vol XXII pp 563–80, Oct. 1887; E. Salmon, *Juvenile Literature As It Is*, Henry J. Drane, 1888; MLM to DUC, 21.10.1887.

as with those who <u>unconditionally</u> love us — as you know we all love you!

    Addio!

      Ever faithfully yours,

        Noel Paton.[56]

Olive had clearly stayed on in Edinburgh to profit from Sir Noel's tuition in painting. There is one later indication that Louisa followed his advice about cultivating her daughter's talent, when she remarked in a note of informal invitation 'Thursday & Friday, Olive is always at the National Gallery.'[57]

The letter from Swinburne that Paton mentioned was one that Louisa found waiting for her on her return to London and which she had obviously enclosed to show him in her own letter of thanks for her visit. It was full of praise for *Four Winds Farm*, published at the beginning of November. In sending out complimentary copies Macmillan had also included Ruskin in his isolation in the Lake District, thinking perhaps that his enthusiasm for Kate Greenaway would inspire a similar warm interest in other children's books. But his reaction was tetchy — he complained about the mixing of vision with reality, criticised Crane's illustrations for being decorative and unreal, not firmly drawn and brightly coloured, said he was in too sorrowful a mood to judge and finally admitted he had not actually read the book as it had been taken away by the children in the house.[58]

In contrast, Swinburne was particularly enthusiastic about the book for personal reasons.

> 'There never was a time when anything affected me so powerfully and delightfully as the wind — by sea or inland — so that no-one could possibly enter into the charm of your story more thoroughly than I.'[59]

An inset story about a seagull appealed to him specially 'for in my boyhood I was always regarded at home as belonging naturally to that

---

[56] Copy of letter shown to RR by CP.

[57] MLM to DUC, 1.12.1887.

[58] Only one letter from Ruskin to MLM survived long enough to be copied by RR. CP told RR there had been several others which Olive had given away. Possibly he alternately scolded and praised MLM as he did Greenaway. For some account of his dealings with the latter, see A. Lurie, 'The Child Who Followed The Piper: Kate Greenaway' in *Don't Tell The Grown-Ups*, Bloomsbury, 1990.

[59] C. Y. Lang, V, p. 168–9.

tribe,' because, although he did not say this in his letter to Louisa, he spent so much of his time playing on the shore and in and out of the sea near his childhood home on the Isle of Wight. As a schoolboy he had climbed the almost vertical Culver cliff alone to prove to himself he was not a coward after the disappointment of his parent's refusal to let him join the army, a request made under the inspiration of the news of the crazily heroic Balaclava Charge. In a letter describing this exploit his identification with seagulls appears — they are 'the others', his brothers and sisters, and 'even a real sea-gull' could not, without using its wings, have managed an overhang he had to turn back from. Henderson's biography of Swinburne significantly entitles the chapter covering the years 1837–49 'Seagull.' The hero of Louisa's simple little story is a young gull who

> 'loved the sea so dearly that while he was still a nestling, peeping out from his home, high up on a ledge of rock, at the dancing flashing waves down below, he longed to be among them. He felt as if he almost would go mad with joy if only his mother would let him dash off with her, whirling and curving about in the air, with nothing below but the great ocean.'[60]

Although there are no grounds for saying that Louisa had Swinburne consciously in mind when writing this story, it echoes the feeling in passages from his early novels marked by his biographer as autobiographical. One example is

> 'he went as before a steady gale over sands and rocks, blown and driven by the wind of his own delight, crying out to the sea between whiles . . . laughing and leaping, envious only of the sea-birds who might stay longer between two waves.'[61]

Such a comparison helps to show why Swinburne loved the *Farm* so much and regarded it as the peak of Louisa's achievement. He told Louisa that he had written a poem to a seagull met at Beachy Head 'the other day.' This too has an echo in her story, for her seagull, rash and over-eager, exhausts itself in a presumptuous flight, is captured lying spent upon the sand and has to pass a winter with its wings clipped in a farmyard. The poet could well sympathise and identify with this situation when he had just written these lines:-

---

[60] MLM, *Four Winds Farm*, Macmillan, [1886], 1887, p. 139.
[61] From *Lesbia Brandon*, quoted in Henderson, p. 12.

When I had wings my brother
Such wings were mine as thine

We are fallen, even we, whose passion
On earth is nearest thine;
Who sing and cease from flying;
Who live and dream of dying
Grey time in time's grey fashion
Bids wingless creatures pine.[62]

The main story of *Four Winds Farm* is that of a child who later becomes an artist of some kind. Although Louisa only called it 'the very opening of the life of a boy who lived to make his mark among men'[63] it is clearly implied by the narrative that this mark would be either in writing or painting. She personified the dreams and impressions which influenced him in four great and beautiful female figures — 'the four winds of heaven.' There is no quotation from George MacDonald at the beginning of any chapter but it is difficult not to believe that there is some influence here from *At the Back of the North Wind*. The author from whose work she did choose an epigraph for the whole book was Walter Pater. She took a sentence from *The Child in the House*, a retrospect of Pater's own child life. 'In . . . his dream he saw a child moving, and could divide the main streams at least, of the winds that had played on him, and study so the first stage in that mental journey.' This may even have been the seed from which the central idea of her book grew, since it is so clearly embodied here. Interestingly, in the first edition, this epigraph appears in very small print on the verso of the half-title page, before the attention-grabbing opening of frontispiece and title-page designed by Walter Crane, as though she wanted it to escape notice. It was perhaps a way of showing that this was a thought more for the consideration of adults than for the children who would move straight to the pictures and the text. *The Child in the House* first appeared in *Macmillan's Magazine* for 1878, and Louisa knew and admired it, as we can see from her having praised it to Swinburne.[64] She also, apparently, knew Pater personally, though the only surviving link between them giving evidence of this, is a note from Pater to one of her daughters, accompanying a novel by Fabre, to whose work he wished to introduce them.[65]

---

[62] A. C. Swinburne, 'To a Seamew', Beachy Head, September 1886, *Poems and Ballads*, 3rd Series.

[63] *Four Winds Farm*, p. 180.

[64] ACS to MLM, 3.7.[1885], C. Y. Lang, V, p. 117.

[65] Pater to Miss Molesworth, 27.7.1891.

In Swinburne's letter praising the 'Farm' he also wrote

'I am very proud and glad to see my poor words of tribute honoured by quotation at the head of the list of your books. (What a fascinating list they make — it is a pleasure merely to read over the titles).'

This is a reference to the passage about Louisa's work in his article on Charles Reade in *The Nineteenth Century* which was reproduced at the end of *Four Winds Farm*. Macmillan's used this passage in the first editions of three other books by Louisa, at the head of their list of her titles in the advertising pages at the back. When Salmon's article was published in October 1887 they quoted a passage from it in *Little Miss Peggy* which came out in December of the same year. But neither passage was used after the fourth appearance of Swinburne's tribute in *Mary*, 1893. Later editions of this book, although retaining the list headed 'Books for young readers. By Mrs Molesworth', had the words of praise removed. One probable reason for this would have been reluctance to quote from increasingly ageing articles in case this made it appear that the books themselves were out of date. Possibly editorial policy changed too, for none of Louisa's first editions published by Macmillan's after 1893 contain any 'blurb', yet other articles about her work had appeared, later than Swinburne's and Salmon's, and could have been used.

On Louisa's return to London in the autumn, the contact with Mrs Ewing's family produced by her article bore fruit in an invitation to a musical party on 22nd November at the house of Alfred Scott-Gatty, Mrs Ewing's brother. There she met for the first time a young man who was to become a great friend. This was Adrian Hope, then about 28, who was secretary to the Great Ormond Street hospital, which would have provided an immediate topic of conversation considering her interest in it. He had been asked to come especially to talk about the hospital to a group of people who, it was hoped, would help to raise money for it. But when Hope wrote to his fiancée, Laura Troubridge, the next day, it was not the hospital he mentioned in connection with Louisa. 'There was such a nice Mrs Molesworth who writes children's books as you may recollect.'[66] Laura was a designer and illustrator, and also a pastelist and portrait painter. A few years later she spent several

---

[66] This and all following quotations from correspondence between AH and LT, and from LT's diary were provided by their grand-daughter, M-J Lancaster, while she was preparing these papers for publication. See also Laura Troubridge, *Life Among the Troubridges*, ed. J. Hope-Nicholson, John Murray, 1966.

weeks on the Isle of Wight doing portraits of Queen Victoria's family. She and Adrian Hope had already been engaged for over three years and lack of money made the prospect of marriage very distant. So his interest in Louisa was not only because she was nice but from the hope that Laura might get work illustrating her books. A week after the party Louisa went to call on him taking Juliet with her, whom Adrian described to Laura as 'a great tall handsome fair-haired daughter'. Louisa talked to him understandingly about his engagement, telling him that a friend of hers, as he put it to Laura 'knew all about you and me'. Laura promptly found out about the friend (a Lady Carnwath) from her sister, discovering that she had been a friend of the Troubridge parents, and said she would 'like to meet that Mrs Molesworth, her books are very pretty.' Over the next two years until the summer of 1888 when they married, Adrian and Laura's letters and Laura's diary show their growing friendship with Louisa, her efforts to make sure Laura did get one of her books to illustrate and her sympathetic interest in the obstacles to their marriage. Adrian in London wrote assiduously to Laura in the country, apparently attempting to tell her everything he did and among it all is a steady flow of references to Louisa. 'I am going to dress for Mrs Molesworth's dinner,' 'I have to go to this dance of Mrs Molesworth's,' 'I wound up by calling on Mrs Molesworth,' 'I rushed off by train to see Mrs Molesworth who was as usual very nice.'

In February 1887 when Adrian was a dinner guest in her house, Louisa agreed to write to her publishers asking that Laura should illustrate her next book. This was not Macmillan's but Hatchards, who were going to produce *The Palace in the Garden* that had been appearing in *Little Folks* during the first six months of 1886. But she was too late and by the time her letter reached Mr Hatchard, he had already asked Harriet M. Bennet to do the work. On hearing this news Laura wrote to Adrian 'I should very much like to have a definite order for a book — especially one of Mrs Molesworth's — her stories are always so pretty.' In the end Laura did not illustrate one of Louisa's books until after she and Adrian were married, but the negotiations started early — the book she did was *The Old Pincushion*, published by Griffith Farran in July 1889, but appearing as a serial in *Little Folks* from July 1887 onwards. Adrian had written to Laura in June, just the month before, 'I must go and see Mrs Molesworth & keep her up to asking that you shall do her next book.' And *The Old Pincushion* would be her next book in the sense that interested Adrian — the next available as 'a definite order' for Laura, even if 'next' meant rather a long wait. There would have been no question of her illustrating any of Louisa's Macmillan titles, although her drawings were shown to them, as both Louisa and Craik were perfectly happy with Walter Crane's work and Louisa's partnership with him would last for several years yet.

Adrian was still angling for the definite order in January 1888 while Louisa continued to be 'very nice' and say how much she wanted Laura to do her next book. She had so many publishing irons in the fire by this time that it was difficult to get anything arranged as quickly as Adrian's impatience wished. One of his detailed letters to Laura gives a tantalising glimpse of a dinner party at Louisa's house on 11ᵗʰ January.

> 'The dinner last night was amusing. All young people. No chaperons at all. I took in a Miss Forster who was tall and pretty. She lives at Pau generally and knew a lot of French people but she was very shy at first because I think she is only just out. Mrs M. never said a word about her books which rather annoyed me for I had fully hoped to be able to write to make you an offer on her part. I shall try to call on her on Sunday. The fog made everyone very late, one man only turned [up] towards the end of dinner.'

London fogs were notorious and Louisa often mentioned them in her books, even writing one complete story about the subject, 'The Mysterious Guide', which makes all too clear the reality that lay behind Adrian's brief comment and in which one of her characteristic personal asides to the reader shows her own experience defictionalised.

> 'One of the peculiarities of fogs — London ones, it seems to me especially — is their extraordinary suddenness. We go to bed, remarking to each other as we say "good-night," "What a lovely, clear starlight or moonlight sky!" and we wake up the next morning thinking we have made a great mistake in waking up at all; that it cannot possibly be "to-morrow morning," or at any rate not to-morrow morning in the sense of getting-up time. And then comes the housemaid's tap at the door; and though still too sleepy to ask any questions, we become slowly aware of the true state of things. For the blinds drawing up makes no difference; the room remains as gloomy as before. "It must be a fog," we murmur to ourselves with a sort of despair.
>
> And much more suddenly than in the course of a night do they come sometimes. I remember once entering a shop in clear, afternoon daylight, and by the time my ten minutes' shopping was over and I turned to leave, lo and behold! the gas-lamps were being lighted along the avenues

of counters, and the street outside was black, as if some ill-natured fairy had suddenly drawn a thick curtain over the roofs of the houses, so as to shut us out from the sky and sun and light altogether.'[67]

Perhaps Louisa had woken up on the morning of that dinner just as she describes here, or had even been out that afternoon on a shopping errand only to be overtaken by the fog that made her guest late. I make no apology for these long and apparently trivial quotations for they help to build up the feeling of what daily life was like for Louisa at that time. Laura finally came to London in February 1888 and Adrian was at last able to take her to meet Louisa whom she liked very much and who offered her several introductions to publishers. They also chatted to Cicely, who told them about a dress she was planning to wear at a Fancy Ball at the Hotel Metropole in a few days time. Adrian reluctantly attended this ball too, taken by the dull sisters of a friend and kept up till 3.0 am 'which was such a bore' as he had an appointment with the chairman of the House Committee of Great Ormond Street hospital the next morning at 9.30. One compensation was a dance with Cicely 'in the frock she had talked to us about in which she looked very pretty.' Louisa and her daughters were clearly in the swing of the season just then — four days after the ball at the Metropole they gave a dance at their own house. Adrian went and found it a bore again, but as he had been suffering from a bad cold for weeks, Laura had just gone back to Norfolk, their marriage seemed as far away as ever and it was bitterly cold and snowing, his opinion was probably not a fair comment on the Molesworths' hospitality. Two days after this Louisa went to call on the cousin with whom Laura had been staying and saw, surprisingly for the first time, some of Laura's drawings which she had left to be looked at. The cousin said 'she liked them <u>very</u> much' and was going to write to Laura. Adrian seems to have made a habit of dropping in to the Molesworths on a Sunday, which was Louisa's regular 'open house' day — 'we are always at home on Sundays' she wrote to Cullum and several other friends and acquaintances.[68] When she wished to discuss anything privately with someone she might suggest they called before 4.0 p.m. when she was more likely to be alone.[69] In March during one of Adrian's calls, Louisa urged him 'to throw everything to the winds' and marry

---

[67] 'The Mysterious Guide. A Story of a London Fog', *Girls' Own Paper*, vol. IX, 1887, p. 67. Later published in *The Story of A Spring Morning, and Other Tales*.

[68] MLM to G. M. C. Cullum, 19.7.[1885], and to DUC, [2.1887].

[69] MLM to JBLW, 3.3.[1886].

Laura at once, promising to help with the house hunting and report back to him. Laura liked this, though doubting the wisdom of it. 'How nice of Mrs Molesworth' she wrote, 'to offer to help to find the little home we want. Darling do you think she quite knew the poverty of the land when she advised our marriage at once! I rather like her for it though — did not you?' But after a few more dinners and calls, this source of detailed glimpses into Louisa's life abruptly ceased when Adrian and Laura married on 2nd August and so did not have to write to each other any more.

11

A New Friend

In order to pursue Louisa's acquaintance with Adrian Hope and Laura Troubridge and the light this shed on her social and daily experience, we moved far on into 1888. Now it is necessary to return to Alfred Scott-Gatty's musical party, on 22nd November 1886, so as to pick up some other threads which became important in her life. A group of guests at this event wanted to help raise money for the children's hospital at Great Ormond Street and Adrian had been asked there to talk to them about it. This was probably one of the origins (a Victorian version of the brain-storming session, perhaps?) of a special appeal in aid of the hospital, to help build a new wing, which was launched by a letter to *The Times* the following February, and in which Louisa played an active part. It was called the Children's Jubilee Tribute because 1887 was the year of Queen Victoria's Golden Jubilee. It was hoped that linking the appeal with this popular occasion would attract more money. And it was through this fund-raising initiative that Louisa came to know a woman who seems to have been her greatest friend in London. Louisa's letters to her are the only ones to a close woman friend that have survived.

This woman was Charlotte Maria Du Cane, who was five years older than Louisa. Her mother, Lady Charlotte Guest, daughter of the ninth Earl of Lindsey, married at the age of twenty-one a man more than twice her age. The match was generally disapproved of by the society of the day, because the husband was 'in trade'. He was John Guest, later a baronet, the great ironmaster with ironworks at Dowlais and an office in London where Lady Charlotte had her own room for her work as his private secretary. She overcame the prejudice against her marriage and established herself as a successful London hostess who yet, on her husband's death, undertook the personal management of the works at Dowlais, with all the accompaniment of business letters, reports and accounts from agents and solicitors about machines and engines, mills and forges, which this involved. She had borne him ten children, of whom Charlotte Maria was the eldest, and had also become famous for her translation of the Mabinogion. Tennyson said 'it was the first book he read after his marriage and that he was so struck with it that it inspired him to write his poem.'[1]

When Louisa met Mrs Du Cane she became acquainted with a family whose contacts stretched all the way from trade and industry, through politics to the court. Mrs Du Cane's eldest brother married the eldest daughter of the 7th Duke of Marlborough, whose nephew was Winston Churchill. One sister married Sir A. H. Layard, politician, diplomat and archaeologist, who discovered the ruins of Nineveh. Her youngest sister was a lady-in-waiting to Princess Christian, third daughter of Queen Victoria. When Macmillan's suggested to Louisa that she should present a complete set of her books published with them to Princess May (this was Princess Mary Victoria of Teck, later Queen Mary), she asked Mrs Du Cane to help her by getting advice on the details of how to do it in accordance with court etiquette from this sister, who, as a member of the royal household, knew Princess May personally. Since the request was made in a letter dated May 1893, it is clear that the books would have been a wedding present on the occasion of Princess May's marriage to the Duke of York, later George V, on 6th July 1893.[2]

Charlotte Maria Guest married Richard Du Cane, her mother's confidential legal adviser and also a cousin of her mother's second husband. Another cousin, the Rev. A. R. Du Cane, was the vicar of Rostherne during the years that Louisa lived at Tabley Grange and High Legh, but Mrs Du Cane's daughter has stated definitely that her mother's friendship with Louisa began over the Children's Jubilee Tribute, so this connection can be no more than a coincidence. In a biography of Lady Charlotte, written by her great-granddaughter who was also Mrs Du Cane's great-niece, Mrs Du Cane is described as having the destiny of 'a high Victorian married lady whose business was good works rather than ironworks.'[3] Both elements had played a part in her life — she

---

[1] Lady Charlotte Schreiber, *Journals 1869–1885* 2 vols, edited by her son Montague J. Guest, John Lane, 1911, vol. 1 p. viii. The poem referred to would have been *Idylls of the King*. Information about Mrs Du Cane and her family has also been taken from *Lady Charlotte Schreiber: Extracts from her Journal 1853–1891*, edited by the Earl of Bessborough, John Murray, 1952.

[2] Letters from MLM to the Du Cane family were lent to RR by Mrs Du Cane's daughter, Julia.

[3] Revel Guest and Angela V. John, *Lady Charlotte: A Biography of the 19th Century*, Weidenfeld and Nicolson, 1989, p. 139.

helped out with the business letters, but also worked for a hospital for incurables at Putney. She was very fond of Angela Burdett-Coutts, whose influence would definitely have been towards charitable work and as we have seen, it was this that introduced Louisa to her.

Louisa's first surviving letter to Mrs Du Cane early in March 1887 suggests that a fair degree of acquaintance already existed. She referred to one of Mrs Du Cane's daughters as 'a very special friend' and confided her plans for moving from Kensington. There is also a reference to a story she was trying to get the SPCK to promise for May — 'otherwise it won't be much use'. Louisa meant by this 'too late to be much use as a money-raiser,' since this was a story she had written specially to help the Jubilee Tribute, called 'A present to the Queen'. It was, as she said in her next letter to her friend, 'exceedingly simple.' It explained in story-form, in very easy terms for quite young children, what 'Jubilee' meant, how the present for the Queen was to be a new wing for the children's hospital, and how children could help by sending for and using collecting cards. On 15th March Louisa sent proofs of this story to Mrs Du Cane, still expecting it to appear in May, although in the event SPCK did better than that and published it in the March number of *The Child's Pictorial*. Louisa thought that the twelve year old Du Cane twins, Isabel and Julia, would like to see it, as well as their mother. She took a special interest in these girls and got to know them well as they too helped with the Jubilee Tribute. A letter of appeal was sent to as many people as those involved could think of, and Isabel and Julia made many copies of it for this purpose, sending some to Louisa for her to send on. Louisa and the Du Canes exchanged lists of possible contributors and news of how their own collecting was going. 'Lionel has already filled two "penny" cards for the hospital,' wrote Louisa on 19th March. In May, taking a bold step she asked the twins 'Will you tell your mother that I almost think a letter might be sent to the <u>Duke of Norfolk</u> — it would have to be written specially on account of the "Sir" at the beginning,' which meant more work for one of the girls. The whole point of this particular appeal, since it was for a children's hospital, was to address it directly to children and involve children in the work. Louisa got Lionel to sign many of the appeal letters.

In the end some £6,000 was raised towards the new wing. This included the proceeds of a concert held at Grosvenor House in March. Cicely went to it with some friends. Louisa could not go, nor could she attend a special meeting on the 17th to do with the hospital, because, she told Mrs Du Cane, she was 'quite ill . . . with a frightful cold.' At the time she wrote this there was also a dense fog and she described its effect on the dog her family had now acquired. ' "Toby" is so terrified by this awful darkness that he looks quite piteous. It is perfectly black here today; I wonder if it is as bad all over London.'[4] The weather was exceptionally bad that year. Humphry Ward wrote in his diary summary of 1887 that 'at least to June it will be known as the coldest, latest, most distressing season within living memory.'[5] But despite the bad weather and her cold, which was 'not yet much better,' Louisa went to Westminster Abbey on 19th March for Bevil's confirmation. She described the occasion to Isabel and Julia as 'a beautiful service — & very nice music.' The previous week Olive had been presented to the Queen at a Drawing-Room and Louisa told the twins about that too.

'Olive enjoyed the Drawing room very much — she was not at all nervous and wishes she was going again next week! Cicely was able to "coach" her exactly what to do, and she took such good care of her that Olive said "I am sure they thought I was Cicely's daughter." If you did not live so very far off we would have asked you to come and see them in their finery.'[6]

At this period there were four Drawing-Rooms a year, always in the afternoon, which was the case throughout Queen Victoria's reign. 'Before a presentation could take place, the names of those involved had to be submitted to the Lord Chamberlain for royal approval, and only then were the relevant cards issued, signifying that the applicants might attend.'[7] Olive was presented by her sister, not by her mother, because Louisa had not been presented at court herself. The finery included a train three yards long 'as prescribed by the official regulation for ladies' court dress,' which involved practising to walk and curtsey gracefully in such an encumbrance. 'The material came in very handy for a ball gown the following year' recalled one debutante when writing her reminiscences. She also described the home gathering for viewing the finery.

'No refreshments were provided at a Drawing-Room, and it was a great relief to get home and have tea, to which many of our friends came, to

---

[4] MLM to DUC, 15.3.[1887].

[5] Sutherland, p. 115.

[6] MLM to I and J DUC, 19.3.[1887].

[7] Horn, p. 77. See the whole of chapter 4 in this book for a detailed account of presentation at Court.

admire our dresses and hear how we had comported ourselves in the presence of Royalty. We called this function 'a Drawing-Room Tea'.[8]

A few years later Louisa wrote a story, *The Girls and I*, in which just such a Drawing-Room Tea, to show off girls who had been presented 'in their finery', was an important part of the plot, as were the extra wraps, needed because putting on evening dress 'in the middle of a March morning was enough to make the stoutest shiver.'[9] The child narrator called the event 'a train show' and it took place at tea-time, accompanied by cakes and ices, when the participants returned from the Drawing-Room. In the story 'three other ladies in trains came too, so there was rather a good show.'[10] Louisa was perhaps thinking of how the tea-party after Olive's presentation might have appeared to Lionel. She combined the Drawing-Room, the 'train show' and the extra wraps to produce a 'lost and found' story about a valuable family heirloom.

This year Louisa was even busier than before, both with original writing and with revisions, proof-reading and all the correspondence generated by such activities. *Marrying and Giving in Marriage*, a book for older girls if not adults, was appearing in *Longman's Magazine* from November 1886 to April 1887, and was published as a single volume in the same month as the last instalment. It was immediately succeeded in *Longman's* by another ghost story, 'The Story of the Rippling Train', which follows so closely a case recounted in a book published in 1886 by the Society for Psychical Research, that it is virtually certain Louisa drew her story from this source.[11] We see from this that she steadily maintained her interest in the psychic and supernatural to the extent of studying current, heavy, academic books on the subject. This was the fourth ghost story she had published and she now opened negotiations with Macmillan's to bring them all out together. These were successfully concluded in November when she wrote to accept the royalty arrangements and *Four Ghost Stories* appeared the following February. She had been keen to find a title that would show it was a book for adults and this was probably preferred to the one she had suggested — *Lady Farquhar's Old Lady and Other Ghost Stories* — because it was shorter.

---

[8] Mary, Lady Trevelyan, *The Number of My Days*. Unpublished typescript at Newcastle University Library, quoted in Horn, pp. 82–3.

[9] Horn p. 82.

[10] MLM, *The Girls and I*, Macmillan, 1892, p. 26.

[11] Gurney, vol. 1, p. 517n. Re-published in *Victorian Ghost Stories*, ed. M. Cox and R. A. Gilbert, OUP Paperback, 1992, 0192829998.

'I think it important' she wrote, 'to show <u>by the title</u> that it is not <u>at all</u> a child's book as my name is so much associated with such, & I shd. be very sorry for anyone to give ghost stories unknowingly to <u>children</u>.'[12]

She was very insistent on not allowing children to read books unsuitable for them and a piece by her expressing this opinion had recently been published in *The Pall Mall Gazette*. She considered that Hans Andersen, Grimm and 'the greater number of the juvenile magazines of the day' were examples of publications where 'one single book may contain stories admirably suited for children and others which one would be sorry for them to read.' Her solution to the difficulty was that 'one should have *two* libraries for one's children — one of books "to read to ourselves" and another of books to be read aloud to them by their mother or someone competent to select, omit or explain.' [13] Probably many parents and teachers now quietly put these principles into practice still, while fashionable standards of political correctness prevent them from saying so. Louisa told Mrs Du Cane that she had not realised her letter would be published in the periodical.

> 'It is very absurd — but I did not know that there was anything of mine in the Pall Mall. The editor wrote to ask me for my "experiences" about children's literature . . . I thought he meant to publish a little pamphlet afterwards on the subject. I don't take the Pall Mall — if you <u>happen</u> to have the one, wd. you let me see it?'

In the letter to which Louisa was replying, Mrs Du Cane had clearly given her the first news she received of her own letter being published and had praised *The Water Babies*, wondering why it had not been mentioned. Louisa took this point up with enthusiasm — 'I quite agree with you about the "Water babies" . . . I think it a marvellous book.' She regretted having left it out, for although she thought it beyond little children, it could have been brought in as suitable for reading to them.[14] The abridged editions of *The Water Babies* that have appeared since then show that many editors and publishers not only agreed with Louisa on this point, but decided not to leave the selecting and omitting to be done by mother.

There were two other pieces in the *Pall Mall* that autumn on the same topic, 'The Best Books for Children', making up a small series,

---

[12] MLM to Macmillan, 11.11.[1887].
[13] MLM, 'The Best Books for Children II', *Pall Mall Gazette*, 29.10.1887 p. 5.
[14] MLM to DUC, 9.11.1887.

and Louisa's was by far the shortest and simplest which makes it seem likely that her letter was just printed as it stood. One wonders if she asked the editor to pay her for his use of what she had thought of as a private letter. This editor was W. T. Stead,[15] famous for his innovating style of 'New Journalism' with sensational campaigns such as his article against child prostitution, 'The Maiden Tribute to Modern Babylon' (1885), which led to a change in the law. He was also specially interested in children's books, and some years after the three 'Best Books for Children' pieces in the *Pall Mall Gazette*, he began to publish *Books for the Bairns*, the first paperback series of books for children, at one penny each. Number ten in the series was *The Christmas Stocking* by Elizabeth Wetherell, which had been among the books recommended by Louisa in her letter. We may recall that Elizabeth Wetherell had been one of her own favourite authors as a child.

Returning to the subject of work that Louisa did intend for publication, *The Palace in the Garden*, which had been serialized in *Little Folks* the previous year, was published by Hatchards in July when Swinburne received his copy with enthusiastic pleasure. 'I could not help beginning a new book of yours at once; I cannot tell you how I am enjoying it.'[16] *The Abbey by the Sea*, apparently not previously published elsewhere, appeared in June, bound up by SPCK with the French street-arab story that Charlotte Yonge had published the December before. Miss Yonge published another of Louisa's stories in 1887 — 'Nesta', which ran from January to June in *The Monthly Packet*. But this had been sent and accepted in June 1886 so it did not form part of the work-load for 1887. Charlotte explained the delay, saying 'Your dear little Nesta is very touching and I will certainly put her in, but I am afraid I must ask you to wait until 1887, as there is a great deal to go into the coming volume.' This was the only other story, apart from *A Christmas Child,* in which Louisa described a child's death, and Charlotte's next sentences make it appear that this too, was about a real child. 'What a fearfully sudden blow it was! But it is one of the hidden treasures to which such sorrows turn.'[17] The Macmillan book for 1887, *Little Miss Peggy*, was finished in August so she had presumably been working on it in the early months of the year. *Aunt Clotilda's Guests* began to appear in the

[15] For more about W. T. Stead, see Sally Wood, 'W. T. Stead and his *Books for the Bairns*', *Newsletter No. 38*, Children's Books History Society, Mar. 1989, pp. 2–6.

[16] C. Y. Lang, V, pp. 197–8.

[17] CMY to MLM, 14.6.[1886].

July number of *Little Folks* and the first issue, in October, of the new periodical for girls, *Atalanta*, edited by L. T. Meade, contained the first instalment of *Neighbours* which ran till the following March so these too must have formed part of her work programme earlier in the year. A second story for the *English Illustrated Magazine*, the short 'That Girl in Black', started in December and ran for three months. And of course alongside all this was the continuing monthly contribution to *The Child's Pictorial*.

In her November letter to Macmillan's about the royalty agreement for *Little Miss Peggy* and *Four Ghost Stories*, Louisa wrote 'I shall take care to keep back my new little novel so as not to clash with it'. She must have been referring to 'That Girl in Black', the only work of hers at that time which could be described as a 'little novel', and thought of as aimed at the same audience as *Four Ghost Stories* — adults, not children or young girls. What she would have been promising was to delay its publication as a book, since she knew the first instalment as a serial was due out very soon. The *English Illustrated*, in which it first appeared, was a Macmillan publication, but it was Chatto that produced 'That Girl in Black' in book form, with another short story, though not until May 1889, thus keeping the promise that it should not clash with *Four Ghost Stories*. This tiny incident is an early sign of a concern that came to a head a few years later. Louisa was writing more and more and the number of different firms that published her work was increasing too — not counting those who had brought out her early novels, during 1887 at least twelve publishers[18] were producing work by her or negotiating with her about future books or serials. Macmillan's was clearly beginning to be a little anxious that this increase might have a deleterious effect on the sales of her books with them. This anxiety developed further later on.

Louisa and the family spent the summer and part of the autumn in Somerset. One meeting worth noting that occurred before this, while the season was still in full swing, took place at a dinner party at Mrs Bishop's. This was the lady Louisa had got to know in Paris as a friend of Mrs Augustus Craven. Sir Mountstuart Grant-Duff wrote in his diary for 12th May, 'Dined with Mrs Bishop, taking down Mrs Molesworth, the author of various stories for children, which are greatly read, and

---

[18] Routledge, SPCK, Hatchards, Longmans, Cassell, Bell and Daldy, Trischler and Co., Griffith Farran, Chambers, Chatto and the publishers of *The Monthly Packet*, *The Contemporary Review* and *The Pall Mall Gazette*.

about one of which, *Four Winds Farm*, my hostess spoke much.'[19] 'Taking down' means that he escorted Louisa in to dinner and that she sat beside him during the meal. Because London houses were tall and narrow, the drawing room was often on the first floor and the dining room on the ground floor — hence 'down'. This entry sounds as though it was their first meeting and there is no other mention of Louisa in the many published volumes of his diary. But considering that her second daughter, Juliet, later married his nephew, that both he and Louisa had a great admiration for Mrs Craven and that he was a close friend of J. B. L. Warren, something she must have known, it is probable that at least an acquaintance continued.

The visit to Somerset seems to have begun early in July, judging by a letter from Swinburne, dated 4th July, 1887, in which he appeared to be responding to an announcement of her imminent departure. 'When I go westward [implying that she had already said she was doing this] — if I do this year — it will probably be to my mother's place in Wiltshire, but I have made no plans yet.'[20] The Molesworths were staying at Bindon House near Wellington, the home of the Lamport family. Charles Lamport, a wealthy shipbuilder from Workington, had bought the house in the late 1870s and added an ornate Jacobean style wing, demolished in the 1930s, so that when Louisa stayed there in 1887, the house was twice as large as it is now. She wrote to Mrs Du Cane from Bindon in October and dated the dedication of *Little Miss Peggy* from there in August. The dedication runs 'To the memory of E. L. the dear young friend who suggested its name to this little story, and from whose late home, so intimately associated with her, this dedication is made.' One of Charles Lamport's four daughters, Ella, died in Alassio in February 1887, aged twenty-three. She, clearly, was the E. L. of the dedication but there is no further information about Louisa's connection with her. It is not even clear, from Louisa's letter to Mrs Du Cane, whether she was staying with the Lamport family or renting the house from them. It was being advertised in *The Times* as 'to let' in October 1887. Yet the tone of the dedication suggests a real friendship. Since Ella was the same age as Cicely, it is possible that they had made friends first, through doing the season together maybe, and that the discussions about the title of *Little Miss Peggy* took place when Ella came to call on or to stay with, the Molesworths. The size of Bindon

---

[19] Grant-Duff, *Diary 1886–1888*, vol. 1 p. 101.
[20] C. Y. Lang, V, pp. 197–8.

house at the time rather speaks against Louisa's renting it. Could she really have wanted or afforded a place in which from the west door to the far conservatory wall there was 'an unbroken vista of 150 feet . . . producing a singularly charming effect . . . when lit up at night time.'[21] It even seems possible that Louisa had stayed at Bindon before, because if she had never seen Ella at home, she would surely not have referred in the dedication to Bindon House having an intimate association with the girl.

While Louisa was still at Bindon, Mrs Craik died suddenly of heart failure, on 12th October, in the midst of plans for her adopted daughter's wedding.[22] The only business letter from Louisa that autumn in the Macmillan archive is addressed to Mr Macmillan, not to Mr Craik. And when, the following February, they were corresponding on business matters again, she made an oblique reference to his loss —

> 'you have had more than enough to put all such little particulars out of your mind. Indeed I think it wonderful & most unselfish of you, never, all this time, to have relaxed in your interest in your friends' affairs.'

Any personal letter of condolence would have been sent to him at home and so would not have been available for preservation by the Macmillan archive. The funeral was on 15th October and attended by many names in the literary world, including Louisa's friends, Sir Noel and Lady Paton.[23] It would have been possible for her to travel from Somerset to London by train for the event, and in view of her admiration for Dinah Maria Mulock Craik and her friendship with George Lillie Craik, it seems likely that she did so. But we don't know.

Louisa wrote to Mrs Du Cane from Bindon on 21st October in a tone of growing intimacy and showing a desire to maintain and increase this.

> My dear Mrs Du Cane,   We are still here you see and very reluctant to leave the country, as we must do before long now! We are not going straight back to London, & there are still visits in prospect

---

[21] From a description of the house by Mrs Foljambe, friend of the Warre family, who owned Bindon after the Lamports, quoted in *Edmond Warre* by C. R. L. Fletcher, John Murray, 1922. I am grateful to Mrs Julia Small who lived at Bindon for 9 years, for information about the house and the Lamport family.

[22] Mitchell, p. 18.

[23] *The Athenaeum*, 22.10.1887, article on Mrs Craik by Frances Martin.

for the girls even when we are, so to say, settled for the winter. But I must be there early next month with some of my young people. We have enjoyed this autumn exceedingly — just now it is perfectly lovely here, though we had snow last week. I have always been meaning to write to my dear little "twins" — but as I think I told you I have suffered a good deal from my head of late & I have been obliged to write as few letters as possible.

We do dread the thoughts of the <u>winter</u> in London — I am afraid we are not getting acclimatised at all. Perhaps we should dislike it less if we lived in a more central position — I do dislike Kensington! — but I have not yet sold my house, & when I do I am not at all sure but that we shall make our headquarters in the country, & only come to town for the season —

I wish we lived nearer <u>you</u>! It is so kind of you to feel so interested in the 19th Century article. It is <u>very</u> nice and gave me extreme pleasure — & it is delightful to find my friends sympathising with me in this —

Cicely & Juliet join me in very kind remembrances to yourself & all of your party whom we know — To the twins I send a special packet of love for themselves. I trust that Julia is <u>quite</u> strong again? Believe me — Yours very sincerely,

Louisa Molesworth

The article referred to is the one by Edward Salmon discussed in the last chapter. It is hardly surprising that Louisa complained of headaches considering the amount of work she was getting through in the year. She was back in London by 9th November when she wrote again to Mrs Du Cane even more affectionately and confidingly.

'I could not but answer your sweet letter — It is very funny — I think there must have been a brain wave of sympathy between us — for I have been slightly troubled in my mind thinking it was rather rude of me to have given you the little book to <u>carry</u>, without any apology for so doing — & last night I asked myself if you wd. think me fantastic were I to write and apologise! Indeed I did not think you "curt", but I too felt that I had a score of things I wanted to say to you — I shd. love to tell you my plans & perplexities if it wd. not bore you. I still feel a little strange in London especially in winter when I have no relations here & indeed I have not yet got accustomed to doing without the constant sympathy & advice that never failed me while my mother lived — just now I <u>cannot</u> make up my mind if we shd. make our headquarters in the country or try to move further in — We <u>do</u> find this "quartier" so gloomy & out-of-the-way!

I am hoping my head is a little better for I am very tired of it — the doctor thinks it is rheumatism, but is not quite sure — & perhaps it is partly the climate — My girls want very much to go to the country & only come up for the season, if we can afford it! I have given you a dose of my own affairs you see!'[24]

Further on in this letter Louisa mentioned arranging to see each other when they were all back home — although Mrs Du Cane had clearly just paid her a visit, she had gone out of town again. Planning meetings was difficult when 'my children are all moving about'. Juliet was soon going to stay with her Molesworth grandmother but at least Cicely and Olive would be at home when Mrs Du Cane returned and Louisa was eager that they should meet the elder Du Cane daughters.

As a postscript to this same letter Louisa wrote 'I do feel very anxious about the Tribute — & I trust something will be suggested by the gentlemen.' In fact she herself did 'something' by writing a long letter to *The Times* about the 'Christmas Treat at the Hospital for Sick Children in Great Ormond-Street.' She was present at this fête and the detailed description she gave of the little patients and their enjoyment of a Christmas tree was well calculated to open purses and pockets. She mingled happy and pathetic glimpses with a practised hand.

> 'My neighbour during this part of the proceedings was a small boy named "Gus", a ci-devant patient only, and who at the first glance bore little trace of ever having been ill. But, alas! there was only one neat little knicker-bockered, red-stockinged leg stretched out on the table where he had been deposited for a few minutes. The other had been amputated for hip disease some months ago. "Gus" however was supremely content, his arms filled with Christmas presents, and evidently cherished none but the happiest reminiscences of the hospital.'

The firm and straightforward appeal with which she ended the letter revealed the cause of the anxiety she had confessed to feeling.

> 'The new wing still hoped for, though the efforts of English children of all classes during the last year have not succeeded in collecting more than a third of the sum required, will be an inestimable boon.'

---

[24] MLM to DUC, 9.11.1887.

She knew the importance of flattering people's practical and economic sense.

'The additional accommodation will actually decrease the cost of each individual cot; wards for accidents, for whooping cough, for the isolation of other infectious diseases, and more ample quarters for the nursing staff, all sorely required, are included in the scheme.'

And a gesture to the empire-building and historical pride of the Victorians also helped. 'The institution in Great Ormond-Street was the first of its kind, "the pioneer and the mother of children's hospitals in all parts of the world." ' The letter was dated 6th January 1888, and appeared in the paper on the 11th. The response was immediate — Louisa was able to tell Mrs Du Cane the next day 'I am so glad you like the letter — it has brought a _few_ cheques already . . . Lord Sligo sent me £10.' The gentlemen who she hoped would suggest something were enthusiastic about what she had actually done herself. Adrian Hope (the hospital secretary) had dined with her on the day her letter appeared — this was the amusing dinner with all young people and no chaperons, mentioned in the previous chapter — and he talked about having a pamphlet made of it. He also wrote to Laura, his fiancée 'Look at yesterday's Times and see Mrs Molesworth's letter about our Christmas Tree. I hope it may bring money.' Laura's answering letter mentioned that she had 'cut out Mrs M's letter about the children — it is so nice.' Mrs Du Cane had obviously relayed some praise from her husband, for Louisa responded 'I hope I may have the pleasure of seeing Mr Du Cane some day as he is so appreciative of my attempt!' [25]

Although Louisa gave to charity, sat on committees and helped with bazaars in the usual way, she saw her own special contribution to charitable work as being through her writing. The story and the letter connected with the Jubilee Tribute were deliberately written with a specifically stated purpose. When the opportunity arose she did the same thing again, as with _Farthings_ (1892), about which she said 'I wrote it for the "Waifs and Strays" at the personal request of the Bishop of Wakefield.'[26] The 'Waifs and Strays' later became the Church of England Children's Society, and in the back of the first edition of _Farthings_ there are advertisements for the Ripon-Wakefield branch of the society, and an appeal form to be detached and returned with a donation. The full title

---

[25] MLM to DUC, 12.[1.1888].
[26] MLM to GLC,. 31.1.[1893].

of Louisa's book was *"Farthings": The Story of A Stray and A Waif* and she incorporated into it a direct reference to the society and its work (although not by name).

> ' "And when I'm a man", Tony went on, "if ever I have money enough, I'm going to look out for other boys left alone like us, and see if I can't help them somehow. Grandy says there's some society begun now for finding out all about them." '[27]

But even when there was no question of such an open appeal, she would address her young readers directly in more general terms asking them to take part in any good and helpful activity they came across, as in *The Oriel Window*.

> 'If ever, or wherever any of you come across this endeavour to brighten and refine dull, ungraceful, and ungracious homes, you will do your best to help it on, I feel sure, will you not?'[28]

As well as this kind of direct address, many of her stories depict charitable, loving, thoughtful action for others with the unspoken corollary that this should be imitated. Louisa herself was well aware of poverty, sickness, unemployment, poor housing and sheer wretchedness as she shows, for instance, in an episode in one of her early novels where the heroine visits a dying child in a hamlet of 'squalid wretchedness.' Louisa identified indifferent, absentee landlords as the underlying cause — 'It belongs to two or three different owners, none of whom live near here, or take any interest in it.' The heroine considers that the death of the child 'is hardly to be called sad' because 'life, so far as we can see, seems sadder than death to most of the poor little children at Notcotts . . . a row of hovels, undrained, unventilated, low-roofed, and dilapidated — so altogether wretched.'[29] Louisa wished to awaken her readers' awareness too, in ways commensurate with their different ages and understanding. Little children might begin to learn something about unemployment with four-year-old Lily in 'No work to do', a simple, short tale in *The Child's Pictorial*, in which an encounter with a small group of men out of work and begging, prompts Lily to offer them her own (needle)work. Her nurse has to explain the mistake and provides her with money to

---

[27] MLM, *Farthings": The Story of a Stray and a Waif"*, Wells, Gardner Darton and Co., [1892], p. 247.

[28] *The Oriel Window*, p. 182.

[29] *Cicely*, vol. II, pp. 142–147.

give them, which 'they'll like . . . much better, you'll see.'[30] More could
be learnt from Louisa's orange Macmillan book for 1887, *Little Miss
Peggy*, which painted a vivid and knowledgeable picture of the hard-
working poor in the Manchester of her childhood. Peggy looked out
from her nursery windows with deep and sympathetic interest at the
daily lives of 'the children at the back.' She played, as far as she could
at the age of five, a friendly part in the way of buns and talk, and
confidently told her mother all the details, not disappointed in her
expectation that Mother would know even more about them and how
to be a kind friend to them. She 'couldn't be a kinder as far as friendly
words and old clotheses goes,' as the mother of the children at the back
put it, even though 'she's a large little family of her own, and not so
very strong in 'ealth, and plenty to do with their money.'[31]

Girls on the verge of adulthood might be roused by this discussion
in *Neighbours*.

> ' "Lavinia doesn't like us to go *much* among the poor; they're so dirty
> . . . and some of them drink even . . . ."
>
> "Of course . . . If they weren't dirty and — not always sober, and if
> they were never ill or in trouble, there'd be no need for us to go to
> them. . . ."
>
> ". . . I don't think you know how bad Leaford is. There's one part
> called the Cross Roads which is really dreadful. The people there are so
> low and degraded and so terribly poor. They say there are little children
> playing about in the gutters some-times, with hardly any clothes on, and
> with dreadful little wizened-up faces, quite unnatural-looking, like old
> fairies." . . .
>
> "Yes . . . it is *very* dreadful. And is nothing done — does no-one try
> to do anything for these wretched people? The little children, oh, to
> think of the poor little children!"
>
> "You don't mean . . . you don't think that we should — that it would
> be right for girls like us to go to places like that? I know that Lavinia
> would never let *us* go." '[32]

The help that Louisa wanted to offer, and to urge others to offer, in
the face of such problems, was of the individual philanthropic kind.

---

[30] *Nesta*, p. 64.
[31] *Little Miss Peggy*, p. 189.
[32] MLM, *Neighbours*, Hatchards, 1889, pp. 137–9.

Political activity to change the structure of society did not form part of her thinking.

> 'Everybody will remember what a long and severe winter we had in the year 1886. And most people not only heard, but saw for themselves how much suffering there was among the poor. Even children did what they could to help, and many pennies and halfpennies were put away that would otherwise have been spent on little pleasures, "for the poor people that have nothing to eat." '[33]

When she wrote a paragraph like that, she was deliberately simplifying for the child reader, but she saw adult activity in response to such a situation as the same in kind, only larger in scale. It is hardly surprising that she thought like this since a large majority of her contemporaries did also. As George Orwell pointed out about Charles Dickens' *Hard Times*, 'its whole moral is that capitalists ought to be kind, not that workers ought to be rebellious.' It should be noted that Dickens had also been a supporter of Great Ormond Street, its 'most devoted and famous patron.'[34] When Dickens attacks society, said Orwell, 'he is always pointing to a change of spirit rather than a change of structure. It is hopeless to try and pin him down to any definite remedy, still more to any political doctrine. His approach is always along the moral plane.'[35]

This approach, we saw in chapter four when discussing Louisa's 'coming out', was also her remedy for the evils of the social system then in force — a moral and individual one. The essay 'Coming out' although drawn upon to illustrate Louisa's own experience at about the age of eighteen, was actually published in *Atalanta* in 1890, that is, during the period of her life we are now considering.

George Orwell, as an active and acknowledged socialist,[36] might have been expected to condemn Dickens' non-political attitude outright but he did not, in fact, do so. Instead, he said

---

[33] *Nesta*, p. 58.

[34] From a leaflet advertising Jules Kosky's *Mutual Friends: Charles Dickens and Great Ormond Street Children's Hospital*, Weidenfeld and Nicolson, 1991.

[35] George Orwell, 'Charles Dickens' in *The Collected Essays, Journalism and Letters of George Orwell Volume I: An Age like this 1920–1940*, Penguin, 1970, pp. 457 and 468.

[36] Orwell wrote in 1946 'Every line of serious work that I have written since 1936 has been written, directly or indirectly, *against* totalitarianism and *for* democratic Socialism, as I understand it.' 'Why I Write' in *Collected Essays*, p. 28.

'it is not at all certain that a merely moral criticism of society may not be just as 'revolutionary' — and revolution, after all, means turning things upside down — as the politico-economic criticism which is fashionable at this moment.' ['*This moment*' was *1940*.]

He identified two viewpoints which 'are always tenable' — 'how can you improve human nature until you have changed the system?' and 'what is the use of changing the system before you have improved human nature?' — and he thought that one or the other was always in the ascendant. The second point of view, which he called moral, might also be described as religious and it motivated a large part of any activity intended to help 'the poor' in Louisa's lifetime.

The acts of Parliament which the famous Victorian philanthropist, Lord Shaftesbury, piloted successfully through the House of Commons to improve the lot of working people with, among other things, the ten hour day and the prohibition of underground employment in mines for women and children, were aimed at forcing the capitalist to be kind, not altering the structure of society. This was the kind of political activity that the new but growing socialist movement was strongly against, thinking that it only strengthened the existing state of society by making things a little more bearable for those who might otherwise rebel. Shaftesbury's acts of Parliament, Angela Burdett-Coutts' model homes and shelter for fallen women, the Church of England Central Society for providing homes for Waifs and Strays (the original name of what became the Church of England's Children's Society), Dickens' emotional appeal to the rich in such books as *A Christmas Carol*, Louisa's and Mrs Du Cane's efforts to raise money for the children's hospital and Louisa's own writing, all form part of the same world view. It is a view that has persisted alongside the idea that health, education and social welfare must be the business of government, because only government has the power and resources to tackle problems of such size. Another woman wrote in her diary in the early eighties, 'Private charity, while I admire it, seems to me utterly insufficient. It is like baling out the sea with a teacup.'[37] But still Societies of Friends of hospitals, children's homes, schools and other organisations have continued to carry out the kind of work Louisa was doing — part-time philanthropic assistance within the limits of her family and social commitments and the conventions of her day. She was

---

[37] Flora Shaw, later Lady Lugard, quoted in Joanna Trollope, *Britannia's daughters*, Cresset Library, 1988, p. 134.

not a pioneer or martyr. Further development of the point is unnecessary, since this is not a history of welfare work but simply an attempt to place one part of her life in context.

The headaches Louisa had mentioned to Mrs Du Cane persisted well into the new year — 'I still suffer a good deal off and on,' she said to Craik at the end of February.[38] Olive too was ill and her mother was anxious about her, not liking to leave her much alone and mentioning in several letters being 'unsettled' and 'worried' by her daughter's state. Although Olive was considered to be getting better by the end of January, from an illness that had started at the beginning of the month, she was 'still quite under invalid orders.' So Louisa, while accepting with pleasure an invitation to dine with Mrs Du Cane on 22nd February, three weeks ahead, thought she would bring Cicely with her and not Olive.[39] It was a pleasant occasion — 'We much enjoyed being with you all — Cicely got no harm as we had a lot of extra wraps sent in the carriage to go home with, but this cold is really rather dreadful.'[40] Just as well that Olive did not go. It was not thought safe either, for her to go to Clifton, which the doctor had specially recommended for her convalescence, until the middle of March. The dreadful cold increased the advisability of keeping her at home. She finally left to stay with her uncle and his family near Clifton on 28th March, a strange period for her, perhaps, since, according to one of his grandchildren, he was a rabid Plymouth Brother.[41] This was her father's youngest brother, Lt. Col. Anthony Oliver Molesworth, and this visit was one of several little signs that Louisa had remained on friendly terms with her husband's family. Another one had been the dedication of *Four Ghost Stories* to her nieces, Lilian and Georgina, the daughters of Richard's second brother, Morgan Crofton, who had died in 1867.

During this time of worry over Olive, Louisa was also anxious about Bevil's future. She confided in Craik about him, though more in personal meetings than by letter. Still, it can be deduced from what she did write that seventeen-year-old Bevil was something of a problem.

> 'It is quite settled for Bevil to begin in the City at Easter. I earnestly trust he will do well & I think he may. I have done my utmost to get this chance for him: when he is older he will understand that such things

---

[38] MLM to GLC, 22.2.[1888].
[39] MLM to DUC, 30.1.[1888].
[40] MLM to DUC, 25.2.[1888].
[41] Personal communication from Beatrix Molesworth.

are not easy! He will be in good hands & under good influence — I
will tell you about it when we meet.'

Louisa had clearly been pulling strings for her son. In this she seems to
have resembled Anthony Trollope's mother, who 'was an uninhibited
string-puller, like all dutiful parents of her class. . . . There was no
embarrassment at all in pulling strings, only in having no strings to
pull.'[42] This letter to Craik was written towards the end of February
and when, two weeks later, she still had not seen him she began to press
for a meeting.

'I hear you are going abroad before long: You won't go without seeing
us? There are several things I shd. like to tell you; about what I am fixing
for Bevil &c. personal things — I don't like to see so little of you & yet
you seem to feel the distance here more than formerly, so I can't ask
you to come.'[43]

It seems as though Louisa may have made rather a fuss about Bevil for
one comment reported about her was 'Here's Mrs Molesworth, Bevilling
again.'[44] She probably found it harder to cope with sons than daughters,
without a husband's support and authority and relied on friends like
Craik for advice and encouragement. It should be remembered that, as
with nearly all Louisa's letters to Craik, the passages quoted above,
mentioning Bevil, come from Louisa's business letters to her publishers,
preserved in the Macmillan archive. Judging by the one private letter
from her to him that I have seen, she was even more confidential when
writing to him at home. Gwen Molesworth thought that 'her boys
worried her' and another of the 8th Viscount's daughters, in a rather
mixed metaphor, said that Louisa 'kept her boys with too tight an eye,
being very much afraid of them overspending.'[45] This particular fear
presumably arose from her experience of Richard's behaviour.

These personal worries and her own illness naturally affected her work.
Macmillan's editor for their foreign language school books, George
Eugene Fasnacht, proposed to Craik that Louisa should write a French
reader for their primary French and German series. Fasnacht had himself
written readers and language courses and produced editions of authors
such as Perrault, Molière and Schiller with notes and introductions. He

[42] Victoria Glendinning, *Trollope*, Hutchinson, 1992, p. 65.
[43] MLM to GLC, 22.2 and 11.3.[1888].
[44] Oral communication from the second Mrs Craik to RR.
[45] GDL to RR, 25.5.1938.

had also been an assistant master at Westminster which suggests the possibility that he might have taught Bevil, whose French was presumably as good as Lionel's, and could thus first have come to a knowledge of Louisa's capabilities.[46] Charlotte Yonge too thought of her as a kind of expert on French matters and applied to her for information.[47] But Louisa, though gratified by the proposal and attracted by a task she saw as 'a very congenial one,' thinking that even the 'vocabulary part' would be 'rather interesting,' felt she was too busy and worried to undertake it. She suggested that her friend Kathleen O'Meara could do the work well.[48] However, having refused Craik's request, Louisa immediately wrote a postscript with suggestions for the book, as though she couldn't bear the idea of letting slip any offer of writing work.

> 'The girls and I cd. do this book next <u>autumn</u>, probably — October to Xmas — I wd. take Paris as the place — bringing in a few historical allusions &c . . . & the little domestic details we know so well, in a series of bright conversational letters from a girl to her English friends.'[49]

And over the next few weeks she pursued the matter, asking twice whether Craik had passed her rough sketch on to Fasnacht and what he thought of it. In the event she did write the reader during the time she mentioned, for she was correcting the proofs in January of the following year and *French Life in Letters* was published in April. The reviewers were favourable and inquisitive — they could not believe she had written such idiomatic French herself.

> 'Has Mrs Molesworth written these letters in English and got them translated or is she as consummate a French scholar as she is a story-teller for children?' 'The writer displays the same brightness of intuition and unrestrained humour that have made her children's stories so charming and attractive. But strange to say her narrative is given in idiomatic French, without the slightest suspicion of Anglicanism [sic]. Can she have written them herself, or has she engaged a sympathetic translator?'[50]

---

[46] Information about Fasnacht from BL catalogue, Macmillan's list of publications 1891 in the back of *Nurse Heatherdale's Story* and tp. of *French Life in Letters*.

[47] CMY to MLM, 6.12.1886.

[48] See the section in chapter 9 on Louisa's friends in France.

[49] MLM to GLC, 4.2.1888.

[50] From *The Journal of Education* and *The Guardian*, quoted in Macmillan's advertising pages at the back of *The Children of the Castle*, 1st edn. 1890, together with extracts from 3 other reviews.

It is to be hoped that these reviews were some comfort to her, for she confessed to Craik that she was very disappointed with the whole transaction. She was paid much less than she expected and the work had been far more trouble than she had anticipated. Beforehand she thought that the French reader would be 'far less strain' than a story, 'almost in some sense a sort of mechanical brain-work.' But afterwards her opinion was just the opposite. Complaining about the size of the royalty, she said it was

> 'considerably less than I have ever had on any book. The S.P.C.K. give me 1^d on a shilling book — & 4^d on a 2/6^d one — And both these books are my regular story books; written without trouble in about an eighth of the time this French book took — You see I had to fill it with idioms — every word had to be considered and weighed.'

She felt that her royalty should be larger than what she received on 'an ordinary little story,' particularly considering that this had been a commission — 'it was proposed to me to do it.' At the end of the letter is a kind of excuse for complaining at all.

> 'I have hesitated to tell you of my disappointment . . . I have so much the habit of frankness with you that sooner or later my feeling wd. have shown itself, so I think I will take the bull by the horns & tell it you right out — Trusting to your preferring this, as I think I shd. in your place.'

She relied completely on his friendly support and understanding.[51]

The complete *volte-face* Louisa performed about the relative strain and difficulty of a story-book and a text-book probably had a lot to do with her state of health. When explaining to Craik why she welcomed the idea of the French reader, she said 'I feel that I could not write a new book just yet.' This was in reference to her proposed Christmas book for 1888, which she wanted to be a collection of previously published stories and not something freshly written. 'After my head got so bad it was a rest to me to feel that I had my 1888 book thus, as it were, ready. . . . I have been told to do as little invention as possible.' Craik did not at first like the idea of a collection. It may be remembered that he was also less than enthusiastic about fairy stories. His preference was clearly for a full-length, real-life story such as *Two Little Waifs* or *Little Miss Peggy*. Louisa mentioned the projected book to him in a

---

51 MLM to GLC, 25.4.[1889].

casual postscript, as something already accepted, simply wanting a suggestion for a title. She had already consulted Crane, who was 'pleased with the idea, as a little variety — But he wd. like to have them earlier than last year.' So she was most taken aback to receive Craik's objections and hastened to justify herself, both with the explanation about her health and by reminding him that

> 'we, you and I, talked about it last year . . . I always meant sooner or later to have a Xmas book of collected stories — I remember your expression was "it is well to gather them up".'

She pointed out that of the thirteen Christmas books she had written for Macmillan's, only one, and that the first, *Tell Me A Story*, had been a collection of short stories. She felt that *Summer Stories* 'does not count, as it was quite an extra', and as for *Four Ghost Stories*, 'I look upon [it] as a completely outside book. It is not the least associated with my children's books.' This is the first mention we have of her careful classification of her books into 'extra', 'outside' and 'regular' ones, which played quite a part in her negotiations with Macmillan's a few years later. At that time Craik was to become seriously concerned lest the amount she was publishing with other firms should spoil their market for her books. She was very conscious of her market value. If Macmillan's refused the collection, she told Craik she would have to publish it elsewhere because 'I shd. be sorry to miss a Xmas just now while I am popular.' But she would much prefer them to bring it out — 'It wd. be something very like a grief to me not to have my Xmas book with you in its red coat as usual.' Another gentle reminder of her popularity was slipped in — 'I very often refuse overtures for children's books.' She was 'just a very little bit anxious' about the matter and offered to visit Macmillan's offices in Bedford Street in order to discuss it.[52]

But all these different forms of pressure do not seem to have been really necessary. Although no letter from Louisa to Craik has survived that directly bears on his capitulation to her defence of the stories which became *A Christmas Posy*, three days after the date of her 'little bit anxious' letter, she wrote to Mrs Du Cane about dedicating the book to the twins, Julia and Isabel, in terms which showed it had definitely been accepted.[53] She herself was pleased with the book, writing to Craik 'The stories are all, I think I may say, very good,' and to Mrs Du Cane

---

[52] MLM to GLC, 22.2.[1888].
[53] MLM to DUC, 25.2.[1888].

'I think it will be quite as pretty a book as any.' 'Pretty' was a catch-all term of approval, in much the same way as 'nice' still is, as can be seen in the quotations from Laura Troubridge's letters, where she refers to Louisa's books as 'pretty' and her letter about the hospital Christmas tree as 'nice'.

By comparison with 1887, Louisa produced very little original writing in 1888. It seems she meant it when she said she really 'could not write a new book just yet.' *Five Minutes' Stories* from SPCK was a collection of pieces that had already appeared in *The Child's Pictorial*. The only other book that appeared that year, apart from those already described that were also collections of previously published material, was *The Third Miss St Quentin*, a novel for girls published by Hatchards. The dedication was dated June 1888 so she may have been writing it earlier in the year — the only piece of invention on her desk. But it is quite possible that this too had been published earlier as a serial though a source has not yet been tracked down. Although an exhaustive bibliography of Louisa's work does not exist, it is clear from her correspondence with Macmillan's and other publishers that it was her practice to have everything re-published as many times as possible — in periodicals, in annuals, as a book, again as a book by another publisher — in order to maximise her income. She made a point of never selling her copyright so as to be able to control, and benefit from, this re-publication activity. The great exception was her series of red-coated Christmas books, which were written for and published by Macmillan's as books the first time round. *A Christmas Posy* was a special case, and we have seen the reason for it. There was one other special case, *Sheila's Mystery* (1895), first published in *Little Folks* and considered in more detail in the next chapter.

An example of her close attention to profit and copyright can be seen in her dealings with Chatto and Windus over 'That Girl in Black'. This was the 'new little novel' which she had promised Macmillan's she would keep back so that it would not clash with the publication of *Four Ghost Stories*. It is possible to reconstruct what happened in some detail from the copies of letters *to* her that survive in the Chatto letterbooks, even though there are no letters *from* her.[54] It was she who approached them, in December 1888 with the offer of two stories. They were dubious about the length but agreed to look at the material. In January

---

[54] Chatto and Windus, Letterbook 21, 1889. Publisher's archives held by the University of Reading Library.

1889, still rather reluctantly, they offered to issue 'That Girl in Black' and 'Bronzie' (which seems not to have been published before) together. It would be a shilling volume they said,

> 'should you be prepared to accept so low a sum as £10 for the remaining rights which we regret is the most we can offer as the market is greatly congested by the recent surproduction of shilling books.'

Louisa immediately sent the letter making this offer to Craik, asking for his advice. She admitted both the truth of Chatto's statement 'that there are far too many of these 1/- books in the market,' and that the 'novelette' was 'a very slight thing.' But she persisted in trying to do something further with the story, after its first appearance in *The English Illustrated Magazine*. 'Still I have my name' she insisted to Craik, '& it is possible this little thing might sell well, even after I am dead!'[55]

The particular matter on which she wanted Craik's advice was whether she could ask Chatto for a royalty on the book after the sale of the first 3000 copies. It would only be a penny in the shilling but that was not the point. She was quite aware of their lack of enthusiasm and the reason for it — 'They are not eager for the book, & I am not surprised: there are such shoals.' But, and this to her was the heart of the matter, 'still I do dislike altogether parting with my rights.' If she simply accepted their offer of £10 for 'the remaining rights' she could then do nothing further with the story should the opportunity arise. Craik obviously advised her to make the suggestion and see what happened, for Chatto then wrote refusing to give her an additional royalty. They explained that this was because 'the expenses of starting and bringing a shilling volume into notice bear so large a proportion to the returns that the sale of 3000 would be scarcely remunerative.' She knew this already, having made that very point in her letter to Craik — 'on a very cheap book I know the initial expenses are greater in proportion, the advertising &c being as dear as for a dear book.' But she would not take no for an answer and suggested they should give her a royalty on every copy sold after the first 5000. Apparently worn down by her importunity, they finally agreed to this, though still reminding her that they did not 'anticipate the possibility of a very large sale' and that 'the prospect of profit is very nearly equal to the risk of loss.' They thought that her motive was only the profit — 'we appreciate however your desire of

---

[55] MLM to GLC, 9.[1.1889].

participating in a decided success.' But she had achieved her aim of retaining her rights and made use of them seventeen years later when offering Macmillan's a collection of short stories for adults which was published as *The Wrong Envelope and Other Stories* (1906). She specifically described the two stories she had argued so hard about with Chatto as 'my own property.' A note of triumph, perhaps, or at least satisfaction. It should be noted that Chatto and Windus need not have published the shilling volume at all if they really felt it would make a loss. Presumably the 'name' that Louisa proudly stressed to Craik, meant something to them, despite their reluctance. We can see from this negotiation over two such slight stories, an insignificant part of Louisa's work as a whole, how great the volume of her business correspondence must have been. It is interesting also that not only was she quite happy to consult a partner in a rival publishing firm over such transactions, but that Craik seems to have been happy to be consulted and to respond with advice — a measure of their private friendship.

Her health and power of invention had recovered sufficiently by the autumn of 1888 for her to return to writing original, full-length stories. *Little Mother Bunch* was issued in *Little Folks* from January to June 1889, and much appreciated by Swinburne — 'I have followed it from beginning to end with unqualified delight.' He had sent one number of the magazine to his mother who praised the instalment of Louisa's story in 'glowing terms of admiration.' 'She thinks with me,' Swinburne added, 'that no-one ever did understand children like you.' Louisa had sent Bertie a copy of *French Life in Letters*, which Swinburne acknowledged in this letter. Bertie and Lionel had never met again, as he made clear. 'I hope Lionel is as well and as prosperous in & out of school as the playfellow of one afternoon whom he has very probably forgotten.' Swinburne the recluse preferred to pursue his friendships by letter. In this one he was lively and detailed about his and Bertie's comparative achievements in languages and science. He was also anxious that Louisa should not stop writing for *Little Folks*, 'my favourite magazine.'[56] Perhaps she had told him she was thinking of giving up working for this particular periodical, but he need not have worried — she contributed four book-length serials to it over the next ten years, as well as short pieces.[57] Swinburne had also been delighted by *A Christmas Posy*, which

---

[56] C. Y. Lang, V, pp. 264–5.
[57] *The Next-Door House*, 1892, *Sheila's Mystery*, 1894, *Greyling Towers*, 1897, *The Three Witches*, 1899.

she had sent him as a gift at the end of November 1888, praising again her 'inexhaustible knowledge and love of childhood' as well as her 'genius for drawing it.' This time he mentioned the literal drawing as well, saying that he, Bertie and Watts all agreed about 'the beauty and charm of the illustrations,' and that Watts in particular admired 'the artist's humorous power of realising character.'[58] Louisa had twice mentioned to Craik that the variety offered by a collection of stories seemed to please Crane when she had discussed the project with him, and this obviously had a good effect on the illustrations he produced.

Over the winter of 1888–89 Louisa also achieved the writing of 'a nice, fresh complete story' for Macmillans as she had promised Craik when persuading him to accept *A Christmas Posy*. The story, *The Rectory Children*, was finished by Shrove Tuesday, 5th March, when she dedicated it to her niece, Helen Walthall, one of her sister Caroline's three daughters. This little link with her family is a reminder, in the almost complete absence of family letters, that she was close to her sisters and missed them. As she had told Mrs Du Cane, she felt strange in London 'especially in winter when I have no relations here,' which implies that in summer, probably during the season, they visited her. A little note to Mrs Du Cane in April indicates both another family link and some of the many social activities the season could bring. She wrote to send tickets for a concert, given to her by her nephew, Herbert Molesworth, the son of Richard's brother, Morgan Crofton Molesworth, and passed on to Mrs Du Cane because she and her daughters already had tickets. She was keen to see her friend during a busy week which included one of the 'train shows' we have already heard about — 'at 5 we are going to see my cousin Mrs Lucas Cocks, to see some of them after the Drawing-room — but they live quite near.'[59]

By now Louisa's relationship with Mrs Du Cane had become very close, so close that she told her about the Stewart family 'mystery', meaning her ignorance of her father's parentage. The two women had been meeting regularly. They had recently had enough private time together for Louisa to unburden herself of 'all those long stories' and now she was writing, in early July, to arrange one last meeting 'before we all disperse,' for the summer away from London. But her confidences at the previous session troubled her, and she wrote:

---

[58] C. Y. Lang, V, pp. 255–6.
[59] MLM to DUC, 30.4.[1889].

'I want to tell you that I have felt perhaps it was foolish & rather selfish of me to tell you all those long stories of my old family troubles & puzzles — . . . But you are so very sympathising and "interested" in your friend's affairs that it led me on — I know I can trust you & I hope you did not think me <u>silly</u>? Sometimes I wonder if it is wrong of me to want to know the whole of the story, as it does not matter now, & as my father & mother never told us all — But I know my father said we might know after his death, & but for my brother's fearfully sudden death, I should have been told all as he promised me — & it is rather fascinating to get to the bottom of a family mystery — We have always been — like most Scotch people — rather proud of our old Stewart ancestry (it is full of romance, as my great-great-grandfather was in the Pretender's army & banished for many years) & I confess I should like to know all about the other side, wh. <u>really</u> is conjecture from the little bits we do know — & I am dreadfully afraid of exaggerating or letting one's imagination run away with one, which very often makes me hesitate in telling even <u>anything</u>. I daresay you know that sort of feeling.'

What Louisa did not know was any of the story about her grandfather and father, related in the first chapter of this book, which had been ferreted out and pieced together by the lawyer, J. P. Bunting, in his efforts to defeat the claim put forward by Louisa's brother Charles, described towards the end of chapter 7. One of the 'little bits' she does seem to have known was her brother's assertion that the Duke of York was godfather to their father,[60] though she and her sisters apparently passed on to their children the story that the royal godfather was the Duke of Sussex. This was an understandable change during the oral handing on of family history, since a Duke whose name included Augustus would have seemed a more likely sponsor for Charles Augustus Stewart. What is more, they also transmitted the story that their father was really the illegitimate son of the Duke and this is what Louisa was to tell Cicely's husband.[61] But it seems to have been more a romantic tale that they liked to think about than a relation of something believed as hard fact. Louisa told Mrs Du Cane that she was proud of her 'old Stewart ancestry' and her grand-daughter once heard her say as a joke that she 'could call cousin with all the Stewarts of Appin.' However, her father could not have been descended from the Stewart clan at all

---

[60] *Claimant*, p. 90.
[61] See the list of *Unpublished Manuscript Sources*.

if his father had really been a Hanoverian. Her sister Caroline's children used to laugh at their mother for telling the royal Duke story, pointing out that if it were true, she was not a Stewart, which she did not like. Perhaps it was as well for Louisa's fascination with the 'family mystery' that she never did hear the true story. To her Victorian mind, an illegitimate royal grandfather would have seemed romantic though scandalous. A military man who supported several other illegitimate children besides her own father would have been scandalous only.

The autumn of 1889 brought Louisa a trouble more real and pressing than 'old family puzzles.' Bevil had not endured his post in the city for long. In November he left England for South America and a ranch in Patagonia. Louisa found his departure very hard to bear.

> 'Bevil goes on Tuesday morning & I am to be away next week till the end, for I think it will be better for me' she wrote to Mrs Du Cane. 'It is a <u>horrible</u> <u>wrench</u> to part with the boy so far — & probably for so long, & these last days he seems to have grown so very <u>near</u> to me . . . I did not think such a great trial was before me — I suppose one's whole life <u>must</u> be discipline of one kind or another.'[62]

Victorian sons were often sent far off, though perhaps more usually to India or South Africa, to sow their wild oats well away from the strict, if two-faced, conventions of Victorian society. If the sowing had already occurred, absence would remove the cause of scandal from their shocked friends and families. A slight hint of this could be deduced from Louisa's sentence 'I think it is for his good in every way, & it is a good chance'. Coupled with her remarks to Craik about his starting in the city, it suggests that at least he was rather wild, in which case the freer, open-air life of a ranch would suit him well. By December he had reached the Cape Verde islands and sent his mother 'very nice letters' from there. The letters in which she told Mrs Du Cane all about this, repeatedly expressed her sense of her friend's kindness and sympathy.

Cicely also wanted to leave home and do something useful. In May 1890, aged 27, she went to train as a nurse. Louisa was doubtful but did not apparently oppose her daughter's wish. 'I <u>very much</u> doubt her being strong enough for the life — but this trial time will show — she has certainly made her offering of herself with the purest motives.'[63] She had expressed a general concern about the arduousness of the life and

---

[62]   MLM to DUC, 21.11.1889.
[63]   MLM to DUC, 22.5.1890.

the danger of starting too young in an article on 'English Girlhood' published the previous October in *The English Illustrated Magazine*. Discussing the need for girls to work, whether to earn their living or to maintain and extend habits of study and regularity and to help others, she added a special warning footnote on nursing as a profession.

> 'Incalculable mischief may be done by its being attempted too young, even if only in the modified form of hospital nursing for a certain period without any intention of devoting one's life to it. . . . Most hospitals refuse to take probationers under the age of five and twenty, but this rule is not, I am sorry to find, universal. And even five and twenty is fully young for the average girl to test her fitness for work so arduous and so peculiarly trying, and assuredly if attempted before that age the risk of lasting injury to health and nerves is exceedingly grave.'[64]

One suspects that she said this kind of thing to Cicely in the discussions that must have taken place before the final decision, and that her know-ledge of the age limit for probationers arose from Cicely's investigations for her own benefit. *The English Illustrated Magazine* published a thirteen page article on 'Hospital Nursing' in March 1891 which no doubt both Louisa and Cicely would have read with interest, Louisa particularly noting the phrase 'Many women break down under the strain of the work.' This article also describes the custom that then prevailed, of having some paying probationers, who, instead of being paid by the hospital and bound by a contract, paid for their instruction themselves, and were able to leave when they pleased. It is likely that Cicely belonged to this class, since Louisa referred to a 'trial time' which matches with the article's description of the 'paying probationer who enters the hospital for a few weeks to see what things are like.'

With Cicely and Bevil both gone, the house in Lexham Gardens was now not only too far out in 'gloomy and out-of-the-way' Kensington which she disliked, but was also 'too big for our diminished party.'[65] She had been talking about moving ever since they first came to live in Lexham Gardens, and this year she actually did it. An interesting aside about Louisa's first home in London is that during the six years she lived there, her neighbours at No. 101 were the Woolf family. When she moved away in 1890, Leonard Woolf was ten years old. There is

---

[64] MLM 'English Girlhood', *The English Illustrated Magazine*, Oct., 1890. Later in *Studies and Stories*, A. D. Innes, 1893, p. 230.
[65] MLM to Cullum, 10.6.1890.

no evidence that the two families ever met, but it is rather a fascinating spatial juxtaposition.[66] Another neighbour for a year was Frances Hodgson Burnett, who took a lease of No. 44 in 1889.[67]

Louisa had been consulting Craik about selling her house as early as 1888 and in February of that year she uttered yet again her wish to be 'further in' when telling him that she had as yet no prospect of selling favourably. In January 1889 he recommended, to help her with assessing the possibilities of moving, someone who sounds like the nineteenth century version of an estate agent. Louisa wrote 'Your "Mann" is coming to see me and this house tomorrow — I think I shall abide by his opinion, & if it is unfavourable as to our chance of letting or selling, we must just settle down here.' It seems that not only did she let the house rather than sell it, but that she kept it over a long period, for in 1911 when sending Macmillan's a list of names and addresses for complimentary copies of her latest book, she showed Cicely's children as living at 85, Lexham Gardens.[68] The actual date of the move is uncertain. The earliest mention of her new address, 19, Sumner Place, was at the head of a letter to Longmans, about a cheap edition of *Neighbours*, on 22nd March 1890. Then the dedication of her 1890 Christmas book for Macmillan's, *The Children of the Castle*, was addressed from there and dated 19th May. But on 10th June in a note to Cullum about a dance, she gave a temporary address, explaining 'we have let our house in Lexham Gardens . . . & our new house — Sumner Place — is not yet ready.' The temporary address, at Tregunter Road, The Boltons, in Kensington, was only a few streets away from the new house, so overseeing the getting it ready would not have been a problem. Both Lexham Gardens and Sumner Place were purely residential streets, with a liberal sprinkling of military and medical men. There was a hospital for consumption and diseases of the chest at the corner of Sumner Place and Fulham Road. Her opposite neighbour was a clergyman.[69]

At the beginning of August, all the family except of course, Bevil, were at Arnside on Morecambe Bay, 'on our way further north' presumably to stay with friends and relations in Scotland. Cicely was there too, and a

---

[66] George Spater and Ian Parsons, *A Marriage of True Minds*, Jonathan Cape and the Hogarth press, 1979, p. 1.

[67] Ann Thwaite, *Waiting for the Party*, Secker and Warburg, 1974, p. 122.

[68] MLM to GLC, 16.1.[1889]; MLM to Macmillan, 11.10.1911.

[69] Information from Kelly's Directories.

letter to a friend in Exeter shows that Louisa was satisfied about both these children just then.

> 'My daughter, who is now a "sister", is with us for her holiday: you can fancy how we enjoy being together, as we are just now, except for my boy in Patagonia. His letters however are most satisfactory.'

She gave her new address in its complete form, which included Onslow Square, and said 'we are so glad to be further in.'[70] To our way of thinking, Sumner Place is not so very much 'further in' than Lexham Gardens, only about one-and-a-half stops on the tube. It runs from north west to south east, linking Brompton Road and Fulham Road, but it is certainly nearer to Knightsbridge and Hyde Park, 'the place where the fashionable world congregated to ride, drive or walk and converse with friends.'[71] In 1902 'the area in London inhabited by what we call Society' was described in an article in *Lady's Realm* as bounded roughly by 'Oxford Street on the north, the House of Commons on the south, Alexandra Gate to the South Kensington Museum on the west, and Regent Street on the east' so the new home was just about within the magic pale.[72] Whenever the actual move took place, on their return from Scotland in the autumn, Louisa and her reduced family were settled in Sumner Place and pleased to be there.

---

[70] MLM to Mrs Rogers, 8.8.[1890]; letter given to RR by Olive M. Rogers, her daughter.
[71] Horn, p. 15.
[72] Lady Jeune, 'The Future of Society' in *Lady's Realm*, Jan. 1902, p. 365.

12

❧✥❧

'Nobody Like You'

In the autumn of 1890, after her return from Scotland, Louisa was thinking and planning about Lionel's future. He would be eighteen in the spring and the possibility of his going to Oxford was being discussed. But when she told Swinburne about this, he advised her against the idea, on health grounds. 'The Thames valley is enough to finish off a delicate boy' he wrote. 'I ought to know, for I was five years at Eton and four at Oxford.'[1] Another aspect of the matter, which gave Louisa concern, was the expense of a university education. She explained to Craik at the beginning of 1893 that she was looking forward to giving up 'all writing except my red Xmas book, before long,' but she could not yet think of doing so because 'I can only meet Lionel's Oxford education by writing more than this.'[2] More, she meant, than just the one book a year at Christmas. But in the event neither the concern about health or about money prevented Lionel's going to Oxford. He was in fact already there, at University College, when Louisa told Craik that it was her writing that helped to cover the cost.

The same month that Swinburne was so discouraging about Oxford, he was full of praise for Louisa's latest books. One, which she had just sent him, *The Children of the Castle*, Macmillans' red book for 1890, he thought beautiful. The other, *The Story of A Spring Morning*, had recently come out in book form, but he had read it some time before, presumably when it was first published in *Atalanta* from July to September 1889. It called forth the greater enthusiasm because he loved the character of Armar, the hero.

> 'What a divine gift it is to be able to create so many of them [sc. children], and to make your readers feel not only a desire to see and hear and hug and kiss them, but a sort of feeling as if one had done so when one shuts the book! I always did say there was nobody like you or near you among

---

[1] C. Y. Lang, VI, pp. 1–2.
[2] MLM to GLC, 30.1.[1893].

writers for and about children, and you are evidently determined to prove
— not merely that I was right, but that it would be frightfully absurd
for anybody to question the fact.'[3]

She must have welcomed his continuing praise and encouragement even
though it was rather gushingly sentimental. The book version of *Spring
Morning* was dedicated to 'my dear cousin Gwen Molesworth,' that
daughter of the 8th Viscount Molesworth who had first got to know
Louisa in France. It helps to support Gwen Molesworth's own statement
when she was an old woman: 'I think after her own daughters she was
fonder of me than anyone.'

The Children of the Castle should have been called *The Princess with
the Forget-me-not Eyes*. This was Louisa's intended title as she explained
to Julia and Isabel Du Cane when sending them the original manuscript
used to set the book in type, which was 'very dirty, but that is the
printer's fault!' It was Walter Crane who made the mistake that caused
the change of title — he 'used the title of the first chapter for the whole
book.'[4] In the published version, the title actually given to the first
chapter, 'Ruby and Mavis', simply used the names of the two girls who
were in fact 'the children of the castle', so that the book and the first
chapter would not have the same title. Crane himself told Frederick
Macmillan that he could not understand how he had come to make
such a mistake. He hoped that Louisa would accept the *fait accompli*,
for he had no time to change his cover design, which emphasised the
children and not the Princess Forget-me-not. It shows two little girls
holding hands, standing beneath a portcullis in a castle archway. Fortunately Louisa appears to have agreed to the alteration with good grace.
The original title emphasised the beautiful and authoritative female
figure with strange powers, who often appeared in Louisa's fantasy
stories. At the beginning of *The Children of the Castle* she informed the
reader that it was one of the stories told by Gratian Conyfer, the hero
of *Four Winds Farm*, thus specifically linking the two books. The latter
has four of these mysterious and lovely creatures, whose powers, like
those of Princess Forget-me-not, are largely dedicated to the moral
and spiritual development of the human beings who meet them. The
godmother in *Christmas-Tree Land* and the white lady who span stories
on her wheel in *The Tapestry Room* were two more of the genre, that

---

[3] C. Y. Lang, VI, p. 1.
[4] MLM to J. and I. DUC, 5.2.[1891].

Louisa had created before *The Children of the Castle*. Often, though not in every case, it was difficult for the children in the stories to tell whether these figures were young or old, ugly or beautiful.

Louisa continued to write of such beings from time to time up to the end of her story-telling life. The spinning-wheel fairy in *The Magic Nuts* (1898) also made stories on her wheel. Another of the group was Cousin Felicity, a strange old lady with magic powers, who never seemed to get any older, in 'The Enchanted Trunks', a story from her last book, *Fairies Afield*. The curiously small old woman in *The Ruby Ring* (1904), who took charge of the various transformations undergone by the hero-ine, was the most nearly religious of the figures, for twice she appeared to be like an angel —

> 'the little old face had taken on a curious majesty. The small almost comical figure seemed to have grown, the sharp, keen eyes shone with a marvellous and beautiful light. The old cloak had disappeared, and in its stead two lovely snow-white wings shaded the gracious form.'

But this vision lasted 'only for a moment.'[5] Any longer and the fairy world of the story would have been shattered by too close a contact with greater realities. Louisa knew that a writer who chooses to take her readers up 'the bonny road That winds about the fernie brae' to 'fair Elfland' should not stray either on to the 'Path of Righteousness' or the 'Path of Wickedness.'[6] Like Dudu the raven, and the cuckoo, these wonderful beings often spoke in riddles, rebuked when necessary and could produce some very tart utterances. They belonged to the same family as Irene's grandmother in George MacDonald's Curdie books. Like her, the Princess Forget-me-not could not be seen by those who did not believe in her and were deliberately doing wrong. Like her, several of Louisa's creations were spoken ill of, and believed to be witches. It is difficult to say definitely whether Louisa was consciously influenced by MacDonald, for such fairy beings, whether called god-mothers, grandmothers or simply old women, abound in traditional folk and fairy tales.

A very different kind of writing was beginning to take up more of Louisa's time and attention. We have noted her two articles on 'English Girlhood' and 'Coming Out'. A third was soon to appear, 'Fiction — Its Use and Abuse', another piece of the same kind, specially directed

---

[5] *The Ruby Ring*, Macmillan, 1904, p. 162.
[6] 'Thomas the Rhymer' in *The Oxford Book of Ballads*.

at young girls. Although the title does not make this clear, its publication in the *Girls' Own Paper* (May 1891), as well as its actual content, shows for whom it was intended. These three essays heralded, over the next ten or so years of Louisa's life, a regular, though not prolific, flow of articles and interviews aimed at helping and interesting young people in life in general and writing and reading in particular. It is clear both from the tone of the writing and from associated correspondence that this kind of work was commissioned. The interviews were definitely requested by the interviewers. She had reached the stage of being sufficiently well-known for her opinion to be sought for its own sake, and for information about her life and methods of work to be seen as helping to sell a periodical. By 1900, she was described with no qualification in one book as 'our most popular writer of children's stories.' Interestingly, this was not a book about children's literature or about writing at all. It was a kind of friendly reference book about the origin of girl's names, with short paragraphs of information about the legendary, historical, literary and contemporary bearers of each name. Louisa had been chosen as an example from the last group for 'Louisa, Louise, Alison.'[7]

In 1890 a contribution from Louisa appeared in *The Art of Authorship* by the Rev. George Bainton, as the result of a request similar to W. T. Stead's, asking her for her ideas on the best books for children. Bainton explained in the introduction that the book was made up of replies from 'authors . . . who have personally contributed, at my request, their reminiscences and advice.' He told the authors to whom he applied that he needed their help in responding to a group of young men who had asked him to talk to them about the art of composition and public speaking. Altogether he obtained and published 178 responses. Louisa's two paragraphs, describing her early experiences of writing and her current methods, appeared alongside pieces from such writers as Robert Browning, Marie Corelli, George Gissing, Rider Haggard, Thomas Hardy, Henry James, George Meredith, William Morris and Christina Rossetti. Some of the contributors were friends and acquaintances of hers — Sir Edwin Arnold, Mrs Craik and Charlotte Yonge among them. Since Mrs Craik died in October 1887, Bainton was obviously collecting his material several years before his book was published. Louisa's own piece was actually written in the autumn of 1887, for she specifically mentions Mrs Craik's death as an event which 'just now we are all deploring.' This was in the context of comparing her own method of

---

[7] Swan, pp. 354–5.

work with her friend's. She said that she herself 'strictly adhered to the rule of never copying. I write at once as I intend the words to stand.' In contrast she related how 'the author of "John Halifax"' had once said to her 'To get a chapter *perfect*, I have sometimes written it over fourteen times.' (Louisa's 'rule' originated in the advice Warren gave her when she was writing her first novel, described towards the beginning of chapter 5.) The book was reviewed unfavourably by *The Spectator* and Bainton was accused of exploiting the contributors by not informing each that he was writing to the others and not letting them know that he intended to make a book out of their letters. Such behaviour again recalls W. T. Stead's dealings with Louisa, although it is fair to record that Bainton denied the charge.[8]

Over the next few years between 1893 and 1898, Louisa wrote another four articles, at much greater length than her short piece in Bainton's book, about her own methods of writing and how she came to write at all. The amount of personal reminiscence and the style varied according to the periodical for which she was writing. 'On the Art of Writing Fiction for Children' in *Atalanta* is the most general, concentrating on advice to 'my dear young friends' on whether and how they should write. For example, she often advised aspiring writers, both privately and in her articles, to form their style by translating. In 'On the Art . . .' she puts it in general terms.

> 'Drill yourself well by *translating*. It is capital training. You know what you have to say, and there is not for the moment the strain of inventing upon you . . . Young writers are usually so full of what they want to say, that they give too little care to how they say it.'

In 'Story-Writing' in *The Monthly Packet* she makes the same point through personal experience — 'the best work I ever did, up to the age of seventeen or so, was translation. It taught me — thanks to the exceptional excellence of the teacher . . . — command of language.' It is clear that when this latter article was commissioned, Louisa was asked for her earliest memories and stories about her childhood and adolescence which had something to do with her development as a writer, while L. T. Meade wanted general advice for the readers of *Atalanta*. In May 1894, in a letter to A. D. Innes, at that time both

---

[8] George Bainton, *The Art of Authorship*, James Clarke and Co., 1900, pp. vii-viii; Louisa's contribution pp. 93–96; review in *The Spectator*, 10.5.1890, pp. 513–5; Bainton's denial in a letter to the editor, 17.5.1890, p. 543.

publisher and joint editor with Christabel Coleridge of *The Monthly Packet*, Louisa referred to her forthcoming article for the periodical and described her feeling about this kind of writing. 'I will try to write my paper soon — What bothers me, in this sort of thing is the being <u>forced</u> to be so egotistical — I suppose one must just put that aside!'[9]

For *Little Folks*, Louisa produced 'How I Write My Children's Stories' another chatty piece full of personal anecdotes. In November 1897 Chambers approached her for a paper on fiction for the young and when accepting the commission she asked for 'a <u>rather</u> more distinct idea of the kind of article' they wanted, herself differentiating between a personal and a general piece.

> 'Should it relate principally to my own experience and "history" so to say, as a writer for children — or should you like it to be more general than this — glancing back at the books of my own childhood & drawing a contrast between them & those of the present day? Of course in an article of only 3000 words a review of this kind would be <u>but</u> a glance.'

It can be seen from 'Story-Reading and Story-Writing' in *Chambers's Journal* that Chambers chose her second suggestion. A good two thirds of the article is about her childhood reading and the final section gives advice on writing for children with some comment on contemporary work in the field and little that is directly personal. This paper was published in November 1898, a year after it was commissioned, because Louisa had other work on hand and could not promise it till the following year.[10] These four articles are, of course, a valuable source for the biographer, particularly in the almost complete absence of family letters, and have been largely drawn on in the writing of this book.

Louisa wrote one other broadly similar piece, 'A Ramble about Childhood' which appeared in the 1898–99 *Girls' Own Annual*. It is similar in its combination of personal reminiscence with general remarks, but differs in that the topic is childhood only and not writing about or for it. It is possible to identify one or two of the anecdotes as the original foundation on which a story was built. Thus a paragraph about a little girl who believed 'that on the 31st of December the "old year" took material human form and strolled about the world in the guise of an aged man' and watched for him from 'a corner of the deep, old-fashioned

---

[9] MLM to A. D. Innes, 12.5.1894, National Library of Scotland.
[10] MLM to Chambers, 30.11.[1897], Chambers Collection, National Library of Scotland.

window-sill of her nursery,' was developed into the story 'Mr Old Year' for *The Child's Pictorial*.[11] And the little boy who, confusing the sense of old as aged with old as worn-out, believed that all old people, even his own grandmother, became destitute and had to beg from house to house, was incorporated into the character of Herr Baby. Although she began this anecdote with the distancing phrase 'a small boy of my acquaintance,' it seems clear from the words 'his dear granny' and 'our carefully-worded explanation of his mistake,' as well as from the later statement of her grand-daughter, 'Herr Baby was Lionel and Bevil mixed up,' that the small boy was one of her own sons. Other memories in *A Ramble* are explicitly taken from her own childhood, the whole being indeed a ramble, or wandering, from one reminiscence to the next, linked by a few more general remarks about the nature of childish thought and experience.

The interviews that Louisa gave, over much the same period of time as that during which she wrote these articles, also contained personal details and reminiscences. The earliest, in *The Westminster Budget* in 1893, was a short, one page piece entitled 'A Popular Writer for Children', on Louisa alone. The two others to appear in periodicals were each part of a long article on a group of writers. One, called 'Some Women Novelists' brought Louisa together with twenty-two others, most of whom did not write for children, the exceptions being Frances Hodgson Burnett and L. T. Meade. The writer, Sarah Tooley, justified including Louisa with authors such as Ouida, Marie Corelli, Rosa N. Carey and Olive Schreiner, by calling her 'the novelist of the little ones' and mentioning many of her 'works of fiction for those of larger growth.' Although the piece was definitely the result of a personal conversation with Louisa, there are several mistakes in the abbreviated account of what she had written. One particularly noticeable error is the statement that Louisa began to write 'Like Mrs Gaskell . . . in order to divert her mind after the death of one of her children.' As we saw in chapter 6, this was not the case — she had begun to write several years before Violet's death. But we cannot know if this was Sarah Tooley's mistake, or Louisa's own, looking back over some 27 years. The other article was specifically on writers for children, entitled 'Children's Classics' by Bella Sydney Woolf. Here Louisa is listed after Lewis Carroll, and her companions include Mrs O. F. Walton, included for *Christie's Old*

---

[11] Later collected in *The Children's Hour*, Nelson, 1899. First published in *The Child's Pictorial*, Jan.-Mar., 1895.

Organ, 'Brenda' for *Froggy's Little Brother,* and Frances Hodgson Burnett for *Little Lord Fauntleroy.* The inclusion of Rosa N. Carey for *Nellie's Memories* seems incongruous as this is a romantic novel for adults or at least girls in their late teenage, while the book for which Louisa was particularly mentioned is *Carrots,* and she was praised because 'among writers of really childlike children's books, [she] stands pre-eminent.' The results of one other interview were published in a book, *Story Weavers: or Writers for the Young* in 1900, offering much the same material.[12]

A further small group of non-fiction pieces came from Louisa's pen during this same period, all to do with charitable work. In 1892 Angela Burdett-Coutts was preparing a report on the philanthropic work of British women to be presented at the Great World Fair opening in Chicago in May 1893, and Louisa was asked to contribute. The book contained thirty-two papers, a statistical survey and an appendix summarizing the work of some 316 organisations and individuals. Louisa's paper, called 'For The Little Ones', concentrated on work for children. One aspect of this was outings to the country for poor children, which she described as 'food, fun and fresh air for the little ones', and which Miss Burdett-Coutts had been one of the first to organise. It seems likely that Louisa was thought of for this part of the report because her book in aid of the Waifs and Strays Society, *Farthings,* came out in 1892 and therefore she would have come easily to mind in this connection.[13] In 1894 the *Newbery House Magazine* published an article by Louisa entitled 'Mrs Molesworth on the Women's Christian Education League',[14] which aimed to raise support for 'The Defence of our National Religion'. This meant, in the context, making sure that children in Board Schools continued to be taught Christianity as part of the curriculum. Another article, 'A Cry from The Far West', published in 1897, was an appeal for the Aberdeen Association, which collected and distributed all kinds of reading matter to educate, interest and amuse the isolated settlers on the Canadian prairie. When the article was published the society had been operating for six years in Canada, but had just opened a branch in London, under the auspices of Lady Aberdeen, 'one of the most

---

[12] Details of all these articles appear in the list of material consulted.

[13] *Women's Mission: A Series of Congress Papers on the Philanthropic Work of Women by Eminent Writers,* arranged and edited with a Preface and notes by the Baroness Burdett-Coutts, Sampson Low, 1893, pp. 13–34. See Edna Healey, *Lady Unknown: The Life of Angela Burdett-Coutts,* Sidgwick and Jackson, 1978, pp. 215–9.

[14] *Newbery House Magazine,* vol. 10, Feb. 1894, pp. 91–8.

philanthropic and energetic of women . . . gifted with great powers of organisation.'[15] Louisa's article was specially to introduce and publicise 'the newly-organised English Collecting Branch of the Society.' She maintained her interest in this work — two years after her article appeared, she mentioned having asked Macmillan's office to send her a list of their new sixpenny series 'as we are thinking of investing in them for the Aberdeen Association'. This was in a letter to Craik approving of his plan to launch *Carrots* afresh in this same series. She was amused at the coincidence. 'It is rather a coincidence that the same day I hear that you think of putting me into it!' ('It' being the sixpenny series.)[16]

One other piece of charitable writing was a pamphlet on the Royal Waterloo Hospital. This was a short history prefaced 'with a little fanciful story of a child's visit to the Hospital.' The hospital secretary, a Captain Houston, had 'urged' and 'teased' her to do it, and then she heard nothing more about it for two or three years. Thinking it had been a waste of time and trouble, she wrote to enquire about the fate of her ms, which prompted the Hospital Board to take action in the form of asking her to arrange for it to be printed. When she told the Secretary 'I had never seen a printer in my life & that I left everything of technical details to my publishers' he asked her for an introduction to her publishers. It is because she wrote to Macmillan's to give warning of the hospital's coming application for help that we know the background to this little pamphlet. After the three years' delay, it was printed very quickly in the end, for just over a month after her explanatory letter she sent Mr Macmillan a copy of the pamphlet.[17]

Louisa's popularity and established position as a writer for children by the last decade of the century is well shown in the commission which resulted in *An Enchanted Garden*. It appeared in May 1892 as part of a series produced by T. Fisher Unwin called *The Children's Library*. The first volume in the series was *The Brown Owl* by the seventeen-year-old Ford Hermann Hueffer (later Ford Madox Ford), published in 1891. His grandfather, the Pre-Raphaelite painter Ford Madox Brown 'was so delighted that he immediately made two illustrations for it, bullied

---

[15] Troubridge (1925), p. 133.

[16] 'A Cry from The Far West', *Macmillan's Magazine*, vol. LXVII, Dec. 1897, pp. 125–130; MLM to GLC, 17.7.[1899].

[17] MLM to Macmillan, 8.11 and 10.12.1907. *Prince's Meadows or Poverty Corner. Being a Short Account of the Royal Waterloo Hospital for Children and Women*, 1907. The 'little fanciful story' was published in *Partridge's Children's Annual*, as 'Bertie's Drive over Waterloo Bridge'.

Edward Garnett into seeing that Fisher Unwin published it and rushed copies to all his friends.'[18] In the event the book had considerable success, but before he could know how it would be received, Edward Garnett was casting round for some better known author to help sell the new series. In February 1891 he urged Unwin to write to Louisa, sending her a copy of the forthcoming *Brown Owl*. The draft letter in which he outlined the approach he thought Unwin ought to make ran, in part, 'We have pleasure in sending you a copy of a <u>Fairy Story</u> by a new writer which will start a Library for Children we have in preparation. It has been suggested by several friends that the Library will be incomplete if it is never to include any story by the author of 'The Cuckoo Clock'.' Garnett's note to Unwin on this draft makes quite clear why he wanted a book from Louisa in the series. 'Rice says that all the booksellers assert a new story by Mrs Molesworth would sell The Children's Library.'[19] With the booksellers agreeing on the pulling power of a book by her, she had arrived indeed. As she had told Craik, she had her 'name'.

Having a name could attract annoyances as well as applause. From the beginning of the 1890s Louisa's letters to Macmillan's complain from time to time about requests for permission to translate her books. She regarded such applications as a nuisance, not as a source of profit, although she did always ask for payment, usually £5, for granting permission, if the book was still within the legal time limit. But this was primarily because 'I think this keeps them out of inferior hands a little.' Very rarely had she actually received such payment. She mentioned having once had £5 for a German translation and also having been paid for two French translations, one by Madame Guizot de Witt, the sister of her friend Guillaume Guizot, who could be expected to behave with meticulous correctness in such a matter, but this was all. By 'inferior hands' she simply meant anyone whose incompetent work would not do justice to a book.

> 'It is well to keep to asking for some payment' she said on another occasion, 'as otherwise I do not know into what hands translations might fall.' 'I dislike translations exceedingly' she wrote, '& you wd. scarcely

---

[18] Arthur Mizener, *The Saddest Story, A Biography of Ford Madox Ford*, quoted in Lurie, p. 75.

[19] Draft letter from Edward Garnett to T. Fisher Unwin in the New York Public Library, Berg Collection. Quoted with permission from Richard Garnett, controller of Edward Garnett's literary estate.

believe the incessant applications of this kind that I have — I prefer my books being read in the original even in foreign countries, for English is now taught to children everywhere.'[20]

This last statement seems rather sweepingly unfair — all children could not be expected to attain in English the standard that Lionel had in French through the special advantage of living in France for so long. It probably arose from her feeling thoroughly fed up with the whole business of translation. 'To tell you the truth' she wrote to Macmillan's after another of the 'so many applications,' 'I am disgusted with would-be translators.' It would be much easier all round, she felt, if people would only read her books in the original. 'I have no great wish for my books to be translated. They lose terribly.' And even the requests for permission were something of a farce, for often, as she pointed out, 'I suppose (as I know many of my books are in Germany) the publishers just wait till the two years have expired and then I get nothing!'[21]

Years later, when replying to Macmillan's about a request from an agency wanting to buy translation rights, she still said 'I am not keen on translations, as the original always suffers' but, she conceded, 'still if in good hands I do not object.' The nuisance value continued to be for her the main characteristic of translations. 'I have been perpetually teazed by would-be translators who always subside if I say I must be paid, even £5! They seem to think I should pay them.'[22] These sentiments are repeated many times in her letters — a demand for some payment to discourage a low standard of work, reluctance to have translations done at all, expectation by would-be translators to be paid themselves and a general disgust with the whole subject. She tried to wash her hands of the matter by getting Macmillan's to answer such applications direct for her, explaining 'I find it best not to answer, myself, as these good people are more in awe of you — & do not go on writing tiresome letters as they would to me possibly.'[23] However, plenty of requests still found their way to her, which she would send on to her publishers, asking them to cope. According to her letters, during her lifetime and with her knowledge, although quite often not with her permission, her books were translated into French, German, Swedish, Japanese and Russian. She mentioned several that she thought had been pirated but could not keep track of.

---

[20] MLM to GLC, 19.1.[189?1], and to Macmillan, 27.8.[1898].

[21] MLM to Macmillan's, 27.8.[1898]. MLM to GLC, Sunday, [?18.1.1891]

[22] MLM to Macmillan's, 6.2.1909.

[23] MLM to Macmillan's, 27.8.[1898].

A request to translate *The Cuckoo Clock* into Japanese seems to have been the only one she welcomed as a compliment rather than feeling it to be an annoyance. She described the letter conveying it as 'extremely interesting and gratifying' and gave her 'hearty consent' to the project. In complete contrast to her reactions to other translators, she wanted to write personally to this Japanese teacher, and arranged to send him a copy of *Carrots*, which he wished to do next, at her own expense.[24] Perhaps the most extraordinary translation story concerned a German lady who approached her for permission to translate *Christmas-Tree Land*. She had already been given permission by Macmillan's, but then wrote direct to Louisa with somewhat fulsome praise of the book. Louisa was justifiably rather suspicious. 'I do not understand the enclosed' she wrote to Macmillan's about the letter forwarded to her.

> 'The lady <u>must</u> know that the permission you gave her, (subject to the conditions of payment which you named) included <u>mine</u> — I am afraid it does not seem quite straightforward of her to write to <u>me</u> about it, after hearing from you ... You see she does not mention payment. It is as if she hoped that <u>I</u> would give the permission with no conditions at all which I certainly will <u>not</u> do.'

The lady then took ten years to find a publisher. By that time someone else had beaten her to it and she wrote to Louisa again, expecting *her* to arrange matters with the other translator. No wonder Louisa exclaimed 'I dread the mention of translations! They are far more trouble than they are worth.'[25]

In 1891 a major change occurred in the red book series. For the first time Walter Crane was not to do the illustrations for Louisa's annual volume. The idea of trying someone else came from Craik and she acquiesced readily — 'I am perfectly satisfied to let you do as you think best about the illustrations' — even offering a reason why Crane might welcome the change — 'Mr Crane is always very busy & <u>perhaps</u> he will not be sorry not to have to do it.' She wondered whether the change of illustrator might be marked by a change in the colour of the binding or something similar, 'to give it the look of a new series as it were?' but this suggestion was not used.[26] Craik was taking a certain risk in adopting as the new illustrator Leonard Leslie Brooke, a young man then, as yet

---

[24] MLM to Macmillan's, 9.7 and 3.10.1907.
[25] MLM to Macmillan's, 29.7.1903; 13.9.1913.
[26] MLM to GLC, 25.4.[1891].

unknown, and Louisa's sentence, quoted above, implies that he had felt some qualms about making the proposal to her. Brooke himself, writing in 1928 at the age of 65, associated the work on Louisa's books with the beginning of his career —

> '. . . small commissions began to arrive from publishers . . . I began drawing for Blackie and Cassells. Also I succeeded Walter Crane as illustrator of Mrs Molesworth's annual story for Macmillan's and held the job for a number of years.'[27]

In one reference book he is said to be 'best remembered as the illustrator of Mrs Molesworth's works.'[28] This comment and another from *The Library* in 1902 show that Craik's choice was justified. *The Library* contributor wrote

> 'the careful un-selfconscious fashion of his [sc. Brooke's] drawing, his understanding of child-life and home-life as known to children such as those of whom and for whom Mrs Molesworth writes, make these pen-drawings true illustrations of the text.'

Looking through the beautiful and touching pictures which Brooke made for Louisa's next eight red books one cannot help agreeing with this writer.[29]

The 1891 Christmas book, the first of Louisa's that Brooke illustrated, was *Nurse Heatherdale's Story*. It was unusual for her, in that the adult telling the story was looking back to a time, not when she was a child herself, but when she was a young nurse taking care of a family of children whose story she told. It was unusual too, in that events were seen from the point of view of a servant, who, respectfully though she did it, was prepared to some extent to criticise and evaluate the attitude of the children's mother towards them. In only one other of Louisa's books was the narrator of the servant class, and that was *A Charge Fulfilled*, for older girls, but by the time she told her story the former nanny had long been a farmer's wife, whereas Nurse Heatherdale had

---

[27] Anne Carroll Moore, 'L. Leslie Brooke', *A Horn Book Sampler*, Boston, The Horn Book, 1959, p. 65.

[28] Simon Houfe, *The Dictionary of British Book Illustrators and Caricaturists, 1800–1914*, Antique Collectors' Club, 1978, p. 246. Brian Alderson comments on this point, 'Houfe is not right — LLB is far better known for his own books, like *Johnny Crow's Garden*, and his various nursery picture books.'

[29] R. E. D. Sketchley, 'Some Children's Book Illustrators', *The Library*, Second Series, Oct. 1902, quoted in Lance Salway, *A Peculiar Gift*, Kestrel Books, 1976, p. 264.

grown old with the the family she served. Louisa took care that the language and style should be consistent with the imagined narrator's status. The exciting adventures and the family's 'Cinderella' change of fortune combine with the everyday details such as learning to knit or spilling ink on an exercise book and the old nurse's homely story-telling manner to make one of Louisa's best real-life books, or 'child-novels'.

Louisa was staying with Mrs Bishop, the friend and biographer of Mrs Augustus Craven, in Tunbridge Wells when *Nurse Heatherdale's Story* came out, in December. It must have been discussed during her visit, because as soon as she was home again she wrote to ask Craik to send her friend a copy of the book. It seems that a fellow guest on this visit was Lucy Bethia Walford, a novelist and critic, for on the same day that Louisa asked for a *Nurse Heatherdale* to be sent to Mrs Bishop, she wrote another separate letter to Craik requesting that a copy should be sent to Mrs Walford 'by first post.' This urgency was because Mrs Walford had 'offered to notice it in her London literary article for the "New York Critic", the best American literary paper — it may be useful to have this notice.' Mrs Walford wrote in her own *Recollections* 'I was for four years, namely from 1889 to 1893, London Correspondent of the *New York Critic*, for which I wrote a fortnightly budget of literary news.' Another link between her and Louisa was that she too was a friend of the Patons. 'We had much pleasant intercourse,' she wrote. 'None of us knew anything about art, but we could talk quite happily with Sir Noel Paton. He was quite simple and frank.' She had also lived in Royal Terrace, Edinburgh as a girl, which would have been around 1855–65, some ten years before Louisa lived there. 'Royal Terrace was not then, and is not now, a fashionable quarter,' she said. They would have had plenty of subjects in common for 'pleasant intercourse', starting with their shared Scottish origin.[30]

Walter Crane did one more piece of work for a story of Louisa's, a single picture as frontispiece for *Studies and Stories* which was published in May 1893. It was an illustration to 'Princess Ice Heart', a fairy story that had first appeared in the *Illustrated London News* Christmas number for 1892, with illustrations by A. Forrestier (who was Special Artist for that periodical from 1882 to 1899). It was the most recently published of those items gathered up in *Studies and Stories*. A. D. Innes, publisher of the book, had already written to Louisa about it at Christmas and

[30] MLM to GLC, 13.12.[1891], 2 letters. L. B. Walford, *Recollections of a Scottish Novelist*, Williams and Norgate, 1910, p. 265, pp. 149–151 and p. 134.

in January 1893 she sent him a parcel of manuscript by registered post. The first intention was to publish these 'five short stories for grown-up people' as she described them in a letter to Craik, in a series by A. D. Innes, called 'The Dainty Books'. This was advertised as 'intended for children of all ages,' though a list of items already published in the series, including Frances Crompton's *Master Bartlemy* suggests that it consisted more of what we would now characterize simply as children's books. In discussing what title might be given to her own book, Louisa spoke very warmly of one by Lucy Walford, *For Grown-Up Children*, in the same series. Innes apparently talked to Craik about this projected book, for the day after she had sent off her registered parcel, Louisa received a letter from Craik with a list of complaints, particularly mentioning it. From her reply, it can be deduced that he said she was writing too many children's books for other publishers, that it was bad for Macmillan's sales of her books if books by her with other publishers appeared at a lower price than that charged by Macmillan's, that her sales had fallen off and what about this book for Innes that was going to be published in a series for children?

Louisa was naturally upset by this letter and sat up very late the night of the day it arrived, in order to answer it at length. She then proceeded to think about it all night and wrote again the next morning with further details she had remembered, relevant to his charges — 'I cd. not help worrying over the temporary complication, asleep and awake!' In reference to the book for Innes she said

> 'Mr Innes must have omitted to mention one important particular — that the book in question is <u>not</u> a child's book . . . It is not the sort of thing I can imagine you wd. care to publish. Nor does it seem likely that there cd. be any <u>possible</u> confusion between it, & my red books with you.'

Yet she was not completely straightforward with Craik about the five stories she insisted were for grown-ups. It is true that four of them were not intended for children, and by her standards were not suitable for them, one in particular being a ghost story, but 'Princess Ice-Heart', the one for which Crane did an illustration, was similar to many of her other fairy stories and perfectly all right for children. And she did not mention that the series itself did include children's books.

She went on to assure Craik that she always tried to see that none of her other books, whether for children or adults appeared 'near the time of my regular Christmas book.' His complaint about lower prices was completely new to her — 'I do not recollect your <u>ever</u> speaking to me of the inconvenience of a book of mine appearing at a lower price than the price of those you publish?' She could only remember one example of such a lower-priced book anyway, and that was *An Enchanted Garden*, which had been a commission from Fisher Unwin. The only other regular children's books she did were the short stories for *The Child's Pictorial*, which were reprinted 'as, so to say, nursery books.' Any other names he saw advertised would have been of books 'for older people.' His statement that her sales had fallen off surprised her very much,

> 'for the two last times I have seen you you told me, to gratify me, that you had been looking through the figures & found the sales kept <u>increasing</u>, & I think I have not received less money of late years? I remember you told me of the steady keeping up of sales, once in my drawing-room, & once when I called at Bedford St for a private talk — & I was very pleased.'

Having thus vigorously defended herself, she made two positive efforts to conciliate him. One was the announcement that her book for the following Christmas was in hand, 'You remember I told you of it, for <u>little</u> children, to be called "Mary".' The other was an offer '<u>to agree to publish no second children's</u> book in the year, without first asking <u>you</u> if you wd. publish it.' She also pointed out the difference between her books for Macmillan's and those for other publishers that has already been noted — 'I think all the children's books I ever published <u>except</u> with you have been reprints of stories that have appeared in magazines.' She had been under the impression that Macmillan's 'wd. not care to publish such.' She herself made a double profit, 'first as serials, then as books,' and what was more, 'I do <u>not</u> find that the sale as book suffers from its having been a serial.'

What kept her awake all night, or at least as long as anyone is awake who says it was all night, was worrying over whether she had listed every single 'outside' children's book, as she told Craik she had done. She remembered three, which were all in some way exceptional. *Farthings*, the book for the Waifs and Strays, written at the request of the Bishop of Wakefield and published the previous October, would have 'helped to give the look of my publishing "outside" children's books.' The next was *Stories of the Saints for Children* published by Longmans, also in 1892. Craik had actually refused this 'to my very great disappointment,' so he could hardly blame her for it. The third was something in prospect, 'for <u>Sunday Schools</u> — on religious lines — but nothing definite, only the magazine that it will appear in, has the right (I mean its editors) of reprinting as book.' This eventually became *Stories for Children in Illustration of The Lord's Prayer.* The first of the eight stories appeared in the periodical *Sunday: Reading for the Young,* published by Wells, Gardner, Darton and Co., in 1895 and the whole group was published in a single volume by the same firm in 1897, just as Louisa said had been arranged. Having unburdened her mind of these books, she repeated the offer about publishing no second children's book in the year 'without <u>first</u> submitting it to you,' this time saying she was prepared to sign an agreement to that effect.

She was relieved to hear from Craik the next day accepting her offer, but not requiring an official agreement about it, and explaining to her satisfaction 'the apparent contradiction about the sales. I am glad this year's seem good.' He must have been relieved in his turn to learn from her third consecutive letter on the subject, that the proposed book with Innes would probably not now be part of the illustrated series 'for children of all ages,' because there was too much material. Although she did not say so to Craik, it also seems likely that once Innes had actually read her stories he felt that, apart from 'Princess Ice-Heart', they were too adult in content. And when *Studies and Stories* did come out, it did not look in the least like a child's book. To the five stories had been added five non-fiction pieces — three being the articles of advice specially for girls already mentioned, one her *Contemporary Review* article on Mrs Ewing and the last a piece from *Time* on Hans Andersen.[31]

It is strange that in all this storm which blew up and then subsided, about her publishing 'outside' children's books, no mention was made of Chambers. Numerically this firm became her second most important publisher, and the one with whom she was to have the longest association after Macmillan's. By the time she died, they had published sixteen titles by her, almost all of which had previously been serialized in periodicals and half of these were definitely for older girls, two categories admittedly which Louisa was sure did not interest Macmillan's. They had also taken over eight books from other firms and re-published them under their own imprint. Most of this was still in the future at the time of the 'temporary complication' with Craik, but she had already agreed with Chambers for *The Next-Door House,* serialised in *Little Folks* the previous year, to be published by them in May 1893 — very definitely an outside children's book. Why did she not tell Craik about this, when

31 MLM to GLC, 30 and 31.1 and 1.2.[1893].

she did say 'I am writing a short novel for girls for "Atalanta",' something that would have given him far less concern? The 'short novel' must have been *White Turrets*, her next story for girls in *Atalanta*, which did not begin to appear until May 1894. Chambers had also asked her for another children's serial story to re-publish as a book even before *The Next-Door House* came out. She choked off this request by saying she would not have one available for a good many months. In fact it was four years before Chambers had another children's serial from her, and her next serial in *Little Folks*, was actually re-published by Macmillan's. This was *Sheila's Mystery* (1895). The two following *Little Folks'* serials went, as before, to Chambers. *Sheila's Mystery* was bound in blue cloth, not red, and it also appeared in May, not at Christmas. These two pieces of evidence make it seem likely that Louisa and Craik did not see the book as part of the 'Carrots' series at all, but as the fruit of their unofficial agreement, that she should publish no second children's book in the year, without first offering it to Macmillan's.[32] It was the only such fruit. Macmillan's continued to publish a children's book by Louisa every year for the Christmas season, with three gaps, until she stopped writing altogether after her last book in 1911. No other second children's book from her in any year appeared under their imprint, so if she did make them the first offer of the collections of stories and the serials re-published by Chambers and others, they were all refused.

The next excitement in Louisa's life was caused by her eldest daughter. In the March of 1893 Cicely was still continuing with the nursing work which she had been doing for three years, as can be seen from a letter to Mr Macmillan in which Louisa, hoping to be able to call on his wife on some future Monday, excused herself for the moment because 'just at present I go on that day every week to help my daughter a little in her rather <u>too</u> hard work.'[33] One wonders what assistance an untrained weekly visitor would be allowed to give. Louisa obviously still felt that nursing was 'work so arduous and so peculiarly trying.' But it was not to last much longer. Cicely got engaged and in June Louisa wrote to Mrs Du Cane 'Thank you so much for your congratulations. Cicely is very, very happy, but I must see you soon & talk about it.' Cicely would be getting married in the same month as Princess May and the Duke

---

[32] *The Carved Lions*, the 1895 Christmas book, was also bound in blue cloth, though afterwards the series continued in red for many years. Possibly just an oversight in processing, because *Sheila's Mystery*, the immediate predecessor, had been blue?
[33] MLM to Macmillan, 3.3.[1893].

of York, and it was in the same letter as Louisa thanked Mrs Du Cane for her congratulations that she also asked for the help briefly described at the beginning of chapter 11.

What she wanted was advice over the details of presenting to the Princess a set of her books published by Macmillan's. They were to be specially bound and have on them whatever arms or monogram the Princess used on her private books, and this needed to be ascertained, as well as correct modes of address. Louisa took a great deal of care over this transaction — there were five letters to Mrs Du Cane on the subject.[34] She was very grateful to Mrs Du Cane for her help in finding out all that was necessary and putting Louisa in contact with the right person. Princess May's personal letter of thanks delighted her — 'I do think it so kind and sweet of her.' Was Louisa then a passionate admirer of the Royal Family, someone who nowadays would read every 'royal' article and watch every relevant TV programme with avidity? There are a few comments to be made here. Since Princess May received something like fifteen hundred wedding presents, it was indeed 'kind and sweet' of her to write personally. Furthermore, the idea of the gift had come from Macmillan's and not Louisa. The special binding and fuss about the details loses some of its particularity when one considers the same kind of episode in the life of Lucy Walford. She was asked by the Queen for one of her novels and wrote about this in her biography, ' "You can't send it in its common binding" pronounced my father . . . "Certainly not. I had 'The Moor and the Loch' beautifully bound. It's only proper respect." '[35] 'Proper respect' also involved the right forms, always confusing to those who are not using them every day — 'How should I begin?', worried Louisa. ' "Madam" or "Dear Madam"? Or "to H.S.H. The Princess May?' Queen Victoria was a stickler for proper etiquette, and thus of necessity all her Court were too — 'the slightest infringements of the freezing rules of regularity and deference were invariably and immediately visited by the sharp and haughty glances of the Queen.'[36] Louisa was only making sure that she conformed to the rules of necessary behaviour accepted by all around her. She was not singular in this.

Cicely's wedding took place on 29th July. Her husband was James Charles Prinsep, from a family with many Anglo-Indian connections. His father, Charles R. Prinsep, had been born in India and his grand-

---

[34] MLM to DUC, 31.5, 3.6, n.d. x 2, and 22.6.[1893].

[35] Walford, p. 251.

[36] Lytton Strachey, *Queen Victoria*, Chatto and Windus, 1921, p 80.

father, John Prinsep, had made a considerable fortune as a merchant, finding the sale of indigo particularly profitable.[37] After the wedding Louisa and her diminished family party spent the late summer and autumn in Malvern, a place they liked so much that they stayed 'till some way on in November' which meant that an invitation from Mrs Du Cane to visit her in Bournemouth where she regularly stayed, had to be refused. The sentence 'A day or two with you wd. have been charming,' betrayed her regret, in one of Louisa's many casual intimate notes, finishing off 'Best love to all, especially my twins.'[38] There were to be more twins soon, whom she would more accurately be able to call 'hers'. Cicely and her husband settled in London so that Louisa was able to visit her daughter often and be a support during her first pregnancy which happened almost at once. 'Cicely depends a good deal on me now' wrote Louisa to Mrs Du Cane in April 1894, and then, on 22nd May, a quick note to her friend announced the birth.

> Dearest Mrs Du Cane, Cicely has twin daughters — born yesterday — It was _very_ bad — We pray and trust that she will go on well — She does not yet know that there are two — I have brought one here. They are well — I will leave word both here & at her house at the door how she is — Will write again if I can
>
> Ever yours very aff. M.L.M.

A day or so later Louisa sent the news to Swinburne who responded just as rapturously to the arrival of real babies in Louisa's family, as to the regular appearance of fictional children.

> 'What a heavenly 'baby story', and how good of you to tell it me! And how good of the elder darling to live and thrive after its drive in the cold before it was six hours old! I do long to be presented to their Graces.'

He reciprocated with a story of a baby in his own family as a sign of friendship.

> 'You see I return your kindness in telling me about those nearest to you by writing to you about those nearest to me. It's the best form of recognition I know.'

---

[37] Burke's _Peerage_, 1939, Brian Hill, _Julia Margaret Cameron - A Victorian Family Portrait_, Peter Owen, 1973, pp. 40–41. JCP's uncle, Henry Thoby Prinsep, married one of the famous Pattle sisters, Sara, and their son, Val Prinsep, the painter and friend of William Morris, Rossetti and Burne-Jones, was thus JCP's first cousin.
[38] MLM to DUC, 3.10.[1893].

Lionel had been enthusiastic enough about the babies for Louisa to comment on it to Swinburne, for he added 'I am glad to hear that Lionel "will adore" his nieces: it does him credit.'[39]

On the same day that Swinburne wrote to welcome the twins, Louisa had become light-hearted enough about her daughter and the babies to indulge in the age-old game of grandmothers — writing as if from the child. Mrs Du Cane had sent the babies a present and Louisa responded with a letter 'dictated' by the elder twin.

My dear Mrs Du Cane,

My grandmother has kindly said she would write to you instead of me, as I have not yet begun even strokes & round O's — to thank you for the lovely little frocks you have sent me. They are just the very thing I needed as my little sister is inclined to keep rather more than her share of our frocks. I hope she will not grow up a selfish little girl. I mean to set her a good example.

I am perhaps to be dressed up nicely tomorrow, & taken to see my mamma as she wants to kiss me very much, & I think I should like to see her. She was rather feverish last night with the joy of hearing about me, though I do not feel at all feverish about having a mamma.

I hope to have the pleasure of seeing Ruth & Daisy & perhaps my young friends who I am told are like my sister and me, tomorrow afternoon. I send my love to everybody & I thank you again very much.

Your loving little Mary Prinsep

I have some other names but I have not yet learnt them.

The twins both had Mary in their names — Venetia Mary Juliet and Mary Eugenia Agneta, so it is not possible to be sure which one Louisa had with her. Cicely gave the names of her cousin (the daughter of Louisa's sister, Agnes), her mother and her sister to Venetia, and it was she who grew up to be such a helpful source of information about her grandmother.

Louisa also wrote as though from the baby staying with her to Swinburne, who replied in kind, enclosing his note in a letter to Louisa.

'I need not ask you to place the enclosed note at once in the honoured hands of the distinguished lady to whom it is addressed. Words fail me to express my sense of her goodness. it is not everybody who can boast

---

[39] C. Y. Lang, VI, pp. 67–8.

of having received a letter — and such a sweet letter, so full of good
sense and good feeling — from a correspondent just six days old. I am
very glad to hear that her mother is better . . . I need not say how I look
forward to kissing the hands (and, if permitted, the feet) of the twins.
Did I ever tell you of the baby girl who said of herself and her sister —
'We's twinges'? It was said to a sister of Mr Watts's who told me — Is
it not a pretty word?'[40]

During this whole period of Cicely's later pregnancy and confinement,
and her own anxiety about and delight in the twins and their mother,
Louisa continued with her usual work. The chances of survival have
permitted six different letters from Louisa to three publishers about a
single ghost story to remain in various archives and libraries as evidence
of the care with which she arranged the fate of even the slightest of her
productions. 'The Shadow in the Moonlight',[41] which eventually became
part of her collection of ghost stories published by Hutchinson in 1896
as *Uncanny Tales*, was first offered to Chambers, before the story was
finished. This was deliberate, since previous negotiations with this publisher had foundered on the question of length, and Louisa was therefore
taking care to check with them beforehand so that she could work to
their requirements. Consequently it is not surprising that she was
annoyed when they refused it for quite another reason. Louisa wrote to
A. D. Innes on 25th May, offering the same story to him because 'The
fact is I wrote it to suit a certain serial & now the (I think) stupid
people will not have it because the ghost is not explained away!'[42] This
was the same day that she wrote to Swinburne and Mrs Du Cane as
from the baby twin she took home with her. It is intriguing to think
of the three letters lying on her desk together. She also wrote to offer
the story to William Blackwood and must have received an encouraging
response for she sent him, and not Innes, her only copy of the manuscript. It seems likely that Innes made her an offer anyway, sight unseen,
for she asked Blackwood twice to make his decision quickly because
'I have had a proposal for it from a serial here for which I have written before . . . but . . . I shd. very much like it to appear in your
magazine.' However, she said, 'if you do not want to use it, I shd. be
sorry to lose the chance' — the chance, of course, to 'gain doubly' by

[40] C. Y. Lang, VI, pp. 68–9.
[41] Re-published in *Terror by Gaslight: An Anthology of Rare Tales of Terror*. Ed. Hugh
Lamb, Constable, Oct. 1992. 0094717206.
[42] MLM to Innes, 25.5.[1894], National Library of Scotland, MS 2875 714/63.

getting the story out in a periodical before it was included in a book.[43]

This same year (1894) saw her starting another kind of work, more routine than writing her own stories. She began to act as a reader for Macmillan's and to send them reports on mss submitted to her, with recommendations for or against publication. She was paid for this work and continued to do it for many years. References to mss received or returned, and occasional copies of actual reports, or enquiries after stories she had particularly liked and hoped would be successful, occur at intervals in her letters to Macmillan's from January 1894 until September 1912. She was also working on *My New Home*, her 1894 red book.

Letters to Mrs Du Cane over the summer and autumn chart the movements of her family and provide continuing evidence of the support and comfort Louisa found in their friendship. In July Sir A. H. Layard, Mrs Du Cane's brother-in-law, died, and at the end of her letter of sympathy Louisa wrote 'Whatever touches you for sorrow or joy will always have my <u>fullest</u> sympathy — This I feel sure you will believe.' She confided details of their worries over the babies.

> 'Little "May" — as they have now decided to <u>call</u> her, is <u>much</u> better — I think she will get on now — It would be really impossible for Cicely to have a wet nurse in that tiny house — but the Doctors do <u>not</u> advise it — I think this illness was to some extent accidental.'

They had obviously been fearing that May's illness was somehow due to Cicely's feeding the babies herself and were relieved by the medical opinion. Mrs Du Cane was being kept *au fait* with every new development. Juliet went off to Norway, Denmark and Holland for the summer with Andalusia Riley, Viscount Molesworth's eldest daughter and Gwen Molesworth's sister, while Olive went to Scotland. Louisa stayed with Cicely and the babies, renting a house at Maybury Hill near Woking. May gave them another fright by getting a chill and a touch of bronchitis. She was turning out to be that great worry of Victorian nurseries, a delicate child. 'She is healthy but not strong, & a trifling cause sends her down. Her extremely sweet, merry nature is much in her favour.'[44] James Prinsep was with them at Woking for some of the time and though we know little of the relationship, two pieces of evidence survive

---

[43] MLM to William Blackwood, 27.5, 30.5 and 13.6.[1894], National Library of Scotland, MS 4621/1–4.

[44] MLM to DUC, 8.7 and 17.7.[1894].

to show that he was on good terms with his mother-in-law. He compiled two large manuscript volumes about his family history, which he called *De Principe*, and Louisa took an interest in this, contributing information about her own family which he incorporated. (It was a useful source for chapter 1 of this biography.) He in turn took an interest in her work, perhaps even giving some advice or assistance, for when *Uncanny Tales* appeared, it was dedicated 'To an otherwise unacknowledged "collaborateur" in these stories, J. C. P.' — i.e. James Charles Prinsep. She had perhaps been writing one of the stories while at Woking that summer — 'Half-way between the stiles' came out in *Longmans Magazine*, 1894–5. The Prinseps moved on to stay with friends at the end of September while Louisa remained to hand over the house at the end of their tenancy. She had hoped to accept Mrs Du Cane's repeated invitation to visit her during the summer, but after making 'a long promised and arranged for visit' in Hampshire she had unexpectedly to return to London earlier than planned. Later she explained to her friend the nature of 'the anxiety which had to do with my giving up thoughts of the visit to you which I had been looking forward to.'

The anxiety was about Bevil. She had been expecting to see him during the winter when he would have to come home for a short time on business. But suddenly while she was still at Woking she heard that he was coming sooner 'partly on account of an accident he has had, which had left an injury.' She worried of course, but managed not to spoil her daughters' holidays with the news, only confiding in that part of the family on the spot — Cicely and her husband. Then Bevil himself arrived on 1ˢᵗ November, 'very well in himself, & in good spirits — business prospects satisfactory.' But it was decided that he had to have an operation, which would not have been necessary if he were remaining in England. From Louisa's rather vague explanation, it sounds as if Bevil had to have his appendix removed.

> 'It is very curious how we are made! I did not understand it at all as I do now the doctors have explained it to me. There are things in our bodies we really should be better without — in ages to come I suppose human beings may grow out of them!'

This was naturally both an anxiety and an expense, in fact a great expense 'as we have gone to a first-rate surgeon.' But Bevil's own attitude made the situation much happier. 'Bevil is very good about it, & so bright & affectionate that we are really enjoying having him in spite of this cloud, & quite cheered by his own good spirits.' She planned to devote the next month or so entirely to Bevil, before he disappeared again to Patagonia. There is an interesting parallel to Bevil's career in the life of Charles Kingsley's son, Maurice, who, a generation earlier, had an urge to become 'a wild prairie hunter.' In 1865, he went up to Cambridge, left without taking a degree, studied agriculture at Cirencester and then 'set off in search of employment on a ranch in the Argentine.'[45] The long letter in which Louisa told Mrs Du Cane about Bevil is the last to her friend that has survived, except for a tiny note from the following year thanking for a tea-table cloth and arranging a meeting. That note ended 'I will write again next week,' but we have no more.[46] Mrs Du Cane died in 1902. So there are no reports on how Bevil stood the operation, no more chatty details about Louisa's daily life.

The only thing we know about Louisa in 1895 is that it was the year she published, and presumably therefore also wrote, *The Carved Lions*, one of her best books, and in some eyes the very best.[47] Set in the Manchester of her childhood, it depicts with a sure and sensitive touch Geraldine's happy, ordinary home-life broken up by her parents' departure abroad because of her father's work and the consequent need to send her to boarding-school. Shy, homesick, tongue-tied, misunderstood and finally completely wretched, Geraldine runs away and by chance takes refuge with the huge carved lions in the furniture shop she had often visited with her mother during happier times. At this crisis the tangle of misery is unwound as deftly as it was created. It is interesting to note that a little episode from the happy recovery period in this book (for Geraldine falls ill as a result of her flight) is treated in much more detail in one of the *Child's Pictorial* stories, published in the August and September issues for 1895, just before *The Carved Lions* came out in October. In order to comfort Geraldine who can't bear to think of going back to school when she is better, her friend Myra tells her that things won't seem so bad when she is better. She supports this with an anecdote —

'I remember once when I was ill — I was quite a little girl then . . . I think it was when I had had the measles, the least thing vexed me dreadfully. I cried because somebody had given me a present of a set of

[45] Susan Chitty, *The Beast and the Monk: A Life of Charles Kingsley*, Hodder and Stoughton, 1974, pp. 243 and 268.

[46] MLM to DUC, 4.11.[1894] and 24.5.[1895].

[47] Green, (1946), p. 114; (1961), p. 59.

wooden tea-things in a box, and the tea ran out of the cups when I filled them! Fancy crying for that!'[48]

In ' "Very ill indeed" ' this incident is expanded to make a story that takes up sixteen pages of *The Children's Hour*, the collection of tales in which it was re-published. On several occasions Louisa used little happenings of this kind twice over in her books, and very often it is these that are founded on fact, as in the episodes from *A Ramble about Childhood*.

The following year, 1896, it was Lionel's turn to get married. His bride was Saba Maud Delves Broughton, the youngest daughter of Sir Henry Delves Broughton, ninth baronet. She was a first cousin of the novelist Rhoda Broughton, and also a relative of Louisa's brother-in-law, Edward Walthall. She herself wrote, later in life, 'I knew Mrs Molesworth when I was quite a child, so that there was no strangeness to either of us, when I became her daughter-in-law. She was always most kind and thoughtful.'[49] Lionel's sister, Cicely, said that 'Lionel was at Oxford when he married — only 21 — & gave up reading for his degree & became a land agent.'[50] Cicely's daughter, one of the twins, enlarged on this, saying that her grandmother thought Lionel was too young for marriage — 'he was only in his early 20's & young for his age,' and that she was disappointed he did not complete his degree. She also said that Lionel did not get on well with his mother, which links up with Gwen Molesworth's remark that Louisa's boys 'worried her.' The date of Lionel's wedding is given in Burke (1939) as 10.11.1896, so he was in fact twenty-three at the time. Swinburne's response to Louisa's letter to him about the marriage was 'I am delighted to hear of Lionel's happy marriage. My old private tutor, the late Bishop (Woodford) of Ely, used to say that nobody ought to marry at a later age than his!!!'[51] One can deduce from this that Louisa, as well as reporting that the marriage was happy, had said something about her feeling Lionel to be too young. Lionel's work took him to Gloucestershire where he was agent for the Elwes family at Rapsgate Park near Cirencester, and to Cheshire, where he acted as agent for his cousin E. C. D. Walthall, Louisa's sister Caroline's eldest son, from 1898 until his death. This cousin was his best man and a great friend. Lionel and Saba's first child, a daughter,

---

[48] *The Carved Lions*, p. 184.
[49] Mrs L. Molesworth to RR, quoted in an unpublished letter from RR.
[50] CP to RR, 1.6.38.
[51] C. Y. Lang, VI, p. 121.

was born in August 1897 and named Violet Saba, after her mother and presumably after Louisa's much loved and still remembered eldest daughter. If this name was chosen as a delicately loving attention to his mother, or even as a peace offering, it suggests that Lionel's relationship with her was improving. On her part, when writing the dedication to her 1898 Christmas book, *The Magic Nuts*, in February, very much in advance, Louisa addressed it to Lionel's daughter.

In March Louisa and Olive were in Ramsgate for their health. Louisa told Mr Macmillan 'I have not been strong this winter, & not able for much, but I think this bracing air has done me good.'[52] She needed any bracing she could get for very soon a blow fell that was still giving her pain years afterwards. Bevil died out in Patagonia on 13th March, 1898.[53] It was totally unexpected — she described it later on as 'his terribly sudden death.' In 1900 in a letter to Craik she used the phrase 'the thought — ever present, of my dear, loyal-hearted Bevil,' and four years later, in a letter of sympathy, she said 'the bitter, bitter grief will often seem unbearable. Oh, how awfully well I know it — my boy's death seems as terrible sometimes as if it had only just happened.'[54]

Even in the midst of grief she went on working. By this time she was using an agent for some negotiations, a Mr Colles of the Authors' Syndicate, though judging by the number of business letters she continued to write personally up to the end of her life, she did not allow him to do much for her. One of her two surviving letters to him shows very clearly her firm intention always to retain control of copyright. She had, in 1892, written a story at the request of a Mr Fitzroy Gardiner, who wanted it for a new periodical he was intending to start. She explained carefully to Colles that single publication of this story, 'The Fairy Godmothers', in the proposed periodical 'was the only right he purchased — as I specially retained, as I always do in the case of serial contributions, the copyright — ie the right to republish in volume form.' But the periodical seems never to have seen the light of day, so the story was not published either, even though Louisa subsequently gave Gardiner 'leave to sell his use of it to some other good serial' so that she could then 'use it in a volume of collected stories for the young.' As long as the story remained unpublished, her hands were tied, which

[52] MLM to Macmillan, 2.3.1898.
[53] Burke, *Peerage*, 1939.
[54] MLM to Macmillan, 20.2.1906, and to GLC, 4.5.1900; MLM to Laura Hope, 1.7.1906. A copy of this letter was given to me by Laura Hope's grand-daughter.

annoyed her, so she was pleased when Colles wrote to say that he had placed it with *Lloyd's Weekly*. She did not know the magazine, but was happy to accept Colles' recommendation. Since she already had nearly enough material for a collection of stories, she was eager for this particular one to appear soon.[55] It was eventually included as one of ten items in *'My-Pretty' and Her Little Brother 'Too'* published by Chambers in 1901. The title story of this book had already appeared in an annual the Christmas before she wrote to Colles, and four of the other items had not only appeared in serials, but had also already been re-published once in volume form.[56] She made everything she wrote work hard for her.

At the end of the year in December, a more cheerful family event took place. Juliet married Julian Grant-Duff Ainslie, the youngest son of Ainslie Douglas Ainslie of Delgaty Castle, Aberdeenshire. Julian's father had dropped the surname Grant-Duff and assumed Ainslie in its place in 1866. His uncle, Sir Mountstuart Elphinestone Grant- Duff, politician and Governor of Madras, retained it. As we have seen, Louisa already knew this uncle and shared with him an admiration for Mrs Augustus Craven. Julian's cousin, Annabel Grant-Duff, wrote of him that he was 'the best shot in the North of Scotland and a charming fellow who writes capital light verse.' He had also been married before, so Juliet acquired two step-daughters, Stella and Alix, on her marriage.[57]

Now only one of Louisa's children remained with her, her youngest daughter, Olive. They became very close. Gwen Molesworth wrote 'later on Olive and she were absolutely one and could not bear to be separated from one another.' Cicely also bore witness to this relationship — 'For many years before her death my mother was wholly devoted to my sister Olive.'[58] On her own account Olive published some poems and stories, including *Tales Told in the Twilight* (1897) and *The Trio in the Square* (1898). She also contributed individual tales to various anthologies and a poem of hers, 'Midnight in Winter', appeared in the *English Illustrated Magazine* for March 1892. When asking Macmillan's help in placing another poem of Olive's, Louisa wrote 'my youngest daughter has now & then been rather successful with "verses" — some of them approved

[55] MLM to Colles, 27.11.[1898], private collection.
[56] 'My-Pretty' in *The Parade*, H. Henry and Co., 1897; 'No Work To Do' and 'A Present for the Queen' in *Nesta*, Chambers, 1889; 'Leo's Post Office' and 'Brave Little Denis' in *The Green Casket*, Chambers, 1890.
[57] DNB; Jackson, p. 173; personal communication from Juliet's grand-daughter.
[58] GDL to RR, 25.5.1938; CP to RR, 1.6.1938.

of by first-rate critics.'[59] But Olive's main occupation was as companion, assistant, secretary and co-writer to her mother. In 1910, a few months before Louisa's seventy-first birthday, she had been unwell and did not feel strong enough to cope with reading and criticising a book on which Macmillan's had asked her opinion. Olive did it for her, and in the letter explaining this Louisa described the help her daughter had for a long time given her.

> 'I may mention that the several books which from time to time you have asked me to read & judge, with a view to publication, have invariably been discussed by us both together, & I have never found her judgement at fault. Besides this, she has for many years been much more than my "secretary", practically my "collaborateur" in writing my own stories.'

Olive criticised her mother's work too — Louisa called her 'my home critic, who is critical.'[60] Olive's role was known to the family — Gwen Molesworth wrote that 'Her daughter Olive collaborated in her later books.'[61]

Although Olive was the closest, Cicely still saw quite a lot of her mother as she too lived in London. A record of one lunch party at Sumner Place was made by Juliet's brother-in-law, Douglas Ainslie, because it was one of the rare occasions when Swinburne came out of his retirement to be present at a social event. His account was of course focussed on Swinburne, the celebrity, whom he saw 'as a great red-plumed eagle pinioned and unable to rise from the ground more than a few feet . . . while his large green eyes blazed with enthusiasms of the past, kindled in the enthusiasms of the present moment.' It so happened, he wrote, that 'this was very evident to me on one of the last occasions that we met in London at a house hospitable also to the poet, Mrs Molesworth's, authoress of the *Cuckoo Clock*.' He explained his own presence there by telling the reader 'Mrs Molesworth's daughter, Juliet, is the wife of my brother Julian,' and then continued with his description of Swinburne's arrival and behaviour.

> 'Swinburne loved Mrs Molesworth's work, about which he has written, and included her in his very short visiting list. On the occasion of this last meeting, I remember his shouting to Watts (both were very deaf) as they entered the room: "Be sure you call the cab and let us get away

[59] MLM to Macmillan, 10.12.1907.
[60] MLM to Macmillan, 14.2.1910, and 14.1.1910.
[61] GDL to RR, 4.5.1938.

immediately after lunch." Watts shouted back in reply that he would not fail to do so.'

Not a very auspicious exchange for a hostess to hear as her guests arrive. And to begin with the course of events matched this unpromising start.

> 'Luncheon . . . was rather a strained meal: I remember Miss Olive Moles-worth's asking which of the tiny twin nieces, Mary or Alice [sic], Swin-burne preferred. At first he did not realise what was meant, but when he did, replied with his usual emphasis: "*Both delightful* children: of course there is *no difference whatever* between them." . . . This was not very encouraging, but after luncheon I managed to get him started on Baudelaire.'

This led to other favourite subjects of Swinburne's, and by the time he was launched on a description of an early morning swim out to sea off the island of Sark, he did not want to leave.

> 'Meanwhile time had been going on, but Swinburne was now wound up, clocks and cabs had no meaning for him, and when Watts came up and discreetly shouted that the cab was waiting, he was waved imperiously away with a single gesture' and the party did not break up until 'far into the afternoon.'[62]

This may well have been Swinburne's first meeting with Cicely's twins, 'whose photographs' he told Louisa, 'are among my treasures.' There had been at least one previous lunch party since their birth, on 4th June, 1896, a day Swinburne thought 'all the more appropriate' for such a gathering, 'as it would remind me of <u>the</u> great annual holiday festival at Eton.' But the children were not there that time.

> 'Of course the absence of the babies is an awful disappointment to me; and though to see them in the autumn, if feasible, would be a treat, I cannot deny that my ambition is always to be presented to children at their youngest possible age, when the notice and patronage of Their Royal Highnesses is most flattering.'[63]

The twins were already two years old when Swinburne wrote this. He continued to tell Louisa about those nearest to him, finishing off this letter with a story about a

---

[62] Douglas Ainslie, *Adventures Social and Literary*, T. Fisher Unwin, 1922, pp. 88–90.
[63] C. Y. Lang, VI, pp. 98–100.

'baby kinswoman' who 'has just travelled from the Isle of Wight to Aberdeenshire, and I am informed that when the 'puff-train' did anything particularly startling or loud she used to say to herself "It's all right, Baby" — reassuring <u>herself</u> so kindly.'

He was quite sure of her interest in such stories and her sympathy with his enthusiasm, merely adding 'I do not apologise to <u>you</u> for intruding an anecdote of a baby.'

During the spring following Juliet's marriage, there was another change. Louisa wrote to tell Macmillan that she was 'just finishing my children's story — "Carrots" series — for <u>next</u> Christmas' on 11th January, addressing the letter from Sumner Place. By the time she came to write the dedication to the book, *This and That*, she had moved house. She dedicated it to the twins, 'To my Mary and May', and the date was their birthday, 21st May. They were five years old, able to enjoy having the story read to them, perhaps even to read some of it to themselves. The Sumner Place house was too large for two women left on their own, so Louisa moved to her third and last address in London, to 'quite a small flat', where she employed only two servants, a cook and a house parlourmaid, with occasional outside help.[64] The flat was one in a block of ten, and evidence survives of her having made friends with at least one of the other occupants. Kelly's Directory for 1902 shows that in one of the apartments lived a Lady Isabel Stewart and Colonel the Hon. Walter Stewart. Louisa gave Lady Isabel a copy of *The Cuckoo Clock*, with the inscription 'For dear Lady Isabel Stewart with love from Mary Louisa Molesworth.'[65] Louisa's address was now 155, Sloane Street and here she was to live for the rest of her life.

---

[64] VMI to RR, 3.1.1952.

[65] This copy survived and is described in a private letter to RR from the present owner.

13

Deaths, Books And Grandchildren

On 2nd April 1900, Louisa's husband died 'at his residence in the Salis-
bury Tower, Windsor Castle,' as *The Times* obituary put it.[1] Richard
Molesworth had been living there for the previous four years, since his
admission as a military knight of Windsor in March 1896. This order
was originally established in the reign of Edward III as a group of
bedesmen,

> 'that is pensioners or almsmen of the same number as the Knights of
> the Garter, who, in return for accommodation and maintenance, were to
> pray daily for the good estate of the sovereign and the Knights Companion
> during life and for their souls after death.'

They were called the Poor Knights, but some sixty years before Richard
entered the order, the name was changed to the Military Knights and
their official dress became, instead of the bedesman's cloak, the normal
uniform of an unattached army officer. This was done at the petition
of the then members of the order who found both the name and the
dress embarrassing.[2] But the original name implied a state of affairs that
continued to exist. Although it was now recognised that those admitted
were retired military men with distinguished and usually long service,
it was also still true that one condition for an applicant was that he
must be 'a gentleman brought to necessity.' A knight was appointed
directly by the sovereign and the official form of appointment stated
'Whereas it hath been made to appear unto Us that [name of candidate]
is a fit object of Our Royal Charity.' Each Knight was allotted a residence
within Windsor Castle, and received an income of £162 13s 5d pa.[3]
The tradition, the title and the attendance in splendid uniforms at all
the ceremonies of the Order of the Garter helped to dress up the fact

---

[1] *The Times*, 6.4.1900.
[2] *The Royal Encyclopedia*, ed. Ronald Allison and Sarah Riddell, Macmillan, 1991, p. 341.
[3] Notes supplied by the archivist of Windsor Castle.

that Richard had applied or been recommended for, and had been granted, an unusual kind of old age pension.

All we know of Louisa's reaction to his appointment is a brief comment from Ranald Paton. 'Somewhat later he was made a Knight of Windsor and I remember Mrs Molesworth's anxiety lest this entailed a real knighthood.'[4] Presumably she did not want suddenly to become Lady Molesworth when she had been living apart from her husband for sixteen years. Too many embarrassing questions might be asked. One letter has survived that shows something of her reaction to his death and her feeling about their marriage. Craik had written to her on hearing the news and she replied immediately, on 4th April, 1900.

My dear Mr Craik,

Thank you, from my heart, for your kind good words; just what I am glad to have from you, who know the whole.

I shall feel grateful to God if perhaps from now I can think of the one who has gone, with all the bitterness of disappointment & weary anxiety, taken away. For surely there was a great mingling of excuse for the faults & follies that fell so heavily on those connected with him.

The thought — ever present, of my dear loyal hearted Bevil — seems somehow to ask this gentle feeling towards his father's memory of me — though my boy was the one who in life found it hard to forgive trouble to me that need not have been — But how can we tell what perception of the larger sight we believe in beyond the grave, may not sometimes be permitted to us though but in gleams?

Thank you again — & always

Yours affectly

Louisa Molesworth[5]

Louisa appears to be saying here that Bevil, right from the days of his making a scene in the streets of Edinburgh about riding in a tramcar that seemed to him an expensive luxury, had been his mother's champion and supporter against his father's 'faults and follies.' There is also what looks like an admission that even up to the time of Richard's death her thoughts of him had been bitter, disappointed and anxious. Now that he had gone, she could afford to look for excuses for the extravagance, the rages and the opinionated combativeness against her father (and,

---

[4] Ranald Paton to RR.
[5] University of Reading Library, MS1448.

probably, others) that had finally caused her to leave him. She wanted to try to forgive him.

Richard seems to have left a very strong memory with at least one of his children. About fourteen years after his death, Juliet and her husband offered hospitality for the night to a Professor who was lecturing in the neighbourhood. Her own daughter tells the story.

'He arrived about tea time, rather a fine looking man with a high forehead and obviously scholarly, — very pleasant, but I remember vividly during tea my mother getting whiter and whiter and leaving before we had finished on some excuse. I knew something was wrong, tho', this sort of behaviour wasn't the least like her. I went after her as soon as I could and found her lying down, she told me she felt very faint and simply couldn't come down and meet the visitor again because he was exactly like her father. That was really the first time I ever knew that he had been separated from my grannie, and my mother obviously didn't want to talk about it. Ordinarily she wasn't the least secretive and in fact rather indiscreet sometimes. As children we never told her anything we didn't want repeated! So she must have felt pretty strongly about her father not to have talked about him.'

The daughter concluded that this strong feeling was one of horror. Juliet was about fourteen or fifteen when her parents finally separated and was thus old enough to retain clear memories. This story fits in with Gwen Molesworth's statement that 'the second daughter told me they were terrified of their father.'[6] But we should not forget that Cicely had wanted to be allowed to live with him. Not all the evidence was against him.

The dedication of Louisa's Christmas book for 1901 helps to show, despite the non-survival of letters or other evidence, that she was keeping up her friendship with Adrian Hope, the secretary of the Great Ormond Street hospital, and his wife Laura, who had illustrated *The Old Pincushion, or Aunt Clotilda's Guests* in 1889. This was the year that the Hopes' first daughter, Jaqueline, was born. As the child grew up she became a devoted reader of Louisa's books and *The Wood-Pigeons and Mary* was dedicated to her as 'my faithful little friend Jaqueline'. Laura and Louisa were anxious to have the child's name spelt correctly.

---

[6] CB to RR, 28.1.1952; GDL to RR, 25.5.1938.

'The name being uncommon', Louisa wrote to Craik, 'Jaqueline's mother asked me to be sure it is not spelt with a "c" — Jacqueline, as happens sometimes. It is a very old Scotch name — She is the daughter of old friends of mine — the Adrian Hopes. . . . It is to be a surprise to Jaqueline.'[7]

Although Louisa was writing to Craik about these details in July, she dated the dedication several months earlier, 19th April, 1901, which was Jaqueline's twelfth birthday, so presumably it was not just a surprise, but a birthday surprise. Later on, after the printer had finished with it, Jaqueline was also given the manuscript. When it was sold at Sotheby's for £380 in 1988, the wrapping label was still attached to it — 'with Mrs Molesworth's love, Miss Jaqueline Hope, More House, Tite Street.' The printer's instructions on the first page of the manuscript were brief. '2 Proofs to Mrs Mo. in one batch. Follow usual style of Mrs Molesworth's works.' This was her twenty-seventh book in the 'Carrots' series for Macmillan's so the printer was well accustomed to the 'usual style.'[8]

The letter in which Louisa wrote to Craik about the dedication of *The Wood-Pigeons and Mary* was a particularly chatty one, mingling business directions and queries with comments on the latest novels just out, remarks about the Hope family, and a reference to an invitation from Craik's second wife, Anna. Louisa was also very pleased with the illustrations to *The Wood-Pigeons*, by H. R. Millar, whose work was new to her. He only did one more of her books, however, *Peterkin* (1902). The six Molesworth titles Macmillan's published between 1897 and 1906 had four different illustrators, a rather uncertain interregnum between L. Leslie Brooke and the illustrator of her last five books, Gertrude Demain Hammond. Another subject discussed was the cheap sixpenny edition of Carrots and its success — 'I knew at first you were very pleased at the way they went off'. It had even penetrated the Boer war — 'I heard of some of the 6d 'Carrots' having found their way to the South African war hospitals, which is nice.' As so often, she combined deference to his judgement on publishing matters with standing up for her own right to adequate financial reward. The idea of another of her books coming out in the cheap edition prompted the following:

---

[7] MLM to GLC, 31.7.1901. Jaqueline's daughter told me that 'the spelling of Jaqueline (without a 'c') comes from a <u>Swedish</u> ancestor who married a Scottish Hope.'

[8] Information from M-J Lancaster, daughter of Jaqueline.

'I should not think of urging a second, for you can judge better. Nor of deciding <u>which</u>. Possibly "Herr Baby" or "Grandmother Dear" or "Us" might be better than a fairy one — (if you <u>do</u> bring out another, I was wondering if perhaps you cd. pay me £60 on it — you don't mind my asking I know — a halfpenny a copy comes to £62.10.)'

She had accepted £50 for an edition of 30,000 copies of the sixpenny *Carrots* so she was asking for another £10 this time and buttressing her request with some careful sums. [9]

The suggestion that any one of the three titles she mentioned might be better than 'a fairy one' implies that Craik was thinking of the obvious follow-up — *The Cuckoo Clock*, now fast catching up on *Carrots* as her most popular book. And he did indeed use *The Cuckoo Clock* as Louisa's second contribution to the sixpenny series, with the result that she had anticipated. It was *not* such a success as *Carrots*, to the extent that when a third title was being considered for the series, she was offered only £40 for an edition of 25,000 copies of *Grandmother Dear*. She accepted this with a good grace, merely hoping it would do as well as the cheap *Carrots*, since Macmillan's intention of bringing out a new issue of that sixpenny edition showed that it, at least, must have been a success in their eyes.[10] The books in Macmillan's sixpenny series were bound in a lightweight paper cover with advertisements. My copy of the paperback *Carrots* features such things as Macassar Oil, Eno's Fruit Salt, Van Houten's Cocoa and Player's Navy Cut tobacco indiscriminately alongside notices of Macmillan's other publications — the sixpenny series itself, books by Rudyard Kipling and Charles Kingsley, and Louisa's own earlier titles. Her most recent volumes were offered at 4/6 and the others at 2/6, so the cheap *Carrots* was a fifth of the price of the hardback version. And the verso of its title-page shows that the first edition had been reprinted twenty-six times.

Such regular sales over a long period indicate her secure position as a favourite children's author. It is worth mentioning, in this connection, a census published by *The Academy* in 1898. This was an analysis of the results of reports from a number of bookshops, both London and provincial, showing the popularity of children's books, judged by the demand. *Alice in Wonderland* (1865) came first, followed by *Robinson Crusoe* (1719), Andrew Lang's Fairy Books (1889), Hans Andersen

---

[9] Clerk's note on MLM to GLC, 17.7.[1899].
[10] MLM to GLC, 22.1.[1905]; MLM to Macmillan, 7.10.1905.

(1846) and *The Water Babies* (1863), in that order. Louisa's books came sixth, ahead of *Eric, or little by little* (1858), *The Jungle Books* (1894), Grimm (1823) and *Treasure Island* (1881). Not top, or even second but steadily doing well.[11]

Some negotiations undertaken by Chambers a few months after the publication of *The Wood-Pigeons and Mary*, also show the constant popularity of Louisa's books and thus their value to a publisher able to get hold of any available titles. Gordon Milligan, the Chambers' representative who mostly handled the firm's dealings with Louisa, wrote to her with an enquiry on this subject. Chambers had already bought stories of hers from other publishers, which he said had done fairly well. They were on the point of re-publishing *Miss Bouverie* (Hurst and Blackett 1880) as a girls' book and Milligan wanted to know whether she had written any more books for other publishers which could be re-issued for young people in the same kind of way. He was hoping to talk the matter over with her personally when he was next in London.[12] The stories that had done fairly well could have been any or all of the seventeen Molesworth titles published by Chambers between 1889 and 1901, when their edition of *Miss Bouverie* came out. Only three of these, *Hoodie*, *Hermy* and *The Boys and I*, all bought from Routledge, had already been published as books (after their first appearance as serials in *Little Wideawake*). The rest had previously appeared in periodicals only, but since Milligan simply refers in his letter to stories, he could have meant either books or serials. The mild description 'fairly well' must have been an understatement, for Milligan would not have asked for more if the previous books had not made a worth-while profit. Buying stories from other houses did not necessarily mean that Chambers purchased the whole copyright. As already noted, Louisa stated several times in letters to Craik and Macmillan that she was careful to retain the right to re-publish a serial in book form herself. Furthermore, a later letter from Milligan to her, on 23rd December 1904, shows that on one occasion Chambers had bought the right to publish certain books of hers in a cheaper form only, but then, overlooking the arrangement, re-published them in another form. Louisa spotted this at once and

---

[11] *The Academy*, 2.7.1898. Where more than one book is indicated, the date given is that of the first in the series, or of the first translation into English. Brian Alderson has pointed out to me that where an established classic such as *Robinson Crusoe* is concerned, one can never be sure that a full text has been read. Respondents to a questionnaire or interview might have been recalling an abridged or adapted version.

[12] GM to MLM, 10.5.[1902], Chambers Collection.

wrote to point out the infringement, which elicited a letter of apology from Milligan and a cheque for a further £60 to cover the remaining rights, so that Chambers would then own the whole copyright. Although the books involved were not named in Milligan's letter, and Louisa's letter of complaint has not survived, this incident was almost certainly to do with *The Blue Baby* which Chambers re-published in 1904. The acquisition date on the British Library copy is 5th December, so Louisa was pretty quick off the mark to get her letter in by 23rd December. Chambers' edition contained, as well as the original stories from the Fisher Unwin edition of *The Blue Baby*, three further stories which, having paid £60 for the right to do so, they had previously re-published in cheap 6d and 1/- editions. These were the title stories from *Nesta*, *The Bewitched Lamp* and *The Green Casket*. Most of her business discussions with Chambers were of this kind — negotiations to obtain further income from material she had already written, sometimes long before.

Louisa's habit, of having her Christmas book for Macmillan's ready well in advance, stood her in good stead in 1902. She dated the dedication to *Peterkin* on May Day, and since she seems always to have completed a manuscript before thinking about the dedication, the story must have been finished by then. If it had not been, a very long gap would have occurred in the series, for in the late summer and autumn of this year, she had an illness serious enough to prevent her from producing any more original writing until her red book for 1904, *The Ruby Ring*. She was well enough in October to write letters but not stories. Craik had written sympathising with her situation and she replied:

> 'I thank you very much for your kind letter and full sympathy. And Anna also, please tell her this with my best love. . . . I will remember your kind offer of help to me just at this time, though I do not know of any special direction for it. . . . My sons-in-law & Lionel are all affectionate & good to me, but they are all very busy with their own affairs. As far as possible I rely on myself, only when illness & weakness come, one feels thankful to know one has friends in the background. . . . Olive has been most devoted to me but the strain has been severe on her. . . . I hope to ask you to come to see me by the middle of November.'[13]

Relying on herself obviously included relying on Olive and we remember that they were described as being one. These personal feelings were

---

[13] MLM to GLC, 28.10.[1902].

mingled with directions for sending off presentation copies of *Peterkin*. The odd business letter about translations and other people's manuscripts was all she could cope with in 1903. As she now did every year, she spent part of the summer at her daughter Juliet's home in Surrey.[14] The village of Hookwood near Horley, where the Grant-Duff Ainslies were living, was close to the border of Sussex, and is now right on the edge of Gatwick airport. Either Louisa's illness was a long one, or she had a relapse, for a note from Watts-Dunton in December 1903, giving news of Swinburne in convalescence, congratulated her on having recovered from her own illness.

In 1904 Adrian Hope died suddenly. Louisa's letter of sympathy to Laura called his death 'too awful a blow', which was hardly surprising since Adrian was only forty-six, and said she had had no idea 'dear Mr Hope' was ill. She was good at writing sympathy letters. One might well envy her final sentence — 'If I do not send this now, at once, to tell you how deeply I sympathize & how earnestly I pray for you, I shall not have courage to intrude on your grief.' But a well-turned phrase did not mean that she was insincere in her expressions or that she did not have a deep affection for both the Hopes. Laura replied to this letter some weeks later and Louisa's answer shows something of this affection and her own religious faith.

Dearest Mrs Hope,

Your letter touches me profoundly — I do thank you for it. Yes — among your many & nearer friends I think there are few, if any, who can more deeply realise your unspeakable loss than I. Long ago, your dear husband confided to me some of the trials he had had when very young even — trials which I understood peculiarly well, & I was filled with admiration of his goodness & unselfishness. And he was so sympathising with me! I was always so delighted to see the perfect happiness that married life brought him — He well deserved it — You both did, & it is strangely sad that God should have seen best to cut it short — but only here — you will as time goes on, feel that you are together still, in one sense, & you will live in the thought of perfect union hereafter — And you have his dear children to care for, to train to be all he could have wished, as I am sure they will be.

You will be, "strong & very courageous," though the bitter, bitter grief will often seem unbearable. Oh, how awfully well I know it — my

boy's death seems as terrible sometimes as if it had only just happened
— I will take my chance some day of seeing you before we go away —
Should we not meet before the late autumn, remember, dear, that I will
never forget to pray for you with loving earnestness — I am glad you
are able to work again —

    Your very affecte
    Louisa Molesworth[15]

Part of the time she was away this summer she spent at Totland Bay
on the Isle of Wight, probably so that the sea air could reinforce her
recovery. We know this from an address on a letter to one of the child
fans who wrote to her. I have seen only four of such letters but she said
she received many and made an effort to reply to them. 'I get a great
many letters from children & I answer as many as I can — For when
I was little, I should have been very hurt if I had written a letter to
which came no reply.'[16]

There were two more deaths in her circle of friends and relations the
following year, 1905. In January it was Lady Molesworth's turn, the
wife of the 8th Viscount who had advised Louisa and Richard to separate.
Louisa wrote to Craik about it.

'You may have seen that our dear kind Lady Molesworth died on Friday.
She was only a few days ill & a strong woman. I was very anxious from
the first. She was one of my best friends & I feel it deeply. It makes a
great difference to my life — practically too, I may say.'[17]

Louisa was friendly with Lady Molesworth's sister too, — Lady Congleton. They had been Agnes and Elizabeth Dove, whose father, Dugald
Dove, had property in County Renfrew. Elizabeth's husband, Henry
Parnell, Baron Congleton was in command of the regiment stationed
at Malta for seven years and she took an interest in the welfare of the
men. On one leave she asked Louisa to help her over getting books for
the soldiers' library there.[18]

Again this year there was no red book for Macmillan's — indeed,
Louisa seems to have published nothing at all in 1905, but a series of
letters from Gordon Milligan about a group of stories which eventually

---

[15] Copies of 2 letters from MLM to LH given to me by M-J Lancaster, Laura's grand-
daughter.
[16] MLM to N. B. Stranach, 1.7.1896. Letter sent to RR by recipient.
[17] MLM to GLC, 22.1.[1905].
[18] MLM to GLC, 17.7.[1899].

became *The Bolted Door* (1906), shows that she did a small amount of original work, as she was actually writing one of the stories during the six months spanned by the correspondence. It is clear from Milligan's letters that her side of it emphasised the number of words in each story in an attempt to boost payment, while he was trying to get as many stories out of her as possible for the one book, sticking all the time to an average price of £10 per story. He insisted that short stories were not as popular as one long one, and not only the more stories in a volume the better, but even the greater the number of words in a story, the more useful it was. He was keen to 'bulk' a volume out, almost as though he was selling packets of detergent with 30% extra. Finally Louisa received £90 for nine stories, eight of which had been previously published in periodicals.[19] With this negotiation satisfactorily concluded, she set off to spend the summer in Germany, returning in the early autumn to stay with Juliet in Surrey before going back to London for the winter and another sad event.

This was the death of Craik himself. In October he was very ill, something Louisa commented on sadly in a business letter to Mr Macmillan. 'I hear to my great sorrow, that he is still very seriously ill . . . I do hope that we may soon hear better reports of Mr Craik's convalescence.' In reply Macmillan held out some hope of his recovery but this did not last long and he died that autumn. An aside in another business letter is the only comment remaining from Louisa on the death of one of her greatest friends and supporters — 'In yours of 9th October (the same letter in which you were still able to give hopes of dear Mr Craik's recovery — hopes so soon to be quenched).'[20] Now that her chief correspondent in the firm was gone, although she was clearly on friendly terms with Frederick Macmillan, who seems to have been the partner she mostly dealt with, apart from Craik, her surviving letters are more strictly business ones.

The first new business matter Louisa engaged in after Craik's death was another book for children, but on different terms. Her illness had made her think seriously about ending her career as a writer. 'I had not intended ever to write another,' she wrote to Macmillan, 'but I am so much stronger now & rather more at leisure that I have been thinking

[19] 6 letters, Milligan to MLM, 12.1904–6.1905, Chambers' archive, National Library of Scotland.
[20] MLM to Macmillan, 7.10.1905, 16.1.1906.

about one.'[21] Up to this time, her financial agreement with Macmillan's had been arranged to provide her with a regular annual income. She received an advance on each new Christmas book in January, together with all royalties due up to the previous June. For instance, in January 1894 she was expecting 'the advance — or rather the "on publication" royalties on my new book — "Mary" — £75' together with £183.4.4 for sales from June 1892 to June 1893. She counted on the arrival of these payments on a particular date to the extent of arranging the dates of payments she had to make herself to fit in with her receipts from Macmillan's.[22] The advance royalty on a new book appears to have been £75 for many years. But now, with her new book for 1906, *Jasper*, she proposed such a radical change that she repeated her wish three times in two sentences, to emphasise that she really meant such a departure from her usual principle.

> 'I should wish to arrange for it on somewhat different terms from hitherto — ie I should propose to sell you the copyright altogether — not to retain any claim in Royalties. Will you kindly let me know, at your leisure, what you could pay me in this case — I to renounce all rights over the book.'

Macmillan in reply urged her to think carefully, because selling the copyright might result in a loss to her.[23] Such consideration for her interests is very different from, for instance, the high-handed treatment meted out to 'lady authors' of girls' stories in the first decades of the twentieth century, by some publishers who bought up copyrights for as little as £30, paid no royalties and made changes to books without consulting or informing the author.[24] But Louisa held to her purpose. 'I do still wish to part with the copyright, though I thank you for what you say as to the possible eventual loss to myself of so doing.' She did not anticipate such a result, which could only happen if the sales were enormous — as good as *Carrots*. Her idea was that *Carrots* had been particularly successful because it 'struck a new vein to some extent' and that 'it is improbable that this new story will have any remarkable sale.' She also explained to Macmillan, in confidence, that she had a special

---

[21] MLM to Macmillan, 20.2.1906.
[22] MLM to GLC, 26.1[1894].
[23] MLM to Macmillan, 20 and 26.2.1906.
[24] See Marjorie Morris, 'Aspects of the Life and Works of Elsie Jeanette Oxenham', in *Newsletter No. 45*, Children's Books History Society, Sept. 1992, p. 4.

reason for completely disposing of this copyright, because she needed a
capital sum and did not wish to sell any of her investments. However,
his warning had affected her enough to make her suggest a compromise
that was in fact agreed on. She accepted £150 for the copyright of *Jasper*,
with the proviso that if it should prove as great a success as *Carrots*,
Macmillan's would give her another £50.[25]

At the same time as the arrangements were being made about *Jasper*,
Louisa also offered Macmillan 'a collection of short stories for <u>adults</u>
which I am anxious to make a little volume of.' Since they had all
appeared before, this would seem at first sight to be the sort of negotiation she usually had with Chambers, and so it would have been, but
for one of the stories. It was really for the sake of that one, that she
was so anxious to have the book published.

> 'I must explain' she wrote, 'that "A ghost of the pampas" was by my
> son in South America — not long before his terribly sudden death —
> it is well written & attracted some notice in the serial in which it appeared
> — I should explain by a little preface or footnote that he was the author.
> You will understand that I am specially anxious to have this story pre-
> served.'

She was also very keen for it to be understood that this book would be
for adults. There was a certain note of resentment at her own image in
what she said on this point.

> 'Of course, it would have to be clearly shown by the title & otherwise
> that the volume is not the <u>least</u> intended or suited for children. People
> are so stupid as to this, as in "Four Ghost Stories" which you published.
> Because I write principally for children they will not understand that I
> may be allowed to write sometimes for adults.'[26]

She had said much the same thing when *Four Ghost Stories* appeared.
But publishers rely on an author's image and reputation to sell her
books, and are not usually pleased when the author becomes restive and
wants to break out in a different line, disappointing or perplexing the
expectations of the public. It is a measure of the value Macmillan's set
on Louisa that they bought the copyright of the stories that made up
The Wrong Envelope and Other Stories for £100 and published it as she
wished without, apparently, any dissentient note. The preface or foot-

[25] MLM to Macmillan, 26.2.1906 and clerk's note on MLM to Macmillan, 1.3.1906.
[26] MLM to Macmillan, 20.2.1906.

note about Bevil that she had mentioned was placed in the position usually held by the dedication in her books and laid out in the same way. It read

> To these short stories I add 'A Ghost of the Pampas' by my son Bevil who died at his ranch in Patagonia seven years ago, at the age of 27.
>
> M. L. M.
>
> SLOANE STREET,
> *April* 24, 1906.

According to Burke's *Peerage*, Bevil died on 13th March, 1898, four months after his 27th birthday on 10th November. The privately produced *Pedigree of the Molesworth Family*, lent to me by a member of the family, also gives 1898 as the year of Bevil's death. So when Louisa wrote that note, he had been dead for eight years.

Two further details of these transactions are typical of Louisa's business habits and relationship with her chief publisher, and are described here to stand for many other such incidents. When she first told Macmillan, in February 1906, that she was thinking of another children's book, she wrote as though it would not be finished for a long time and had perhaps not even been started.

> 'I have been thinking about one [sc. another book for children] . . . Not a fairy story; rather more in the style of "Carrots" — I might let you have it in time to get it ready for the so-called Christmas books this year — Possibly for next year only.'

But Frederick Macmillan knew her ways. During the week after he received Louisa's letter he offered the commission to illustrate *Jasper* to Gertrude Demain Hammond and in her letter of acceptance she spoke of being able to have the illustrations ready by the end of July if she received the story early in May. They were justified in their assumption when Louisa wrote again at the end of March saying 'I am glad to say that "Jasper" is practically finished — sooner than I had hoped.' She always liked to get ahead with her work. The other characteristic appears in her next sentence — 'Shall I send it to you next Monday? — by registered parcel post is perfectly safe I suppose — (I have no duplicate, so I am extra careful about M.S.S.)' This anxiety about the safety of parcels and letters occurred again and again in the long history of her dealings with Macmillan's and other publishers. She sent all the material for *The Wrong Envelope* to the office in St Martin's Sreet on Monday 26th February and on Wednesday 28th she pursued it with a postcard — 'I posted an important parcel to Mr Macmillan on Monday — & shd. like to hear of its having been safely received.' Macmillan himself replied to her that same day and the next day, 1st March, she wrote, on a slightly apologetic note, 'I was in no hurry for any reply to my letter but as I have had some disagreeable experiences of letters &c going astray I am always a little anxious about "copy".' This feeling persisted throughout her life — the very last letter she ever wrote to Macmillan's, in the year of her death, contained the sentence 'postal miscarriages are not infrequent still and I confess to being nervous about any letter of importance.'[27] She even wrote a story called 'Miss-sent letters', which appeared in *The Blue Baby* and contained two separate tales about unhappy events narrowly averted by great efforts in pursuing letters that had gone astray.

Around the time that *Jasper* was published, Louisa was disturbed by an article on children and their needs which she interpreted as being in some way either an attack on her personally, or at least on the kind of books she wrote. She was sufficiently upset to consult Rudyard Kipling (whom she already knew) about a possible reply to the criticism. He responded kindly and at some length, dismissing the article and saying that he felt she need take no action and should not worry about it.

Private
[Telegraph] Burwash   Batemans
[Station]   Etchingham   Nov 15 1906   Burwash
Sussex
Dear Mrs Molesworth,

Your letter gives me a chance to thank you from my heart for the debt I and my children owe the authoress of *Carrots* and *The Cuckoo Clock*. It is a debt of two generations, not made lighter by time.

I confess I don't see wherein the article needs an answer. It is just the sort of obvious stuff that any man or woman might write round the subject without touching the root of the matter: & least of all can I see how it affects you. Grown ups are always explaining what children want in one way or another and children are always putting grown-ups aside and quietly taking what they want where they find it. I fancy that grown

---

[27] MLM to Macmillan, 27.1.1921.

ups are apt to forget that a child's scope nowadays is a little wider than it was — the writer of the article gives a very funny instance of it himself without seeing the drift of his example i.e. the case of the children who read about the railway accident. Children live in a world of <u>allusion</u> as much as <u>illusion</u>. The illusion they make for themselves — the allusion (among grown ups) the half caught words & hints of the life to which they are growing up makes yet another world. Remember Griselda in *The Cuckoo Clock* — or take the mental matter of any child over eight years old. It is always seeking for more light on the manners & habits of the grown ups. So I am afraid I rather regard the article as what is vulgarly called "skittles". He ends with a very nice platitude about a Renaissance etc. Excellent! We all want a renaissance every five minutes in something or the other and we mostly lift up our voices to say so. So in that way the world is supposed to progress but again, I cannot see why you of all people should be in any way moved. With the sincerest respect & admiration believe me dear Mrs Molesworth yours very faithfully

    Rudyard Kipling

This was the sort of affair about which she used to consult Craik, who had himself been linked with Kipling in a small way, since he was a cousin of two ladies, Miss Mary and Miss Georgiana Craik, with whom Kipling had often stayed during his holidays from school, in Warwick Gardens. Their father, the literary historian G. L. Craik, was his uncle.[28] It is interesting that Louisa felt able to appeal to Kipling instead. Her connection with him, though at least sixteen years old by this time, does not seem to have been more than one of friendly acquaintance, judging by the surviving letters, although her turning to him over this problem suggests that there might have been a little more to it than we can now discover. He had written to her in October, 1899, thanking her for a copy of *This and That*. He added

> 'I must thank you by the same token for this and that when I was a youngster. *Then* the Cuckoo Clock much of which even now I know by heart — item "Carrots" & "Herr Baby", & for "Grandmother dear". Now I have a small three year old of my own we'll begin all your books over again together.'

---

[28] R. L. Green, *Kipling and the Children*, Elek Books, 1965, p. 74; Charles Carrington, *Rudyard Kipling: His Life and Work*, revised edition, Macmillan, 1978, p. 74–5; Mitchell, p. 14.

The three year old was Elsie, born in 1896. His eldest child, Josephine, the 'best-beloved' of *The Just-So Stories*, had died of pneumonia in New York six months previously, and John, the youngest, was not yet old enough to appreciate stories. The sentiment of gratitude was the same as that which introduced his later letter, though it is interesting to learn that he knew *The Cuckoo Clock* well enough to have much of it by heart. This private comment to Louisa is supported by a public reference in one of the articles Kipling sent back to newspapers in India during his long journey to England via the Far East and North America in 1889. Describing a visit to the shop of a Japanese dealer in curiosities, he presented himself with humourous exaggeration as a barbarian blundering into an immaculate dolls' house and said

> 'Do you recollect Mrs Molesworth's *Cuckoo Clock*, and the big cabinet that Griselda entered with the cuckoo? I was not Griselda, but my low-voiced friend, in his long, soft wraps, was the cuckoo, and the room was the cabinet.'[29]

But one wonders why, if he was that fond of *The Cuckoo Clock*, he did not mention it in *Something of Myself*, along with Mrs Ewing's *Six to Sixteen*, which, he said, he also knew 'almost by heart'. He could not, in fact, have read *The Cuckoo Clock* during the six years that he and his sister were boarding unhappily in Southsea, which was when he came to know *Six to Sixteen*, for it was not published until 1877, and that year their mother took them away to spend it with her. But a newly-published copy might have come his way over Christmas just before he went to school in January 1878.

Louisa's eldest daughter made a rather strange comment when explaining how Kipling and her mother had met. 'Mr Kipling (in the early '80s almost unknown) was introduced to my mother by the Macmillans — & used to come to tea on Sundays sometimes.' Certainly he was unknown in the early *eighties*, having returned to India straight from school in 1882 to a journalist's post when he was not quite seventeen. Louisa was in France at that time and when she settled in London in 1884 after her seven years in Europe, he was still in India and did not himself arrive in London until October 1889, and in January 1892 he married and then went to live in Vermont for four years. So he could

---

[29] Rudyard Kipling, *From Sea to Sea and Other Sketches: Letters of Travel*, Macmillan, 1900, vol. 1, p. 320. I am grateful to Professor Thomas Pinney for giving me this reference.

only have visited her over a period of about two years, and Cicely's comment was irrelevant, unless of course, as is possible, 'the early '80s' was a slip for 'the early '90s'. She also said, in conversation, that Kipling was a 'rather shabby young man' when her mother first knew him, and 'glad to come to the house on Sundays.'[30] In view of the speed with which Kipling became popular after his arrival in London, if Cicely's recollections are to be trusted, they must apply to the early months of his sojourn there. The house of Macmillan got to know him at once — a long ballad of his appeared in *Macmillan's Magazine* the month after his arrival — which makes his early introduction to Louisa perfectly possible. An editor who met him that autumn described him as wearing 'a rather shabby tweed overcoat' and as 'young, very poor, and (in this country) quite unknown,' which does fit with what Cicely remembered.[31] It is clear from Carrington's biography that, despite his almost instant fame, Kipling was lonely and homesick for India during the winter of 1889–90, feelings that would, presumably, have made him 'glad' of any friendly hospitality. One further interesting detail is that when his parents came home on leave in May 1890, they stayed first at Wynnstay Gardens and later in Earl's Court Road,[32] both addresses within a few streets of Lexham Gardens. So it would have been particularly easy for Kipling to call on Louisa on his way to or from his parents' house, without making a special journey.

Returning to 1906, Louisa's response to Kipling's efforts at reassurance over the article that had worried her, was to offer him a copy of *Jasper*, her current book. He accepted it for John, and gave further comfort for her apparently reiterated concern about the article.

> 'My John I am sure would be delighted with Jasper & we should be most honoured if you would send him a copy. Never mind about "Renaissances". It's a blessed word like "Mesopotamia" and it means something that one would like to do if one knew how but not knowing how one generally hits about & bleats, as someone else. It's just the same as "Reform" in politics or "technique" in art — a club wherewith to hammer the man who is trying to do something or — worse still — doing it.'

---

[30] Conversation between CP and RR, who made notes at the time. (1938, when CP was 75).

[31] The editor was Sidney Low. D. Chapman-Huston, *The Lost Historian*, (a memoir of Sir Sidney Low), quoted in Carrington, p. 178.

[32] Carrington, p. 203.

John was by this time nine years old, certainly of an age to enjoy *Jasper*. When the book arrived Kipling's letter of thanks promised that John would write himself to thank for it from Cape Town. At this period of their lives the Kiplings were spending every winter in South Africa, in a house lent to them by Cecil Rhodes. *Jasper* was to be saved for John until Christmas 'which is generally spent on a steamer on or near the equator' wrote Kipling. And that is all that remains of the acquaintance between Kipling and Louisa. By 1906 he had written all his books for children except *Rewards and Fairies*, and she must have read them, but what she thought we don't know.[33]

An increasingly important part of Louisa's life by the beginning of the new century was her growing number of grandchildren. She may not have been 'a kissing or petting' sort of person, but she loved them very much. One of Cicely's daughters wrote

> 'a more dearly loved grandmother never lived ... I can hear her voice saying 'Is that you, darling' with the same clearness as if I were standing at her door today.'

Yet Juliet's daughter, Cynthia, while supporting this picture in her own way by describing Louisa as 'not a cosy person,' then said 'we weren't particularly fond of her.' Her cousin's description continued

> 'She was the "gentlest" grandmother possible — in all the 27 years I knew her I never remember the smallest criticism or disapproval in voice or manner.'

But this same grand-daughter, the twin Venetia known as 'May', slightly contradicted herself by telling little anecdotes which show criticism in a mild and joking form.

> 'It was a family joke that she liked "dogs in their proper place —" "And little girls too?" "Yes my dear and you are not in yours, sprawling on the floor!" '

---

[33] Kipling's letters to MLM of 29.10.1899, 15 and 17.11.1906 were owned by CP and destroyed by her. RR copied them c. 1938. A few sentences have been quoted in Green (1965), p. 200, with acknowledgement to RR for 'transcripts generously supplied'. I am grateful to Professor Pinney for a copy of the 4th letter, 3.12.1906, which is at Cornell University Library, held in the Rudyard Kipling Papers (#4610) in the Division of Rare and Manuscript Collections. The article that worried MLM has not been identified. Kipling's letters and most of the accompanying text were published in an article in *The Kipling Journal*, Dec. 1997. I am grateful to the editor for permission to re-publish.

She maintained her own ideas of proper behaviour in every detail, which 'May' reported with loving amusement.

> ' "Granny in all the years we have been down Sloane Street we have never seen you leaning out of the window." "Ladies never lean out of windows." "But Granny if they had to see something?" "They would put on their bonnets & go out & see." (She always wore a bonnet even in 1920 — never a hat — & never a cap indoors.)'

She liked to give her grandchildren treats, however strange they were.

> 'One of our greatest treats was "to go to Harrods with Granny." She would patiently go from counter to counter having saved up her shopping to give us as many things to buy as possible.'

Harrods, of course, was within walking distance from the flat in Sloane Street. She kept promises to the children over the kind of detail that is often forgotten in family life. 'May' admired a little bronze statuette belonging to Louisa who promised that she should have it to keep 'when I go to heaven.' After her death it was found among her things marked 'For May' with the date when the promise was made. This is the meticulous payer of bills and answerer of letters, who expected others to be as reliable as she was herself.

Another treat was the same she had given to her own children and her nieces and nephews — to listen to a new story and be asked for helpful suggestions. This was so much a part of the children's picture of their 'Granny' that they could not believe it was in any way unusual. 'One of my young cousins once said "When we go to tea with X we are going to ask her granny to read us her stories",' remembered 'May'. ' "But perhaps she doesn't write stories",' was the adult rejoinder. ' "What! Don't all grannies write stories?" ' This young cousin was probably Juliet's daughter, Cynthia, who in later life wrote about her grandmother's annual visits when she brought with her the manuscript of the book or short story she was writing at the time.

> 'All her books were in her own clear legible writing with hardly an erasure and they went to the publishers like this. . . . We used to sit round her in a circle on the lawn, sometimes our cousins — children of her elder daughter — would be staying, and we all loved to be the first to hear a story which no one else knew about. She read in a soft voice full of expression which made it all very alive.'

Cynthia's cousin 'May' thought just the opposite on this last point. She considered that their grandmother 'was not a good "reader aloud" — her voice was too level, & she didn't dramatise herself.' The two cousins obviously had different standards for what constituted good reading aloud.

Cynthia's description continued,

> 'Sometimes she was still in process of writing and would ask our advice and quite often took our suggestions. I remember this particularly in a book of short stories called 'Fairies Afield'. The particular story was called 'Ask the Robin'. She said she wasn't quite sure how to go on with it and I remember saying 'Oh Grannie I know exactly. Of course her guardian angel would be there to help.' My grannie was not quite sure if Guardian Angel was what she wanted but to please me she put it in, qualifying it by saying "Fairy Queen or Guardian Angel." '

And certainly at a crisis in this story, the robin of the title, in explaining to the little heroine something of the recent history of the part of the forest where she lived, referred to a ban pronounced by 'Our queen — call her fairy queen, or guardian angel as best pleases you.'[34] It is clear that Louisa only put this in to please her grand-daughter Cynthia, for the actual helper and guide throughout the story is the robin himself. But Cynthia remembered that she had suggested other parts of the story too.

> 'I told her what I thought would happen to the little girl in question, who had a difficult and rather exacting task set to her, to repair the cruelty committed by another, as a result of which a spell had been cast on a wood and no robins could sing there until it was removed. Grannie used all I said, and told me afterwards it should have been my story. I was rather sorry she had dedicated the book she wrote before this one, 'Fairies of Sorts' to her nine grandchildren, 'The Three Threes', of which we are the middle three in the dedication; this was published in 1908. I much preferred the stories in 'Fairies Afield', perhaps because I had had more to do with their writing, and had asked her to write one about a Weather House. But most of us had sat round her listening to the earlier book, so she had dedicated that one to us.'[35]

The dedication referred to runs:

---

[34] *Fairies Afield*, p. 32.
[35] Account sent to RR by CB and quoted in part by Green (1961).

To Three Threes
Mary, May, Carola
Stella, Alix, Cynthia
Violet, Roger, Delves

The first three were Cicely's daughters, the second Juliet's step-daughters and daughter, and the third Lionel's children, all set out in order of age. Louisa sent the manuscript of this book to Macmillan's in February 1908, saying that she wanted to add a dedication 'but that will be time enough when I get the proofs, no doubt.'[36] So the children had sat around her listening to *Fairies — Of Sorts* the previous summer, in 1907. The twins by that time were thirteen and their sister Carola eleven. Cynthia, who was then seven, had already had one book dedicated to her more or less at birth, *The Blue Baby and Other Stories*, which was inscribed 'To *our* baby Cynthia Juliet Grant-Duff Ainslie Advent Sunday 1900'. She remembered being 'rather proud' of having a book specially dedicated to her, as no doubt all the children were. Her step-sisters had also had a book of their own in 1899, *The Children's Hour*, a collection of some of the *Child's Pictorial* stories, dedicated 'To Stella and Alix for their own hour.' Lionel's two eldest both had their own books in the year of their birth. His second child was the first boy among Louisa's grandchildren, so she proudly wrote at the front of *'My-Pretty' and Her Little Brother 'Too'*, 'To my first grandson Roger Bevil Molesworth.' Louisa would have been pleased at the revival of the name of her lost Bevil. Perhaps Lionel was being tactfully sympathetic again. Roger Bevil was six and his sister Violet ten in the summer of 1907, but their brother Hender Delves was the only one who could not have listened to *Fairies — Of Sorts* because he was only born that year. Although he was fourteen months by the time Louisa sent off the copy of the dedication in April 1908, the name he was to be called by had not been definitely fixed and last minute alterations were necessary. In the copy she sent, the last line read 'Violet, Roger, Hender' and in June she had to write again saying 'Is it too late to alter <u>one</u> of the names of my grandchildren in the dedication of "Fairies — of Sorts"? I find that the youngest of them is to be known by his <u>second</u> name "Delves", not "Hender".'[37]

Cynthia's final comment on Louisa was

---

[36] MLM to Macmillan, 18.2.1908.
[37] MLM to Macmillan, 9.6.1908.

'I think really to sum up, we regarded my Grandmother with a sort of awed interest, but she didn't touch our lives nearly tho' we felt quite proud to have our opinions asked and used and to have her as a relation.'

This attitude of awed interest is reflected in 'May's' comment 'My grandmother was not an easy person to know. She was v. reserved and not at all gushing.' Gwen Molesworth, too had given evidence that Louisa was awe-inspiring — 'Her manner was distant and one worshipped from afar.' But it *was* possible to get to know her. The difference between Cicely's and Juliet's children in their relationship with their grandmother was that the former lived in London and saw her often — 'we lived so near her for most of my unmarried life' said 'May', 'that very few letters ever passed.' Visiting so often that Louisa, on hearing the noise of a child at the door merely said 'Is that you, darling?' 'May' had the opportunity to observe her grandmother's writing methods and question her about them. As a result, she had much the same to say on the subject as interviewers and Louisa herself in her semi-autobiographical articles.

'She wrote regularly for 1 hour at least every day. If at the end of one hour inspiration wouldn't work she gave it up. I asked her once if she found it difficult to write — she said no, once started her children's adventures unrolled themselves before her — they practically "took over". I believe many authors find this.'

Cynthia, too, recognised the closer ties between Louisa and Cicely's children, writing ' "the twins" saw <u>much</u> more of Mrs Molesworth than we ever did & I am sure knew her much better.' She also added 'My mother [sc. Juliet] adored her and she obviously inspired great affection in people.' She used the same strong word about Olive, describing her as 'her favourite daughter . . . who lived with her and adored her.' Time and propinquity produced the intimate knowledge that led to deep affection.

There is not much other documentation of Louisa's 'annual visits' to her daughter Juliet's home, described by her grand-daughter Cynthia. Only a few addresses at the head of her business letters and odd references in them to her movements so that manuscripts or proofs could be forwarded, remain as evidence of these and other journeys and visits. We know from this source, for instance, that in 1907 she spent two or three weeks in Paris in May, and most of September in Cornwall, partly with Andalusia and Athelstan Riley, and partly in a hotel in Newquay.

Andalusia was the eldest child of the 8th Viscount Molesworth and the sister of Gwen, Louisa's great friend in her husband's family. During August she was with Juliet and her family, who had moved from Surrey to Sussex and were now living in Hellingly, a village about eight miles from Eastbourne. The readings to her grandchildren on the lawn that summer came from one of the two groups of tales Cynthia particularly remembered hearing — the stories which would make up *Fairies — Of Sorts*. At the same time she was also getting another book ready for publication in December, as one of her red book series. The book in preparation, *The Little Guest*, had two German villages in the early chapters of the story which bore very similar names — Winkenthurm and Winkenberg — to that of the Ainslie's house in Hellingly, Winkenhurst. Although there is no outside evidence to support the idea, I feel certain in my own mind that she invented these names to please and amuse her grandchildren.[38]

The small heroine of *The Little Guest*, Elinor, was still young enough to make mistakes in pronunciation and stumble over difficult words, producing sentences such as 'I fink she's razer better', and making two shots at saying 'porridge' but managing no better than 'poddidge' and 'pollidge' because 'though she otherwise spoke so clearly, she was not very strong on her "r's".'[39] Louisa had obviously taken great care in reproducing the kind of speech she thought realistic and suitable for six-year-old Elinor, and was annoyed when the proof-reader corrected the deliberate errors to standard English. In a letter of complaint to Macmillan's about this proof-reader's work, she said 'In most instances his corrections are quite wrong . . . young children do not talk perfect English & cannot be represented as doing so.'[40] This is the only direct comment Louisa made on the subject of what is usually called 'baby-talk' that has survived. 'Baby-talk' is really something of a misnomer, for in ordinary speech the phrase is normally used to describe the kind of language addressed by adults to very small children, who cannot yet talk at all. A literary example from a well-known author would be the chapter in *Barchester Towers* called 'Baby Worship', in which Eleanor Bold talks to her infant son in such phrases as 'Diddle, diddle, diddle, diddle, dum, dum, dum', 'a dawty little bold darling,' and 'his little 'ittle,

---

[38] MLM to Macmillan, 21 and 26.8.1907, addressed from Winkenhurst, Hellingly, Sussex with the instructions 'adding to my name "care of J. Grant-Duff Ainslie Esq."'
[39] *The Little Guest*, p. 138.
[40] MLM to Macmillan, 2.4.1907.

'ittle, 'ittle nose'.[41] Recent research into the subject has put baby-talk on a respectable level. An international team, headed by an American neuroscientist, has put forward the view that 'the urge . . . to talk apparent gibberish to babies' is an important response to the needs of this very early stage in language development. 'Parentese', as the team named baby-talk, 'is not simply babble or affectionate endearments, but near-normal language spoken slowly in sing-song style, with key sounds stretched out to make comprehension easier.' It is necessary and valuable to the development of babies that they have, from some adult, this experience of language sounds which then appear in their own babbling.[42] When children actually begin to speak, they do not talk 'parentese'. To adults their mistakes in learning to talk correctly may sound both sentimentally sweet and comic but to the children it is a serious matter. David Crystal makes this clear in his *Listen To Your Child*, subtitled *A Parent's Guide to Children's Language*. Children practise their language over and over, and the mistakes they make are consistent, logical steps in their advance to perfect speech. A simple, easily illustrated example is the way most children learn the regular past tense form first — I play, I played. Then for a while they try to make all verbs in the past tense fit this pattern, which leads to mistakes such as I throwed, she buyed, that adults might find amusing. Louisa used this kind of mistake in the following exchange from *Carrots*. ' "Have you thinkened, Floss?" he asked, eagerly. ' "Thought," gravely said Floss, "not thinkened, what about?" ' Similar examples occur in several of her other books where the child concerned is young enough to warrant it — four year old Baby in *Herr Baby* says, 'beginned', 'comed', 'keeped', little Steph in *Summer Stories* says 'he flewed', six year old Humphrey in *The Children's Hour* uses 'runned' and 'knowed'.[43]

Six seems to have been something of a watershed in Louisa's eyes. Although it is dangerous to make statements of the 'all' kind, after a careful examination of her books, I would say that in every one where there was a child of six or under, she reminded the reader of its age through phonetic reproduction of mispronunciation and a certain amount of grammatical error. The occasional child she described as speaking perfectly under six, or imperfectly over that age, was mostly

[41] Anthony Trollope, *Barchester Towers*, OUP, World's Classics edn., 1960, pp, 131–2.

[42] *The Times*, 1.8.1997, p. 6.

[43] *Herr Baby*, pp. 97, 157 and 173; *Summer Stories*, p. 51; *The Children's Hour*, p. 109.

commented on as unusual. The hero of *Jasper*, for example, was scorn-fully told by his sister — ' "What awful grammar, Japs . . . You really should know better at seven years old." ' By the very end of the story he was eight and his improved speech was also remarked on — 'his English by this time being almost quite "grown-up" '.[44] At the other end of the scale, Maud, in *The Girls and I*, whose speech at 6 was perfectly accurate and quite complex, was called 'very grown up,' 'the oldest of us all,' 'terrible old-fashioned' and described as having 'her quiet little particular way.'[45] Carrots was closer to Louisa's idea of an average child, in that by the time he was seven, during the last four chapters of the book, he had lost all trace of child language and spoke in complete correct sentences. The one exception was a small mistake which, significantly, he made while upset just after hearing of his mother's serious illness. In this context David Crystal gives an example of a child who still occasionally made a particular mistake at the age of eleven, 'especially when she was tired or irritable.'[46] He says, too, that even the best of pre-school children 'won't have mastered all the do's and don'ts until around age 9,' although he also comments on the remarkable progress most of them have made by four. But, just because so much of what a four or five year old says is correct, the errors are more conspicuous. In addition, the rate of language development differs, of course, from child to child.[47] So Louisa's presentation of the age range for language error matches quite well with observations in the field of language acquisition research.

Even in books for teenagers and adults, where, if children were in-volved at all, they played a minor role, she used realistic child speech. When she was writing her early three-volume novels, Louisa had no thought of publishing books for children, but in *Not Without Thorns* for instance, a five-year-old caught cutting up worms was made to retort when rebuked, ' "I ain't nasty. And you're cwueller to shoot pwetty birds and bunnies." ' And in a brief incident at the beginning of *Cicely*, when the heroine's five-year-old nephew was dying, the child's imperfect speech was touched on. ' "I asked him if he felt very 'sore', that is his word for 'ill'," she explained with a faint little smile, " and he said,

---

[44] *Jasper*, pp. 7 and 234.

[45] *The Girls and I*, pp. 1, 5 and 65.

[46] David Crystal, *Listen To Your Child: A Parent's Guide to Children's Language*, Penguin, 1986, p. 156.

[47] Crystal, pp. 151, 154 and 33.

'Not so wenny bad, Cissy.' He calls me 'Cissy'." [48] In *Meg Langholme*, a book for older girls, the heroine narrated the main part of the story in the first person as an adult. But, at the beginning, she described herself as a small child in the third person, reporting her own speech in such phrases as 'I do wiss papa would tum out again,' 'Is they nice?' and 'Where are your house?' to underline her youth. [49] The youngest child in 'The Shadow in the Moonlight' from *Uncanny Tales*, which Louisa definitely intended as a book for adults, was shown as having a lisp. The child was a boy old enough to be doing lessons with a governess, and, though his age was not given, since the next sibling was fifteen, he was probably at least eleven or so. The narrator was his eldest sister and in reporting his description of a ghostly experience, she repeated and commented on his mistakes. ' "I've felt a — a sort of *breaving*" — Dormy was not perfect in his "th's" — "like somebody very unhappy." ' [50] His part in events was small but significant, since he was the first person to experience the ghost, and it seems that the point of emphasising his imperfect speech was to bring out his youthfulness and inexperience. The plot was so structured, as often in ghost stories, that each uncanny happening was experienced by someone older and more suspicious than the person who met the ghost on the previous occasion. This gradation stands out the more clearly because of the emphasis on Dormy's youth through his speech. In another book for older girls, *Philippa*, where children, though mentioned, did not even appear, Louisa still made any reference to what a young child said include childish errors. A mother, for instance, describing some newly met relations, said ' "They have all three got dark hair, as smooth as — oh, I can't trouble to find a comparison — "as smoove as smoove" as Bonny says — dear Bonny!" ' [51] Here, the loving reference to her child and its faulty expression underlines the mother's loneliness amongst new relations whom she had to impress, and her longing for her home and children.

So, from Louisa's comment to Macmillan's and from her actual practice we can see that she thought child speech should be represented as realistically as possible, but she did not believe this involved writing every word as a particular child of the relevant age would have said it. Indeed, in one book she commented on how difficult this would have

---

[48] *NWT*, vol. 2, p. 20; *Cicely*, vol. 1 p. 90.
[49] *Meg Langholme*, pp. 10, 12, 13.
[50] *Uncanny Tales* p. 14.
[51] *Philippa*, Chambers, [1896] 1897, p. 102.

been. The youngest child aged six, said 'It's full of fairies' and his older sister, the narrator, wrote 'He really said "wairies," but I can't write all his speaking like that; it would be so difficult for you to understand.' Another slight example from *Carrots* illustrates the same point. ' "About a plan," replied Carrots. He called it "a pan" but Floss understood him.'[52] It seems that Louisa intended to include enough mispronunciations and grammatical errors to maintain a consistent and realistic picture of a young child's speech patterns, but not so many as to be annoying to the reader. As we shall see later, this aim did not succeed with all readers.

In her books for children Louisa not only showed the younger characters using imperfect speech, but also trying and wishing to improve it and being corrected by others, as for instance in the 'poddige/porridge' example from *The Little Guest*, and the 'thinkened/thought' one from *Carrots*, mentioned above. 'Not yet six' Jack in *Opposite Neighbours* was corrected by his brother for saying 'took' instead of taken, with the comment ' "Jack doesn't speak good grammar . . . Papa's rather vexed about it." ' The four-year-old heroine of *Mary* found it difficult to say 'g'. She was trying to guess about something special that would happen on her birthday and said ' "For us all to be d—." ' Then with a great effort, for Mary was growing a big girl and wanted to speak quite rightly, "to be g-ood all day. Kite good." ' In her next speech the hesitation was repeated, "g-go away" but after that, although she made plenty of other mistakes, Mary was shown as able to use the hard 'g' sound in words like 'get', 'go' and 'good' perfectly well.[53] A similar example of correction and improvement occurs in one of the little *Child's Pictorial* stories, about mice. The child said

> ' "There must be a front door to one of the mouses' houses there, I think." "Mice, not mouses," corrected Mamma. "I meant to say mice," said Leonard. It was not often he made mistakes, for he was seven now.'

Then on the next page the correction was shown taking effect — ' "Have the mou- the mice been good to-night, Mamma?" '[54] This is the same kind of mistake, caused by over-generalisation, as the 'flewed' and 'comed' ones given earlier. The child learns that many nouns form their

[52] *The Boys and I*, p. 197; *Carrots*, p. 24.
[53] *Opposite Neighbours*, p. 40; *Mary*, p. 17.
[54] *Twelve Tiny Tales*, p. 73.

plurals by adding 's' and assumes he can use the rule for all nouns.[55]

Objections to her practice started early. Edward Salmon, in his article 'Literature for the Little Ones', said 'It may be asked whether it is wise to write for children precisely as children speak. Would not Mrs Molesworth's works serve a more useful end if her children said 'dreadful' instead of 'dedful'?' But his reason was not because he found the mistakes irritating or that they made the books more difficult to read. Indeed, he felt that omitting the child language would deprive the stories of 'their most humourous side and their full realistic charm.' But he was prepared to put up with this for the sake of improving their 'educational value' and 'lucidity'. In other words, he was afraid that real children might be encouraged not to bother about trying to improve their speech if they read stories where fictional children made the same kind of mistakes. He does not seem to have noticed that Louisa's characters made positive efforts to improve. It should be noted that Salmon omitted this passage when the article was re-published in his book, *Juvenile Literature As It Is.*[56]

Later critics objected for different reasons. Marghanita Laski commented on 'the phonetic reproduction of the most peculiar child language' as 'one of Mrs Molesworth's most trying little tricks . . . that maddens the reader' and also, she thought, produced sentences 'impossible to read aloud to children as they stand.' She pointed out that 'no two children misuse language in quite the same way,' giving this as a reason for condemning, as 'a stylistic error,' any attempts to reproduce it.[57] Louisa had in fact noticed this, and to a certain extent, conveyed it. For example, in *A Christmas Child*, when the hero, Ted, was very young he used 'thoo' for 'you' but later in the book his little sister said 'zoo' for the same word. Several of Louisa's child characters used 'werry' for very, but Racey, in *The Boys and I* said 'vrezy'.[58] The kind of language she gave to her fictional children was not, of course, peculiar at all. David Crystal shows that such errors, with variations, are common to all children. As for the impossibility of reading such words aloud, children themselves, and those who have most to do with them, are completely used to hearing words like 'nucken', 'somesing' and 'werry' all the time

[55] Crystal, pp. 13–14.
[56] Salmon (1887), p. 579.
[57] Laski, p. 64.
[58] *Christmas Child*, pp. 7 and 9; p. 123; *Carrots*, p. 97, *Herr Baby* p. 15, *The Boys and I*, p. 233.

and take them for granted. Laski's basic objection seems to be that she herself finds the practice irritating. Another who felt the same way wrote that Louisa 'was a most capable storyteller, and her great success was in revealing very young children and their feelings', but then added 'although their baby talk becomes at times a little tiresome.'[59] The two-page entry on Louisa Molesworth in *The Dictionary of British Women Writers* includes the statement that although *Carrots* and *Herr Baby* are 'well worth reading,' they are 'slightly marred by the irritating device of using baby-talk.'

What is it, exactly, that these writers find so irritating and tiresome? They make no moral objection, as Salmon did, no pronouncement about damage to the educational progress of young readers. It appears to be a reaction from personal taste — they do not like seeing wrongly spelt words and wrongly constructed sentences on the page and find them an annoying barrier to ease of reading. But the same objection could be made, for instance, to the Uncle Remus stories. When the first book appeared in 1880, it 'became, overnight, one of the famous American books of the nineteenth century' although it was written in 'accents of English few had ever heard outside the South and which none had ever seen in print.' Sentences such as this — 'he laff en laff twel he hatter hug a tree fer ter keep fum drappin' on de groun'' — need some consideration at a first reading before they become clear. But the initial difficulty did not prevent the stories from becoming 'hugely popular' and having a great influence on later writers such as Kipling, Milne, Potter and Grahame.[60] I am not saying that Louisa's books bear any similarity to the Uncle Remus stories, but that the dialect used by Joel Chandler Harris is at least as difficult to understand and get used to as printed baby-talk. It can be done, so that the stories can be read with ease, but it needs familiarity.

R. L. Green, in *Kipling and the Children*, discussing the use of dialect in writing 'intended for those more sophisticated and cultured readers who did not use it in real life' said that it became 'almost a disease by the end of the century.' He saw literal presentation of child-speech as an aspect of the great popularity of dialect.

'Another branch of this disease of language was the reproduction of the conversation of small children for sentimental adults which also owed its

[59] M. F. Thwaite, *From Primer to Pleasure*, The Library Association, 1963, p. 150.
[60] John Goldthwaite, *The Natural History of Make-Believe*, OUP, 1996, pp. 254–5, 257, 281.

main impetus to American writers, headed by John Habberton whose *Helen's Babies* (1876) . . . overflowed both with luscious sentiment and an abundance of 'baby talk' which set a fashion that was to run riot for twenty years until the publication of Kenneth Grahame's epoch-making presentations of real children in *The Golden Age* (1895).'[61]

Louisa does not fit into this scenario in that she did not write for 'sentimental adults' but for children, and she warned several times in her published articles and interviews against the assumption that all books about children are suitable for them. Her own use of child speech was very unlikely to have been influenced by Habberton. *Carrots* was published in the same year as *Helen's Babies*, and, as we have seen, in that book and in her early novels, she had already established her practice based on the principle that 'young children do not talk perfect English and cannot be represented as doing so.' There is no positive evidence that she read *Helen's Babies* but in one of her articles, just after insisting that Florence Montgomery's *Misunderstood* was never meant for children, she wrote something that suggests it.

> 'There are books . . . in which none of the characters are children, none of the scenes those of the nursery or school-room, which are better, more wholesome reading than others I could also name peopled almost entirely by small personages, and dwelling principally on their sayings and doings.'[62]

She may not have been thinking of *Helen's Babies* itself among the 'others I could also name' but her description fits it and books of the same type.

Despite the tone of the quoted passage, Green himself did not dislike baby-talk, at least in Kipling's books. Writing in 1965, he said

> 'Baby-talk has, for some reason, become almost impossible to take nowadays, and some adult readers find 'Wee Willie Winkie' sentimental. Here personal taste and personal prejudice must be accepted: in a sense these stories have dated — though it should be possible to accept them now as 'period' pieces like any other children's classics of last century. . . . Kipling's child stories . . . were treasured favourites of my own childhood —and enjoyed every bit as much by my father when he read them to me.'

---

[61] Green (1965), p. 83.
[62] 'Story-Reading', p. 774.

He maintained that, in contrast not only with *Helen's Babies* but also
with Louisa's *Herr Baby*, when writing 'baby-talk' Kipling had not
'simply imitated from literary sources, but observed and then made his
own phonetic transcript of what he actually heard.'[63] This implies that
he was prepared to accept baby-talk if it was accurate. But Louisa
represented child-speech, as shown by the comparative examples quoted
from Crystal, with errors in grammar and pronunciation common to
children observed in real life. She did not make them up out of her
own head, or copy literary sources.

   Other criticisms appear to stem from the idea that all writers who
use baby-talk must be pandering to a low taste in their readers (and
perhaps themselves as well) for indulgence in sloppy sentimentality or
finding comic enjoyment in children's errors. One of the supporters of
this line of thinking wrote of 'Mrs Molesworth . . . represent[ing] the
speech of small children in this glutinous fashion.' Presumably, since
'glutinous' means sticky or gluey, he had the association of sticky with
sweet in mind, and meant to imply that stories using baby-talk were
unpleasantly sweet and sentimental. A further charge was added —
'no-one before her seems to have realised its commercial potential. Once
she had done it, the idea became immensely popular.'[64] It is true that
the late Victorian and Edwardian popular image of the ideal child was
of a dear, trustful, innocent, pretty creature, with indistinct speech.
This change from the eighteenth and earlier nineteenth century view of
children as ignorant beings needing instruction or sinners to be saved
is well illustrated in the change of a particular periodical title. In 1881
The Children's Treasury became *Our Darlings*.[65] And as Gillian Avery put
it, in *Childhood's Pattern*, 'Other writers lost their sense of proportion.'[66]
Baby-talk was indeed used by authors like Stella Austin, Ismay Thorn
and Yotty Osborne precisely because of its sickly-sweet appeal. And they
probably were influenced by the immense popularity of *Carrots*. We
saw that Louisa remarked to Macmillan 'it has been *greatly* copied.' But
she herself continued to use imperfect child-speech because she thought
it realistic. The book in which it was most conspicuously present was
Herr Baby and she never used it again so much in any one story. Even

---

[63] Green (1965) p. 88.

[64] Humphrey Carpenter, *Secret Gardens*, Allen and Unwin, 1985 p. 106.

[65] Information from bookseller's catalogue, Talatin Books, no. 32, Jul. 1997, nos.174–5 and 31.

[66] Avery, (1975), p. 150.

here and in *Carrots*, there were several older children who spoke correctly to counterbalance the imperfect utterance of the two heroes. But surely, if Louisa had wished to exploit baby-talk commercially, seeing it as a money-spinning device, she would have used it more and more, instead of interspersing books for and about small children among those for older ones. Of her full-length 'child-novels', only six have a principal character consistently using imperfect language throughout the story,[67] although, as already noted, it occurs in her other books and short tales wherever the child concerned is young enough to justify it.

Louisa was accused of exploitation by more than one writer. The following quotation implies a misuse that was emotional rather than commercial.

> 'She increasingly, as time went on, exploited the inadequacies and errors of children's language in order to provide amusement for those whose superiority in that regard could be felt to be unchallenged.'

In other words, for adults. This point was hammered home by another sentence in the same paragraph — 'she exploited the comic possibilities of children's language relentlessly.'[68] It should be noted that the passage chosen to illustrate the topic comes from *Herr Baby*, quite an early book, published only six years after Louisa's first children's book and thirty years before her last, and also the only one, as mentioned above, in which baby-talk is so heavily used. The piece runs,

> '"Werry well. If him's a goose him won't talk to you, and him won't tell you somesing *werry* funny and dedful bootiful that him heard in the 'groind room."'[69]

This shows several well-documented and common errors for three and four year olds. There is confusion between the subject and object forms of the pronoun ('him' for 'he'), reference to self in the third person, difficulty in pronouncing 'v' and 'th' and one complete mispronunciation of a long word. Sorting out pronouns takes a long time for a child once it has started to use them.[70] If these mistakes, then, are all 'real' and 'natural', what is wrong with putting them into a child's mouth in a story? The trouble probably is that there are too many different kinds

---

[67] These are: *Carrots, Herr Baby, Us, Little Miss Peggy, Mary*, and *This and That*.
[68] Wall, B., p. 83.
[69] *Herr Baby*, p. 8.
[70] Crystal, p. 132, 90.

of mistake in one speech. It is overloaded. Louisa achieved a much better effect in *Us*, where the twin hero and heroine consistently misuse the pronoun 'us' in referring to themselves, but otherwise only stumble over 'th'. The reader remains aware of the children's age but is not 'maddened' by too much misspelling or bad grammar.

The passage selected as an example of relentless exploitation is the same as that used by the author of the remark about 'glutinous' language to illustrate his theme, (and the list of secondary sources shows that his book was one of those consulted). These two writers would have had difficulty in finding a speech from one of Louisa's later books as densely packed with childish errors. As time went on, in fact, she was increasingly careful when she wrote about children under six to present merely a suggestion of what their language was really like. I believe Louisa did not at all intend to provide amusement for adults, although they may have found it in her books, as Salmon indicated when he expressed himself ready to sacrifice humour and charm for the sake of educational values. On the contrary, she presented sympathetically the distress and puzzlement of children being laughed at by adults for their 'funny ways' and speech, as in the following example.

> 'Nurse laughed; and Fanny, the under-nurse, laughed too. "What a cure the child is, to be sure!" said Fanny, pertly. Hermy took her solemn eyes off nurse and turned them upon Fanny. She would have liked to ask her what she meant — she knew what "a cure" was: medicine was a cure for being ill, dock-leaves were a cure for nettle-stings; but how she — Hermy — could be a cure passed her comprehension altogether — but she knew it was useless. Fanny would not explain, and she and nurse would only laugh the more loudly. Oh, that laughing! How Hermy disliked it! She was thinking to herself that a world where nobody was allowed to laugh — no big people at least — would be a very nice place, when nurse interrupted her.'[71]

In another incident, from *A Christmas Child*, an adult was shown deliberately trying not to hurt a child's feelings over this very point. '"Not quite so bad as that," said his father quietly, for he did not want Ted to see that it was difficult not to smile at his funny way of speaking.' In the same book another adult, not so considerate or understanding, did try to extract amusement from the child's mistakes, and Louisa was very clear about what she thought of such behaviour.

---

[71] *Hermy: The Story of a Little Girl*, Routledge, [1880] 1881, p. 15.

'He looked at Ted in a rather queer way as he said it. The truth was that Mr Brand, who though so big was not very old, was carried away by the fun (to *him*) of watching the puzzled look on the child's face, and forgot that what to him was a mere passing joke might be very different to the tender little four-years-old boy.'[72]

I have dwelt at some length on this matter of imperfect speech or baby-talk because, in the reaction to the 'Isn't it sweet' school of thought, dismissive contempt, or, at the least, irritation, seems to me to have held sway for a long time, and I felt Louisa deserved some serious consideration of her practice and intention in this area. The book which had elicited her only direct surviving comment on the matter, *The Little Guest*, was published in the autumn of 1907. It was, she thought at the time, 'very probably the last complete story I shall ever write.'[73] Her illness and age (she was now sixty eight) were apparently making her feel that her writing career was at an end.

---

[72] *Christmas Child*, pp. 28 and 52.
[73] MLM to Macmillan, 18.2.1907.

14

Last Years

Louisa did not after all end her writing career with *The Little Guest*, as she had suggested to Macmillan's might be the case. Of course, she already had most of the tales for *Fairies — Of Sorts* ready and waiting when *The Little Guest* was published, but that was a collection and she had been thinking of the latter book as her last 'complete story.' *Fairies — Of Sorts* was her Christmas book for 1908. However, she did then write another full-length story, *The February Boys*, which was published in 1909 — with Chambers. This is the only time a complete new book of hers, which had not previously appeared in a periodical, was published by any house other than Macmillan's. Chambers, while continuing to negotiate for re-issues of her earlier books, had been pressing her to let them have something totally new. She suggested to them in January 1908 that they should bring out *Sweet Content* (which they did) and *The Little Old Portrait* (which they did not). When thanking her for these ideas, Gordon Milligan also repeated that he would be very happy to consider a new story by her, similar to the ones she had written for Routledge which Chambers had re-published — *Hermy* and *Hoodie*.

In July she promised him that Chambers should have the first offer of her next new story, if she ever wrote another. And, at the very end of the year he was able to write and thank her for giving Chambers the first chance of a new story. He offered her £200 for the complete copyright and when she accepted it, she told him that this had been the sum she had had in mind herself. This was in January 1909, but, at her request, the money was not to be paid until 7th April, presumably for tax reasons. Milligan wrote, when agreeing to this arrangement, that he understood her reasons for wanting to postpone the payment. She had complained to him about tax before and received an understanding response.[1]

Meanwhile, in March 1909, Frederick Macmillan asked if Louisa

---

[1] GM to MLM, 31.1, 14.3, 1.7 and 31.12.1908, and 4.1.1909, Chamber's Collection.

could let his firm have another book, but her reply was discouraging.

> 'I am sorry to say that I see no chance of my having a book ready . . .
> for this year's production. Some months hence, or perhaps twelve months
> hence, I may have another, but I don't think it could possibly be for the
> autumn season this year.'[2]

Naturally there was 'no chance', because she had already sold her new
book for the year to Chambers, but she said nothing about this to
Frederick Macmillan, and there is no mention of *The February Boys* in
any of her surviving letters to Macmillan's. One wonders what their
reaction was when it appeared the following September. It is possible
that she was trying to nudge Macmillan's into paying her more, while
they seemed to feel she had passed the summit of her popularity. As
evidence of this, we can look in detail at her response to the terms they
offered her in February 1907 for *The Little Guest* (without seeing the
manuscript).

> 'I very much deprecate any appearance of "bargaining" about my books,
> especially with such old friends as yourselves,' she wrote. 'But I am sure
> you will not misunderstand my entering into a few details, in reply to
> your letter just received — In the first place "£60" is a smaller advance
> than I have ever had from you. It has always been £75, & naturally with
> my present standing, I should not like to accept lower terms than for
> more than — I think — 30 years! Then as to the £150 for the entire
> copyright, I think I must tell you that for years another firm has been
> pressing me to let them have my new "Christmas book," and judging
> by what they have already distinctly offered, I have every reason to believe
> they would pay £200 (for all rights) for my present book. But I very
> much prefer its being published by you — Will you kindly consider the
> matter again. If I retain the copyright I had been thinking of an advance
> of £100 — you see I am no longer either a young author or a young
> woman — & the amount I make is, of course, of some consequence to
> me, writing as little as I now do, to ensure no risk of deterioration in
> my book through overtasking myself — as it seems to me so many
> popular writers do.'

The other firm to which she referred was clearly Chambers, while the
argument based on overworking implied that if she did not receive as

---

[2] MLM to Macmillan, 3.3.1909.

much as she needed from Macmillan's, she would have to write more so as to earn more, at the risk of a drop in quality. Her 'old friends' capitulated completely and at once, as is clear from her next letter, dated only the day after the one quoted above. In it she agreed 'to retain the usual interest in copyright,' and was 'glad to have £100 advance.' A clerk's note added later to the head of her letter recorded that the royalty was 6d.[3] We may note that, despite Macmillan's complete acceptance of her terms, and her firm statement that she preferred to have her new books published by them, she did not go back on her agreement with Chambers, to let them have *The February Boys* in the following year. It seems likely that, as well as using Chambers to keep Macmillan's up to the mark, she may have thought it a good idea to gratify the former with the new book for which they were pressing, because she was doing so much business with them over re-issues and buying up rights of her books from other firms.

The February Boys looked quite different from Louisa's orange series with Macmillan's. This had now anyway become blue and gold, with *Fairies — Of Sorts*, a change she approved of — 'I am delighted with my new book's garb and pictures.'[4] But these pictures were still in black and white, as the illustrations for her Christmas books had always been since the unfortunate *contretemps* over *Herr Baby*. Chambers asked Mabel Lucie Attwell to illustrate *The February Boys* with startling effect. Moreover, the illustrations were in colour, and the green or blue cover displayed the coloured figure of a child, in outline with no background, in complete contrast to the black embossed designs on orange cloth which had for so long been the hallmark of her "Carrots" series. With this production Chambers had moved 'Books by Mrs Molesworth' into the twentieth century. This book was also the story about Carrots grown-up with children of his own, asked for thirty years before by the then Crown Prince of Italy. Looking at first editions of the two books together gives a strong sense of totally different eras.

During her correspondence with Gordon Milligan about *The February Boys* and the re-publications of that year, Louisa asked him to consider some stories by Mrs Hohler. This was her niece, Venetia Goring, her sister Agnes' only child, who had married a Mr Edwin Hohler. Although the reply was that Chambers would be happy to look at the stories, they never in fact produced anything by Mrs Hohler. She had already

[3] MLM to Macmillan, 20 and 21.2.1907.
[4] MLM to Macmillan, 12.10.1908.

had eight books published when Louisa made this request. Her first three, all dated 1898, were brought out by three different firms — Macmillans, SPCK and Nelson. Since these three firms had also all published books by Louisa, it is possible that she had recommended her niece's work to their notice. The British Library catalogue lists five other titles by Mrs Hohler, published by Macmillan, Blackie, Constable and Nelson. The last one is dated 1907, the year before Louisa made her application to Chambers on her niece's behalf.[5] So it may be that she hoped to get Chambers to do for Venetia what they were already doing for her — to buy up titles from other firms and reissue them. Venetia's son, who used, as a child, to visit his Great-Aunt Louisa and Cousin Olive regularly in London, thought that Louisa had inspired his mother to write her own children's books,[6] and whether or not this was the case, she apparently made an effort to help her niece with getting her work reissued. This is a trivial incident, but it serves as a reminder, in the absence of letters or diaries, that Louisa maintained contact with her own family. She had dedicated *The Children of the Castle* to Venetia, and two other books to three of her sister Caroline's children. Caroline lived in Wales to the end of her life, and Louisa remained in touch with her. It was, for instance, from Caroline that Louisa obtained a copy of one of her out-of-print books when Macmillan's wanted to re-publish it in 1915.[7]

Louisa finished the writing of both her two last books in the summer of 1909, despite her off-putting remark to Frederick Macmillan only a few months previously about possibly having something ready 'twelve months hence.' This was the final, most extreme result of her passion for preparing everything well ahead of time. She did not tell Macmillan's about them in detail until January 1910. George Macmillan wrote in December 1909 enquiring about another book and in her reply she admitted she could promise them *a* book for 1910 which would be available in April. But first she wanted to reach 'a mutually satisfactory arrangement.' Apart from her particular desire for a single capital sum

[5] Books by Mrs Edwin Hohler:- *For Peggy's Sake*, Macmillan, 1898; *The Green Toby Jug and The Princess Who Lived Opposite*, Nelson, 1898; *The Picture on the Stair*, SPCK, [1898]; *The Bravest of Them All*, Macmillan, 1899; *Mark's Princess or Noblesse Oblige*, Nelson, 1904 [1903]; *The Deserted Palace*, Blackie, [1904]; *Peter: A Christmas Story*, Constable, 1906; *Dick's Angel*, Constable, 1907. The BL catalogue lists no other titles by her.
[6] C. G. Hohler to RR, 16.6.1938.
[7] MLM to Macmillan, 23.10.1915.

when *Jasper* was published, she had always clung to the royalty system, with her books as far as possible under her own control. Now, with her advancing age, she changed her mind.

'When Mr Frederick Macmillan wrote to me last March about a book for this Christmas, I explained to him that though I had none for you this year, I should like to write for you again, but that my views are now altered as to terms. He replied (March 4th) that you would do your best to meet my wishes. These I will recapitulate. You see I am now far from young, & as we are such very old friends I will frankly tell you, that it is now of much more importance to me to enjoy personally the products of anything I write, than to leave a few pounds a year more to my heirs. So I wish to give up the royalty system. Will you therefore consider and let me know the largest sum you can offer me for the entire copyright? . . . As this is really a business matter of importance to me, you will not, I feel sure, misunderstand my mentioning that other firms offer me very much higher terms for copyright than any you have yet seen your way to propose but I really infinitely prefer publishing with yourselves; our association is of such very long standing that I should like it to continue to the end of my writing.'

She had said most of this to Frederick Macmillan the previous March, except that she had specified the much higher terms as 'offers of from £200 to £300.'[8]

While waiting for a reply, she also wrote to Gordon Milligan, asking what Chambers could give her for another new book. In response he regretted that they were not able to offer her any increase on the amount they had paid for *The February Boys* — that is, £200. She was not trying to sell the same book to two different buyers however, as appeared in her next letter to George Macmillan accepting his proposal, also of £200, 'for entire copyright of a children's book for next Christmas.' She thought she would be selling Chambers and Macmillan's one book each, unless Macmillan's was prepared to take both. It was at this point that she explained to George Macmillan that she had two books quite ready.

'But I have something more to ask you. As a matter of fact I have two children's books ready — I completed them last summer. One is a story of real life, I call it "The Story of a Year" — 49,000 words. The other consists of four long fairy tales — tales in which real life mingles. I have

---

[8] MLM to Macmillan, 28.12 and 3.3.1909.

called it "Fairies Afield", but this can be changed. It is 52,000 words
long. I believe the stories in it are <u>really</u> "original" & not commonplace.
My home critic, who <u>is</u> critical, says she thinks both books are as good
as anything I have ever done. But it is <u>absolutely certain</u> that they are
my <u>last</u>. I have not had at all a good winter & the doctors entirely
prohibit any more "work" for the rest of my life. I have to take things
very quietly. As I said before I began with your house & I should like
to end with it, & I think your kind father would have wished this to
be so.'

This was a reference to Alexander Macmillan, who, with his brother
Daniel, started the firm in 1843. He had died in 1896, but had before
then transferred all power and action to his own and his brother's sons
and their partners.[9] Since this transfer took place gradually, between
1871 and 1888, Louisa could have had some dealings with him over
her early books, but as we have seen, her chief contact and correspondent
in the firm, until his death, was George Craik.

What she wanted from Macmillan's was an agreement to take both
books, one for Christmas 1910 and one for 1911, both on the same
terms, £200 for each, both sums to be paid in mid-April of the relevant
year. The agreement was to include an arrangement by which the money
would still be forthcoming even if she died before the final payment
was due. Chambers had also offered her £200 for a new book, she
explained, but she was not going to reply until she had heard from
Macmillan's. She pointed out that if she did sell one of the two books
to Chambers 'I could not debar them from publishing <u>next</u> Christmas,
& for every sake it is best not to have two of my books appearing
simultaneously.' This last sentence also suggests the very probable reason
for her not letting Macmillan's have a book for Christmas 1909, even
though she had finished two during the previous summer. She would
not have wanted to have *The February Boys* competing with another of
her books from a different publisher during the same holiday season.
Of course George Macmillan agreed to all she asked and four days after
putting this double proposal to him, she was thanking him for his 'most
satisfactory reply.' She arranged to transfer both mss to his keeping as
soon as possible. Since she and Olive were staying at a hotel in Worthing
for a time, she asked for a special messenger to be sent as soon as possible
after their return to London to collect the papers, as had often been

---

[9] For the early history of Macmillan's, see Charles Morgan, *The House of Macmillan.*

done before. This was yet another example of her anxiety about the safety of mss — 'I confess to being very nervous about the safe transit of my M.S.S. as I keep no copies I mean duplicates.' And when notifying Macmillan's of her presence in Sloane Street again, she made a little pun, half laughing at her own nervousness, saying 'I shall be glad when the M.S.S. are safe in your safe!'[10]

Olive was right to think that her mother's two last books were as good as anything she had ever done. *The Story of A Year,* first of the two to be published, has a similar plot structure to *Two Little Waifs* and *The Carved Lions.* There is a gradual, inevitable build-up of increasingly distressing circumstances which culminates in the characters' running away to the relief of safety and happiness. The whole strength of the book lies in this contrast between the life endured by the heroine and her mother with a half-crazed, miserly relation whose meanness over food and heating during a cold winter makes the child ill, and the sudden, delightful, move to pretty, healthy quarters with kind people and plentiful food. Against the darkness and cold, the lack of colour and the sour discord of the miser's house, depicted strongly enough to convey a sense of horror, are set the freshness, warmth, brightness and loving-kindness of the dwelling to which the child and her mother escape. In this story the running away is not a child's whim but an adult's considered reaction to unbearable circumstances. Cicely said that the portrait of the miser in this book was based on someone her mother had known in Edinburgh. It is both vivid and restrained, and the events that lead up to what, so briefly summarised, must sound like a melodramatic climax, are in fact so well told, with such quiet detail added to detail from the child's viewpoint, that it carries complete conviction. When the child discovers that she and her mother will never have to return to the house of her miserly great-aunt, her reaction is a one sentence summary of the whole story. '"It is almost," I thought, "almost worth while to have been in that terrible house for the joy of the difference."'[11] The book is one of Louisa's first person narratives, related, like *The Carved Lions,* by an adult looking back on special events of her childhood, and written down for the benefit and at the request of her own children, now themselves grown-up. It is also one of her very best books.

Fairies Afield too, the four long fairy tales, stands comparison well

---

[10] MLM to Macmillan, 14, 18 and 28.1.1910.
[11] *The Story of a Year,* p. 167.

with her other fairy and fantasy tales. Louisa dedicated this last book 'To one who loves fairy stories, the Reverend John Cyril Howell.' In the letter telling Macmillan's she would probably want to add a dedication to this book, she described that dedication as 'very special and rather important.'[12] At the time *Fairies Afield* was published, the Rev. Howell, a man then in his late thirties, was vicar of St Mary's, Graham Street, Pimlico. This church, although not the nearest to 155, Sloane Street, was still within easy walking distance. The block of flats where Louisa and Olive lived lay between Wilbraham Place and Sloane Terrace, at the Sloane Square end of Sloane Street, and Graham Street links Eaton Terrace and Holbein Place, which runs into the south east corner of Sloane Square. It would have been quite easy for Louisa to attend St Mary's and it is clear that she became friendly with its vicar. Gwen Molesworth wrote that 'many of the clergy were among her friends' mentioning particularly a Father Maturin, who was the priest of the Roman Catholic church in Cadogan Street, an extension of Cadogan Terrace which runs into Sloane Street practically opposite number 155. She knew yet another clergyman who had lived nearby when she first moved to Sloane Street, this time a connection too. The Reverend Henry E. J. Bevan was the husband of Charlotte Molesworth (and thus Gwen Molesworth's brother-in law) and in 1902 he was living at number 141 Sloane Street, just opposite Louisa. Gwen remembered that Louisa had attended a course of divinity lectures he gave and had described them as 'witty, spiritual and learned.' The closest grand-daughter said that when she lived in Sloane Street, Louisa sometimes attended a nearby Scottish Presbyterian church but that she went more often to High Anglican services. Little trace has survived of Louisa's personal religious beliefs, but the following paragraph from a letter to Craik shows that they existed.

'Yes — I think that the line of demarcation between those who realise that this life is not all, & those who put away all such thoughts, is growing stronger. But I do not think that the former class is lessening — very much the contrary I trust & believe.'[13]

The first word indicates that this was part of an on-going discussion between her and Craik, even in an ostensibly business letter. It is clear also, that she belonged to the 'former class'. These were important matters to her.

---

[12] MLM to Macmillan, 4.3.1911.
[13] MLM to GLC, 22.2.[1888].

There is other evidence too of her links with the Anglo-Catholic wing of the Anglican church — in one business letter she referred to 'my dear friend The Reverend Mother' as someone she wanted to receive a copy of her latest book. She also wrote, on request, a little address to children for Holy Innocents Day, not a subject readily compatible with the strict Calvinism of her childhood.[14] Again, the whole tone of her 1892 book, *Stories of the Saints for Children*, shows her sympathy with and interest in High Church beliefs and practice. She commented on the history of the early martyrs 'For through and by these very sacrifices did the Church take root and gather strength,' which is not the attitude of a Scots Presbyterian, and phrases such as 'our own branch of the Catholic Church' and 'those wonderful earliest days of Christianity' indicate where her loyalty now lay. It would have been difficult for any one in the late nineteenth century to relate some of the legends of the early saints and martyrs without admitting that many of them are pure fiction. But while Louisa was careful to talk of legends, to say 'we do not know,' 'it is believed,' 'all that is sure is,' and to explain some of the more extreme tales, such as St George and the dragon, as allegories, she was positive and almost affectionate in her attitude. A good example is her remark about St Cecilia.

> 'Not very much is known of her as certain fact, but through all the legends that have gathered round her sweet name, many of them very charming, some of them almost as fanciful as fairy tales, enough can be gathered to give us a just idea of her true history.'

She betrayed a particular affection for St Cecilia in the phrase 'or, as we love to call her in our English tongue, S. Cicely,' an affection probably arising from the fact that St Cecilia was her eldest living daughter's name-saint.[15]

Although *Fairies Afield* really was Louisa's last new book, she continued to take an interest in new issues and editions of her stories and to read and criticise mss for Macmillan's. The firm regularly sent her new novels for her own pleasure, and sent copies of her books on her behalf and at her request to charitable appeals and sales. Most of her correspondence with Macmillan's now was about such topics and usually sent to George Macmillan. For instance, just at the time that *Fairies Afield* appeared, he asked her permission to include abridged

---

[14] MLM to GLC, 28.10.1902; 3 letters to J. F. Bullock, Bodleian.
[15] *Stories of the Saints*, pp. 2, 231 and 40.

versions of some of her books in their new series, *The Children's Classics*. She was quite happy about this, as long as she did not have to work on the abridgements herself and was paid in advance. The latter proviso was explained by her wish to have all business arrangements completed as quickly as possible, leaving nothing pending to cause problems at her death. She did not mind saying quite openly 'I am old and in somewhat uncertain health.' As to whether such abridgements might interfere with the sale of her regular books and how much she should be paid, she relied on Mr Macmillan's judgement. Despite her efforts, previously described, to get them to pay her more from time to time, she did feel the firm had always been fair to her.

> 'I think', she told George Macmillan, 'you & all the members of your firm realize that from the very first of my connection with it, now so many years ago, I have always thoroughly trusted your regard for my interests as well as for your own, in respect of equitable payment'

— a tribute that any publisher might be proud of. The sum agreed was £10 for each abridgement.[16]

At this point a friendship should be mentioned which had clearly stretched over many years, but of which the only remaining evidence is a letter from this year, 1911. It was addressed to Elizabeth Haldane, who was distinguished both as an author and for her public work, the first woman to receive the honorary degree of LL.D. from St Andrews University (in 1911) and the first to be made a J.P. in Scotland. The three columns about her in the DNB detail her eminence further. Louisa was writing to thank Elizabeth for her help. It is clear from the tone and details of the letter that this was more than mere acquaintance.

> My dear Elizabeth,
>
> I must send you one word of heartiest thanks for your most kind intervention on the Riley boy's behalf.
>
> It was more than good of Lord Haldane to take the trouble he did, & his information & advice have been of the greatest assistance. I must say that it seems to me that the position was very much less "tragic" than was represented to us, but Athelstan Riley is absolutely an ignoramus as regards army matters. Then again there are side issues which you will sympathise in, as making Olive and me more anxious to help. I fear that the boy's mother has but a few weeks to live, & the satisfaction of

---

[16] MLM to Macmillan, 24.10.1911.

knowing that everything that could be done in the matter <u>has</u> been done, is greatly cheering her.

I cannot say how much we think of you just now, with the feeling upon you of almost needing to be in two — or more — places at once! I do trust dear Mrs Haldane feels peaceful & restful. It is very nice that you have such a thoroughly good nurse, & one that she likes.

When you are up here again I should like you to see our twins. Olive & I are rather silly about them! They are so sweet & so pretty & <u>very</u> well endowed with brains too. Cicely was asking about you the other day, & sympathising about your mother — I am so glad you think my fairy stories attractive. I am pretty sure that this is my <u>last</u> book.

With best love & repeated thanks

Ever your affectionate Louisa Molesworth[17]

'The Riley boy' was one of the five sons of Athelstan Riley and Andalusia Molesworth, the eldest child of the 8th Viscount. It is not clear which son was involved, but since Louisa was particularly interested, it might have been her godson, Laurence to whom she dedicated *Greyling Towers* when he was ten. He was now twenty-three and, as implied by Louisa's letter, must have got into some mess in the army out of which Lord Haldane helped to pull him. Viscount Haldane was Elizabeth Haldane's elder brother, at this time Secretary of State for War and much involved in the legislation for army reform. The following year he became Lord Chancellor. Louisa was instrumental, or partly so, in focussing a very big gun indeed on the Riley boy's problem, whatever it was. His mother, Andalusia, did, as expected, die very soon, in February of the following year. Mrs Haldane was Elizabeth's 86 year old mother, who, at such an age, might well need a nurse, and yet she lived to be 100. The twins, Venetia and Mary, Cicely's children, were now seventeen, and although it sounds as though Elizabeth had never met them, she obviously knew their mother.

One of Elizabeth's two other brothers, Sir William Haldane, when asked about Louisa in 1938, remembered both her and her daughters well, and their staying at Cloan, Auchterarder in Perth, the Haldane family home. He described Louisa as an extremely pleasant lady. When Louisa mentioned visits to Scotland in her letters to Craik or the Macmillans, she would have meant not only her own family and the Patons, but the Haldanes as well. Lady Haldane said that Louisa was a very

---

[17] MLM to E. Haldane, 12.11.1911, National Library of Scotland, MS 6023/58–9.

great friend of her mother's, Mrs Nelson, the wife of the publisher. The publisher referred to was probably Thomas Nelson, 1822–1892, whose wife, Jessie Kemp, came from Manchester, but unfortunately nothing further has been found relating to this friendship.[18]

Since Louisa's links with an eminent family have just been described, this would seem as suitable a place as any for mention of that very sensitive subject — snobbishness and class-prejudice. Louisa has often been accused of snobbishness, but before we can decide, or even discuss, whether she was snobbish or not, we need some working definition of the word. People can get confused and think that writing *about* snobbishness *is* snobbish. Certainly discussions on the subject do not always produce a clear statement of what the participants mean by snobbishness. In *Hathercourt Rectory*, Louisa seems to think it is snobbish when well-educated and well-born people are despised and ostracised because they are poor, thus implying that snobbery means estimating people's value by their wealth alone. And this theme of course occurs in all sorts of fiction — school stories, popular romance *and* Bronte and Austen (Jane Eyre and Fanny Price, for example). But this is surely only one aspect of the subject. Charlotte Yonge gives a better, because broader, definition in her description of a character thought to be snobbish — 'she was understood to be unduly bent on county and titled society, and to be exclusive towards inferiors.'[19] This matches up with the OED definition of a snob as 'one whose ideas and conduct are prompted by a vulgar admiration for wealth or social position,' which also implies the opposite of admiration for the absence of those two qualities.

The only published accusation of snobbishness in Louisa's personal life, as opposed to her writing, occurs in Marghanita Laski's *Mrs Ewing, Mrs Molesworth and Mrs Hodgson Burnett*. Apart from the first edition of R. L. Green's *Tellers of Tales* (1946), which contained the barest minimum of biographical facts and no character assessment, this was the first piece of writing about Louisa in modern times — that is, since the Second World War. As such, it may have carried a disproportionate weight, particularly as no biography has since appeared to give a broader picture. Unfortunately it presents her as 'not herself a very likeable personality' — a judgement based on a single anecdote from her youngest grandchild, Lionel's second son Hender Delves, who was 14 when she died. This anecdote turns specifically on snobbishness. Delves took

---

[18] Letter from Haldane's secretary to RR, 6.5.1938.
[19] *Modern Broods*, Macmillan, 1900 p. 78.

a school-friend to have lunch with his grandmother, who, on learning that the friend was a doctor's son, is supposed to have said "Is it really necessary to be friendly with doctor's children?" The story is not consistent with her life, for, as was related in the account of her years in Edinburgh, the Molesworths were friendly there with their family doctor and his wife and children. It is also possible that the grandson's memory was not very reliable, for he told Laski that he remembered his grandfather 'as a charming old man who occasionally presented expensive boxes of chocolates from Fortnum and Mason.' But Richard died in 1900 and Delves was not born until 1907. Nor did he know or remember enough about his grandmother's life to correct mistakes such as Laski's statement 'Her childhood was spent in High Leigh [sic] in Cheshire.' As we saw, Louisa was in fact brought up in Manchester, and her parents did not move to High Legh until after she was married. Delves' knowledge of his great-aunts and uncles was clearly sketchy, for Laski was only able to say that Louisa 'had at least one sister'. She also asserted that Louisa divorced Richard, which was not so, and that when they got engaged he was heir to Viscount Molesworth, which was not true either.[20] We may therefore fairly doubt the accuracy of the story showing Louisa looking down on a doctor's son.

But Gillian Avery, in *Nineteenth Century Children*, charges Louisa with snobbishness in her stories. 'With tremendous pleasure Mrs Molesworth snubs the vulgar, sometimes using methods almost as vulgar herself.'[21] This is a comment on *Mary*, which to my mind involves an actual misreading of the text. The four-year-old heroine, waiting in a confectioner's shop for her mother, who has just gone back to a previous shop to retrieve her purse, is so frightened by a boy who is rude to her that she runs away. The boy's mother only laughs and shows no concern until the shopwoman tells her that the child is 'little Miss Bertram of the Priory.' Avery does not mention that, when the woman apologises by declaring 'if they had only known who the young lady was, they would never have made so free as to disturb her' Mary's mother says 'I think you should teach your son to be gentle and polite to everybody, especially little girls, *whoever they are*.' The last three words of this speech are italicised in the story. There *is* snobbishness here, but on the part of the shopwoman and the boy's mother, whose attitude well illustrates the OED definition — 'vulgar admiration of . . . social position,' and

---

[20] Laski, pp. 58, 56, 57.
[21] Avery (1965), p. 201.

the author does not approve of it. Nowadays we would be more likely to disapprove of the fact that the mother left the child at all, and echo the child's appeal '"please, mamma, let me *always* stay 'aside you when we go to shops."'[22] But in those days, in a country village, people did not dream of such a thing as danger to a child among the local inhabitants who mostly all knew each other.

It seems to me that, far from illustrating Avery's accusation of vulgarity, this episode supports a statement made by Margery Fisher, that Louisa was a liberal-minded author who 'accepted the structure of society of her time, but . . . was sensitive in the way she presented it in her books.'[23] The illustration Fisher was herself commenting on here, comes from *A Christmas Child* and shows an uneasy consciousness in Ted, the hero, of the difficult relationship between employers and servants. At family prayers 'it gave him somehow a little uncomfortable feeling to see the servants quite by themselves, as it were, so separated from the family, and he had got into the way of sitting between the two sets of seats.'[24]

Avery also criticises Louisa for

> 'constantly creating situations where dishevelled children of gentle parents are at first taken by servants for 'poor children'. The servants, brusque and unmannerly at first, soon change their tune when they hear the children's 'pure accents'.'[25]

There are indeed several incidents of this kind throughout Louisa's books, from *Carrots* (1876) to *Peterkin* (1902). The relevant episode in *Carrots* shows Floss and Carrots arriving at their aunt's house, looking such 'a dilapidated little couple' that the manservant who opens the door thinks they are poor children sent with a message and does not associate then with the 'young lady and gentleman . . . expected on a visit.' In *Peterkin*, Giles, the narrator, calling at a strange house in London with his brother and another child, is afraid that the parlourmaid answering the door will think they are beggars, because they 'looked a funny lot.' In the first instance the children are recognised through Carrots' courage and trust in making a clear statement of their identity to their cousin Sybil, but Giles certainly attributes his civil reception to

---

[22] *Mary*, p. 125.
[23] Margery Fisher, 'Stories from a Victorian Nursery', *Signal 69*, Sep. 1992, p. 180.
[24] *Christmas Child*, p. 137.
[25] Avery (1965), p. 201.

his accent — 'I suppose my way of speaking made her see we were not beggars' — backed up by the fact that he had not arrived on foot — 'perhaps she caught sight of the four-wheeler, looming faintly through the fog.' However, I would dispute the interpretation that, in this kind of incident, Louisa is just conveying 'without shame, the innate snobbery of children.' It seems to me that there are two ways of reading these events, one literary and one social. It is part of human nature to take pleasure in being proved right after all and this feeling appears in litera-ture in the recognition scene. Heroes and heroines in all kinds of writing — spy thrillers, crime stories, novels, — are often presented at a disad-vantage and mocked or ignored or imprisoned, only to be justified by the appearance of an authority figure who supports them, or through the gradual manifestation of their own ability and virtue or credentials. This is what happens in *The Boys and I*, a further example of the dishevelled children mistaken for beggars type of episode. At first the children, also calling at a strange house in London, are told roughly by a manservant to 'get off the steps . . . My lady can't have beggars loitering about.' Then, attracted by the disturbance, a lady comes to the door who recognises the children and invites them in, saying ' "I know who you are — I remember. Come in — come in out of the cold, and tell me all about it." ' Finally Louisa makes the narrator comment on the discomfiture of the manservant. 'James, who had become particularly meek — I suppose he was rather ashamed of having taken us for little beggars, now that he saw the young lady knew us — did as she told him.'[26]

Children would see as little (or as much) snobbery in 'The Princess and the Pea' or the princess unrecognised in the guise of a dirty kitchen-maid[27] as in *Little Miss Peggy*, where the heroine, who had run away and 'looked miserable enough with her torn clothes, and scratched and tear-stained face' was rescued by someone who saw 'in a moment that she was a little lady.'[28] The whole point of 'The Princess and the Pea' is the recognition of the heroine's high rank because of her incredibly sensitive skin. It was discovered that Cinderella was the right bride for the prince because her feet were small enough to fit the glass slippers.

---

[26] *The Boys and I*, pp. 179–182.
[27] For example, 'Donkey Skin' in *The Grey Fairy Book*, 'The Many-Furred Creature' in *The Green Fairy Book*, both edited by Andrew Lang, 'Allerleirauh' from Grimm's Fairy Tales and many other versions.
[28] *Little Miss Peggy*, p. 182.

White, tender skin, small hands and feet, 'pure accents', beauty, were all traditionally marks of the aristocrat and of royalty and as such were unashamedly the stock-in-trade of fairy tales. The discovery episodes in Louisa's books which Avery condemns as snobbish can be read as fairy-tale recognition scenes.

Of course that is not the whole story. There is the social interpretation too, which does not exclude, but can be used alongside the literary one. In real life the relationship between children and servants was very complex and Louisa not only experienced it herself, as child and adult, but also wrote about it with understanding. Servants were in a position of authority over children both because they were specifically given this position by the parents and because they too were adults. But children were superior to servants because they would one day become fully paid-up members of the middle or upper class, and employ servants themselves. This dual role could give rise to tension and uncertainty. In the happiest circumstances, the relationship could be loving and fruitful, and Louisa illustrated this, for instance, when describing the old nurse in *Carrots* and *The February Boys* who was loved and trusted by two generations of children. But she knew that servants could be spiteful or neglectful, standing on their own dignity and domineering over the children in their charge, and children could be disobedient, rude and downright tormenting. Usually she showed only one side behaving badly at a time, as for instance in *Rosy*, where the 'self-willed and queer-tempered' heroine is treated patiently and kindly in her sulks and tantrums by the good-humoured nurse. The opposite situation occurs in *The February Boys*, where the butler loses both his temper and his dignity when the children's attempt to get catalogues for making scrap-books results in an avalanche of mail and the unexpected visit of three travelling salesmen. It is not just chance that the example of the unkind servant is not a nurse. Louisa showed very few unpleasant nurses, and those she did present were marginal — heedless and deceitful nurse-maids, soon dismissed, or older ones who were set in their ways and past their work. Presumably she did not want to alarm and frighten her young readers by suggesting that having an unkind nurse was such a common event, it might happen to them.

Victorian employers thought of and treated servants and children as, in many ways, belonging to the same class. They spent most of their time in separate quarters — the children in nurseries at the top of the house, and the servants behind the green baize door. Both groups were supposed to be seen and not heard, and, as one employer put it, showing clearly that she thought of them as in some sense the same, 'Servants, as well as children, require to be managed with *kindness* and *firmness*.'[29] All this underlay those episodes in Louisa's books where servants mistook dishevelled children for beggars. Each group naturally wished to justify itself in the eyes of adult authority as against the other group. In such episodes Louisa has combined the literary pleasure of a recognition scene with the social reality of the relationship between children and servants. But it should be added that in the three incidents described, as in other, similar ones, not mentioned, the overriding pressure of the narrative is to get the children on the doorstep inside to warmth and safety, away from the cold, hunger and fear of being lost that they are experiencing outside. The servant-child relationship is secondary.

Quite a lot of good sense and justice on the snobbery/class question emerges from Louisa's adult novels and books for teenage girls. For instance, in her second triple decker, *She Was Young and He Was Old*, she made the comment 'wrong, however, as all must be who persist in the absurd attempt to define vulgarity or refinement as a distinction common to the class, instead of a characteristic peculiar to the individual.' *Hathercourt Rectory* has several references to 'contemptible class-prejudice.' The heroine scorned the hero for having, as she believed, tried to separate her sister from the man who loved her simply because they came from different classes. Later she condemned herself for indulging in 'a kind of class-prejudice' because she saw she had come to assume that 'people who were different from us externally — people who had fewer struggles and more luxuries than my parents — must of necessity be narrow-minded and self-absorbed and unsympathising.' [30]

Louisa's presentation of snobbishness in *Blanche* well illustrates the OED definition. This book explores the subject of class distinctions, showing right and wrong ways of reacting to them. Their existence is taken for granted and only the vicar's wife is allowed to pay no heed to them. Even this amount of liberty is disapproved of by one particularly starchy character, who remarks 'But the vicar's wife, you know, Sir Adam, doesn't count in that way. It's her role, or she thinks it is, to ignore all class distinctions.'[31] The narrative turns on the discomfort of a family that finds itself uneasily placed in a new neighbourhood between two classes, neither of which understands clearly the family's true social

---

[29] Pamela Horn, *The Rise and Fall of the Victorian Servant*, 1986, p. 129.

[30] *Hathercourt Rectory*, pp. 214 and 217.

[31] *Blanche*, p. 327.

position. The events that precipitate this situation are perfectly plausible, given the social structure of the time. Hardly anyone now could read this novel with much sympathy, simply because that structure and the assumptions that went with it have gone, and we can hardly bear to consider the details about 'tone' and not falling into a lower social position that were so important then. Gillian Avery made an aside very relevant to this point in *Nineteenth Century Children* — '(for we are now so very squeamish where class is concerned).' But since that is the way things were, it is interesting to see what Louisa offers as the right attitude to take up. Blanche is the heroine with whom the reader is expected to identify, and Louisa makes her declare that internal qualities are independent of class. In talking of a titled woman who has been rude, overbearing and patronising to her and her family, Blanche says 'She would be a common-minded, inferior woman in *any* class. . . . I believe that is the truth of it all: there are refined and charming natures to be found in every class, and there are the opposite.' But, as with her attitude to the problems of poverty, described in Chapter 11, Louisa was not revolutionary about class. She accepted the existing situation. And so, when the more excitable younger sister reacts to Blanche's declaration that there were charming people in every class with the suggestion that they should hunt up a few of these in the class below their own, Blanche calmly replies 'It is one's duty to live in one's own class unless one is plainly shown it is necessary to leave it.'[32]

In this discussion, there is a relevant point to be made about Dickens. No-one appears to condemn him as snobbish for his horror at associating with those beneath him in the blacking factory where he had to work at the age of twelve, because of his father's imprisonment for debt. 'Again and again he emphasises the "degradation" involved in his companionship with these working class boys. They were "common men and boys", "common companions", to be associated with whom was "shame" and "humiliation".'[33] Orwell, however, does point out that in *Great Expectations*, Dickens identifies with Pip's attitude to Magwitch which is at bottom snobbish, and he makes that marvellous comment about David Copperfield, 'it is the thought of the pure Agnes in bed with a man who drops his aitches that really revolts Dickens.'[34] But one does not sense here the kind of blame that Laski, Avery and others seem

---

[32] Avery, (1965), p. 189; *Blanche*, p. 118.
[33] Ackroyd, p. 77.
[34] Orwell, pp. 477 and 481.

to attach to Louisa simply for being middle-class herself and writing about what she knows. It would have been very extraordinary if she had *not* included the nannies and servants, the contrast between middle and lower class in clothing and accent, the consciousness of 'gentlemen's children' and 'poor children' which were part of the very structure of the society in which she lived.

Orwell makes one comment about Dickens which applies very well to Louisa.

> 'However much Dickens may admire the working classes he does not wish to resemble them . . . Dickens is quite genuinely on the side of the poor against the rich, but it would be next-door to impossible for him not to think of a working-class exterior as a stigma.'

Surely this comment describes all the shrinking from 'vulgar accents' and anything 'which Mamma could possibly have disliked,'[35] that in so many nineteenth century people, writers or not, is accompanied, to us paradoxically, by a real concern and active work for the disadvantaged, and a consciousness of their worth. In her stories Louisa showed that she well understood and sympathised with the situation of poor people, even portraying their justifiable bitterness, as in the following example. Two poor children are discussing a rich family who, by their failure to return, have involved their own family in expense. One child tries to excuse them by supposing someone is ill. The older child responds cynically.

> ' "Dead perhaps," said Selma with a sort of bitterness in her tone. "No, that is not likely. When rich people are ill they have doctors and plenty of medicine, and good food and warm fires, to make them well again." '[36]

This speech has a special bite to it because the children's own father has been ill throughout the winter without any of the things Selma mentions. This kind of sympathy did not prevent Louisa from being, in her personal life, 'decorous and correct,' and 'hating vulgarity,' as her grand-daughter described her.

It has often been said that Louisa's books and others like them in content, portraying a middle-class milieu with nannies, servants and so forth, cannot be re-published now because they are out of date and children would not be able to identify with such surroundings. But

---

[35] Orwell, p. 478; *The Carved Lions*, p. 188.
[36] *Summer Stories*, p. 236.

these comments seem to have a very disapproving tone — in some sense, it is implied, nannies are wrong and we are virtuous in abstaining from them. But we indulge in *au pairs*, and all the domestic technology we can afford, a situation clearly reflected in contemporary writing for children. Because I have a washing machine and therefore do not need a washerwoman, does that make me better than a nineteenth century employer of domestic labour? If I had lived then, I would certainly have employed a washerwoman if I could have afforded one. Fisher, in the article quoted above, asks whether

'in today's tales for the middle years, . . . the sometimes cringing self-consciousness about ethnic minorities, the finicking inverted snobbery sensed in many descriptions of school classroom alliances or streets of terraced houses [is] any more acceptable than the confident use of the hierarchy of classes'

that we seem to disapprove of so much in the books of Louisa and her contemporaries.[37] Naomi Lewis has a very telling paragraph addressing this point in her preface to *Twentieth-Century Children's Writers*. 'Publishers and librarians' she says, 'are known to pause doubtfully at this or that text, murmuring the unlucky verdict: "too middle-class."' But if this is restrictive, she continues, the opposite can also be so. 'To present life only in terms of council houses and supermarkets, is to shut the child, mentally speaking, in a viewless if conventionally furnished cell.'[38]

If we think of snobbishness and class-prejudice as a clear recognition of class boundaries in one's own contemporary social structure, defined by differing habits of speech, style of dress and personal behaviour, a decision to remain within them and to describe them as they exist, then Louisa was snobbish. If, however, we see it as making up to those who derive power from their wealth and social position, and despising those whose poverty and lower rank make them comparatively powerless, then she was not.

As she grew older, Louisa had got into the habit of spending September with Olive in one of the watering places on the south coast — Bournemouth, or Eastbourne, or Folkestone. They were in Folkestone just after the outbreak of the First World War and stayed on to try to help. When

---

[37] Fisher, p. 180.
[38] Naomi Lewis, in *Twentieth-Century Children's Writers*, ed. Tracy Chevalier, St James Press, 1989, p. ix.

writing to George Macmillan at the end of October, Louisa said 'We were at Folkestone for many weeks, seeing & hearing many sad (& even horrible things) — & glad to do anything we could.' She shared the feelings of most people as the awful nature of this war became apparent — 'I suppose the war is going well, but at what a cost! One dreads to open the papers.' Many of her own family were fighting — 'I have three very dear nephews at the front — & ever so many less close to us — one grand-nephew of only 19 — over a dozen at least in all!'[39] The three nephews were the sons of her sister Caroline, and the grand-nephew would have been her brother Charles' grandson, Godfrey Stewart, whose father Noel was a soldier too. Her own son, Lionel, was 41 at the outbreak of war and also ill, so he could not have been called up.

Louisa continued to live in Sloane Street throughout the war and her contribution to the war effort was to help with making hospital supplies. There is an eyewitness account of her at this time, offering

'a picture in my memories of the war years: It is that of a charming, quiet little old lady seated at a table busily occupied in one of the rooms at the late Lady Sclater's War Hospital Supplies Depot in Pont Street. She was making dressings and pneumonia jackets for the wounded. I was told she was Mrs Molesworth, and looked at her with reverence and admiration that she should, at her age, come and work so regularly; and with gratitude for the lovely books she had written for children. If I remember rightly she was accompanied by her daughter.'

Pont Street crosses Sloane Street almost exactly in the middle, three blocks from No. 155, so Louisa and Olive could have walked there quite easily. One of Louisa's letters to Macmillan's in 1916 with arrangements about times for a messenger to call, makes it clear that they were at the Depot daily between noon and seven in the evening.

In 1916 too, Macmillan's re-published Louisa's story of the French Revolution, as both she and they felt it was a suitable book for war-time. It was first published by the SPCK in 1884 and had been out of print for many years. It was probably a letter from an admirer, asking about the book, which first gave Louisa the idea. For in her reply, suggesting that the woman should write direct to the SPCK herself, which might encourage them to bring the book out again, she said 'I think it would be very appropriate in these present stormy, revolutionary times.'[40] Only

---

[39] MLM to Macmillan, 31.10.1914.
[40] MLM to unnamed correspondent, 3.7.1915. Privately owned.

after the Society had replied to Louisa's own request, saying that they did not see their way to re-issuing *The Little Old Portrait*, did Louisa suggest it to George Macmillan. She said she had received several enquiries about it. 'A good many of my younger friends who had it in their childhood ask me how to get it for their children.' She was pleased at the idea of a story which, when it first came out, 'was much liked,' being re-published by Macmillan's rather than the SPCK. 'I am not very sorry for their not doing it,' she wrote, 'as I never thought the cheap form in which it appeared quite did it justice.'[41]

The original edition was a thin little book in small print, and the illustrations, appearing only around the initial at the head of each chapter, were in delicate sepia tones, just tinted in places with green. My own copy is bound in a pale green cloth, and though this was probably once brighter, the whole book has a reticent air that explains Louisa's feeling. Macmillan's version, with larger print and thicker paper, and eight full page illustrations by Gertrude Demain Hammond, was bound to match Louisa's last three books, in blue cloth with the same geometric design, but in black, not gold. It gives an altogether more substantial impression and Louisa was pleased — 'The story shows to great advantage in its new dress, & the illustrations are charming.'[42] She had offered to lend the original portrait, on which the story was based, to be photographed for the illustrations, but it does not appear that this was done.[43] When it came to providing the text from which the new edition could be printed, neither the SPCK nor Louisa herself had a copy, and eventually she got hold of one from her sister Caroline. The new title, *Edmée: A Tale of the French Revolution*, was Louisa's own suggestion and she also offered to (and did) correct the proofs, saying 'I should be glad . . . to feel that I have done them myself.' So she was still taking a great interest in the production details of her books, although again remarking 'At my age life becomes a very uncertain forecast.'[44]

She might also have commented on the extra uncertainty of life in wartime. When she first offered *The Little Old Portrait* to Macmillan's in October 1915, she and Olive were in Folkestone again. 'We have had Zeppelin raids very close at hand —' she wrote, 'I don't think one place is any safer than another!' Most people had somebody at the front

---

[41] MLM to Macmillan, 18.10.1915.
[42] MLM to Macmillan, 3.10.1916.
[43] See the end of chapter 8 for Louisa's purchase of this portrait.
[44] MLM to Macmillan, 30.10.1915.

to worry about, though she hoped George Macmillan had escaped the worst of this.

> 'I trust you are not in any closely acute anxiety in connection with this awful war — Like almost everyone we have several very near & dear to us in France, or worse, at the Dardanelles — & some whom we shall never see again.'

His reply, expressing an interest in the book, clearly also gave news of personal bereavement, for she responded

> 'I am indeed grieved to hear that you have suffered so terribly in your family circle through this horrible war — Our own anxieties at the present moment are principally centred in the Dardanelles — We must all sympathise beyond expression with each other, & I think we all <u>do</u>.'[45]

Anyone who had friends or relations involved in the disastrous Dardanelles campaign certainly had reason to be worried.

But the bereavement Louisa did suffer was not because of the war. Her second son, Lionel, died on 23rd December, 1916, after a protracted illness. It was, she told George Macmillan, 'a <u>very grievous sorrow</u>, almost an inexpressible one.' She had not realised how seriously ill he was, and now she felt great concern for the financial situation of his widow and children.

> 'He had been ill for over two years, hopelessly so, I now see, yet the shock seems sudden when the end does come. He was obliged to give up his excellent post, or posts, more than a year ago, a terrible disappointment to him, & anxiety as he leaves three children, a daughter of 19 & two dear boys just growing up. You may remember that he married very young & was only 43 when he died — I am thankful to know that he did not suffer acutely, & he quite realised his condition & met death bravely & resignedly — It cannot but add to my own responsibilities & cares, as I cannot but wish to do all I can for my daughter-in-law & the children.'

Her immediate reaction to the family's needs was to ask if she could not be paid more for *Edmée*, as it seemed to have been a success 'if one can judge by the very numerous & favourable reviews of it,' and to offer Macmillan's some of her other out-of-print SPCK books. Neither of these efforts bore fruit, and she resignedly attributed *Edmée's* lack of

---

[45] MLM to Macmillan, 18 and 23.10.1915.

financial success 'to these terrible war times.' The war had, for her as for so many others, a decidedly adverse effect on her income, something she commented on several times. 'I am of course quite aware that the great drop in my Royalties is accounted for, like many other losses, by this terrible war & its results — disastrous taxation &c.' It was not only her royalties that had fallen — 'the present upheaval of everything is <u>very</u> seriously affecting my income,' which would have included interest on investments.[46]

Even war cannot prevent happiness from breaking in occasionally, and a few months after Lionel's death Louisa's closest grand-daughter, Venetia Prinsep, now Mrs Inglefield, gave birth to a great-grand-daughter, Verity. One of the few surviving family letters, written to a child in Edinburgh, mentions the baby with great interest. It was Louisa's habit to give copies of her books to all her young relatives at Christmas and for birthdays, and this letter, quoted below, begins with enquiries about which books the young recipient would like.

November 9 1917

My dear Jean,

Though I have no <u>new</u> books of mine to send you, as I have quite left off writing, I would still like you & Bell to have one at Christmas to remind you of your old Great Auntie. So will you look over the list which I think you will find at the end of "Edmée", & tell me the name, or names, of any you have <u>not</u> had, or would like. Have you had "Fairies Afield" or "Fairies of Sorts"? They are the most recent of my fairy tales. I don't know if you & Bell like fairy stories or real ones best?

Tell your Granny and Mummy that Olive keeps better, I am glad to say, & we both are working again daily at our Depôt, where the need of workers is very great. Also they will like to hear that my little <u>great</u>-grand-daughter "Verity Inglefield" is very well indeed, & her mother says "gets pink with her valiant efforts to <u>speak</u>." She is 8 months old. The sad thing is that her father is still in hospital, very little, if any, better. She and her mother are still in the Isle of Wight with Mary Prinsep, now the head of the Tennyson hospital.

Give my "much love" with Olive's to everybody.

Your loving Great Aunt Louisa

We have had some terrifying raids <u>quite</u> close to us, but we are not nervous. Still it is not pleasant to be up at night for hours. It will interest

---

[46] MLM to Macmillan, 27.1.1917; 30.10.1915.

your grandfather to hear that the Head of the London Aircraft Defence has just taken the very top flat of this house. General Ashmore.[47]

Jean's Granny was the Minnie Wilson Morgan who had been married in 1875 from Louisa's home in Conwy, North Wales, and had been so much a part of her family that Charles Augustus referred to her in his will as 'like a daughter.' Minnie was herself the grand-daughter of Louisa's aunt, her mother's sister Mary Miller, *née* Wilson. So thirteen year old Jean and her sister Bell were not really Louisa's great-nieces, but more distant relations — in fact first cousins three times removed. Mary Prinsep, who was distinguishing herself in the nursing field, was the twin-sister of Venetia. Though no other correspondence with this branch of the family survives, we can see from the kind of detailed news Louisa was giving, that she kept in close touch with them.

At this period air-raids were quite frequent. Louisa mentioned them again in a letter to Macmillan's early in December.

'We had another raid last night or early this morning, as of course you know, but so far we have heard no particulars — The officer in command of the London gun defences, has just come to live in the <u>top</u> floor of these flats. He must have been up all night!'[48]

Throughout the war too, Louisa continued to take an interest in various East End parishes and to help them by sending signed copies of her books to their sales. She was particularly inclined to help one such very poor parish because both the vicar's children were specially involved in the war — 'his son has done (& suffered) gallantly at the Front, & a daughter is a devoted nurse in France.'[49] So her attitude to the war was the traditional one, that although it was awful and terrible, one's duty was to contribute as best one could.

Louisa only lived for a few more years after the war was over, but she kept up to the end an interest in her books and possible new ways of bringing them before the public. In 1919 Chambers responded to her simple request for a copy of *The February Boys* with enough interest to induce her to look round for more of her out-of-print titles for them. They wanted children's stories, not adult or teenage novels, so they refused *The Laurel Walk*, but accepted two out of three books she had first published with Longmans. She wrote to this firm herself, asking

[47] Privately owned. I am grateful to Fiona Bickersteth for allowing me to copy this letter.
[48] MLM to Macmillan, 7.12.1917.
[49] MLM to Macmillan, 4.11.1918.

that the rights of these three, in which Longmans were obviously no longer interested, should be made over to her. Chambers' representative read *The Palace in the Garden* and *The Story of A Spring Morning* with much pleasure, saying that the books appealed to them greatly, and offering her £50 for the two. But the third book, *Silverthorns*, was refused for an interesting historical reason. They felt that it would not be acceptable because more time was needed before the public would countenance stories involving German lessons and German teachers. One of the mainsprings of the plot was the rivalry between two girls in a German class and their efforts to win a special end-of-term German prize for composition. The teacher too, was a native German with an unmistakably German name — Herr Märklestatter. The war was too recent for publishers to be able to approve of a positive presentation of such a theme. Louisa apparently offered to alter the story, for in a later letter Chambers said that if she did anything with the book, they would be glad to consider a different version. She would probably have substituted a French class, teacher and prize for the German ones, but illness intervened.[50]

Her last successful, documented business transaction concerned the publication of *Carrots* by G. Bell and Sons in their Queen's Treasures Series, with the delightful illustrations by M. V. Wheelhouse. When Macmillan's wrote to tell her of the offer, in February 1920, Louisa had to dictate her reply to her daughter because of illness. She was pleased at the proposal because 'it shows that "Carrots" still holds its own.' But she was particularly concerned to receive her share of the proceeds as soon as possible, not waiting for the actual publication which she was sure would be delayed 'as coloured illustrations always take time.' The expenses of her illness and the after-effects of the war had made her very worried over money matters, as she explained to George Macmillan.

'I have had a serious attack of bronchitis lately, affecting my heart. I am better now, but it has made me realize as never before (not even in the strain & sorrows of the war) my advanced age. And material life I am finding very difficult & not likely to improve much in my time. So I am grateful for any little addition to my income. I do hope you will not think me grasping or unreasonable.'

Mr Macmillan's reaction to this appeal was to endorse her letter with a note 'We will send the cheque and recover from Bell,' and to do so

---

50 Chambers to MLM, 25.2, 12, 17 and 30.5, 4, 6 and 11.6.1919. Chamber's Collection. MLM to Longmans, 13.5.1919, Publisher's archive, University of Reading, 62/143.

within a week. Louisa was most grateful for this act of kindness and said she was 'very glad' to have the money. She had calculated that in the normal course of things she would not have received it until January 1922, commenting that this was 'rather a long way ahead for me at eighty.' She was quite right, for by that date she had been dead for six months.[51]

A codicil to her will dated May 1920 confirms that her worries over expense were justifiable. It considerably reduces the amounts of two cash legacies 'owing to the great expenses incurred in my present illness' and in order to avoid realising any of her investments 'at their present low values' — a direct result of the war. Her solicitor would have advised her on this matter — it was not simply the excessive anxiety sometimes experienced by old people. The witnesses to this codicil were her niece, Venetia, who was presumably paying her a visit — she lived just nearby in Cadogan Place — and a trained nurse, which suggests the seriousness of this illness. The will itself had been made when she was staying with Juliet and her husband the previous year. Just before the war they had moved from Winkenhurst when Julian Ainslie had become manager (or perhaps owner) of the big water mill at Hellingly, near Eastbourne, and had taken up residence in The Old Mill House, Horsebridge, adjacent to the mill. It was a flour mill, and one of the witnesses to Louisa's will that August was William Wallace, who was described as a flour miller, living in Hailsham. A photograph of the mill workers taken about 1915, shows Juliet and Julian Ainslie, and also gives the name of one of the workers as Wallace. The other witness, Mary Ann Noble, kept the village shop, Central Stores, Horsebridge, which was just opposite the mill. We may assume that two of the nearest available independent people were asked in to the Old Mill House as witnesses when her solicitor brought the completed will down from London.

A new venture was suggested to Louisa in 1920. She wrote to tell Macmillan's that her agent, Mr Colles of the Authors' Syndicate, 'proposes to "film" some of my stories. It is quite a new idea to me. It appears that there is a demand for cinemas [sic] suitable and desirable for children.' She was very pleased to agree to this proposal, particularly as Colles had told her that filming her stories might lead to increased sales of her books. George Macmillan responded generously and with great interest to this idea. He told Louisa she could regard all her Macmillan books as her own property for the purposes of filming whether in fact she or the firm actually owned the copyright. He also

---

[51] MLM to Macmillan, 13, 20 and 25.2.1920.

advised her to retain the copyright on any films made, a piece of advice she accepted whole-heartedly. It appears from her response that he thought filming her books might be quite a profitable venture for her. She wrote 'What you say makes me hope that some substantial benefit may come to me through this unexpected source.' She wrote at once to Colles with 'a complete list of all the books the Macmillans have published for me.' Reading through this list before sending it prompted her to add 'It is rather appalling to realize the number I have written! Considering that though my chief, the Macmillans are not my only publishers.' She probably did not realize that the number of her Macmillan titles — forty, including two collections of stories for adults and the French lesson book — was exceeded by the sixty-one shared out among her twenty other publishers. This project did not materialize during her lifetime. Her very last letter to George Macmillan in January 1921, enquiring about her royalty cheque in just the same handwriting as ever, has a rueful postscript: 'I have been meaning to tell you that so far nothing has come of Mr Colles's efforts as to my stories being "cinemated". I begin to think nothing will. I suppose they are not dramatic enough.'

Louisa died at her flat in Sloane Street of heart failure on Wednesday 20th July, 1921. A requiem mass, 'attended by many literary friends,' was held for her at Holy Trinity Sloane Street on 23rd July, and she was buried in Brompton Cemetery.

It was her youngest daughter, Olive, the closest to her, who inherited the copyrights of Louisa's books and continued to give permission for their re-issue over and over again. Macmillan's went on re-printing the most popular titles in the smaller formats bound in red with black and gold decoration, or blue with a diaper pattern, so familiar to collectors now. After World War II they published some facsimile editions, *Carrots* for instance, in 1957 and *Christmas-Tree Land* in 1981. Other firms too felt that Mrs Molesworth was a name worth having in their lists, and Dent included *The Cuckoo Clock* (1954) and *The Carved Lions* (1964) in their Children's Illustrated Classics Series, while *My New Home* appeared in the Gollancz revival series in 1968. The Faith Press and the Harvill Press also brought out some titles, including *The Ruby Ring* and *The Tapestry Room*. But *Carrots* and *The Cuckoo Clock* have always been the ones most re-issued. The latter book was a Puffin classic in 1988.[52] It was also produced by Macmillan's in a beautiful new

---

[52] Jane Nissen Books is re-publishing it in September 2002.

edition in 1931 with illustrations by C. E. Brock. The reviewer in the Christmas number of *The Bookman* was very enthusiastic and his words make a fitting final comment on Louisa's working life. 'There is a new generation always ready for Mrs Molesworth's stories, and there could be no more attractive edition of the story of Griselda and her cuckoo than this one ... It has always, we think, fallen to Mrs Molesworth's lot to be interpreted by sympathetic artists and no-one could have done better for her than Mr C. E. Brock has done here ... this book ... was published first in 1877, but its charm has not faded and Griselda ... and her journeys with the cuckoo are here waiting to win and enthral fresh readers.'[53]

For a last opinion of her as a person, we should turn again to her friend Ranald Paton, whose father was also one of her greatest friends. 'Mrs Molesworth remained my friend for life,' he wrote. 'Believe me, her friendship was worth having. A lovely character, I have never met anyone to equal her.'

---

[53] *The Bookman*, Christmas No., Hodder and Stoughton, 1931, p 164.

LIST OF BOOKS AND ARTICLES BY
MRS MOLESWORTH

I believe this to be a complete list of Mrs Molesworth's books with dates of first publication only, but it does not include uncollected stories, nor the bibliographical details of first publication in periodicals. Articles listed are all those that have so far been traced. Items marked thus, *, have not been mentioned in the text.

A — CHILDREN'S BOOKS

A Christmas Child: A Sketch of A Boy-Life, Macmillan, 1880.
A Christmas Posy, Macmillan, 1888.
A House To Let, SPCK, 1889.
An Enchanted Garden: Fairy Stories, Unwin, 1892.
Carrots: Just A Little Boy, Macmillan, 1876.
Christmas-Tree Land, Macmillan, 1884.
Family Troubles, SPCK, 1890.
"Farthings": The Story of A Stray and A Waif, Wells, Gardner Darton and Co., [1892].
Fairies Afield, Macmillan, 1911.
Fairies — Of Sorts, Macmillan, 1908.
Five Minutes' Stories, SPCK, 1888.
Four Winds Farm, Macmillan, [1886], 1887.
French Life in Letters, Macmillan, 1889.
Friendly Joey, and Other Stories, SPCK, 1896.
'Grandmother Dear': A Book for Boys and Girls, Macmillan, 1878.
Great-Uncle Hoot-Toot, SPCK 1889.
Greyling Towers: A Story for the Young, Chambers, [1898].
Hermy: The Story of A Little Girl, Routledge, [1880] 1881.
Hoodie, Routledge, 1882.
Jasper: A Story for Children, Macmillan, 1906.
Little Miss Peggy: Only A Nursery Story, Macmillan 1887.
Little Mother Bunch, Cassell, 1890.
Mary: A Nursery Story for Very Little Children, Macmillan, 1893.
Miss Mouse and Her Boys, Macmillan, 1897.
My New Home, Macmillan, 1894.
'My-Pretty' and Her Little Brother 'Too' and Other Stories, Chambers 1901.
Nesta; or Fragments of A Little Life, Chambers, 1889.
Nurse Heatherdale's Story, Macmillan, 1891.
Opposite Neighbours and Other Stories, SPCK, 1895.
Peterkin, Macmillan, 1902.

Robin Redbreast, A Story for Girls, Chambers, 1892.

Rosy, Macmillan, 1882.

Sheila's Mystery, Macmillan 1895.

Silverthorns, Hatchards, 1887.

Stories for Children in Illustration of The Lord's Prayer, Wells, Gardner, Darton and Co.,1895.

Stories of the Saints for Children, Longmans, 1892.

Studies and Stories, A. D. Innes, 1893.

Summer Stories for Boys and Girls, Macmillan, 1882.

Sweet Content, Griffith Farran, 1891.

Tell Me A Story, Macmillan, 1875.

The Abbey by the Sea, SPCK, [1887].

The Adventures of Herr Baby, Macmillan, 1881.

The Blue Baby and Other Stories, Fisher Unwin, 1901.

The Boys and I: A Child's Story for Children, Routledge, 1882.

The Bolted Door and Other Stories, Chambers, 1906.

The Carved Lions, Macmillan, 1895.

The Children of the Castle, Macmillan, 1890.

The Children's Hour, Nelson, [1899].

The Cuckoo Clock, Macmillan, 1877.

The February Boys: A Story for Children, Chambers, 1909.

The Girls and I: A Veracious History, Macmillan, 1892.

The Green Casket and Other Stories, Chambers, [1890].

The House That Grew, Macmillan, 1900.

The Little Guest: A Story for Children, Macmillan, 1907.

The Little Old Portrait, SPCK, 1884.

The Lucky Ducks and Other Stories, SPCK, 1891.

The Man with the Pan-Pipes and Other Stories, SPCK, [1892].

The Magic Nuts, Macmillan, 1898.

The Mystery of the Pinewood and Hollow Tree House, Nister, 1903.

The Next-Door House, Chambers, 1893.

The Old Pincushion, or Aunt Clotilda's Guests, Griffith Farran, [1889].

The Oriel Window, Macmillan, 1896.

The Palace in the Garden, Hatchards, 1887.

The Rectory Children, Macmillan, 1889.

The Ruby Ring, Macmillan, 1904.

The Story of A Spring Morning, and Other Tales, Longmans, 1890.

The Story of A Year, Macmillan, 1910.

The Tapestry Room: A Child's Romance, Macmillan, 1879.

The Thirteen Little Black Pigs and Other Stories, SPCK, [1893].

The Three Witches, Chambers, 1900.

The Wood-Pigeons and Mary, Macmillan, 1901.

This and That: A Tale of Two Tinies, Macmillan, 1899.

Twelve Tiny Tales, SPCK, 1890.
Two Little Waifs, Macmillan, 1883.
"Us": An Old-fashioned Story, Macmillan, 1885.

B — ARTICLES

'A Cry from the Far West', *Macmillan's Magazine*, vol. LXVII, Dec. 1897, pp 125–130.

'A Ramble about Childhood', *The Girls' Own Annual* vol.20, Oct. 1898–Sep. 1899, Feb. 4 1899 pp 292–4.

'Coming Out', *Atalanta*, May 1890. Later collected in *Studies and Stories*, A. D. Innes, 1893.

'English Girlhood', *The English Illustrated Magazine*, Oct. 1890. Later collected in *Studies and Stories*.

'Fiction: Its Use and Abuse', *Girls' Own Paper*, May 1891. Later collected in *Studies and Stories*.

'How I Write My Children's Stories', *Little Folks*, 1894, p 16.

'Mrs Ewing's Less Well-Known Books' *The Contemporary Review*, 49, May 1886. Later collected in *Studies and Stories*.

'Mrs Molesworth on the Women's Christian Education League' *Newbery House Magazine*, vol. 10, Feb. 1894, pp 91–8.

'On the Art of Writing Fiction for Children', *Atalanta* VI, May 1893.

Prince's Meadows or Poverty Corner. Being a Short Account of the Royal Waterloo Hospital for Children and Women, [21-page pamphlet], 1907.

'Story-Reading and Story-Writing', *Chamber's Journal*, 75, 5.11.1898, p. 772–775.

'Story-Writing', *The Monthly Packet*, no. 522, vol. 88, Aug. 1894, pp. 158–165.

'The Best Books for Children II', *Pall Mall Gazette*, 29.10.1887.

C — ADULT NOVELS AND SHORT STORIES

Cicely: A Story of Three Years, Tinsley Brothers, 1874, 3 vols.
Four Ghost Stories, Macmillan, 1888.
Hathercourt Rectory, Hurst and Blackett, 1878, 3 vols.
Lover and Husband: A Novel, by Ennis Graham. Charles J. Skeet, [1869] 1870, 3 vols.
Miss Bouverie, Hurst and Blackett, 1880, 3 vols.
Not Without Thorns: A Story, by Ennis Graham. Tinsley, 1873, 3 vols.
She Was Young and He Was Old: A Novel. By the author of 'Lover and Husband', Tinsley Brothers, 1872, 3 vols.
That Girl in Black, and Bronzie, Chatto and Windus, 1889.
The Wrong Envelope and Other Stories, Macmillan, 1906.
Uncanny Tales, Hutchinson, 1896.

D — TEENAGE NOVELS AND STORIES

'One Sunday Morning', *The Monthly Packet*, 1, no. 1 [January 1851]. Later published in *Blanche*.

A Charge Fulfilled, SPCK, [1886].

Blanche: A Story for Girls, Chambers, [1893] 1894.

*Imogen, or Only Eighteen, Chambers, 1892.

*Leona, Cassell, 1892.

Lettice, SPCK, 1884.

Marrying and Giving in Marriage, Longmans, Green and Co., 1887.

Meg Langholme or The Day After Tomorrow, Chambers, 1897.

Neighbours, Hatchards, 1889.

*Olivia, A Story for Girls, Chambers, [1894], 1895.

Philippa, Chambers, [1896] 1897.

*The Bewitched Lamp, Chambers, [1891].

*The Grim House, Nisbet, 1899.

The Laurel Walk, Isbister, 1898.

*The Red Grange, Methuen, 1891.

The Third Miss St Quentin, Hatchards, [1888].

White Turrets, Chambers, [1895], 1896.

LIST OF BOOKS AND ARTICLES CONSULTED

A — BOOKS

A Pictorial and Descriptive Guide to Edinburgh, Ward, Lock and Co., 1907.

Ackroyd, Peter, *Dickens*, Sinclair Stevenson, 1990.

Adams, W. E., *Memoirs of a Social Atom*, 1903, 2 vols.

Ainslie, Douglas, *Adventures Social and Literary*, T. Fisher Unwin, 1922.

Allison, Ronald and Sarah Riddell, eds., *The Royal Encyclopedia*, Macmillan, 1991.

Altick, Richard, *The English Common Reader*, 1957.

Atkinson, C. J., *A History of the Royal Dragoons*.

Avery, Gillian, *Childhood's Pattern*, Hodder and Stoughton, 1975.

Avery, Gillian, *Nineteenth-Century Children*, Hodder and Stoughton, 1965.

Bainton, George, ed. *The Art of Authorship*, James Clarke and Co., 1890.

Battiscombe, Georgina, *Charlotte M. Yonge*, Constable, 1943.

Beveridge, David, *Between the Ochils and Forth*, Edinburgh: Wm. Blackwood and Sons, 1888.

Bishop, M. C., *A Memoir of Mrs Augustus Craven*, Richard Bentley, 1894, 2 vols.

Blunt, Wilfred Scawen. Ms diaries, quoted Fiona MacCarthy, *William Morris: A Life for Our Time*, Faber, 1994.

Bowerbank, John, *An Extract from a Journal Kept on Board HMS Bellerophon (from Saturday July 15, 1815 to Monday August 17 1815)*, London, Whittingham and Arliss, 1815.

Bratton, J. S., *The Impact of Victorian Fiction*, Croom Helm, 1981.

Briggs, Asa, *Victorian Cities*, Penguin, 1982.

Briggs, Julia, *A Woman of Passion*, Hutchinson 1987.

Brill, Barbara, *William Gaskell 1805–1884*, Manchester Literary and Philosophical Publications, 1984.

Burdett-Coutts, Angela, *Women's Mission: A Series of Congress Papers on the Philanthropic Work of Women by Eminent Writers*, arranged and edited with a Preface and notes by the Baroness Burdett-Coutts, Sampson Low, 1893.

Burnett, F.H., *The One I Knew the Best of All*, Frederick Warne, 1893.

Butts, Dennis, *Mistress of Our Tears: A Literary and Bibliographical Study of Barbara Hofland*, Scolar Press, 1992.

Carpenter, Humphrey, *Secret Gardens*, Allen and Unwin, 1985.

Carrington, Charles, *Rudyard Kipling: His Life and Work*, revised edition, Macmillan, 1978.

Catt, George R., *The Pictorial History of Manchester,* reprinted from 'The Pictorial Times, [1844].

Chalmers, Peter, *Historical and Statistical Account of Dunfermline*, 2 vols, 1844 and 1859.

Cherry, D., *Painting Women: Victorian Women Artists*, Routledge, 1993.

Chitty, Susan, *The Beast and the Monk: A Life of Charles Kingsley*, Hodder and Stoughton, 1974.

Chorley, Katharine, *Manchester Made Them*, Faber and Faber, 1950.

Cohen, Morton N. and Anita Gandolfo, eds., *Lewis Carroll and the House of Macmillan*, C.U.P., 1987.

Coleridge, Christabel, *Charlotte Mary Yonge*, Macmillan, 1903.

Crane, Walter, *An Artist's Reminiscences*, Methuen, 1906.

Crystal, David, *Listen to Your Child: A Parent's Guide to Children's Language*, Penguin, 1986.

Curtis, Bill, *Fleetwood — A Town is Born*, Lavenham; Terence Datton, 1986.

De Blowitz, H. G. S. A. Opper, *My Memoirs*, Edward Arnold, 1903.

Drummond-Hay, The Right Hon. Sir John, *A Memoir Based on his Journals and Correspondence*, London: John Murray, 1896.

Farwell, Byron, *For Queen and Country: A Social History of the Victorian and Edwardian Army*, Allen Lane, 1981.

Faulkner, Peter (ed.), *Jane Morris to Wilfred Scawen Blunt*, University of Exeter, 1986.

Fletcher, C. R. L., *Edmond Warre*, John Murray, 1922.

Fonds Ancien de Littérature pour la Jeunesse: Catalogue de Livres Imprimés Avant 1914, Paris, Bibliothèque de L'Heure Joyeuse, nd.

Gaskell, Mrs, *Mary Barton and Other Tales* Smith Elder, nd, pocket ed.

Gaskell, Mrs, *The Life of Charlotte Bronte*, Smith, Elder, 1857.

Gatty, Horatia, *Juliana Horatia Ewing and Her Books*, SPCK, 1887.

Gerin, Winifred, *Anne Thackeray Ritchie: A Biography*, OUP, 1981

Gerin, Winifred, *Charlotte Bronte*, OUP paperback, 1969.

Gerin, Winifred, *Elizabeth Gaskell: A Biography*, OUP, 1976.

Glendinning, Victoria, *Trollope*, Hutchinson, 1992.

Goldthwaite, John, *The Natural History of Make-Believe*, OUP, 1996.

Gosse, Edmund, *The Life of Algernon Charles Swinburne*, Macmillan, 1917.

Grant, James, *Cassell's Old and New Edinburgh*, 3 vols. Cassell and Co., 1883.

Grant-Duff, Sir M. E., *Notes From A Diary*, John Murray, 1897 etc., *1851–1872*, 2 vols, 1897; *1873–1881*, 2 vols, 1898; *1886–1888*, 2 vols, 1900; *1889–1891*, 2 vols, 1901, *1896–January 23, 1901*, 2 vols, 1905.

Green, R. L., *Kipling and the Children*, Elek Books, 1965.

Green, R. L., *Mrs Molesworth*, The Bodley Head, 1961.

Green, R. L., *Tellers of Tales*, Kaye and Ward, 1969.

Greenwood, Walter, *History of Lancashire*, County Books Series, 1951.

Griest, Guinevere G., *Mudie's Circulating Library and the Victorian novel*, 1970.

Guest, Revel and Angela V. John, *Lady Charlotte: A Biography of the 19th Century*, Weidenfeld and Nicolson, 1989.

Gurney, Edmund, Frederic W. H. Myers and Frank Podmore, *Phantasms of the Living*, Rooms of the Society for Psychical Research and Trubner and Co., 1886.

Haldane, M. E., *A Record of a Hundred Years*, Hodder and Stoughton, 1925.

Healey, Edna, *Lady Unknown: The Life of Angela Burdett-Coutts*, Sidgwick and Jackson, 1978.

Henderson, Ebenezer, *The Annals of Dunfermline*, Glasgow: John Tweed, 1879.

Henderson, Philip, *Swinburne: The Portrait of a Poet*, Routledge and Kegan Paul, 1974.

Hill, Brian, *Julia Margaret Cameron — A Victorian Family Portrait*, Peter Owen, 1973.

Hogben, J., *Richard Holt Hutton of 'The Spectator'* Edinburgh, Oliver and Boyd, 1899.

Holman-Hunt, Diana, *My Grandfather, His Wives and Loves*, Columbus Books, 1969.

Horn, Pamela, *High Society: the English Social Elite, 1880–1914*, Alan Sutton, 1992.

Horn, Pamela, *The Rise and Fall of the Victorian Servant*, Alan Sutton, 1986.

Houfe, Simon, *The Dictionary of British Book Illustrators and Caricaturists, 1800–1914*, Antique Collectors' Club, 1978.

Jackson, Annabel Huth, *A Victorian Childhood*, Methuen, 1932.

Jevons. *Letters and Journal of William Stanley Jevons*, edited by his wife, Macmillan, 1886.

Kipling, Rudyard, *From Sea to Sea and Other Sketches: Letters of Travel*, Macmillan, 1900.

Lang, Andrew, *History of English Literature*, Longmans, 1912.

Lang, C.Y., ed., *The Swinburne Letters,* vols I–VI, Yale UP, New Haven, 1982.

Laski, M., *Mrs Ewing, Mrs Molesworth and Mrs Hodgson Burnett* Arthur Barker Ltd., 1950.

Linton, E. Lynn, *The Autobiography of Christopher Kirkland*, Richard Bentley, 1885, 2 vols.

Lockett, Alan, *Ports and People of Morecambe Bay*, North Lonsdale Publications.

MacBeth, George, ed., *The Penguin Book of Victorian Verse*, 1969.

Maxwell, Christabel, *Mrs Gatty and Mrs Ewing*, Constable, 1949.

Mitchell, John Fowler and Sheila Mitchell, *Monumental Inscriptions (pre–1855) in West Fife*, Scottish Genealogy Society, 1972.

Mitchell, S., *Dinah Mulock Craik*, Boston, Twayne Publishers, 1983.

Molesworth, Mary, *A Stumble on the Threshold: A Story of the Day*, Charles Ollier, 1848.

Molesworth, Mary, *Claude or the Double Sacrifice,* Henry Colburn, 1850, 2 vols.

Molesworth, Mary, *Stray Leaves from the Tree of Life*, London: William Mackintosh, Brighton: G. Wakeling, 1869.

Molesworth, Mary, *The Great Experiment*, Newby, 1860.

Moore, D. L., *E. Nesbit: A Biography*, Ernest Benn, 1933.

Moore, George, *Literature at Nurse or Circulating Morals: A Polemic on Victorian Censorship*, edited with an introduction by Pierre Coustillas, The Harvester Press, 1976.

Morgan, Charles, *The House of Macmillan,* Macmillan and Co. Ltd., 1943.

Muirhead, F., and M. Monmarche, *Southern France*, The Blue Guides, Macmillan, 1926.

Nesbit, E., *Long Ago When I Was Young*, Ronald Whiting and Wheaton, 1966.

Noel-Paton, M. H., *Tales of a Grand-daughter*, 1970, published by subscription.

Pemberton, W. Baring, *Battles of the Crimean War*, B.T. Batsford Ltd., 1962.

Porter, John, *History of the Fylde of Lancashire*, Fleetwood and Blackpool, 1876.

Potter. *The Journal of Beatrix Potter*, F. Warne and Co., 1966.

Pride, Glen L., *The Kingdom of Fife*, Architectural Guides to Scotland, RIAS 1990.

Ritchie, Hester, ed., *Letters of Anne Thackeray Ritchie*, Murray, 1924.

Robson, Isobel Stuart, *Story Weavers: or Writers for the Young*, Robert Culling, 1900.

Ryan, Rachel, *A Biography of Manchester*, Methuen, 1937.

Salmon, Edward, *Juvenile Literature As It Is*, Henry J. Drane, 1888.

Salway, Lance, *A Peculiar Gift*, Kestrel Books, 1976.

Schreiber, *Lady Charlotte Schreiber: Extracts from Her Journal 1853–1891*, edited by the Earl of Bessborough, John Murray, 1952.

Schreiber, Lady Charlotte, *Journals 1869–1885*, 2 vols, edited by her son Montague J. Guest, John Lane, 1911.

Shercliff, W. H., *Manchester, A Short History of Its Development*, Public Relations Office, Manchester, 1977.

Spater, George and Ian Parsons, *A Marriage of True Minds*, Jonathan Cape and the Hogarth Press, 1979.

Spear, Percival, *A History of India*, Penguin, 1965, vol.2.

Stewart, Alexander, *Reminiscences of Dunfermline*, Edinburgh: Scott and Ferguson, 1886.

Strachey, Lytton, *Queen Victoria*, Chatto and Windus, 1921.

Sutherland, J., *Mrs Humphry Ward*, OUP, 1991.

Swan, Helena, *Girls' Christian Names*, Swan, Sonnenschein and Co., 1900.

Swindells, T., *Manchester Streets and Manchester Men*, Manchester, Morten, 1906, series two.

The Victoria History of the County of Lancashire, Constable, 1906.

Thurman, Judith, *Isak Dinesen: The Life of Karen Blixen*, Penguin, 1984.

Thwaite, Ann, *Waiting for The Party*, Secker and Warburg, 1974.

Thwaite, M. F., *From Primer to Pleasure: an Introduction to the History of Children's Books in England, from the Invention of Printing to 1900*, The Library Association, 1963.

Trollope, Joanna, *Britannia's Daughters*, Cresset Library, 1988.

Troubridge, Laura, *Life Among the Troubridges*, ed. J. Hope-Nicholson, John Murray, 1966.

Troubridge, Laura, *Memories and Reflections*, Heinemann, 1925.

Uglow, J., *Elizabeth Gaskell*, Faber, 1993.

Walford, L. B, *Memories of Victorian London*, Edward Arnold, 1912.

Walford, L. B., *Recollections of a Scottish Novelist*, Williams and Norgate, 1910.

Wall, Barbara, *The Narrator's Voice*, Macmillan, 1991.

Wall, Stephen, ed. *Charles Dickens: A Critical Anthology*, Penguin, 1970.

Ward Lock's *Guide to Edinburgh*, 1906.

Warren, Hon. J. Byrne Leicester, *The Flora of Cheshire*, with a biographical notice of the author by Sir Mountstuart Grant-Duff, Longmans, Green and Co., 1899.

Warren, M. L., *Diaries*, 2 vols, 1924, printed for private circulation.

Wetherell, Elizabeth, (pseudonym of Susan Bogert Warner), *The Wide, Wide World*, edited by Joyce Lankester Brisley. University of London Press, 1950. First published in 2 vols, 1852, 'edited by a clergyman of the Church of England.'

Wilberforce, Samuel, *Agathos, and Other Sunday Stories*, Thames Ditton, 1840.

Wilson, Maurice James Hartley, *Pressed Leaves from the Forest of Dunfermline*, Dunfermline: A. Romanes and Son, 1937.

Wordsworth. *The Letters of Mary Wordsworth 1800–1855,* selected and edited by Mary E. Burton, Oxford: Clarendon Press, 1958.

Yates, Edmund, *Recollections,* Harper, 1885, 2 vols.

Yonge, C. M., *The Pillars of the House*, Macmillan, 1873, 2 vols.

B — ARTICLES

Beerbohm, Max, 'No 2, The Pines' in *And Even Now*, Heinemann, 1920.

Cooper, J., 'Penny Plain or Twopence Coloured?', *Newsletter No. 55*, Children's Books History Society, July 1996.

Cooper, J., ''Just Really What They Do' or, Re-reading Mrs Molesworth', *Signal 57*, September 1988.

'English Publishing and the Mass Audience in 1852' in *Studies in Bibliography 6*, 1954.

Fisher, Margery, 'Stories from a Victorian Nursery', *Signal 69*, September 1992.

Forbes, Archibald, 'How I Became a War-Correspondent', *English Illustrated Magazine*, April 1884.

Gosse, Edmund, 'Lord de Tabley: A Portrait', *The Contemporary Review*, vol. 69, 1895, pp. 84–99.

Jeune, Lady, 'The Future of Society', *Lady's Realm*, Jan. 1902.

Lauterbach, C.E. and E.S., 'The Nineteenth Century Three-Volume Novel' in *Papers of the Bibliographical Society of America 51*, 1957, pp. 263–302.

Lewis, Naomi, in *Twentieth-Century Children's Writers*, ed. Tracy Chevalier, St James Press, 1989.

Lurie, Alison, 'The Child Who Followed the Piper: Kate Greenaway', in *Don't tell the grown-ups*, Bloomsbury, 1990.

Martin, Frances, *The Athenaeum*, 22 Oct., 1887, article on Mrs Craik.

Moss, Anita, 'Mrs Molesworth: Victorian Visionary', *The Lion and the Unicorn*, vol.12, no. 1, June 1988, pp. 105–110.

Morris, Marjorie, 'Aspects of the Life and Works of Elsie Jeanette Oxenham', *Newsletter No. 45*, Children's Books History Society, Sept. 1992.

Orwell, George, 'Charles Dickens' and 'Why I Write', in *The Collected Essays,*

Journalism and Letters of George Orwell Volume I: An Age like this 1920–1940, Penguin, 1970.

'Porcelain Children: 'Hummel-Figures' from the Goebel Factory', *Newsletter No. 39*, Children's Books History Society, September 1989.

Quiver. Woolf, Bella Sydney, 'Children's Classics', *The Quiver*, vol. 41, 1906, pp. 674–6.

Salmon, Edward, 'Literature for the Little Ones', *The Nineteenth Century*, vol XXII, Oct. 1887.

Salmon, Edward, 'What Girls Read', *The Nineteenth Century*, vol. XX, Oct. 1886.

The Saturday Review, 15.6.1872; 1.2.1873.

Sircar, Sanjay, 'The Victorian "Auntly" Narrative Voice and Mrs Molesworth's *Cuckoo Clock*,' *Children's Literature*, 17, ed. Butler, Higonnet and Rosen, Yale University Press, 1989 by The Children's Literature Foundation.

The Spectator, 22.1.1870; 8.2.1873.

Swinburne, A. C., 'Charles Reade', *The Nineteenth Century*, Oct. 1884, vol. XVI.

Watts, Theodore, 'Lord de Tabley', in *The Athenaeum*, No. 3553, 30.11.1895, pp. 754–56.

Westminster Budget. F. H. L., 'A Popular Writer for Children: Mrs Molesworth', *The Westminster Budget*, 20.10.1893, p. 24.

Wolff Janet and Caroline Arscott, 'Cultivated Capital', *History Today*, vol. 87, Mar. 1987.

Woman at Home. Tooley, S. A., 'Some Women Novelists', *The Woman at Home*, Dec.1897, pp. 193–195.

Wood, Sally, 'W. T. Stead and his *Books for the Bairns*', *Newsletter No. 38*, Children's Books History Society, March 1989.

INDEX

Compiled by Jane Cooper

Since Mrs Molesworth is the subject of this book, there is no separate entry for her in the index. Unqualified entries refer directly to her; e.g. Appearance, Children, Education, Religion, Writing methods etc. The main text and the footnotes have been indexed, but not the preliminary material or the book lists and family trees.

Abbey by the Sea, The, 271
Aberdeen Association, 303–4
Adventures of Herr Baby, The, 200, 203, 214, 230, 302, 350, 357–9; problems w. illustration of, 215–7
Agent, *see* Colles
Ainslie, Cynthia (later Bruce, grand-daughter), 202, 344, 345–6, 347–8
Ainslie, Douglas (brother-in-law of Juliet Molesworth), 324–5
Ainslie, Julian Grant-Duff (son-in-law), 323, 333
Ainslie, Stella & Alix (step-grand-daughters), 323, 347
Ancestral pride, 291
Animals & pets: attitude to, 200, 218–9, 220–1, 344
Appearance, 73
Army postings, with RM on, 85
Arnold, Edwin (later Sir Edwin), 253–4, 299
Art of Authorship, The, 299
'Ask the Robin' (*Fairies Afield*), 346
Atalanta, 272, 300, 313
Attwell, Mabel Lucie (illustrator) 363
Aunt Clotilda's Guests see *The Old Pincushion*
Aunt Judy's Magazine, 197, 213, 229, 251
Avery, Gillian, 357, 373–4, 378

Baby-talk, 349–360
Bainton, George, 299, 300

Barbour, Robert (employer & partner of CAS), 20–21, 56
Bereavement, reaction to: Violet's death, 134–5, 136, 138, 139–40, 148, 168–70; AJS, 231–2; Bevil, 322, 334–5; RM, 328–9
Beresford, James (CAS' stepfather), 11, 12, 13
'Best Books for Children, The', 270–1
Bindon House, 273–4
Birth, 18
Bishop, Mrs M. C. (*née* O'Connor), 226, 272, 309
Black, Agnes (MLM's g.aunt), 1, 53n.(1), 62
Black, Nancy, *see* Wilson
Blackwood, William (publisher), 317
Blanche, 377–8
Blue Baby, The, 333, 340, 347
Blue Dwarfs, The, (*A Christmas Posy*), 213
Bolted Door, The, 336
Boys and I, The, 47, 217, 332, 352–3, 354, 375
Boys' attitude to girls in MLM's books, 36–7
Brock, C. E. (illustrator), 389
Brooke, L. L. (illustrator), 307–8, 330
Broughton, Edward W. D. (brother-in-law, later Walthall), 138, 164, 165, 321

Broughton, Saba M. D., *see* Molesworth

Bunting, J. P., 171, 175, 291

Burnett, Frances Hodgson, 25–6, 33–4, 43, 294, 302, 303

Business methods (*see also under* individual publishers): anxiety about safety of mss, 230, 339–40, 366–7; classification of books, 286, 311–12; copyright, retention of, 159, 218, 287–9, 322, 332–3, 337–8; getting ahead with work, 229, 285, 333, 339, 364; playing one publisher against another, 214–5, 229, 286, 362–3, 365–6; money, 218, 229, 287–9, 317, 336, 361; re-publication, 159, 287, 318, 322, 332–3, 336; royalty system, 337–8, 365

Caen, 203–7 *passim*, 232; Maison du Chanoine, 204, 209, 211

Carroll, Lewis, 215

Carrots, 3n.(11), 39, 40, 47, 53, 165, 190–3, 204–5, 340, 350, 351, 353, 357–8, 374, 376, 386; publication & success, 192, 337, 388; sixpenny series, in, 303, 330

Carved Lions, The, 23, 24–5, 56–7, 313n.(32), 320–21, 367, 388

Chamber's Journal, 159, 301

Chambers (publishers), 234, 301, 312–3, 317, 332–3, 361–365 *passim*, 385–6

Character, 73–4, 76–7, 114, 142, 147–8, 169–70, 194, 220, 344, 345, 348, 379, 389

Charge Fulfilled, A, 250, 308

Charitable work, 250–1, 265, 267, 276–9, 385; articles on, 303–4

'Charlie's Disappointment', (*Tell Me A Story*), 185, 219

Chatto & Windus (publishers), 272, 287–9

Children of the Castle, The, 294, 296, 297, 364

Children (*see also under* individual names): education, 189–90, 234, 246, 254; upbringing & relationship w., 108, 131, 140, 184–5, 200, 218–221, 234, 246, 292; sons a worry, 283

Children's Hour, The, 321, 347, 350

Child's Pictorial, The, 240, 249, 267, 272, 278, 287, 311

Christmas Child, A, 91, 209–11, 236, 271, 354, 359–60, 374; review, 210

Christmas Posy, A, 285–7, 287, 289

Christmas-Tree Land, 230, 250, 297, 388

Cicely, 188, 351–2; plot & characters, 180–1; publication, 178

Class prejudice, *see* Snobbishness

Claimant, The, 171n.(30)

Clergy, friendships with, 368

Colles, Mr (agent), 322–3, 387–8

Colville, Alexander (husband of MLM's aunt), 6–7, 65

Colville, Catherine, *see* Wilson

Colville, John Wilson (cousin), 62, 100–101, 172, 177

'Coming Out': 74, 280; MLM's attitude to system, 74–6, 280

'Con and the Fairies' (*Tell Me A Story*), 185

Concealment: burning JBLW's letters, 104; hiding his books from RM, 112, 117

Contemporary Review, The, 252

Countryside: British, love of, 29–30; southern European, love of, 70–71, 105

Courtship & engagement, 78, 80–84

Coutts, Angela Burdett-, 267, 281, 303

Craik, Anna (GLC's 2nd wife), 187, 283n.(44), 330, 333

Craik, Dinah Maria Mulock, 173, 187,

188, 227–8, 253, 299–300; death, 274

Craik, George Lillie, 173, 215, 216, 310–12, 341; death 336; MLM's reliance on, 200–1, 229, 283, 284, 288–9, 294; preference for real-life stories, 229, 250, 285; relationship w. MLM, 187–8, 229, 274, 283, 289

Crane, Walter (illustrator), 182, 188, 216, 230, 262, 286, 290, 297, 307, 309

Craven, Mrs Augustus, 225–6, 272

'Cry from the Far West, A', 303

Cuckoo Clock, The, 20, 84, 196–7, 209, 326, 340; Japanese cabinet's influence on, 31–2, 196; Kipling, love for & knowing by heart, 341, 342; popularity, 192, 331, 388–9; publication, 195; sixpenny series, 331

Cullum, G. Gery Milner-Gibson-, 223, 241, 246, 249

Death, 388

De Mallets, 92, 94, 221–2

De Principe, 1n.(3), 319

Dessert, going down to, 41, 128–9, 130

De Tabley, see Warren

De Witt, Henriette Guizot, see Guizot

Dickens, Charles, 280–1, 378, 379

Divorce, see Separation

Drummond-Hay, E. W. A. (AJS' godfather), 7, 8, 9

Du Cane, Isabel & Julia, 267, 268, 286, 297, 315

Du Cane, Mrs (Charlotte Maria), 265–7, 270, 274–6, 290–1, 314–320, passim

Dunfermline, 1, 2, 3, 5, 6, 7, 16, 17, 41, 173

Dyson-Laurie, Gwen, see Molesworth

Edgeworth, Maria, 5, 45, 59

Edinburgh: 25, Royal Terrace, 188–9; move to, 176, 177, 188; visits to, 44, 61–3, 256

Edmée: A Tale of the French Revolution, see The Little Old Portrait

Education, 65–7; abroad, 68–70; early, 29, 43–4, 45; translation in, 65

Enchanted Garden, An, 304, 311

'Enchanted Trunks, The' (Fairies Afield), 298

'English Girlhood', 293

English Illustrated Magazine, 249, 272, 288, 293, 323

Ewing, Mrs (Juliana Horatia), 42–3, 59, 83, 131, 186, 229, 260, 312, 342; MLM's appreciation of, 252–3; article on, 252

Fairchild Family, The, 5, 6, 33, 45–6, 47–8, 54–5, 58, 59

Fairies Afield, 298, 346, 366, 367–8

Fairies – Of Sorts, 346–7, 361, 363

Fairy godmother figures, use of, 297–8

Fairy-tales, MLM's love of, 33, 42, 49–50, 250

Fan letters, 335

Fantasy, see under Writing, kinds of

Farthings, 277–8, 303, 311

Fasnacht, G. E. (French editor), 283–4

Fears, childhood, 18, 34–5, 51

February Boys, The, 205, 361, 362, 363, 365, 376

'Felix: An Outcast' (Abbey by the Sea, The), 251, 271

Feminism, 46, 227, 228

'Fiction: Its Use and Abuse', 298–9

Filming MLM's books, 387–8

Fisher, Margery, 374, 380

Five Minutes' Stories, 287

Fleetwood (seaside home), 38–40, 56, 108, 141, 142, 151, 170, 177

Fog, 249, 262–3, 268

Forbes, Archibald (RM's batman), 86–7

'For the Little Ones' (*Women's Mission*), 303

Four Ghost Stories, 269, 272, 286, 338

Four Winds Farm, 250, 253, 256, 257–9, 260, 273, 297

France, knowledge & love of, 167, 175, 181, 205, 225–6, 284

French Life in Letters, 283–5, 289

Gaskell, Mrs, 24, 59–61, 67, 77, 78, 90, 135, 160, 163, 224, 302

Gaskell, William (teacher), 59–61, 65–7, 68, 77, 135, 153, 224

Gatty, Alfred Scott-, 260, 265

Gatty, Mrs, 128–9, 252

Germany (*see also* Thuringia), 20; visits to, 212, 217, 246, 336

'Ghost of the Pampas, A', 338–9

Ghost stories, *see under* Supernatural

Girls and I, The, 269, 351

Girls' Own Annual & *Paper*, 299, 301

'Goblin Face, The' (*Five Minutes' Stories*), 34

Goethe, interest in, 147–8

'Goodnight Winny' (*Tell Me A Story*), 129–31, 132–3, 182, 184–5, 186, 239

Goring, Agnes, *see* Stewart

Goring, Craven Charles (brother-in-law), 110, 126, 148–9, 223

Goring, Venetia (niece, later Hohler), 165, 363–4, 387

Gosse, Edmund, 145, 146, 237–8

Graham, Ennis (pseudonym), 4n(13), 150, 153, 181, 184

Grandchildren, relationship with, 344–8, 349

Grandmother Dear, 3n.(11), 4, 42, 56, 201–2; sixpenny series, 331

'Grandmother Dear's Old Watch', 232–3

Grant-Duff, Sir M. E., 225, 272, 323

Great Ormond Street Hospital, 250–1, 255, 260, 265; Dickens as patron, 280; *Times* letter, on behalf of, 276–7

Green, R. L., 21n.(10), 22, 56, 197, 355–6, 356–7, 372

Grief, *see* Bereavement

Guizot, Guillaume, 226–7, 231–2

Guizot, Henriette (later De Witt), 227, 305

Haldane, Elizabeth & Haldane family, 370–2

'Half-way between the stiles' (*Uncanny Tales*), 319

Hammond, G. D. (illustrator), 330, 339, 382

Hatchards (publisher), 261, 271, 287

Hathercourt Rectory, 188, 201, 377

Helen's Babies (John Habberton), 356, 357

Hermy, 214, 217, 332, 359

Hettier, Madame (relative), 205

High Legh: Westfield: building, 138, 143, 151; moving in, 166–7; sale of, 174; West Hall, 107–8, 124, 126–7, 130, 132, 133, 136, 138, 141–4 *passim*, 166, 167, 170–1; household, 127–8

Hillside (home of MLM's aunt & grandmother), 6–7, 17, 41, 49, 64

Hofland, Mrs, 5, 45, 46–7

Holland (*see also* Rotterdam), 1, 7, 13, 17, 18, 31, 35, 318; MLM's love of, 19–20

'Honest Little Man, An' (*A Christmas Posy*), 128

Hoodie, 185, 214, 217, 332

Hope, Adrian, 260–2, 263–4, 277, 329, 334

Hope, Jaqueline, 329–30
Hope, Laura (*née* Troubridge), 260–2, 263–4, 277, 329–30, 334–5
House That Grew, The, 47
'How I Write My Children's Stories', 301
Hutton, John & Lucy (*née* Jevons. Parents of T. G. Hutton), 209, 210
Hutton, Mary Josephine, 153, 209, 210
Hutton, Richard Holt, 152–3, 179, 209
Hutton, Thomas Grindal, 153, 209–11, 219

Illness, 131, 133, 139, 140, 143, 150, 151–2, 198, 267, 275, 276, 282, 285, 333–4, 386, 387
Illustrated London News, 309
Ingelow, Jean, 249
Inglefield, Verity (great-grand-daughter), 384
Inglefield, V. M., *see* Prinsep
Innes, A. D. (publisher), 300–301, 309–10, 312, 317
Innes, Isabel (mother of CAS), 10–16 *passim*
Italy, Crown Prince of, 204–5, 363

Jasper, 337–8, 343–4, 351
Jevons, Thomas Edwin, 210
Jevons, William Stanley, 153, 210–11
Juvenile Literature As It Is, 255, 354

Kipling, Rudyard, acquaintance w. & letters to MLM, 340–44
Knutsford, attitude to, 160–4

Lacretelle, J-E. (painter), 223–4
'Lady Farquhar's Old Lady' (*Four Ghost Stories*), 173
Lamport family, 273–4

Laski, Marghanita, 80, 197, 354, 355, 372–3, 378
Lettice, 234
Lewis, Naomi, 380
'Literature for the Little Ones', 255–6, 354
Little Folks, 41, 240, 271, 272, 289, 301, 312, 313
Little Guest, The, 55–6, 349, 361, 360, 362; Winkenhurst as origin of names in, 349
Little Miss Peggy, 24, 30, 36, 260, 271, 272, 273, 375
Little Mother Bunch, 289
Little Old Portrait, The, 234, 361; purchase of original picture, 202–3; re-published as *Edmée*, 381–2, 383
Little Wideawake, 214, 217, 332
Loneliness as a child, 35–6
Longmans (publisher), 294, 311, 385–6
Longman's Magazine, 269, 319,
London: 19, Sumner Place, 294, 295; 85, Lexham Gardens, 234–5, 293–4; 155 Sloane St., 326; Kensington, dislike of, 235, 275, 276, 293; paying calls, 246–7; 'the season' & Society, 245, 268–9, 295; social life & contacts, 245, 246, 253–5, 262, 263, 290
Lorimer, Bell & Jean (cousins), 384–5
Lover and Husband: first attempts, 99, 101, 105; character, not plot, 155–7; influenced by 3 vol. convention, 117; MLM's interest in, 120, 131, 135, 139, 141–2; success, efforts to ensure, 142, 152–3; publication, 149–50, 159–60; reviews, 152–3, 179

Macdonald, George, 259, 298
Macmillan's, 178, 183, 192, 234, 330, 366, 388; anxiety about no. of

Macmillan's – *cont.*
    MLM's books w. other publishers,
    272, 310–312; financial
    negotiations, 330–1, 337–8, 362–3,
    365–6, 370, 383–4, 386–7; MLM
    reading mss for, 318; MLM's
    relationship w., 195–6, 214–5, 286,
    337, 338, 370, 382–3, 386–7;
    second children's book in year, 311,
    312, 313
Macmillan's Magazine, 240, 241, 259,
    343
Magic Nuts, The, 298, 322
Manchester, 25; Chorlton, 23–4;
    Church Croft, 72, 82n.(22); gloom
    & dirt, 22–3, 25–7; Dover Terrace,
    63–4; Rusholme Rd. house, 21–2;
    society, 77–8; Whalley House, 89
Marriage, 82–3, 85; breakdown of,
    feeling about, 208, 328
Marrying and Giving in Marriage,
    269
Mary, 260, 311, 353, 373–4
'Mary Ann Jolly' (*Tell Me A Story*),
    3–4, 185
May, Princess (Mary Victoria of Teck,
    later Queen Mary), 266, 313–4
Meg Langholme, 80–81, 91, 352
Meldrum, George, 44, 53, 62, 64,
    176, 190
Meldrum, Marion, *see* Wilson
Memories, earliest, 18–19, 300
Millar, H. R. (illustrator), 330
Miller, Mary, *see* Wilson
Miller, Rev. Ebenezer, 7, 20, 64
Milligan, Gordon (publisher), 332–3,
    335–6, 361, 363, 365
Milner-Gibson, Mrs, 222–3, 224, 225,
    246
Miss Bouverie, 205, 209, 332
Miss Mouse and Her Boys, 37
'Miss-sent Letters' (*The Blue Baby*),
    340

Mohl, Mme (*née* Mary Anne Clarke),
    224, 244
Molesworth, Andalusia, *see* Riley
Molesworth, Lt. Col. Anthony Oliver
    (RM's brother), 282
Molesworth, Capt. the Hon. Anthony
    Oliver (RM's father), 78, 82
Molesworth, Cicely (daughter), 131–2,
    263, 267, 282, 318, 321, 342–3;
    appearance, 97, 182, 232, 245;
    attitude to RM, 85, 193, 208, 329;
    birth, 87; character, 124, 130;
    childhood, 89, 128, 167, 184–5;
    marriage, 313, 314–5; nurse
    training, 292–3, 294–5, 313;
    presentation at court, 218;
    relationship w. MLM, 108, 184–5,
    218, 220, 292, 315; scarlet fever,
    140; twin daughters, 315
Molesworth family, relationship w.,
    206
Molesworth, Grace (*née* Crofton, RM's
    mother), 86, 89
Molesworth, Gwen (later Dyson-
    Laurie, RM's cousin), 84–5, 205–6,
    247, 283, 297, 323, 324, 329,
    348
Molesworth, Hender Delves
    (grandson), 347, 372–3
Molesworth, Herbert (nephew),
    290
Molesworth, Juliet (daughter), 129,
    131, 202, 225–6, 318; appearance,
    182, 232, 245, 261; attitude to RM,
    193, 329; birth, 89; marriage, 273,
    323; homes in Surrey & Sussex &
    visits by MLM, 334, 336, 348, 349,
    387; relationship w. MLM, 181,
    348
Molesworth, Lady (the first, Georgina
    Gosset), 86, 218n.(33)
Molesworth, Lady (the second, Agnes
    Dove), 218n.(33), 335

Molesworth, Lilian & Georgina (nieces), 282

Molesworth, Lionel Charles (son), 212, 246, 254, 302, 316, 321, 333; birth, 170; death 383; marriage, 321; Oxford, 296;

Molesworth, Mary (writer, d.1869), 88, 92–5, 146

Molesworth, Morgan Crofton (RM's brother), 92, 94, 282, 290

Molesworth, Olive (daughter), 131, 212, 282, 318; appearance, 245; birth, 96; collaboration in MLM's books, 250, 323–4; presentation at court, 268; publications, 323; relationship w. MLM, 323, 333, 348

Molesworth, Rev. Samuel, 8th Viscount (RM's cousin), 83, 86, 206

Molesworth, Richard (husband): character, 79, 84–5, 114–5, 124, 150, 175, 193, 206; death, 327; extravagance, 141, 193–4, 206; Knight of Windsor, 327–8; military career, 78–80, 85, 87, 88, 140–1, 174; relationship w. AJS, 112–3; relationship w. CAS, 113–4, 116; wound, effect on, 84–5; MLM's relationship w., 83, 112, 115, 126, 136, 142, 190, 198–9; separation from MLM, after, 211

Molesworth, Richard Bevil (son), 193, 246; appendix removed, 319–20; birth, 165; character, 168, 282–3, 292; death, 322, 339; 'Ghost of the Pampas, A', 338, Patagonia, 292, 295; Westminster, 246

Molesworth, Richard Pigot, 7th Viscount (RM's uncle), 83, 88–9, 146–7

Molesworth, Richard Walter (son), 142, 143, 146

Molesworth, Roger Bevil (grandson), 347

Molesworth, Saba M. D. (née Broughton daughter-in-law), 321, 383

Molesworth, Violet (daughter), 91–2, 126, 131–2, 184–5; birth, 85–6; character, 97, 124, 130, 135; illness & death, 133–4, 140

Molesworth, Violet Saba (grand-daughter), 321–2, 347

Monthly Packet, The, 251–2, 271, 300, 301

Morgan, Mary Wilson (Minnie, cousin), 64, 384–5; legacy from CAS, 176; wedding, 176

Mourning, see Bereavement

'Mr Old Year' (The Children's Hour), 301–2

Mudie's, 153–4, 159

My New Home, 318, 388

'My Pink Pet' (A Christmas Posy), 33, 197–8

'My-Pretty' and Her Little Brother 'Too', 323, 347

'Mysterious Guide, The' (Story of a Spring Morning), 262–3

Nature and Love (poem), 184

Needlework, attitude to, 222

Neighbours, 272, 279

Nesbit, E., 197

Nesta, 271, 333

Newbery House Magazine, 303

Next-Door House, The, 199, 312

Nineteenth Century, The, 235, 236, 255, 256, 260

'No Work To Do' (Nesta), 278

Not Without Thorns, 4n.(13), 168–9, 170, 180, 351; review, 179

Novel: three-volume, 117, 153–4; Victorian attitude to, 154–5

Nurse Heatherdale's Story, 91, 308–9

O'Meara, Kathleen, 224–5, 284
Old Pincushion, The or Aunt Clotilda's Guests, 261, 271, 329
'On the Art of Writing Fiction for Children', 300
'One Sunday Morning' (*Blanche*), 251
Oriel Window, The, 278
Orwell, George, 280–1, 378–9

Palace in the Garden, The, 30, 240, 249, 261, 271, 386
Pall Mall Gazette, The, 270–1
Paris: addresses in, 211–2; departure from, 234, 249; move to, 209; social circle in, 221–27; visits to, 68–9, 244, 348
Pater, Walter, 259
Paton, Lady Margaret Gourlay, 173, 201, 274
Paton, Ranald, 193, 211, 389
Paton, Sir Noel, 172, 173, 178, 181, 188, 190, 274, 256–7, 309
Pau, 192, 203; visit w. Agnes, 1868, 100, 104–105; move to, 1877, 198, 200; Villa Marie-Jeanne, 201
Peterkin, 330, 333, 334, 374–5
Philippa, 352
Pine, Lady, 221
Pine-woods, MLM's passion for, 19, 213–4, 230
Playthings: dolls, 32; dolls' house, 27–8 reels, 32–3, 35; shells, 33; toys, 31, 57
Politics: JBLW as Liberal candidate, RM on Conservative side, 113–4; spite in, 161–2
'Poor Miss Crawfurd', 36
Popularity of her books, 192, 286, 304–5, 331–2
'Present to the Queen, A' (*Nesta*), 267
Prince's Meadows (pamphlet) 304

'Princess Ice Heart' (*Studies and Stories*), 309, 312
Prinsep, Cicely, *see* Molesworth
Prinsep, James Charles (son-in-law), 314–5, 318–9, 333
Prinsep, Mary Eugenia (granddaughter), 316, 384–5
Prinsep, Venetia Mary (later Inglefield. Grand-daughter), 316, 318, 345, 346, 348, 384–5
Pseudonym, *see* Graham, Ennis

Quiver, The, 251;article on MLM, 302

'Ramble about Childhood, A', 301, 321
Reading: books read, 45–6, 48–50, 66, 147; in childhood, attitude to, 43, 50, 51–2; in later life, attitude to, 48, 76–7, 270
Rectory Children, The, 27–8, 290
'Reel Fairies, The' (*Tell Me A Story*), 32–3, 35–6, 185, 197–8
Religion: in her writing, 55–7, 76, 251, 369; faith & practice, 76, 127, 226, 250, 334–5, 368–9; upbringing, 54–8
Riley, Andalusia (*née* Molesworth), 318, 348–9, 370–371
Riley, Athelstan, 205n.(5), 222n.(45), 348, 370–371
Riley, Laurence (godson), 370–371
Ritchie, Anne Thackeray, 244–5
Robin Redbreast, 100
Rosy, 217
Rotterdam, 1, 7, 9, 13–14, 15, 16, 18, 20, 64, 213; 75, Westnieuwland (MLM's birthplace), 15, 16, 18
Routledge (publisher), 214, 217–8
Royal Waterloo Hospital, pamphlet on, see *Prince's Meadows*
Ruby Ring, The, 186n.(20), 298, 333, 388

Ruskin, John, 257
Rutherford, Henry (husband of MLM's aunt), 7, 9, 10n.(37), 13, 14, 15–16
Rutherford, Marion *see* Wilson

Sale of own books, interest in, 195, 201, 288, 311, 312, 369, 385, 386
Salmon, Edward, 1, 252, 255, 256, 260, 275, 354, 355, 359
Saturday Review, The, 152, 153, 156, 179, 180, 206
Scotland (*see also* Dunfermline; Edinburgh), 3, 5, 13–16 *passim*, 53, 54, 71, 166, 173, 177, 190, 219; visits to, 37, 41, 58, 61, 78, 80, 188, 255, 294, 318, 371
Second sight, *see under* Supernatural
Separation from husband, 199; advocated by 7th Viscount, 206; legal status of, 208; not divorce, 209; Victorian attitude to, 206–8
'Shadow in the Moonlight, The' (*Uncanny Tales*), 317, 352
Sheila's Mystery, 186n.(20), 287, 313
Sherwood, Mrs, see *The Fairchild Family*
She Was Young and He Was Old, 157, 158, 180, 181, 377; publication, 160; review, 179
Silverthorns, 100, 256, 386
Skeet (publisher), 139, 149, 159, 170, 183
'Some Women Novelists' (*Woman at Home*), 302
Snobbishness, 372–80; personal, 372–3; in writing, 373–80
Social problems, attitude to, 279–82
SPCK (publisher), 234, 240, 249, 267, 271, 285, 381, 382
Spectator, The, 152, 153, 179, 209, 234, 300
Stead, W. T., 271, 299, 300

Stewart, Agnes (sister, later Goring), 61–2, 98, 100, 101, 104, 107, 131–2, 142, 175; birth, 31; character, 194; courtship, 109–10, 130; marriage, 148
Stewart, Agnes Janet (*née* Wilson, mother): birth, 1; books read, 5; character as grandmother, 201–2; childhood, 3–6; death, 231; France, move to w. MLM, 199; ill-health in later life, 168, 176; marriage, 16; MLM's love for, 233; Paton, link w., 173; portrait of, 8; Tangier, visit to 8–9; stories heard, 6; Ulverston as home, 177, 194
Stewart, Caroline (sister, later Broughton/Walthall), 53, 62, 116, 130, 138, 164–5, 174, 176, 194, 196, 290, 364
Stewart, Charles (brother), 62, 101, 170–1; Barbour's firm, partner in 166; birth, 21; birth of children, 151; China, visit to, 166; engagement, 109; illness, 125–6, 171; legitimacy claim, 171–3; marriage, 124, 125; death, accidental, 175; will, 172–3
Stewart, Charles Augustus (father): Australian Stewarts, relship. w., 16–17; baptism, 10–11; childhood, 12–14; death, 170; education, 14; England, move to, 20; illegitimacy & attitude to, 10, 16, 54, 71; illness, last, 168; legacies, 171; marriage, 16; MLM's relationship w., 50–51, 95–6; prosperity, increasing, 9–10, 20–21, 72, 83; religion, 56; Rotterdam, work in, 9–10; 15
Stewart family mystery, 54, 71–2, 175–6, 290–2
Stewart, James Horne (legitimate son of WS), 17, 53–4, 71, 86

Stewart, John Wilson (brother), 17, 53, 62, 64
Stewart, William (MLM's paternal g.father): military career, 10–12, 14, 15; illegitimate children & attitude to, 11, 17, 53–4; Lt. Gov. New South Wales, 14; marriage, 12; MLM writing to, in childhood, 44–5;
Stewart, William Wilson (brother), 31, 98, 124, 166, 175, 232
Stories for Children in Illustration of the Lord's Prayer, 311–12
Stories of the Saints for Children, 311, 369
Story of a Spring Morning, The, 19, 296, 386
Story of A Year, The, 47, 365, 367
'Story of the Rippling Train, The' (*Four Ghost Stories*), 269
'Story-Reading and Story-Writing', 301
Story-telling: Nancy Black, 41–2; MLM: to siblings, 42–3; to children, 89–90, 178, 181–2, 198
Story Weavers: or Writers for the Young: interview w. MLM, 303
'Story-Writing', 300
Studies and Stories, 309, 312
Summer Stories, 186, 212, 286, 350, 379
Supernatural, interest in the: ghost stories, 173, 241–2, 249, 269, 352; second sight, 102, 223, 250
Sweet Content, 361
Swinburne, A. C., 145, 236–41, 254, 257–9, 321; Beerbohm's account of visit to, 242–4; praise of MLM, 235–6, 257, 260, 271, 289–90, 296–7; love of babies & children, 237–8, 244–5, 315–6, 316–7,

325–6; lunch party at Sumner Place, 324–5

Tabley Grange, 87, 88, 127, 130; building on to, 98, 107, 118; leaving, 136–7, 138
Tabley House, 90–91
Tapestry Room, The, 42, 204, 297, 388
Taylor, Dr & Mrs William (family doctor in Edinburgh), 190, 199–200, 208
Tell Me A Story, 3n.(11), 182–3, 286; publication, 178, 187; success 187
'That Girl in Black', 272, 287–9
Third Miss St Quentin, The, 287
This and That, 326
Thuringia, 212–4, 230, 241–2
Tinsley (publisher), 160, 170, 173, 183–4
'Too Bad' (*Tell Me A Story*), 185–6
'Toymakers of Bergstein, The' (*Summer Stories*), 212, 379
Toys, *see* Playthings
Translation of MLM's books, 305–7
Transy (home of AJS as a child), 2, 5, 6, 7
Troubridge, Laura, *see* Hope
Two Little Waifs, 229, 367

Uncanny Tales, 317, 319, 352
Uncle Remus stories, 355
'Unexplained' (*Four Ghost Stories*), 240, 241–2
Unwin, Fisher (publisher), 240, 304–5, 311, 333
Us: An Old-fashioned Story, 4n.(15), 239, 359

'Very ill indeed' (*The Children's Hour*), 321

Wales: holidays in 116–7, 249; move to, 174

Walford, L. B., 48, 309, 310, 314
Walthall, E. C. D., (nephew), 232, 321
Walthall, Edward W. D., *see* Broughton
Walthall, Helen (niece), 196, 290
War, First World, attitude to & life during, 380–5
Ward, Mrs Humphry, 254
Warren family, relationship w., 90, 97, 103–4, 127, 137–8, 161
Warren, George, 2nd Baron de Tabley, 87, 93, 95, 130, 136–7, 165
Warren, J. B. L., (later 3rd Baron de Tabley): advice to MLM on writing, 99, 101–2; character, 111–2, 117, 132, 145–6, 147–8; children of MLM, attitude to, 98, 130; confidant & adviser on MLM's family problems, 109–110, 113–4, 116, 136–7; first novel, MLM's interest in publication, 110–12; Grant-Duff, friend of, 111n.(9), 127n.(3), 195, 273; help to MLM on publishing her 1st novel, 118, 119–20, 142, 152–3; love affairs & marriage possibility, 103, 106–7, 122; MLM's farewell to, 165; MLM's relationship with & analysis of this, 87, 97–8, 100, 115–6, 120–3, 157–8, 194–5; mother's death, 125, 131; upsets w. MLM, 118–20, 133–4, 143–6; Welsh holiday, joins Molesworths for, 116–7
Warren, Margaret (sister of JBLW), 97, 137, 144, 162
Watts, Theodore (later Watts-Dunton), 145, 195, 236, 238, 243, 244, 253, 254, 290, 317, 324–5, 334
Westfield, *see* High Legh
West Hall, *see* High Legh

Westminster Budget, The: article on MLM, 302
'What Girls Read', MLM's reaction to, 255
Wide, Wide World, The, 58–9
Widow, described as, 212
Will, 387
Williamson, William Crawford (Stewart family friend), 68
Wilson, Agnes Janet, *see* Stewart
Wilson, Catherine (later Colville, MLM's aunt), 2, 6, 17, 44, 64
Wilson, John (MLM's maternal g.father), 1, 5, 6
Wilson, Marion (later 1 Rutherford, 2 Meldrum, MLM's aunt), 2, 7, 15–16, 27, 44, 53, 62, 64, 176, 190
Wilson, Mary (later Miller, MLM's aunt), 2, 7, 20, 64
Wilson, Nancy (Mary, *née* Black, MLM's maternal g.mother), 1, 6, 41–2, 46, 53
Winkenhurst, see *The Little Guest*
Woman at Home, The: 'Some Women Novelists', article on MLM, 302
Women's Mission, contribution by MLM, 303
Wood-Pigeons and Mary, The, 329–30
Wordsworth, Dorothy, servant of, as MLM's nurse, 28
Wordsworth, William, 28
Writing: advice to others on, 65, 300, 301; audience, 129; beginning, 59–60, 67; for children, why published, 178, 187; RM's attitude to, 150; style, 71, 181, 186–7, 198
Writing, kinds of: commissioned articles & interviews, 298–9, 300–304; fantasy & fairy tale, 42, 196–7, 213, 250, 297–8, 367–8; realistic story, 42, 129, 217

Writing methods: need for critical feedback, 158, 188; 'never copying' rule, 101–2, 105, 300; plots, crisis in, use of, 47; trying out mss on children, 181–2, 345–6; regularity, 170, 247–8, 317, 348; real-life events & people as source, 3n.(11), 31–3, 35, 38–9, 40, 70, 129, 149, 165, 182, 185, 191, 192–3, 196, 200, 201–2, 203, 219, 232–3, 262–3, 301–2, 321; same incident in different stories, 34, 320–1; translation good training in, 65, 300; 'working' vs. 'thinking', 158–9, 248–9

Wrong Envelope, The, 289, 338–9, 340

Yonge, Charlotte M., 47, 76–7, 199, 219, 225, 251–2, 271, 284, 299, 372